THE EVOLUTION OF
LIBRARY AND MUSEUM
PARTNERSHIPS

Recent Titles in
The Libraries Unlimited Library Management Collection

THE EVOLUTION OF LIBRARY AND MUSEUM PARTNERSHIPS

Historical Antecedents, Contemporary Manifestations, and Future Directions

Juris Dilevko and Lisa Gottlieb

**LIBRARIES UNLIMITED LIBRARY MANAGEMENT COLLECTION
GERARD MCCABE, SERIES ADVISER**

A Member of the Greenwood Publishing Group

Westport, Connecticut • London

British Library Cataloguing in Publication Data is available.

ISBN: 1–59158–064–1
ISSN: 0894–2986

First published in 2004

Libraries Unlimited, 88 Post Road West, Westport, CT 06881
A Member of the Greenwood Publishing Group, Inc.
www.lu.com

Printed in the United States of America

The paper used in this book complies with the
Permanent Paper Standard issued by the National
Information Standards Organization (Z39.48–1984).

10   9   8   7   6   5   4   3   2   1

CONTENTS

PREFACE

This book is about the nature of museum-library partnerships and collaborative efforts at the beginning of the twenty-first century and about what the library-museum relationship could be in the future. The background to this topic lies in the increasing number of joint-use libraries in North America, Sweden, Australia, and New Zealand. As defined by Alan Bundy, joint-use libraries are facilities in which "two or more distinct library services providers, usually a school [library] and a public library, serve their client groups in the same building, based on an agreement that specifies the relationship between the providers."[1] Kathleen Imhoff speaks of "two or more libraries of different types coming together to provide services in a single building operating cooperatively to provide resources, such as curriculum support, bibliographic instruction, and information literacy to the general public and/or students, faculty, and administrators."[2] While joint-use agreements between public and school libraries are the most common, academic and public libraries also have established joint-use partnerships. If joint-use facilities were, at the beginning, typically found in rural areas that had difficulty in financially sustaining separate public and school libraries,[3] they are increasingly appearing in urban areas where municipal governments and educational entities at all levels are facing the type of financial constraints that make resource sharing in one building an attractive option. Such joint efforts have not been without controversy, as demonstrated by Natalie Reif Ziarnik in her overview of the tensions between school and public librarians in the United States in the twentieth century and by Beverly Goldberg in her account about opposition to a university-public joint-use library.[4] Nonetheless, examples of innovative joint-use facilities, both rural and urban, abound:[5] Loup County, Nebraska;[6] Washoe County, Nevada;[7] Broward Community College,

Florida;[8] the University of Washington–Bothell;[9] Florida Atlantic University;[10] Pinellas County, Florida;[11] Fort Collins, Colorado;[12] San Jose State University, California;[13] Härnösand Library, Sweden;[14] Almedal Library, Sweden;[15] and Pinnaroo School Community Library, South Australia.[16]

While financial exigencies and other practical concerns may have been the immediate cause for the implementation of library-library joint-use facilities, it soon became apparent that they also provided "more opportunities for the development of information literacy and lifelong learning" than separate facilities.[17] If this is true for library-library shared buildings, it could be argued that library-museum joint-use buildings are the natural next step in the creation of a citizenry committed to knowledge acquisition and lifelong learning. In other words, the reasons for the development of joint-use facilities between various types of libraries are equally applicable to the development of joint-use facilities between libraries and museums. To be sure, there were some initiatives in this direction at the end of the twentieth century—for example, the now-closed Exploration Center implemented by the Enoch Pratt Free Library of Baltimore at the Port Discovery children's museum and the Sahara West Library and Fine Arts Museum in Las Vegas. Yet, on the whole, such library-museum joint-use facilities are few and far between. More popular have been library-museum partnerships, in which institutions work together on stand-alone digital or on-site projects contingent on dedicated funding, but with no guarantee that the ties thus tenuously forged will evolve into an ongoing or permanent arrangement. In addition, some of these museum-library partnerships display a tendency toward "edutainment" or "infotainment"—loosely defined as entertainment masquerading as education or information—that speaks to the existence of new social forces impinging upon the cultural landscape of museums and libraries. Accordingly, while we wish to point out the importance of library-museum partnerships on a general level, we also want to make clear that we want to argue for the establishment of a very specific type of library-museum partnership: a library-museum hybrid located in the same building that does not succumb to the temptations of edutainment.

Toward this goal, we examine the context for the growth of museum-library partnerships in chapters 1 and 2, situating them as both a reaction to, and part of, what has been called the edutainment trend in the digital age. In chapter 3, we look at various contemporary manifestations of museum-library partnerships—including online partnerships—by focusing on projects sponsored by the Institute of Museum and Library Services between 1998 and 2003. After describing these projects, we examine the extent to which they can, in fact, be called partnerships and the extent to which they partake of edutainment-type features. We try to answer the question of whether libraries have moved away from an emphasis on the strength of their collections—an inexhaustible source of detailed information about social and cultural questions of all kinds—in the rush to establish partnerships with museums. In chapter 4, we approach museum-library partnerships from a historical perspective, showing that library-museum partnerships—in the form of library-museum hybrid institutions—have a long and rich tradition. We propose that, instead of libraries entering into partnerships with museums where library contributions are minimal, libraries should develop a significant museum function, in effect taking over the role of the museum based on historical antecedents, especially the "cabinet of curiosities" model, broadly defined as a collection of books and objects. In this way, library collections can be physically adjacent to museum objects in order to provide substantial opportunity for indepth intellectual juxtaposition. Chapter 5 sketches a vision of this new library-museum hybrid as a physical entity—one in which linked or closely proximate rooms or designated areas/wings/floors (divided, for example, according to Dewey Decimal or Library of Congress classifications) contain an intermixture of museum objects arranged in so-called visible storage centers[18] and text-based materials arranged on shelving units. While we recognize the existence of digital museum-library collaborations and their claim to provide seamless hybridization, we nevertheless believe that, because the edutainment model has become the reigning paradigm in many existing on-site and online cultural institutions and collaborative efforts, our proposed on-site library-museum hybrid may have its advantages. Chapter 6 provides an ideological framework for our ideas; we suggest that libraries and museums that understand their role to be edutainment-based public spaces are abrogating their fundamental role as educational entities committed to rigorous learning, that they are, to borrow the words of Jean Baudrillard, contributing to "a radical loss of meaning."[19]

NOTES

1. Alan Bundy, "Joint-Use Libraries: The Ultimate Form of Cooperation," in *Planning the Modern Public Library Building*, ed. Gerard B. McCabe and James R. Kennedy (Westport, CT: Libraries Unlimited, 2003), 129–30.

2. Kathleen R. T. Imhoff, "Public Library Joint-Use Partnerships: Challenges and Opportunities," in *Joint-Use Libraries*, ed. William Miller and Rita M. Pellen (Binghampton, NY: Haworth Press, 2001), 18–19.

3. Bundy, "Joint-Use Libraries," 130–34.

4. Natalie Reif Ziarnik, *School and Public Libraries: Developing the Natural Alliance* (Chicago: American Library Association, 2003), 1–19; Beverly Goldberg, "Faculty Object to Shared San Jose Library: Joint University–Main Public Library Facility," *American Libraries* 29 (December 1998): 21–22.

5. For an extended bibliography of such libraries, see American Library Association, *Combined Libraries: A Bibliography* (ALA Library Fact Sheet Number 20); for a list of public and school library joint-use facilities, see the appendix in Shirley A. Fitzgibbons, "School and Public Library Relationships: Essential Ingredients in Implementing Educational Reforms and Improving Student Learning," *School Library Media Research* 3 (2000), http://www.ala.org/ala/aasl/aaslpubsandjournals/slmrb/slmrcontents/volume32000/relationships.htm. In addition, Bundy's "Joint-Use Libraries" and Fitzgibbons's "School and Public Library Relationships," both cited above, contain extensive historical and bibliographical information about the development of, and scholarship about, joint-use libraries.

6. Jerome Lobner and Lillian Kaslon, "School/Public Library Combinations," *Nebraska Library Association Quarterly* 31 (summer 2000): 17–21.

7. Sharon Honig-Bear, "School-Public Library Partnerships in Washoe County, Nevada," in *Joint-Use Libraries*, ed. William Miller and Rita M. Pellen (Binghampton, NY: Haworth Press, 2001), 5–16.

8. Julia A. Woods, "Joint-Use Libraries: The Broward Community College Central Campus Experience," in *Joint-Use Libraries*, ed. William Miller and Rita M. Pellen (Binghampton, NY: Haworth Press, 2001), 41–54.

9. Cynthia Fugate, "Common Ground: Making Library Services Work at a Collocated Campus," in *Joint-Use Libraries*, ed. William Miller and Rita M. Pellen (Binghampton, NY: Haworth Press, 2001), 55–64.

10. Patricia Roshaven and Rudy Widman, "A Joint University, College and Public Library," in *Joint-Use Libraries*, ed. William Miller and Rita M. Pellen (Binghampton, NY: Haworth Press, 2001), 65–88.

11. James Olliver and Susan Anderson, "Seminole Community Library: Joint-Use Library Services for the Community and the College," in *Joint-Use Libraries*, ed. William Miller and Rita M. Pellen (Binghampton, NY: Haworth Press, 2001), 89–102.

12. Karen A. Dornseif, "Joint-Use Libraries: Balancing Autonomy and Cooperation," in *Joint-Use Libraries*, ed. William Miller and Rita M. Pellen (Binghampton, NY: Haworth Press, 2001), 103–16.

13. Christina Peterson and Patricia Senn Breivik, "Reaching for a Vision: The Creation of a New Library Collaborative," in *Joint-Use Libraries*, ed. William Miller and Rita M. Pellen (Binghampton, NY: Haworth Press, 2001), 117–30.

14. Elsa Gomez, Eila Hultén, and Ulla Drehmer, "A Joint Library Project in Härnösand, Sweden," *Scandinavian Public Library Quarterly* 31 (1998): 22–24.

15. Annina Rabe, "A Library in Balance," *Scandinavian Public Library Quarterly* 35 (2002): 31–33.

16. Alan Bundy, *Widened Horizons: The Rural School Community Libraries of South Australia* (Adelaide, Australia: Auslib Press, 1997), 191–220.

17. Charles Kratz, "Transforming the Delivery of Service," *College and Research Library News* 64 (February 2003): 100.

18. Celestine Bohlen, "Museums as Walk-in Closets: Visible Storage Opens Troves to the Public," *New York Times*, 6 May 2001, B1.

19. Jean Baudrillard, *Simulacra and Simulation*, trans. Sheila Faria Glaser (Ann Arbor, MI: The University of Michigan Press, 1994), 80.

ACKNOWLEDGMENTS

Parts of chapters 1, 2, 4, and 5 are revised versions of an article that originally appeared as "Library-Museum Hybrids: Resurrecting and Updating a Neglected Idea" in *Library Quarterly* 73 (April 2003): 160–98. © 2003 by The University of Chicago. All rights reserved. We thank Perry Cartwright, manager, Contracts and Subsidiary Rights, for granting us permission to make use of this article in the present book. We would also like to thank Gerard McCabe, Series Adviser for the Libraries Unlimited Library Management Collection, and Barbara Ittner, Acquisitions Editor for Libraries Unlimited, for their many kindnesses throughout the course of this book project.

1 MARKETING MUSEUMS AND LIBRARIES: AN INTRODUCTION

Robert Martin, director of the Institute of Museum and Library Services in the United States at the beginning of the twenty-first century, identifies both museums and libraries "as . . . primary social agenc[ies] in support of education, providing resources and services that complement the structures of formal education and extend education into an enterprise that lasts the length of a lifetime."[1] As individuals increasingly rely on Internet-based information sources, museums and libraries have had to adapt to the redefined service expectations of patrons by providing their resources and services online. Museum Web sites typically offer online catalogs of their collections, and many institutions at the beginning of the twenty-first century already had undertaken digitization projects that added images to their catalog entries. The American Museum of Natural History in New York City, to take just one example, was developing "a searchable online catalog of the whole museum, with images and text."[2] Museums were also linking their collections through databases, creating "a kind of digital global museum."[3] In addition to searching online catalogs, library patrons were "increasingly requesting that their questions be answered by the Internet even when more advantageous (print) sources [we]re available."[4] Digital reference systems in libraries became commonplace. And just as digitization initiatives enabled museum patrons to create self-guided armchair visits of museum collections, online encyclopedias, stock quotes, company data, and ebooks caused "average citizens...to consider themselves 'do-it-yourself' librarians."[5]

The proliferation of electronic resources resulted in what many commentators described as "changing patterns of use" among library and museum patrons—changes that drastically altered the role of these institutions in their communities.[6] Students with remote access to academic library databases per-

1

ceived the library more as a virtual resource for online research materials than as a physical destination on campus. At the University of Idaho, "door counts and book circulation…decreased by more than 20 percent" in the period 1997–2000, but "since 1999, the number of electronic articles that Idaho students retrieved went up by about 350 percent."[7] Augusta State University in Georgia reported that gate counts were down from 402,361 in 1992–1993 to 217,977 in the 2000–2001 academic year, but that "online traffic has increased dramatically."[8] One Augusta State student "managed to get through two years of college…without ever borrowing a book from the library."[9] Similar scenarios were unfolding in public libraries, which were "being disintermediated by full-text access to a growing virtual library of journal and magazine articles"—a situation that placed an "even greater control of information in the hands of potential clients, making them less likely to utilize the bricks-and-mortar library."[10]

As museums and libraries expended time and money to develop resources and services that coincided with new technology-based structures of both traditional and distance learning, they faced another challenge: how to remain a physical presence in their communities. If people could access museum and library collections remotely, what incentive do they have to visit the buildings that house these collections? Librarians and museologists began to pose such fundamental questions as "To what degree is a library or museum a physical space?" and "What is the community role of libraries and museums?"[11] Ray Lester pointedly asks, "In a society where—in principle—everyone, everywhere throughout the globe will have direct online access to digital representations of exactly the sort of artefacts which have traditionally been collected, looked after and made accessible within our memory institutions, what future roles are there then for those institutions?"[12]

Some indication of the changing community roles of libraries and museums can be found in Martin's description of these institutions as not only primary social agencies "in support of education," but also "social settings for numerous community activities" that provide "extraordinary opportunities for recreation and enjoyment."[13] At the same time that museums and libraries struggled with how to use their collections to educate and inform the public in the digital era, they also had to contend with competition from countless entertainment venues that recognized that "well-packaged education is compatible with pleasurable experience and may enhance it."[14] As popular attractions such as Disney World and Sea World combined education and sensation, museums and libraries also sought to increase the entertainment value of what they offered the public. While their proposed solutions provided social settings and opportunities for recreation and enjoyment, in many cases these solutions had little to do with the educative function of museum and library collections. Instead, libraries and museums followed the lead of other leisure-time venues and offered a range of entertainment-based services and experiences.

The tension between educating and entertaining the public was captured in the term *edutainment*. Stephen Asma explains that the concept of edutainment, as defined in the museum world, can be reduced to a simple formula: "By making the educational function of the museum more entertaining, [museum] leaders...hope to boost admissions." This formula has proved to be as controversial as it is straightforward. Museum professionals worried that, "by mimicking the commercialism of the theme park world," the edutainment model diminished scholarship. An exhibit at the Field Museum in Chicago entitled Dinosaur Families (1997) was, according to Asma, "remarkably lame": in an attempt to mine the popularity of Steven Spielberg's movie *Jurassic Park*, the exhibit "consisted of shopping-mall dinosaur robots that squeaked and jerked about in a manner so gripping that my niece fell asleep as we watched it."[15] Art museums adopted similar tactics, only to suffer similar criticisms. Jed Perl equated the museum's appeal to popular themes with the demise of its traditional educative role—a process he referred to as "the Disneyization of the museum world."[16] Hilde Hein made a more sweeping indictment, commenting that the trend to edutainment represented "a decline in the respect paid to specialized scholarship and a corresponding elevation of experiential knowledge held accessible to everyone."[17] For Hein, the "elevation" of the everyday ultimately prefigured the redefinition of the museum as simply another form of mass entertainment.

A vivid illustration of these concerns can be seen in the controversy swirling around the Chocolate exhibit at the American Museum of Natural History (AMNH) in New York in 2003. As recounted by Julie Salamon in an article with the deliciously astute—as well as ironically subversive—headline "Museums Defend Fudge Factor,"[18] some individuals saw Chocolate, originally curated by the Field Museum in Chicago, as a valuable undertaking for museums. David Helfand, chairman of the astronomy department at Columbia University, commented favorably on the exhibit's drawing power: "It frightens me to think about the gap between scientific content and decisions that need to be made and the scientific knowledge of the population at large [and so] I think if chocolate pulls them in the door, it's great." Charles S. Spencer, chairman of the AMNH's anthropology department—observing that "every exhibit is a balancing act.... We try to make things educational but also to present it in a way that is entertaining and not boring"—remarked that lectures such as "Can Chocolate Save the Rain Forest?" offset "weekend chocolate tastings" and chocolatiers molding chocolate animals. And Sophia Siskel, director of exhibitions and education at the Field Museum, while conceding that "for some people the exhibition might be sugar-coated," defended it on the grounds of relevancy: "But if we don't make ourselves relevant and exciting to a general audience, we become the dinosaurs that we house."

At the same time, there were other aspects of the exhibit to which due attention should be given. Chocolate, we are told, was originally conceived as a "tiny" exhibition "containing some dried botanical specimens," but "when the museum briefly described the proposed display in a listing of future events, the positive feedback from the public was huge, more than for any other [proposed] show." The initial plans for a small-scale exhibit were, logically enough, rethought. The exhibit was also commercialized; after all, "museums now design their gift shops as carefully as their exhibitions." But what was particularly striking about the Chocolate commercialization was its invasively tentacular and grating scope. Numerous visitors complained about it. For example, despite the fact that her children happily "watched videos in a setting designed to look like a giant box of bonbons, listening to testimonials about the pleasures of chocolate," Judy Colp Rubin was "not enthralled" because "the gift shop loomed inescapably beyond the exit; she could see shelves full of Godiva for sale. She said with a sigh: 'All I've been hearing is, "When can we buy the chocolate?"'" Another parent angrily asked, "Is no place sacred from the heavy sell jobs we're faced with 24 hours a day in our lives?"

Even those who did not complain were blissfully swept away by the exhibit. Despite the presence of "exhibits explaining where cacao beans grow and how the chocolate trade once encouraged slavery," children and adults tended, on the whole, to agree with a boy who—while lining up at the gift shop cash register after selecting candy bars and boxes of chocolate—bluntly stated, "The best part of the exhibit is here." And if the views of Katharine Ho about the exhibit were slightly more nuanced than those of the enthusiastic—though no less pragmatic—boy, they nonetheless partook of the same sensibility. Admitting that she probably would not have come to Chocolate except for "a newspaper photograph of the hot chocolate bread being sold in conjunction with the exhibition," Ho felt somehow obligated to endure the exhibit before she went to the specially constructed café. "'It looked like bread with fudge in the middle,' she said with a beatific expression. 'But to go directly to the café without going through the exhibition would have been too gluttonous.'"

On reading these statements, perhaps the right question to ask, along with Salamon, is, "Does it matter if Chocolate feels more akin to the Food Network than [to] *Nova*?" And yet even she, in the course of her article, cannot hide her ambiguous feelings about whether it does, or does not, matter. On the other hand, it is clear that the criticisms of Asma, Perl, and Hein cannot be dismissed as the musings of cantankerous traditionalists and out-of-touch curmudgeons condemned to fight a losing intellectual battle. Many of their fears are substantiated by Chocolate as the AMNH and other museums "fudge" their educative missions in quest of attendance figures, popular renown as an entertainment venue, and income to "offset cutbacks in government funds, reduced private giving and the post-Sept. 11 loss of tourism." If Chocolate can be said to be representative, museums, at the end of the twentieth century and the beginning of the twenty-first century, not only made it general practice to rely on customer feedback to choose and prioritize the subject matter of future exhibits, but also were deliberately oblivious to the implications of attracting customers who—like Rubin's children and Katharine Ho—were more interested in the commercial and entertainment aspects of the museum function than in its ability to serve as a primary agent "in support of education, providing resources and services that complement the structures of formal education and extend education into an enterprise that lasts the length of a lifetime." Accordingly, Helfand's comment that "I think if chocolate pulls them in the door, it's great" is, at best, disingenuous, and, at worst, naive, given that, although customers like Ho are "pulled in the door" by Chocolate, it is only to race through the exhibit as a sense of duty to justify their real reason for going to the museum—the treats at the café and the gift shop.

Libraries too have attracted their fair share of criticism for becoming what some perceive to be rudderless entertainment centers. Consider Hal Niedzviecki's eloquent and politically charged article "Libraries Need to Mind Their Own Business."[19] Niedzviecki, founder of the Canadian alternative publication *Broken Pencil: The Magazine for 'Zine Culture and the Independent Arts*, is anything but a traditionalist curmudgeon, but he comes very close to having the same views about the role and obligations of public libraries as Asma, Perl, and Hein have about museums. The fact that libraries are no longer vital institutions in the public consciousness, he writes, is the fault of libraries themselves. To be sure, some libraries are success stories—for example, the Toronto Public Library can proudly say that it circulates the most books (in more than one hundred languages) in North America, and the Halifax (Nova Scotia) Public Library was honored in 2002 by the American Library Association "for outstanding achievement in the promotion of library services"—but he detects a general malaise and confusion among librarians about the real purpose and social role of their institutions. "Libraries are...venturing into murky waters," in large part because "they are attempting to be everything to everybody, particularly at a time when higher usage is often rewarded with higher levels of funding support from government." Listing some egregious examples of services and programs—the Canada Taiwan Bird Fair at the Vancouver central library, a course about Feng Shui in the Bedroom at the Edmonton library, and lectures at the Toronto library about small business plans and film festivals—Niedzviecki squarely places this "truly strange" array of offerings against the context of competition in which the existence of an organization is associated with measurable outcomes. In the case of private-sector firms, an important measurable outcome is profit figures; in the case of nonprofits, important measurable outcomes include circulation and attendance statistics. In a world of zero-sum financial balance sheets, libraries feel that they must demonstrate their utility in relation to other public services. The higher the attendance statistics that libraries can point to, the better their chances of extracting funding from governmental entities. Thus, to generate these statistics, libraries compete for the attention span of consumers who have an almost limitless range of entertainment options. After all, their potential patrons can attend such outsized cultural and corporate events as the International Festival of Authors or "the celebrity-cookbook author [that] Indigo [a Canadian bookstore chain] is bringing to a suburb near you" instead of coming to the library. Libraries thus assume the trappings of their competitors; they become the same kind of edutainment-based activity centers as museums. In so doing, they lose an essential part of their identity as they blithely schedule events that they hope will periodically entice crowds away from the local equivalent of Indigo, Disney theme parks, or other contemporary amusements.

All this is bad enough on its own, but Niedzviecki deserves considerable praise for understanding that promotions such as "vote for the best book" contests or campaigns that focus on selecting a single book for an entire city to read are, structurally, on the same level as entertainment-based programming and events. These contests and campaigns are especially insidious because libraries are positioning books as "mere cogs in the machine of capitalism" and, instead of being "oases of non-commercial activity," are participating in "what is essentially book-industry marketing."

> At the library, if nowhere else, all books should be considered equal regardless of how much press an author is getting, or what awards are dispensed. If the public library can't stay out of the fame game, it becomes an adjunct to the book industry, and not a last bastion upholding our collective right to free access to information.

As Niedzviecki recognizes all too well, the book industry is part of the vast entertainment complex—"that interlocking world of books, articles, TV shows, movies, radio, pop music, and Web sites"—dominated by a handful of corporate conglomerates that practice what commentators such as Robert McChesney and André Schiffrin identify as vertical integration and market censorship to predetermine what books ultimately appear on library shelves.[20] To take one small example, large publishers can afford to send hundreds of free review copies to influential critics and tastemakers, while smaller publishers cannot afford to do so.[21] Libraries feel they have very little choice but to buy these heavily promoted items because their patrons are clamoring for them, but the clamor itself has likely been artificially created. In sum, librarians and libraries often fail to realize just how deeply imbedded they are within this corporate nexus, how "[t]he books that are finally chosen by libraries have...already been chosen by others who have financial and corporate influence."[22] Many librarians thus follow the principles of the "responsive public library collection" as articulated by, among others, Sharon Baker and Karen Wallace, in which selection and purchasing decisions are based on "product analysis" and "marketing-based" principles about what is popular and what is not.[23] The result is creeping homogeneity of collections—something that Baker and Wallace implicitly admit when, citing studies showing that approximately 30–35 percent of borrowers are responsible for 78–80 percent of circulated books, they recommend that libraries "maximize limited resources by concentrating major efforts on the core market while simultaneously using a limited number of well-considered, targeted efforts to reach individuals who currently lack motivation to use the library."[24] When libraries try to appeal to core markets by spending a significant percentage of their acquisitions budget on cultural products generated by corporately controlled media, there is scant room for "creative forms largely shut out of the mass media...[such as] shot-on-video documentaries, avant-garde post rock..., and books on how to start your own lo-fi radio station—the kind of stuff, in other words, that slips through the corporate cracks, the kind of stuff you won't find at the local HMV or Blockbuster."[25] As a result, libraries neglect their role as "frontline facilitators for media literacy...[who] focus on teaching us how to interpret and speak back to the media system."[26] The trend toward edutainment-based activities is therefore very much a political question. By emphasizing edutainment or infotainment as a response to competition from other entertainment options, museums and libraries forego the opportunity to emphasize that which is not edutainment or infotainment and to provide opportunities for patrons to acquire meaningful knowledge and develop critical inquiry skills.

This brings us back to the Feng Shui in the Bedroom course at the Edmonton Public Library. Not only are such courses examples of edutainment, but they also raise some of the same kinds of political issues as library emphasis on bestsellers. Kimberly Lau explains how many individuals in advanced Western capitalist societies—caught in the transition from industrial society to what Ulrich Beck has called a "risk society," defined as a society that seeks to protect itself, in multiple ways, against "the techno-industrial processes that sustain modernity"—have co-opted Eastern health and wellness traditions such as yoga and tai chi in their attempts to develop "social responses" to the ills of modernity.[27] Feng shui can also be inscribed as part of this Eastern wellness tradition. But this alternative social response is, in reality, a fundamental part of the way global capitalism sustains itself by framing alternative practices of all kinds as "alternative *purchasing* practices" that give individuals the "impression" that they are taking some sort of "positive social action" through consumerism [original emphasis]. Traditions such as tai chi, yoga, and feng shui are thus positioned as "commodified bits of difference" in a world where "[d]ifference has become a highly marketable commodity" that has been "sanitized and *neutralized* for easy consumption" [original emphasis].

But, as Lau caustically observes, "the shift from ostensible status symbols to understated ones does nothing to redistribute wealth, nor to make health, wellness, and spirituality equally accessible. Consumption is obviously not political action, despite the popular New Age discourses aspiring to make it so." In other words, "[a]ttention to class and equality issues is supplanted by concern for individual and planetary wellness, considerations that are easily accommodated through consumption as a mode of social action." The result of such "disturbing self-absorption"—manifested as self-discovery and self-healing—is that individuals start to believe that the "commodified discourses" of alternative health are political and that alternative health consumption is a "political action"—a circumstance that, ironically, leads to inaction and self-satisfaction because it "obscures the issues of power and inequality at the core of class society."

Just as important, these alternative health traditions become "orientalist fascinations" that "pass for political corrections" inasmuch as they perpetuate "the common tropes of popular orientalism which entangle the East in a romanticized past: the East as a timeless place that transcends the problems of this world, a place where the West can escape from its ills, a place where the West can seek peaceful solace." Accordingly, India and China are transformed from "contemporary modern world economies to nations of spiritual peasants"—a way of thinking that, again, enforces long-standing stereotypes about the hierarchy of civilizations. Just as their emphasis on bestsellers and best-books lists po-sitioned libraries as "mere cogs in the machine of capitalism," so do such courses as Feng Shui in the Bedroom. Instead of the "oases of non-commercial activity" that Niedzviecki would like them to be, libraries participate in consolidating ex-isting power relations and the inequality that results from such hierarchies through edutainment-based programming, events, and experiences.

In the words of Sallie Tisdale, libraries have become entertainment cen-ters,[28] so much so that "the ability to research, read, and reflect...is nonexistent in an institution so conceived [because] [i]t is like studying at the mall."[29] As we have seen, the same could be said about museums. And so it is logical to ask whether there is an overarching sociopolitical explanation for this transforma-tion of libraries and museums. Basing his argument on the work of such scholars as Herbert Schiller,[30] Juris Dilevko suggested that the rise of the library-as-enter-tainment-center was closely connected with the increasing reliance of libraries on corporatized and commodified technologically based information and media resources that brought about, among members of the public, "a packaged con-sciousness emanating from corporate ideology" and "the commercialization and industrialization of the mind."[31] All this, in turn, was linked to a "neo-liberal deficit culture" that preached the "supremacy of market imperatives" and gave rise to a "politics of scarcity" and "economic rationalization" whereby govern-ment spending is allocated only on the basis of performance measures and is no longer "squandered on costly social programs with egalitarian impacts."[32]

As John Buschman forcefully argues, libraries were no longer seen in terms of their contribution to an independent, inclusive, and critical public sphere consisting of "fully informed participants, and acting as a space apart from the commodification that characterizes [contemporary] culture," but in "economic terms" such that "discussion of and decisions about libraries are being made in the context of economic instrumentality."[33] Libraries were thus positioned within "the dominant new public philosophy trends" that assigned overall value to institutions based on their economic contributions.[34] This regime of informa-tion capitalism was achieved through an emphasis on technological and net-worked resources, which were viewed as the best way for individuals to become lifelong learners who would contribute to the economic renewal promised by an information-based society.[35]

Because the obsession with cutting deficits reduced the total amount of money available to fund public services at all levels of government, the level of base operating funds received by any service or entity became subject to quan-tifiable outcome measures that could demonstrate the ongoing relevance and ef-ficiency of that service or entity within a given community in comparison with other services or entities. For libraries, this meant that the "funding of *additional* technological resources is *not* being funded with additional [total] resources," and so there was less money for such things as increased service hours and print collections, to name only a few [original emphasis].[36] Naturally enough, most services and entities experienced shortfalls. Libraries—as well as other cultural and educational institutions—were compelled to seek money from other sources, especially competitive grants from private companies and philanthropic foundations such as the Bill & Melinda Gates Foundation. Because these private-sector organizations are interested in "furthering the agenda of wealth creation and protection under information capitalism,"[37] they were strong advocates of the viewpoint that, no matter the field or area, technological innovations and solutions lead to significant productivity and performance increases, variously measured. Competing for private funding against other cultural institutions on a regional or national scale, libraries typically asked for money for projects that were "deemed marketable and catchy, and the overwhelming hype and public relations surrounding networked technologies fits that bill and makes libraries seem relevant and contemporary."[38] Moreover, libraries that were successful in attracting private money used their success to "leverage" additional public tax support and competitive governmental grants.[39] The ideology of private capital, with its "strong biases" toward technological innovation, began to dominate the cultural and educational landscape.[40]

But all this comes at a cost: the "public sphere function of libraries subtly but surely changes...from a space for research, reflection, and reading to part of a community's 'social capital'" so that libraries are redefined "as part of a community's (or a university's or a school's) economic assets to lure wealthier home-owners or students or businesses."[41] Accordingly, for libraries to be perceived as valuable and relevant participants in the new information economy, they are forced to demonstrate their drawing power by emphasizing "marketable and catchy" technologically based information and media solutions capable of drawing large numbers of individuals into the library and thus meeting performance measures that qualify them for future funding. The result is a wide range of infotainment- and edutainment-oriented resources, events, and programs that purport to stimulate learning but are, more often than not, the antithesis of the type of serious study, knowledge acquisition, reflection, contemplation, and critical inquiry with which libraries—and museums—are traditionally associated. In their "unthinking shift" to the "entertainment resources and products of the 'new' economy" and in their rush to become "extension[s] of the media entertainment empire in order to 'survive,'" libraries—and museums—abrogate their function of being sites for "rational discourse—or the potential for [such] discourse,"[42] in effect precluding the establishment of a critical public sphere.

Little wonder, then, that some commentators have begun to worry about how cultural institutions can increase "deepened curiosity and prolonged, complex attention"[43]—the kind of "deep looking"[44] at objects that "holds promise of decentering us at a radical moment of unselfing, encouraging us to endeavor to respond objectively to these works of art...and to experience them as beautiful and to experience beauty as leading to caring, even justice"[45] but that the distractions of edutainment-based events and displays all too often preclude. Although these remarks by John Walsh and James Cuno, respectively, apply to art museums, the underlying issue, we believe, also has resonance for libraries and museums of all kinds. How can museums—and by extension, libraries—bring about a situation in which, rather than emphasizing edutainment-based events, they offer patrons objects "that exist outside of us, in themselves, and resist the commonplace; that have us leaving, as the poet Peter Sacks says, 'at a different angle' to that in which we came..."?[46] How can they navigate the "seductive dynamism of the marketplace" and lay claim to being legitimate agents of the type of intellectual "nourishment" that will make them "worthy of the public trust"?[47]

As museums and libraries struggled with such questions—and as some of them developed, separately, a series of edutainment strategies to remain relevant at the beginning of the twenty-first century—they also embarked upon a variety of partnership arrangements. Quite simply, the thinking was that the power and resources of two institutions are better than the power and resources of one. But just as the edutainment phenomenon has implications for libraries and museums viewed separately, so does it have implications for museum-library partnerships, especially in light of the questions broached in the previous paragraph. In chapter 2, we will touch in greater detail on some of these consequences.

NOTES

1. Robert S. Martin, "Welcoming Remarks" (presented at the 21st Century Learner Conference, Washington, DC, November 2001), par. 4, http://www.imls.gov/whatsnew/current/sp110701-3.htm (accessed September 6, 2003).

2. James Gorman, "In Virtual Museums, an Archive of the World," *New York Times*, 12 January 2003, par. 3–4, http://www.nytimes.com (accessed January 12, 2003).

3. Ibid., par. 7.

4. Bernard Vavrek, "Wanted! Entertainment Director," *American Libraries* 32 (June/July 2001): 69.

5. Ibid.

6. Karen Brown and Miriam Pollack, "Illinois Libraries and Museums: Connecting and Collaborating for the Future," *Illinois Libraries* 82 (summer 2000): 211.

7. Scott Carlson, "The Deserted Library: As Students Work Online, Reading Rooms Empty Out—Leading Some Campuses to Add Starbucks," *The Chronicle of Higher Education*, 16 November 2001, par. 6, http://chronicle.com/free/v48/i12/12a03501.htm (accessed November 29, 2001).

8. Ibid., par. 21.

9. Ibid., par. 2.

10. Vavrek, "Wanted!" 69.

11. Brown and Pollack, "Illinois Libraries and Museums," 212.

12. Ray Lester, "The Convergence of Museums and Libraries?" *Alexandria* 13 (March 2001): 184.

13. Martin, "Welcoming Remarks," par. 4.

14. Hilde S. Hein, *The Museum in Transition: A Philosophical Perspective* (Washington, DC: Smithsonian Institution Press, 2000), 81.

15. The three previous quotes are from Stephen T. Asma, *Stuffed Animals and Pickled Heads: The Culture and Evolution of Natural History Museums* (Oxford: Oxford University Press, 2001), 15, 35, 45.

16. Jed Perl, "Welcome to the Funhouse: Tate Modern and the Crisis of the Museum," *The New Republic*, 19 June 2000, 32.

17. Hein, *The Museum in Transition*, 48.

18. All quotations describing the Chocolate exhibit are from Julie Salamon, "Museums Defend Fudge Factor," *New York Times*, 30 July 2003, B1, B7.

19. Unless indicated otherwise, all quotations in the following paragraphs are from Hal Niedzviecki, "Libraries Need to Mind Their Own Business," *The Globe and Mail*, 27 October 2003, R3.

20. For an overview of these issues, see Juris Dilevko and Lisa Gottlieb, "The Politics of Standard Selection Guides: The Case of the *Public Library Catalog*," *Library Quarterly* 73 (July 2003): 289–337.

21. For a revealing look at how demand was created for Margaret Atwood's book *Oryx and Crake*, including a description of the strategy of sending advance copies to more than 300 people on a "big-mouth list" (defined as "anyone who can help create a buzz by word of mouth"), see Don Gilmor, "Anatomy of a Best-Seller," *Toronto Life*, September 2003, 86–92.

22. Ibid., 295.

23. Sharon L. Baker, *The Responsive Public Library Collection: How to Develop and Market It* (Englewood, CO: Libraries Unlimited, 1993); Sharon L. Baker and Karen L. Wallace, *The Responsive Public Library: How to Develop and Market a Winning Collection*, 2nd ed. (Englewood, CO: Libraries Unlimited, 2002).

24. Baker and Wallace, *The Responsive Public Library*, 12, 21.

25. Niedzviecki, "Libraries Need to Mind Their Own Business," R3.

26. Ibid.

27. All quotes in this and the two following paragraphs pertaining to alternative health practices are from Kimberly J. Lau, *New Age Capitalism: Making Money East of Eden* (Philadelphia: University of Pennsylvania Press, 2000), 7–12, 14, 135–40. Lau quotes Ulrich Beck, a German sociologist who has written a book called *Risk Society*, and refers to Stuart Hall, a Marxist media analyst.

28. Sallie Tisdale, "Silence, Please: The Public Library as Entertainment Center," *Harper's*, March 1997, 65–74.

29. John E. Buschman, *Dismantling the Public Sphere: Situating and Sustaining Librarianship in the Age of the New Public Philosophy* (Westport, CT: Libraries Unlimited, 2003), 73.

30. Herbert I. Schiller, *Culture, Inc.: The Corporate Takeover of Public Expression* (New York: Oxford University Press, 1989).

31. Juris Dilevko, "Why Sallie [Sally] Tisdale is *Really* Upset about the State of Libraries: Socio-political Implications of Internet Information Sources," *Journal of Information Ethics* 8 (spring 1999): 37–62. Dilevko quotes Schiller, *Culture, Inc.*, 89–90.

32. Dilevko, "Why Sallie [Sally] Tisdale is *Really* Upset," 50, 54. Dilevko's argument relies on Isabella Bakker, "Introduction: The Gendered Foundations of Restructuring in Canada," in *Rethinking Restructuring: Gender and Change in Canada*, ed. Isabella Bakker (Toronto, ON: University of Toronto Press, 1996), 3–25.

33. Buschman, *Dismantling the Public Sphere*, 37, 38, 48.

34. Ibid., 73.

35. Ibid., 57–62.

36. Ibid., 72.

37. Ibid., 69.

38. Ibid., 70.

39. Ibid.

40. Ibid., 71.

41. Ibid., 73.

42. Ibid., 74.

43. John Walsh, "Pictures, Tears, Lights, and Seats," in *Whose Muse? Art Museums and the Public Trust,* ed. James Cuno (Princeton, NJ: Princeton University Press, 2004), 88. Walsh quotes Philip Fisher.

44. Ibid., 88.

45. James Cuno, ed., "The Object of Art Museums," in *Whose Muse? Art Museums and the Public Trust* (Princeton, NJ: Princeton University Press, 2004), 51.

46. Ibid., 52.

47. James N. Wood, "The Authorities of the American Art Museum," in *Whose Muse? Art Museums and the Public Trust,* ed. James Cuno (Princeton, NJ: Princeton University Press, 2004), 108–9, 125, 127.

2 MUSEUMS, LIBRARIES, AND POSTOBJECT ROLES

The controversial tenure of Lawrence M. Small as secretary of the Smithsonian Institution is a good place to begin examining the museum edutainment model. Leaving the corporate sector to join the Smithsonian in 2000, Small became "the first non-academic and only the second non-scientist to lead the institution"; he had the dubious distinction (in the museum world) of not having an advanced degree.[1] His contentious relationship with curators and scholars at the Smithsonian, however, had less to do with a lack of academic credentials than with his wealth of business experience. As Small himself stated, he wanted the Smithsonian to focus on the "two M's: modernization and money."[2] Employing a "corporate vision and blunt, sometimes combative management style," he proposed increasing private fund-raising and corporate partnerships, "the mounting of more crowd-pleasing blockbuster exhibitions," and the "renovation of what he calls shabby buildings."[3] At the same time, Small developed plans for unpopular cost-cutting measures directed at research projects—plans that he subsequently withdrew to quell a "rebellion" led by Smithsonian scientists and curators over what they saw "as an assault—under the cover of modernization—on the institution's research function."[4] As Elaine Sciolino explains, "The clash pits a purist notion of intellectual pursuit against the need to operate efficiently, raise money and draw audiences to compete with the Internet and popular tourist attractions like Disney World."[5]

Warfare (internecine or otherwise) waged against an economic backdrop is an appropriate metaphor not only for the controversies at the Smithsonian, but also for the challenges facing museums generally. According to Neil Cossons of the London Science Museum, "The battlefield will be the marketplace and the casualties will be those museums that fail to adapt."[6] If the marketplace is the battlefield, then the object of the battle is to attract consumers who have the discretionary spending power of time. To compete, museums have embraced a "marketing mode...concentrated on first trying to discover and then attempting to satisfy...public needs and interests."[7] Deborah Solomon calls it "the revenge of the focus groups," noting that "museums are obsessed with audience response, relying on attendance forecasting and visitor research (a field that barely existed 20 years ago) to plan their shows."[8]

Attendance forecasting and visitor research are often used to develop block-buster exhibitions, a concept rooted in congressional legislation supported by the museum community. Introduced in the House of Representatives in 1975, the Arts and Artifacts Indemnity Act permitted "the Federal Council on the Arts and Humanities to indemnify works of art, printed matter, other artifacts and objects and motion pictures or recordings which have educational, cultural, historical or scientific value, and whose exhibition is certified by the Secretary of State as being in the national interest."[9] Instrumental in lobbying Congress to pass the legislation was J. Carter Brown, director of the National Gallery of Art in Washington, D.C. from 1969 to 1992, who recognized that museums, once freed from prohibitive insurance costs, would be able to exhibit important objects from other institutions' permanent collections.[10] This enabled American museums to create shows centered on famous, attention-drawing masterpieces from around the world, rather than having to depend solely upon their own collections for exhibitions. It also meant that a popular show, developed through the collaborative efforts of the host and the lending institution, could easily be mounted at a series of museums in the United States. The end result was the concept of the traveling blockbuster.

The repute of the objects that comprise blockbuster shows pleases not only museum patrons but also administrators, who are well aware that famous artworks and artifacts attract enormous crowds and, therefore, revenue. The year after Congress passed the Arts and Artifacts Indemnity Act, the National Gallery served as the first host of the Treasures of Tutankhamen show, "which brought more than 8 million people to museums in seven American cities" and was "largely credited with ushering in the era of blockbuster museum shows."[11] In 2003, about 4,000 people per day visited the Matisse Picasso exhibition at the Museum of Modern Art in Queens, while 800,000 individuals traveled to the Los Angeles County Museum of Art over a period of 17 weeks in 1999 to see the works of Vincent van Gogh.[12] And, in the ultimate sign that exhibitions of all kinds would assume even bigger blockbuster proportions, the maximum insurance coverage for museum exhibitions was raised to $600 million as part of a revision to the Arts and Artifacts Indemnity Act in 2003.[13]

Although Solomon identifies museums' recipe for blockbusters as shows "that appeal to the broadest audience and ideally feature at least one French Impressionist,"[14] blockbusters can transcend genres of art and artifacts. A case in point was the 2003 display of the Dead Sea Scrolls at the Public Museum of Grand Rapids, Michigan. The museum anticipated that 225,000 individuals would view the scrolls, a figure substantially above the usual target audience for its exhibits.[15] Planning for an exhibition of this magnitude entailed a series of changes in the museum's operations, including "a marketing campaign more aggressive than anything [the museum] has done in the past," additional security, and extended hours, as well as "a special gift store that sells tote bags, neckties and silk scarves decorated with images from the scrolls" and a museum restaurant menu "adjusted to include Middle Eastern dishes."[16] The scope of these changes prompted the institution's director to conclude, "We're a 149-year-old museum that has just reinvented itself."[17] This reinvention encompasses not only the adjustments made for the Dead Sea Scrolls exhibit, but also changes in the perception of the museum itself. The publicity generated by the exhibit—and visitors' accolades—raised the profile of the museum in its community. This praise and publicity, in turn, created a heightened profile of the institution in the museum community as a whole: "The Dead Sea Scrolls show means that museum professionals will probably never again think of Grand Rapids as having no more significant [a] cultural destination than the Gerald R. Ford Presidential Museum."[18]

THE CONTROVERSY ABOUT BLOCKBUSTERS

The success of blockbuster exhibits that display the art of Matisse, van Gogh, and Picasso or artifacts such as the Dead Sea Scrolls raises the question of why this approach to attracting museum visitors is controversial. Notwithstanding some critics' labelling of French impressionist blockbuster shows as hackneyed, could it nevertheless be argued that these exhibitions present a neutral territory on which intellectual purists and marketing pragmatists could meet? The answer to this question has little to do with the art or artifacts on display, and that itself is the source of the controversy. In other words, blockbuster shows are about more than the prominent treasures on display. Consider the exhibit of the Dead Sea Scrolls at the Public Museum of Grand Rapids, where the gift shop sold souvenirs with the religious texts emblazoned on them and the museum restaurant offered a specially devised Middle Eastern menu. These extra amenities signify that a visit to the exhibit involves not only seeing the scrolls, but also shopping and eating—activities that, critics would argue, have no intrinsic connection to the presumed reason for the visit. No matter how enjoyable these experiences might be, buying a silk scarf and sampling falafel do not enhance one's appreciation or understanding of the Dead Sea Scrolls.

What critics of blockbuster exhibits decry is the evolution from museum displays that focus exclusively on specific artworks or objects to a packaging of various experiences that museums now create for their patrons—experiences that, while intended to increase the enjoyment of the visit, are often commercial in nature. In essence, blockbuster exhibits are more spectacle than traditional exhibit, with such unavoidable features as timed, advance-sale tickets and snaking lines ushered by docents and security guards. In another example, the Royal Academy of Arts in London hosted a blockbuster show in 1999 entitled Monet in the 20th Century, whose record 813,000 visitors over a period of 12 weeks made it "the most popular art exhibition ever held in Britain."[19] Popularity led to prosperity, with revenue generated by both tickets and merchandising, enabling the academy to clear existing debts.[20] Reacting to the exhibit, the art critic of the *London Evening Standard* wrote that the academy "seems determined to make money and be vulgarly popular rather than conscientiously promote scholarship, connoisseurship and genuine esthetic excitement."[21] Offering a different perspective, a trustee of the academy conceded that, in order to attract visitors, "you have to put on shows that people want to see."[22]

Arguably, scholarship and popularity mesh more easily in impressionist paintings than in examples of recent blockbuster exhibits based on popular media, such as The Adventures of Wallace and Gromit hosted by the Museum of Fine Arts in Boston (1998) and *Star Wars:* The Magic of Myth, whose stops included the San Diego Museum of Art (2000), the Minneapolis Institute of Arts (2000), and the Brooklyn Museum of Art (2002). Because museums use market research techniques such as focus groups to determine what "people want to see," blockbuster exhibits become not only popular attractions, but also encomiums of popular culture—what Perl condemns as the selection of a themed exhibit "on the basis of how closely it resembles what people are seeing in the Multiplex or on Cable TV."[23] Frequently offering the cultural flavor of the month, blockbuster shows promise a spectacle comprising comfortably familiar experiences—popular themes, shopping, and eating—that characterize other entertainment venues.

The emphasis, in blockbuster exhibits, on providing visitors with varied experiences and a sense of spectacle also applies to how museums function in general. Museums assume what Douglas Davis terms *postobject* roles, serving as a "medium of information and pleasure as well as a repository providing first-hand access to the sacred object."[24] Or, as Stephen Weil explains, the "age of stuff" of museums "is slowly evolving into an 'age of nonstuff,' an age not of things but of interactions and processes."[25] In the age of stuff, the primary objective of the museum was "the growth, care, and study of its collection,"[26] whereas in the age of nonstuff, museum collections are relegated to a secondary role. Describing the shift from authentic object to authentic experience, Hein notes that the museum's goal now "is the achievement of an experience that is genuine, but undergoing such an experience does not depend on meditation by an authentic object."[27] Consequently, the notion of authenticity differs in the context of the age of stuff as opposed to the age of nonstuff. When applied to a museum's collection, a label of authenticity assigns value based on the rarity, novelty, or historical significance of the objects. What makes experiences authentic is the degree to which they both reflect and involve the museum visitor, irrespective of the objects on display.

THE EDUTAINMENT PHENOMENON

A good place to begin examining the various types of "interactions and processes" of the postobject museum and their relationship to the edutainment phenomenon is the museum itself—that is, the building, rather than the collection. Despite, or perhaps because of, competition for patrons' time and attention, museums are embarking on projects for new or renovated facilities—a building boom that can be explained, in part, by the fact that new buildings or building additions attract money from both donors and visitors. As Michael Kimmelman remarks, "It is always easier to commission an architect and raise money for a building than it is to amass a first-rate collection, because, among other reasons…patrons are generally happier to see their names engraved in large letters in stone than to see them printed in tiny wall labels next to paintings."[28] Buildings appeal to potential donors not simply as personal, philanthropic trophies, but as a means of raising corporate and civic profiles and revenues—the same factors that motivate the museums themselves to break ground on new projects. Attracted to an attention-grabbing new structure, visitors can revitalize not only the lagging finances of the museum, but also the economy of the surrounding community. As a result, museums "are competing with one another to produce the most striking buildings," asking "renowned architects…to come up with buildings so unusual that they may become tourist attractions in their own right."[29] Simply put, everyone wants to be the next Bilbao.

Designed by architect Frank Gehry and completed in 1997, the Guggenheim Museum in Bilbao, Spain, is perhaps the most conspicuous example of the museum building as tourist attraction. Kimmelman incisively cuts to the heart of the matter: "Bilbao has become the ultimate dream of museum entrepreneurs. You don't even need a collection. You can borrow one. The goals are now civic luster and economic improvement—decent goals but, aside from the aesthetics of the building itself, not artistic ones."[30] While Gehry's signature design of undulating titanium appeals to architectural critics and visitors, it eclipses, in terms of the public's collective consciousness, the collection it houses. Guggenheim Bilbao embodies the experience/object dichotomy, giving visitors a spectacle worth seeing, but one that, at the same time, is curiously disconnected from the museum's collection. Perl is scathing in his assessment of this trend: "Nobody goes to Guggenheim Bilbao to see the art. Looking at art is just something you ought to remember to do while you are there, like going to the bathroom or taking your vitamins."[31]

With its high profile, Guggenheim Bilbao has certainly become the poster child for a new generation of museums whose identity, as Victoria Newhouse observes, is more closely linked to the container, not the contents.[32] But it did not originate this trend. That distinction is held by the Centre Georges Pompidou, which opened in Paris in 1977. Architects Renzo Piano and Richard Rogers described their creation as a "live center of information and entertainment" and as "a cross between an informational Times Square and the British Museum."[33] This hybridization combined a modern art collection with an open-access public library, an experimental music center, a children's museum, movie screens, cafés, restaurants, and gift shops. As originally envisioned, this amalgamation of cultural and popular attractions signalled the Pompidou's role as "the anti-Louvre—a freer, friendlier, multi-use museum for a freer, friendlier, multi-use

Paris."[34] As Vera Zolberg explains, "By comparison with the usual French art museums, the Centre Pompidou...is unique in its deliberate commitment to attract a large public by providing the atmosphere of a supermarket of events and exhibitions. It shows art forms and styles that incorporate everyday experience...and 'marginalized art' that may be understood without reference to the scholarly aestheticizing discourse of modern art."[35] The Pompidou center sought to fulfil its populist mandate by validating art forms that reflect "everyday experience"—a policy consistent with the democratization-of-institutions movement promoted by cultural theorists at the time and summarized by Kimmelman as "down with elitism, question authority."[36] But at the same time, the Pompidou's user-friendliness equates populism with choice and interactivity—the "interactions and processes" of authentic experiences—by offering what Zolberg refers to as "a supermarket of events and exhibitions."[37] In other words, the Pompidou center is consciously unscripted. Just as the modern art collection is to be interpreted within the context of everyday experience, independent of scholarly narration, the choice of what to experience within the Pompidou center is left to the visitor.

Twenty years later, the concepts of choice and interactivity also characterize the Pompidou's successors. Consider the J. Paul Getty Center in Los Angeles, designed by architect Richard Meier and, like the Guggenheim Bilbao, completed in 1997. Describing the trip from parking lot to museum, Newhouse explains that "every four minutes throughout the day a tram leaves the 1,200-car garage, transporting visitors on the scenic, uphill trip to a museum that is, in effect, the most rarified version of the theme park formula yet devised."[38] This formula also applies to the scene presented to visitors once they disembark: The tram "deposit[s] you in an open plaza where you are surrounded by several buildings and therefore several options. You can stroll in one direction toward the restaurant, with a view of the ocean. You can peruse the gardens. There is a study center for scholars, and in yet another building is a hall for lectures and performances."[39]

Kimmelman's observation that the museum at the J. Paul Getty Center "is the major attraction at the site, but not the only one"[40] can be applied to the Pompidou center as well—with one qualification. The Pompidou center's successors have reinterpreted the idea of creating egalitarian and entertaining museum experiences. Rather than providing visitors with popular cultural options, as was the guiding principle of the Pompidou in 1977, the new generation of museums gives visitors options that are deemed commercially popular. As with the spectacular buildings prominent architects are enlisted to design, these new museum experiences are, at best, tangentially related to the museum collection. More often, they reflect the fact that museums increasingly are run like businesses, with the interconnected priorities of catering to the customer and generating revenue. In some instances, patron experiences revolve around the museum's "ancillary business activities like restaurants, museum shops, online sales and licensing."[41] Reflecting how the role of museums has evolved since the "anti-Louvre" Centre Pompidou, I. M. Pei's glass-pyramid addition to the Louvre is yet another example of the container as tourist attraction. Intended to be an inviting gateway to the museum, critics have assailed its "airport aesthetic,"[42] a criticism directed at both the actual design of the pyramid and the fact that it is the "centerpiece of a new complex of ticket windows, shops and restaurants that attracted visitors who never bothered to see the art."[43]

In addition to restaurants and gift shops, museums offer patrons other activity-based experiences that, in the words of one museum administrator, are "chang[ing] the nature of the way people experience the museum."[44] The Dallas Museum of Art offers tai chi classes Saturday mornings. The Walker Art Center in Minneapolis has Walker After Hours—"monthly evenings aimed at younger members with films, videos and music" and a specially concocted "martini of the month."[45] The Brooklyn Museum of Art has First Saturdays, with a different schedule of events each month. According to the program for August 2003, patrons were "taken on a musical journey around the world—from the Balkans to the Caribbean" by two Brooklyn bands.[46] In addition, visitors were "invited to sketch charcoal portraits from a live model," view the film *It Came From Outer Space*, or attend a lecture on "the influence of pulp art on computer game designs" before rounding out the evening with a dance party from 9:00 to 11:00 P.M.[47] In an intriguing twist on the notion of museums furnishing patrons with "interactions and processes," these evening programs have emerged as a popular social scene, highlighting "the marketing potential of museums as promoters of relationships."[48] As the director of the Brooklyn Museum of Art commented, "The reason we started First Saturday was not for a dating opportunity. But with the emphasis on inclusion rather than exclusion, the evening really has become a comfortable meeting place for everyone in the community and it lends itself to those options."[49]

INTERACTIVE DISPLAYS AND EXHIBITS

Much like the way that museums use architectural attractions and entertainment-oriented activities, permanent exhibits are also vehicles for providing patrons with authentic experiences. In this context, the traditional model of exhibits composed of labelled artifacts has given way "to less directed and more multi-sensory approaches."[50] Consider the somnolent mechanical dinosaurs that Asma encountered at the Chicago Field Museum's Dinosaur Families exhibit. One can imagine that 20 years ago this exhibit would have consisted of painted displays and stationary models. Not only are the themes of popular media frequently presented in exhibits, but the mode of presentation is also media based. Not limited to science museums, media-based presentations are "the essence of the new age of edutainment: the dazzling star show, the Hollywood star narration and the personalized, motivational delivery of scientific information.... Where once [museum] exhibitions were static, comprising artifacts in glass cases and wall-mounted captions, today they are increasingly cinematic and interactive 'experiences.'"[51] For example, dwindling attendance has prompted the directors of Mount Vernon in Virginia to infuse twenty-first-century technology into the life of George Washington. As executive director James Rees commented, "Our idea now is to find ways to show that he was the most robust man of action you can imagine. We're going to use film, sound, lights, and every other technique we can think of."[52] Ideas generated so far include "holograms, computer imagery, surround-sound audio programs and a live-action film made by Steven Spielberg's production company. The film may be shown in a theater equipped with seats that rumble and pipes that shoot smoke into the audience."[53]

Interactive exhibits in the postobject museum do not simply combine multiple media; they also incorporate technologies that enable patrons to actively participate in, rather than passively view, displays. Just as there is a contingent of prominent museum architects who produce tourist-attraction buildings, the "edutainment boom has…given rise to a new generation of exhibition designers" who specialize in the experiential.[54] One of these individuals is Edwin Schlossberg, who designed the Pope John Paul II Cultural Center in Washington, D.C. Describing the various experience-based activities available, Peter Hall reports that "visitors to the John Paul Center are encouraged to design a stained-glass window out of available motifs on a digital kiosk, practice bell-ringing and create a giant collaborative collage by floating designs onto a video wall. Visitors can record their testimonials and creations by swiping a card through a scanner and review them later at interactive stations in the café."[55] Another of the new-generation design firms, DMCD, developed "experiences" for the new Kalamazoo Air Zoo—a name that, while somewhat obscuring the Air Zoo's identity as an aviation museum, does suggest the interactive extravaganzas that compose its exhibits. As DMCD explains on its Web site, "The new Air Zoo…will set a new standard combining the learning discovery of interpretive centers with the joyful excitement of theme parks. Similar to a world-class aviation museum, the Air Zoo will interpret its outstanding collection of vintage aircraft. Like a popular theme park, the Air Zoo will engage visitors of all ages in the sheer exhilaration of flight through the latest in presentation technology."[56] These technology displays include "a 'solo coaster' for visitors to fly around the collection of warplanes, and a simulated World War II bombing run over Germany, where they have a 50 percent chance of being 'shot down.'"[57]

The phrase *interpretive center*, used by DMCD to characterize the Air Zoo, is similarly applied by Ralph Appelbaum, arguably the best known of this new generation of museum designers, to describe his company as "the largest interpretive museum design firm in the world."[58] The concept of "interpretive museum design" becomes clear in his work for the Newseum, "an interactive museum of news" located in Arlington, Virginia, from 1997 to 2002 and scheduled to reopen near the Washington Mall in 2006. In Appelbaum's view, museums "don't bring objects together, they bring people together."[59] In the case of the Newseum, this philosophy is manifested in "the building's transparent design and place in the heart of the news capital of the world," both of which, in turn, "constantly invite the visitor to relate the exhibition experience inside to the historic locale and news-making world outside."[60] According to the Newseum's Web site:

Visitors to the Newseum will be greeted by an expanded presentation of the Newseum's popular "Today's Front Pages" display, which features newspaper front pages from all 50 states and the District of Columbia as well as countries around the world. Inside, visitors will enter the 90-foot-high atrium and then begin exploring the museum's six levels of displays and experiences including a 17,000-square-foot News History Gallery; nine themed or changing exhibition galleries; a series of 60-seat orientation theatres; an expanded Interactive Newsroom; a state-of-the-art broadcast studio and control room with a smaller studio overlooking Pennsylvania Avenue; and familiar icons from the original Newseum including Pulitzer Prize-winning photojournalism, a memorial dedicated to the more than 1,400 journalists who died while reporting the news, and segments of the Berlin Wall.[61]

While the technology involved in the Newseum displays offers interactive experiences for its visitors, what makes the Newseum an interpretive museum is the sense that patrons are encouraged to relate the various displays not only to the "news-making world outside," as Appelbaum suggests, but also to their own personal experiences. For instance, a popular feature of the original Arlington-based Newseum was the interactive kiosks where visitors entered their date of birth and received a personalized, complimentary edition of "The Birthday Banner," described as "an authentic-looking front page with news that happened on the day they were born."[62]

In the same way that museums provide choices to patrons through their ancillary businesses and evening programs, interactive displays allow visitors to customize their museum experience, making it authentic according to an individual's personal tastes and interests. The ability to customize experiences within the display using what Sharon Macdonald identifies as "less directed and more multi-sensory approaches"[63] empowers the patron with a sense of control. Yet, as with the shopping and programming options available outside of the exhibition area, this sense of choice and control reifies the museum experience as a consumer experience far removed from traditional object-based displays. This process is readily apparent in Macdonald's description of a permanent exhibition at the Science Museum in London entitled Food for Thought: The Sainsbury Gallery, which opened in 1989. Sponsored by Britain's Sainsbury grocery-store chain, the exhibit highlights various processes and concepts related to food production and consumption, such as canning, pasteurization, and nutritional value. Macdonald observes that the design of the exhibit itself simulates the experience of being in a store by employing "supermarket strategies": it "avoids having a single 'storyline' which visitors must follow in order, but instead has themed areas, rather as supermarkets have shelves and counters devoted to particular products."[64] The concept of choice is incorporated into the exhibit to give visitors options about how to proceed through the displays, allowing them to control through selection the experience of the exhibit, just as the use of shopping metaphors directly equates this form of visitor empowerment with spending power. Museum visitors assume the role of consumers not only in their initial choice of visiting the museum, but also in their ability to pick and choose among the various displays or, as Macdonald writes, "to 'shop around' in the exhibition, to make their own selections, to 'decide for themselves' what they wanted to 'take home' from their museum experience."[65]

Solomon has suggested that "we're in an age when people want their own experiences, however personal, to be instantly historicized."[66] This historicizing process drives interactive displays such as the Newseum's Birthday Banner kiosk and the personalized, ready-to-scan, stained-glass window designs at the Pope John Paul II Cultural Center. Echoing Macdonald's comparison of the Food for Thought exhibit to a shopping experience in which patrons decide what museum experiences they want to take home, art museums are "allowing visitors to use their hand-held computers to download information about an entire collection or a single object,"[67] with the result that patrons can literally bring their museum experience home with them. At the Exploratorium in San Francisco, staff members developed the "Electronic Guidebook Project, which...not only allow[s] visitors to download additional material on their hand-held computers, but also create[s] a password-protected personal Web page, meaning people can revisit their own selection of the museum's collections from any computer."[68] These types of interactive displays and amenities underscore the idea that museums "cannot afford to presume a single visitor's perspective."[69] Instead, museums create exhibits that can accommodate any number of different viewpoints, employing what Elaine Heumann Gurian refers to as "storytelling in tangible sensory form."[70] Museum exhibits are not only incorporating technology that can be controlled by the patron, but also incorporating the patron into the narrative fabric of the display, thus making the displays both interactive and interpretive. Ostensibly about the news or about food production and consumption, the displays at the Science Museum in London are really about the museum visitors' experiences—their lives, viewpoints, and preferences—which, in turn, are being instantaneously packaged into a museum experience. As Weil concludes, museums in the age of nonstuff "do not so much recreate or represent the past as they legitimize the present,"[71] whether it be the large-scale popular cultural themes presented in blockbuster shows or the more personal themes of daily life.

What makes museum experiences authentic, then, are their levels of interactivity—the interactions and processes incorporated into a specific exhibit as well as the activities available outside the display areas—and the degree to which these experiences relate to, reflect, and, ultimately, can be controlled by the patron. Offering these interpretive and interactive experiences necessitates, by definition, a removal from authentic objects, whose interpretive context is formed and explicated by scholars and curators. Museum professionals "have come to understand that their mission is to meet the needs of their audience as much as it is emphasizing their collections and scholarship."[72] The erosion of the interpretive context that museums traditionally created for their collections and the simultaneous emphasis on patrons' self-directed museum experiences raises the fundamental question: What exactly is the role of museums in the age of edutainment? Are not interactive displays where "the visitor would be buffeted by cold air like a pea being frozen"[73] and simulated bombing raids much closer to the entertainment side of the equation than the educational one?

AUTHENTIC EXPERIENCES AND CULTURAL PRODUCTS

Of course, this is not to suggest that all museums are evolving into the Magic Kingdom. In fact, many institutions implement educational programs as a way to reconnect with the museum-going public. The San Francisco Museum of Modern Art opened a Learning Lounge adjacent to its primary exhibition space, which provides "computer kiosks, movable film screens and sofas, where visitors can read books and catalogs, watch videos, tap into multimedia presentations about museum offerings and talk to education resource staff members."[74] The Denver Art Museum introduced a children's Backpack Program: "Backpacks loaded with games and activities that encourage children to find patterns, animals, and unusual beadwork [that] show an unusually young audience that art and a museum need not be intimidating."[75] At the same time, marketing tactics associated with the edutainment movement such as blockbuster shows and technology-driven displays are not necessarily incompatible with a museum's educative mission. For an exhibit developed by the Minneapolis Institute of Arts in conjunction with the *Star Wars: The Magic of Myth* blockbuster show in 2000, curators supplied visitors with a "treasure map" that linked "archetypal themes" from the *Star Wars* displays to "21 specially labelled pieces from the museum's collection of paintings, textiles, sculpture and 20th-century art."[76] The lead curator of the exhibit was impressed by "the rapt attention of visitors connecting [the] permanent collection to the 'Star Wars' exhibit."[77]

The concept of choice—whether in the selection of amenities at a museum or how to proceed through an exhibition—also cannot be dismissed as a mere marketing tool. Indeed, the idea of incorporating multiple perspectives in displays can create challenging and engaging museum experiences. The National Museum of Australia uses its "multinarrative exhibitions...to convey that there are several, sometimes conflicting stories of the country's history."[78] Other art museums, including the modern art department at the Pompidou center, the Tate Modern in London, and the Denver Art Museum, are experimenting with what is known as "the nonchronological hang," arranging their collections according to a thematic principle rather than the time period in which the artworks were created.[79] By eschewing the chronological tradition, museums explicitly recognize that art can be viewed through many lenses, "that there is no one true history, but rather many."[80]

But conservative art critics are just as dismissive of the nonchronological hang as they are of blockbuster shows and architecture that upstages a museum's collection. Perl argues that "chronology, that backbone of the historical sense, has been collapsed into some kind of postmodern time warp. And out of that time warp comes the new funhouse museum, where art past and art present are no more than raw materials, to be bifurcated and cloned in order to produce bigger museums or smaller museums—whatever the market will bear."[81] Yet, while some see a connection between arranging art thematically and theme parks—"the new funhouse museum," as Perl calls it—there is a significant distinction: the nonchronological hang still centers on the museum's traditional mandate of "the growth, care, and study of its collection."[82] This same distinction characterizes the Minneapolis Institute of Arts's use of a pop culture blockbuster show to highlight its own collection, the Denver Art Museum's backpack program, and the Learning Lounge at the San Francisco Museum of Modern Art. These are all programs or exhibits that use a museum's collection to both entertain and inform. As Newhouse remarks, "Entertainment can be a welcome alternative to the museum/mausoleum, but when mishandled it quickly degenerates into crass commercialism that diminishes the art"[83]—or artifacts, or historical materials, or whatever it is that the museum collects. From one perspective, the ability to navigate this boundary successfully—to entertain and inform patrons by providing them with valuable experiences rather than simply popular choices—corresponds to the ability to relate the experiences to the museum collection.

It is also the objects in their collections that make museums unique. Weil is adamant about this point: "What museums have that is distinctive is objects, and what gives most museums their unique advantage is the awesome power of those objects to trigger an almost infinite diversity of profound experiences among their visitors."[84] The problem with the commercialization associated with edutainment has less to do with conflicting notions of taste or with a cultural dichotomy between populism and elitism than with what George Ritzer terms "the dedifferentiation of consumption."[85] Alan Bryman explains that this dedifferentiation signifies "the general trend whereby the forms of consumption associated with different institutional spheres become interlocked with each other and increasingly difficult to distinguish."[86] In other words, the goods and services provided by such seemingly diverse venues as shopping malls, casinos, amusement parks, and educational settings—just a few of the examples provided by Ritzer—are becoming increasingly indistinct.

It is not difficult to see how museums in the age of edutainment fit into this trend. By focusing on providing authentic experiences for patrons through ancillary services and activities such as shopping, yoga classes, martini menus, and technology-driven spectacles, rather than on explicating their permanent collections, museums do little to differentiate themselves from other entertainment venues. At the same time, marketing tools such as traveling blockbuster shows that move from museum to museum—as well as the emphasis placed on attracting visitors with museum buildings rather than collections—are making it increasingly difficult to distinguish one museum from another. What Perl identifies as "an international trend toward satellite museums and museum franchises"[87]—Guggenheim New York, Guggenheim Bilbao, Guggenheim Las Vegas—exacerbates the situation, as does the sheer range of projects for which experiential museum designers create what the firm DMCD calls "a total visitor experience."[88] The postobject museum delivers customization through a formula—one that is being applied in countless entertainment venues. The experiences museums provide in the realm of edutainment might be authentic in their ability to focus on and be controlled by the patron, but, unlike authentic objects, they are not unique.

LIBRARIES AND EDUTAINMENT

Just as museums are being packaged as cultural products for customers with discretionary spending power, libraries too are adopting marketing jargon and techniques to attract patrons. Maureen Brunsdale urges academic libraries to adopt a private-sector mind-set that includes "aggressive promotion within a definite marketing plan" to win over customers so that they "buy in" to the library and become regular users of its "largest product," which is "usually equated with some combination of collection and services."[89] But the marketing strategies embraced by many other libraries completely reconfigure the notion of product. The proliferation of information available online and the subsequent reduced role for libraries as physical spaces has prompted both public and academic librarians to ask, "What if librarians stopped fighting a losing battle in the information wars, and instead began devising a new vision" of the library, one in which "librarians continued to do what they already do, but for marketing purposes reinvented their institutional image as entertainment centers?"[90] If questions like these are any indication, libraries—much like museums—are embracing postobject roles, promoting entertainment-based experiences more vigorously than they do their traditional "product": their collections and services.

While museums that stake their future on edutainment are accused of emulating theme parks, the library doppelgänger is the megabookstore with coffeehouse, typified by such chain behemoths as Barnes & Noble and Borders. With their plush chairs and café ambiance, these bookstores provide not only unhurried book browsing and Internet connection time, but also a place to socialize. The strategy for creating a "new vision" of the academic or public library is to entice patrons with the same kind of social venue model. Consider the alterations made in the library at Texas Christian University: "Dead ahead of the main entrance, an espresso machine hisses and sputters as students line up for Starbucks lattes and Krispy Kreme doughnuts before heading off, snacks in hand, to the library's study areas. In the main reading room, students sprawl on couches and plush chairs, as a Mozart divertimento pipes in through speakers overhead."[91] A recent addition to the library at Georgia College and State University included not only new computer labs and display areas, but also a cybercafé.[92] Public libraries are considering relaxing restrictions on coffee in the library to accommodate "a new breed of library patron" accustomed to the idea, promoted by bookstores, "that books and coffee go together."[93] Libraries have become part of a general trend in which cultural institutions "[cater] to the public's wants as well as its needs."[94]

Ironically, the Barnes & Noble model is actually derived from libraries. Barnes & Noble wanted to re-create the ambiance and décor of an "old-world library, with wood fixtures, antique-style chairs and public tables" that would evolve into a welcoming space where customers would want to linger.[95] Bookstores also incorporated a facet of the modern library: programming. Each Barnes & Noble superstore employs a community relations coordinator who schedules book talks, demonstrations, discussion groups, and performances.[96] Paradoxically, libraries are promoting themselves as social venues not only by cloning the bookstore's reinterpretation of the old-world library, but also by replicating the nature of bookstore programs. To be sure, libraries have a long tradition of both adult and children's programming, but in the postobject world, library activities are selected with an eye toward showcasing an institution's "entertainment value." In the long run, there is a good chance that the notion of entertainment value will, quite simply, become the library's raison d'être.

Two programming types can therefore be identified in contemporary libraries: programs that reflect the traditional range of educational services offered by libraries and programs that, to borrow Zolberg's description of the Pompidou Center, infuse the library with "the atmosphere of a supermarket of events and exhibitions."[97] In the latter category, we may place the Cuyahoga County Library System in Ohio, where patrons have learned to belly dance, listened to stand-up comics and rock and roll bands, and attended talks "by a local paranormal investigator."[98] In the Queens Borough Public Library system, comedians—in this case, amateurs at open microphone night—regale patrons, and classes offer instruction in merengue, ballroom dancing, and yoga.[99] And in Edmonton, Alberta, the public library offers courses such as Feng Shui in the Bedroom,[100] something we discussed more extensively in chapter 1.

Just as academic libraries are renovating to create areas conducive to coffee drinking and socializing, the influx of programs in public libraries has created a need for new spaces. Dean Murphy observes that "programming has become so essential to the library experience in Queens and elsewhere that new library buildings typically include large spaces not intended for books"; one library branch "has meeting rooms with collapsing walls and a 223-seat auditorium, including a performance stage and advanced sound system."[101] Enhanced facilities not only provide a venue for library-sponsored programs, but are also rented out for social functions. A 1999 issue of the *Unabashed Librarian* included a discussion about the positive aspects of hosting wedding ceremonies and receptions. Noting that libraries in central Arkansas have held "a memorial service, one prom, class reunions and a host of other functions," an enterprising area librarian recommended that staff members should "start cultivating a list of accepted caterers."[102]

To accommodate their new role as entertainment centers, libraries have begun to imitate museums when it comes to architectural design and presence. Libraries too are positioning themselves as tourist attractions in a postobject universe. Nowhere is this more evident than in the Seattle Public Library (SPL) designed by Rem Koolhaas. SPL has been rapturously praised by architectural critics—the highly regarded Herbert Muschamp gushes that "in more than 30 years of writing about architecture, this is the most exciting new building it has been my honor to review,"[103] and the no less highly esteemed Paul Goldberger writes that it is "the most important new library to be built in a generation, and the most exhilarating."[104] Although the commentators regard it as a building in which "social, technical and psychological goals are fused into a comprehensible form," SPL is nevertheless the library equivalent of the next Guggenheim Bilbao. That is, it is less concerned with books (the assigned area for which takes up only 32 percent of its total square footage) than with the spectacle of its "pure bling-bling" and with defining itself as "a series of episodes in urban space [in which] there are crowd scenes and moments of intense solitary absorption, [where] intense vertigo gives way to erotic stimulation [such that] over here, you're an actor, over there a spectator."[105] SPL prides itself on being a public space that conveys "dazzling energy."[106] It contains a café, "sound domes" ("individual pods reminiscent of giant hair-dryers that will enable young users to listen to music, either their own or the library's"), a "meeting platform" ("a cluster of closed conference rooms off a labyrinthine series of narrow corridors painted bright lipstick red, like something out of a David Lynch movie"), a portentously named "mixing chamber" (what used to be simply called the reference desk) with a view "so vertiginous that you want to scream...as if you're gazing up into a building from where a basement used to be before it was washed out to sea," a pretentiously named "living room" masquerading as an entrance lobby, and staff members equipped "with state-of-the-art Vocera digital walkie-talkies" lest patrons lose their way among the stairs and escalators painted bright chartreuse or "the fat columns thrust up and inward at an assortment of splayed angles, like the trunks of some exotic tree."[107] Yet, for all its seemingly sophisticated and up-to-the-moment trappings and its claim to be "the first library of the twenty-first century,"[108] it embodies the same experience/object dichotomy as the Guggenheim Bilbao, so that looking at the art or browsing and reading among the books "is just something you ought to remember to do while you are there, like going to the bathroom or taking your vitamins."[109]

When the type of architectural design and postobject philosophy evident at the SPL is combined with the programs and services available in the libraries of Cleveland, Queens, and countless other cities and towns, "a major shift...away from strictly scholarly pursuits toward functions once associated with community centers, religious and business organizations, [and] the YMCA" has occurred.[110] These new functions constitute a form of dedifferentiation not only between libraries and a variety of social organizations, but also between libraries and museums, since both sets of institutions have expanded their community roles through entertainment-based programs that are disconnected from their respective collections. Activities such as yoga and tai chi are no longer confined to recreational facilities; they are also readily available at museums and libraries. Museums with evening programs of music and martinis resemble eating establishments, while libraries with espresso machines look like bookstores and coffee bars.

Dedifferentiation in museums and libraries can be traced not only to the interactive social activities that both institutions provide for their patrons, but also to interactive technology. Of course, technology in libraries is hardly a new concept, and it does not have the same sense of novelty that characterizes its more recent introduction into art museums and historical sites. Yet technology in libraries today functions not simply as an information tool but as a vehicle for entertainment and spectacle. One example is the presence, in public libraries, of "NatureMaker" trees—leafy, life-size, "sculpted trees" composed of handcrafted "composite 'bark' over an intricately welded, steel sub-structure."[111] Trees that incorporate "seating and interactive touch screens" have been installed in libraries in Los Angeles, Tulsa, and Florence, Alabama.[112] Echoing the philosophy of museum designer Ralph Appelbaum, NatureMaker's cofounder Gary Hanick explains that "the whole idea is to create an 'experience.' It's all a means of bringing people in."[113] But this particular "experience" is not exclusive to libraries; it can also be found at the MGM Grand Hotel in Las Vegas; the Galleria shopping center in Scottsdale, Arizona; the corporate offices of Eastman Kodak in Massachusetts; the Los Angeles International Airport; the Mercy Clinic in Lake Geneva, Wisconsin; Walt Disney World; three houses of worship in California; and the Natural History Museum of Los Angeles[114]—a list that echoes what Ritzer identifies as venues that are gradually blending into one undifferentiated locus.

Underscoring the postobject marketing techniques of libraries is the idea that, by increasing the library's visibility in a community through new roles, it is simultaneously increasing access to its collections. As Gary Strong of the Queens Borough Public Library explains, "It is like retail philosophy: If you don't get someone walking into the store they are not going to buy anything."[115] Patrons seem to be "buying" in Queens: its system ranked second in circulation statistics and program attendance for libraries with population service areas of over 1,000,000.[116] The Cuyahoga County Public Library system— home of the belly dance—ranked fourth in both categories for libraries with a population service area ranging from 500,000 to 999,999.[117] The social venue model, however, is not universally successful. Since Krispy Kreme doughnuts, Starbucks coffee, and plush chairs were installed in the library at Texas Christian University, library traffic has doubled in terms of visits per week, but circulation statistics decreased.[118] And, in a sign that the general public may be becoming disenchanted with the "dedifferentiation of consumption" edutainment principles that are the hallmark of many publicly funded cultural institutions, residents of Contra Costa, California, opposed an initiative in 2000 to raise taxes as a means of generating revenue for their libraries, arguing that "public money should not be spent on institutions that have evolved into entertainment centers."[119]

On the one hand, assuming the functions of an entertainment center is a tacit admission on the part of libraries that they can no longer rely on their collections alone to bring people inside their walls. On the other hand, serving as a social venue does not automatically translate into actual use of the library's collections and, as the Contra Costa example demonstrates, can prompt a backlash among citizens who no longer see a distinct role for the library in their communities. The question then becomes, What exactly are libraries providing access to in the current climate of edutainment? Discussing the efficacy of the new postobject roles of museums, Kimmelman astutely writes that "the question should not be how many people visit museums but how valuable are their visits."[120] The same is true of libraries.

FOR BETTER OR WORSE: PARTNERSHIPS

Another way in which libraries are offering authentic experiences not unlike those available at museums is the blockbuster exhibit. As with programming and technology, libraries traditionally have gallery space that is used to mount in-house exhibits of books or photographs. What distinguishes library blockbusters from library displays, however, is that these traveling exhibits are based on the same marketing plans and ancillary activities that characterize museum blockbusters. When the Northwestern University Library hosted the 2000 Bologna Illustrators exhibit from Italy, the library used this exhibit of original children's book art to develop a seven-week series of programs entitled The Art of the Story, which included a display of "African-themed children's books drawn from both Africa and the United States" and an evening of storytelling by a member of the university's theater department.[121] The mounting of the Bologna Illustrators exhibit and the related programming entailed the creation of not only an exhibit space for the artworks themselves, but also a stage for live performances, a café, "a bookstall to sell outstanding examples of children's literature," and catalogs based on the exhibition.[122] The librarians at Northwestern observed that the "library—almost Cinderella like—was transformed into an art gallery and gathering spot" for the duration of the exhibit.[123]

Just as the Northwestern University Library welcomed the Bologna Illustrators exhibit as a chance to "transform itself into a cultural meeting place for students, staff, and the general public,"[124] the Louisville (Kentucky) Free Public Library hosted the Gutenberg Millennium Exhibition with the twin goals of increasing both "the library's recognition as a quality cultural institution" and the "perception of the library as a valuable community asset."[125] Billed by the library as "a blockbuster exhibit," the eight-week show traveled from the Gutenberg Museum in Mainz, Germany, and included "a full-size Gutenberg replica press that printed souvenir Gutenberg pages on site, numerous documents and artifacts, rare examples of 15th-century printing, and some stunning examples of the manuscript arts before Gutenberg."[126] The show's more than 100,000 visitors each received "a free poster, exhibition guide, and souvenir replica page from the Gutenberg Bible."[127]

Traveling exhibits like those hosted by the Northwestern University Library and the Louisville Public Library come to fruition through a series of partnerships. Generating the necessary funding for The Art of the Story exhibit meant enlisting partners and sponsors from both for-profit companies and nonprofit organizations. Northwestern librarians recalled how they "made lobbying visits to the Illinois Humanities Council and the Art Institute of Chicago. We networked at local children's-book events and receptions, spoke with local children's-book publishers, and began a temporary business partnership with a local bookstore known for its selection of children's literature.... In the end, $80,000 was generated in sales revenue and gifts from foundations, organizations, a local bank, and publishers, and from within the university, allowing us to keep the project within budget."[128] Organizers of the Gutenberg exhibit note that "marketing, communications, and advertising were funded with approximately $170,000 in donated and allocated resources. Meeting outcome goals meant getting maximum exposure out of every dollar."[129] Much of the donated resources involved sponsorship plans with local media. The *Louisville Courier-Journal* "donated approximately 70% of the cost in exchange for sponsorship recognition," while a local television station "provided free production services for 30-second and 10-second commercials."[130]

For both museums and libraries, partnerships—whether corporate sponsorship to raise money for a project or collaborations with other institutions and organizations to attract patrons—are relationships borne of competitive necessity. Yet, while museums and libraries join forces to develop "new marketing approaches" to counteract the "increased competition for the public's time,"[131] the partnerships themselves can create competition among project collaborators. Only a thin line separates the cooperative spirit from the competitive spirit of partnerships. The library community recognizes this dichotomy. Discussing various "partnership initiatives" proposed for Illinois museums and libraries, Brown and Pollack question whether "large and small museums or libraries that have overlapping collection areas [can] collaborate and avoid competition."[132]

Competition among project collaborators is fuelled in part by disagreements over institutional autonomy and control. The friction that these issues can create is especially apparent in corporate-museum partnerships. Weil concludes that "the greater the extent to which a museum might seek corporate funding—particularly for its program activities—the more important will be that museum's ability to assure prospective sponsors that its programs will attract a wide audience."[133] This relationship results both in the choice of market-tested and consumer-driven exhibition themes and in a loss of control over how those themes are presented and explicated to the audience. Museums can find themselves in a situation in which donors overrule curatorial decisions, as was the case with the proposed "Hall of Fame of American Achievers" at the Smithsonian Institution's National Museum of American History. The original source of funding for the hall, which was to display the "life stories of eminent Americans,"[134] was a gift of $38 million from businesswoman Catherine Reynolds. The gift, however, was contingent on Reynolds's ability to "apply her own definition of achievement" through the selection of the individuals represented in the exhibit.[135] Reynolds withdrew funding for the project in 2002 after her list of candidates—predominantly business and entertainment figures such as Steven Spielberg, Oprah Winfrey, Martha Stewart, and Federal Express founder Frederick W. Smith—caused an uproar among the Smithsonian's curators. Her decision reflected the fact that "the philosophy of the scholars at the institution turned out to be so at odds with her own views on how an exhibit honouring American Achievers should be staged."[136]

While the pressure to defer to corporate sponsors in implementing projects can result in a loss of autonomy for museums, these partnerships also contribute to a dedifferentiation among museums competing for corporate dollars. In order to meet sponsors' expectations, museums gravitate toward exhibitions that are guaranteed to be popular. Asma explains that "the more dependent that museums become on fast-food corporations, oil companies, movie tie-ins, and bloated marketing strategies, the less likely they will be to take risks. Just as in the case of Hollywood movie studios, if museums move increasingly toward blockbusters, the huge investments these require will inevitably force them to move increasingly toward formula exhibits."[137] On the one hand, museums' dependence on corporate sponsorship produces a limited range of formula exhibits. As Perl observes, "museums are so anxious to upstage one another or to collaborate with one another, that almost everything you see reminds you of something else."[138] On the other hand, corporate sponsorships can also alter the identity of a museum within its community. In the most literal sense, there is a loss of identity that comes from the name changes that are an inevitable consequence of corporate sponsorship. For instance, the name of Kenneth Behring, a real estate developer who has donated $100 million to the Smithsonian Institution since 1999,[139] appears on the Kenneth E. Behring Family Hall of Mammals at the Smithsonian's National Museum of Natural History, and the Smithsonian's National Museum of American History is called the Behring Center. The main exhibit space for the Smithsonian's National Air and Space Museum is called the Steven F. Udvar-Hazy Center in honor of its magnanimous donor.

A more insidious effect of corporate sponsorship on institutional identity is the weakening of a museum's educative role. Consider the recent acquisition by the Field Museum of Sue, "the biggest and most complete *Tyrannosaurus rex* ever excavated."[140] To finance this $8 million purchase, the Field Museum formed corporate partnerships, including one with the fast-foot restaurant giant McDonald's.[141] McDonald's imprint was considerable. Museum patrons could watch Sue being prepared for display in the McDonald's Fossil Preparation Laboratory; McDonald's received two life-size replicas of the dinosaur "that will travel nationally and internationally"; and the Field Museum sported a new "Dino McDonald's" in which mini-Sues were offered as McDonald's Happy Meal toys.[142] In many respects, Sue is not really a part of the museum's collection. Instead, she evolved into a marketing product that blurs the line between the operations of an education-based institution and those of its corporate sponsor.

The ramifications of corporate partnerships—dedifferentiation among institutions, challenges to institutional autonomy, redefinition of community identity—should also be examined in the context of museum-library partnerships. In July 2002 the Enoch Pratt Free Library in Baltimore closed the Exploration Center that it had opened in the Port Discovery children's museum four years earlier. Developed in partnership with Port Discovery "to expand and enhance the educational themes of the museum,"[143] the Exploration Center provided access to a collection of 5,000 books, 12 computer stations, "a separate play space and an arts and crafts area," and it was "staffed by three specially trained children's librarians and an aide."[144] Critics of the Exploration Center—the most vocal of whom were members of the Baltimore library community—questioned this expenditure of resources in terms of both the size and demographics of the branch's user community. Jane Shipley, a member of the organization Save Libraries/Save Lives, summarized the concerns as follows: "The Exploration Center is invisible from the street, its book collection was chosen to meet the needs of a children's museum rather than of a local school or neighborhood branch library, and children can't get there on their own. In fact, since half of the visitors to Port Discovery are from out-of-state, it is fair to say that the Exploration Center is simply a tourist attraction."[145] Citing the fact that other Baltimore library branches were in dire need of additional books, computers, and staff, Shipley construed the Exploration Center as an example of how the Enoch Pratt library system was "abandoning our neediest neighborhoods only to . . . pamper tourist attractions."[146]

Museum-library partnerships in general are susceptible to the criticisms made by Shipley, who argued that "librarians in a public library should respond to the expressed needs of their patrons, not those of a museum."[147] Although Betsy Diamont-Cohen, the manager of the Exploration Center, defended "the collaboration between the Pratt Library and Port Discovery [as] a good example of the kind of 'creative problem solving' and 'thinking outside of the box'" that libraries are encouraged to explore,[148] the Baltimore controversy illustrates how museum-library partnerships can create, rather than solve, problems. The issue of institutional autonomy and identity raises important questions. How are the roles of each institution construed in museum-library partnerships? Who are the beneficiaries of these programs? These concerns are amplified in the current climate of edutainment. Museums and libraries individually are attenuating their identity as distinct institutions with unique collections and services by emphasizing experiences that imitate and replicate the experiences available at entertainment-based venues. But what happens when museums and libraries, already independently pursuing a postobject agenda of authentic experiences, decide to collaborate? What methods will be used to achieve the partnerships' goals of increasing the visibility of museums and libraries and providing access to information?

NOTES

1. Elaine Sciolino, "Smithsonian Chief Draws Ire in Making Relics of Old Ways," *New York Times,* 30 April 2001, A1.

2. Adam Goodheart, "Smithsonian's Veteran Man-in-the-Middle Stands His Ground," *New York Times,* 24 April 2002, E2.

3. Sciolino, "Smithsonian Chief Draws Ire," A1, A15.

4. Bob Thompson, "History for Sale," *Washington Post,* 20 January 2002, par. 23, http://www.washingtonpost.com (accessed January 20, 2002).

5. Sciolino, "Smithsonian Chief Draws Ire," A1.

6. Andrew Barry, "On Interactivity: Consumers, Citizens and Culture," in *The Politics of Display: Museums, Science, Culture*, ed. Sharon Macdonald (London: Routledge, 1998), 101.

7. Stephen E. Weil, *Making Museums Matter* (Washington, DC: Smithsonian Institution Press, 2002), 31.

8. Deborah Solomon, "Tastemaker, New in Town, Dives into a Cauldron," *New York Times*, 2 May 2001, D1.

9. U.S. Congress, *Bill Summary and Status for the 94th Congress*, HR 7216, 94th Cong., 2nd sess., http://thomas.loc.gov (accessed September 6, 2003).

10. Michael Kimmelman, "J. Carter Brown, Who Transformed the Museum World, Dies at 67," *New York Times*, 19 June 2002, par. 32, http://www.nytimes.com (accessed June 19, 2002).

11. Jacqueline Trescott, "Egyptian Exhibit to Rival Tut Show," *Washington Post*, 4 June 2002, par. 1–2, http://www.washingtonpost.com (accessed September 13, 2003).

12. Bonnie Rothman Morris, "Lots of Rubbernecking in These Traffic Jams," *New York Times*, 23 April 2003, F4.

13. Carol Vogel, "House Approves Increase in Insurance for Museums," *New York Times*, 18 September 2003, B5.

14. Solomon, "Tastemaker," D1.

15. Stephen Kinzer, "The Dead Sea Scrolls: Middle West Miracle," *New York Times*, 23 April 2003, F9.

16. Ibid.

17. Ibid.

18. Ibid.

19. Alan Riding, "The Royal Academy Puts On a New, Fresher Face," *New York Times*, 21 April 1999, D7.

20. Ibid.

21. Ibid.

22. Ibid.

23. Jed Perl, "Welcome to the Funhouse: Tate Modern and the Crisis of the Museum," *The New Republic*, 19 June 2000, 32.

24. Douglas Davis, *The Museum Transformed: Design and Culture in the Post-Pompidou Age* (New York: Abbeville Press, 1990), 35.

25. Stephen E. Weil, *A Cabinet of Curiosities: Inquiries into Museums and Their Prospects* (Washington, DC: Smithsonian Institution Press, 1995), xv.

26. Weil, *Making Museums Matter*, 28.

27. Hilde S. Hein, *The Museum in Transition: A Philosophical Perspective* (Washington, DC: Smithsonian Institution Press, 2000), 8.

28. Michael Kimmelman, "All Too Often, the Art Itself Gets Lost in the Blueprints," *New York Times*, 21 April 1999, D7.

29. Stephen Kinzer, "It's Museum Time in the South," *New York Times*, 18 December 2001, E1.

30. Michael Kimmelman, "Museums in a Quandary: Where Are the Ideals?" *New York Times*, 26 August 2001, sec. 2, 26.

31. Perl, "Welcome to the Funhouse," 31.

32. Victoria Newhouse, *Towards a New Museum* (New York: Monacelli Press, 1998), 220.

33. Ibid., 193.

34. Perl, "Welcome to the Funhouse," 34.

35. Vera L. Zolberg, "An Elite Experience for Everyone: Art Museums, the Public, and Cultural Literacy," in *Museum Culture: Histories, Discourses, Spectacles,* ed. Daniel J. Sherman and Irit Rogoff (Minneapolis: University of Minnesota Press, 1994), 58.

36. Kimmelman, "Museums in a Quandary," 26.

37. Zolberg, "An Elite Experience," 58.

38. Newhouse, *Towards a New Museum,* 211.

39. Kimmelman, "All Too Often," D7.

40. Ibid.

41. Bernard Stamler, "Temples of Culture Are Needy, Too. Tai Chi, Anyone?" *New York Times,* 23 April 2003, F2.

42. Newhouse, *Towards a New Museum,* 173.

43. Kimmelman, "All Too Often," D7.

44. Stamler, "Temples of Culture Are Needy," F2.

45. Neal Karlen, "Displaying Art with a Smiley Face," *New York Times,* 19 April 2000, D17.

46. Brooklyn Museum of Art, "First Saturdays at the Brooklyn Museum of Art: August 2 Schedule of Evening Programs," http://www.brooklynmuseum.org (accessed July 29, 2003).

47. Ibid.

48. Kimberly Stevens, "The Name May Be Artsy, But It's Still Date Night," *New York Times,* 24 April 2002, E25.

49. Ibid.

50. Sharon Macdonald, ed., "Exhibitions of Power and Powers of Exhibition: An Introduction to the Politics of Display," in *The Politics of Display: Museums, Science, Culture* (London: Routledge, 1998), 13.

51. Peter Hall, "Now Showing: Something Dazzling," *New York Times,* 2 May 2001, D17.

52. Stephen Kinzer, "Mount Vernon, Alarmed by Fading Knowledge, Seeks to Pep Up Washington's Image," *New York Times,* 29 July 2002, par. 19, http://www.nytimes.com (accessed July 29, 2002).

53. Ibid., par. 3.

54. Hall, "Now Showing," D17.

55. Ibid.

56. DMCD Incorporated, "DMCD Overview May 2001," http://www.dmcd.com (accessed September 9, 2003).

57. Hall, "Now Showing," D17.

58. Newseum, "Newseum Design Unveiled: Museum Will Be Expanded and 'Reinvented' Next to the National Mall," par. 12, http://www.newseum.org (accessed July 29, 2003).

59. Deborah Solomon, "He Turns the Past into Stories, and the Galleries Fill Up," *New York Times,* 21 April 1999, D12.

60. Newseum, "Newseum Design Unveiled," par. 11.

61. Ibid., par. 13.

62. Ralph Blumenthal, "A Press Pass to the Workings Behind the Headlines," *New York Times*, 12 April 2001, B2.

63. Macdonald, "Exhibitions of Power," 13.

64. Sharon Macdonald, ed., "Supermarket Science? Consumerism and 'The Public Understanding of Science,'" in *The Politics of Display: Museums, Science, Culture* (London: Routledge, 1998), 123.

65. Ibid.

66. Solomon, "He Turns the Past into Stories," D12.

67. Karen Jones, "New 'Smart' Galleries, Wireless and Web-Friendly," *New York Times*, 24 April 2002, E27.

68. Ibid.

69. Hall, "Now Showing," D17.

70. Elaine Heumann Gurian, "What Is the Object of This Exercise? A Meandering Exploration of the Many Meanings of Objects in Museums," *Daedalus* 128 (summer 1999): 181.

71. Weil, *A Cabinet of Curiosities*, 13.

72. Karlen, "Displaying Art with a Smiley Face," D16.

73. Macdonald, "Supermarket Science," 123.

74. Tessa DeCarlo, "A Place to Hang Out and Learn a Thing or Two," *New York Times*, 23 April 2003, F16.

75. Elizabeth Heilman Brooke, "Car Showrooms Give Way to Cultural Showcases," *New York Times*, 3 June 1999, B2.

76. Neal Karlen, "A Curator Puts 'Star Wars' in Turnaround," *New York Times*, 19 April 2000, D17.

77. Ibid.

78. Hall, "Now Showing," D17.

79. Sarah Boxer, "Snubbing Chronology as a Guiding Force in Art," *New York Times*, 2 September 2000, A19.

80. Ibid., A21.

81. Perl, "Welcome to the Funhouse," 31.

82. Weil, *Making Museums Matter*, 28.

83. Newhouse, *Towards a New Museum*, 191.

84. Weil, *Making Museums Matter*, 71.

85. George Ritzer, *Enchanting a Disenchanted World: Revolutionizing the Means of Consumption* (Thousand Oaks, CA: Pine Forge, 1999), 134.

86. Alan Bryman, "The Disneyization of Society," *The Sociological Review* 47 (February 1999): 33.

87. Perl, "Welcome to the Funhouse," 31.

88. DMCD Incorporated, "DMCD Overview."

89. Maureen Brunsdale, "From Mild to Wild: Strategies for Promoting Academic Libraries to Undergraduates," *Reference and User Services Quarterly* 39 (summer 2000): 332.

90. Bernard Vavrek, "Wanted! Entertainment Director," *American Libraries* 32 (June/July 2001): 69.

91. Scott Carlson, "The Deserted Library: As Students Work Online, Reading Rooms Empty Out—Leading Some Campuses to Add Starbucks," *The Chronicle of Higher Education,* 16 November 2001, par. 38, http://chronicle.com/free/v48/i12/12a03501.htm (accessed November 29, 2001).

92. Ibid., par. 12.

93. Julia Browne, "Coffee, Tea and/or Literacy: The Public Library's Role in Accommodating Today's 'Average Joe,'" *Current Studies in Librarianship* 24 (spring/fall 2000): 81.

94. Ibid., 80–81.

95. Steve Coffman, "What If You Ran Your Library Like a Bookstore?" *American Libraries* 29 (March 1998): 40.

96. Ibid.

97. Zolberg, "An Elite Experience," 58.

98. Tom Breckenridge, "Check It Out—Libraries Shelve Stuffy Image for Broader Appeal," *The Plain Dealer,* 14 January 2002, B5.

99. Dean E. Murphy, "Moving Beyond 'Shh' (and Books) at Libraries," *New York Times,* 7 March 2001, A1, A20.

100. Hal Niedzviecki, "Libraries Need to Mind Their Own Business," *The Globe and Mail,* 27 October 2003, R3.

101. Ibid., A1.

102. "Weddings at the Library?" *The Unabashed Librarian* 112 (1999): 19.

103. Herbert Muschamp, "The Library that Puts on Fishnets and Hits the Disco," *New York Times, sec. 2,* 16 May 2004, 1.

104. Paul Goldberger, "High-tech Bibliophilia: Rem Koolhaas's New Library in Seattle Is an Ennobling Public Space," *The New Yorker,* 24 May 2004, 90.

105. Muschamp, "The Library that Puts on Fishnets," *sec. 2,* 31. The figure of 32 percent of square footage area comes from a graphic that accompanies Muschamp's article.

106. Goldberger, "High-tech Bibliophilia," 91.

107. Quotes are taken from Muschamp, "The Library that Puts on Fishnets," *sec. 2,* 31, and Andrew Gumbel, "The Perfect City Library: Rem Koolhaas's Design for the Seattle Library Was Initially Derided," *The Independent* (London), 25 May 2004, http://www.lexis.com (accessed July 13, 2004).

108. Ibid.

109. Perl, "Welcome to the Funhouse," 31.

110. Murphy, "Moving Beyond 'Shh,'" A1.

111. NatureMaker, "Company Profile: Worldwide Makers of Museum-Quality Sculpted Trees," http://www.naturemaker.com (accessed September 6, 2003).

112. Craig Wilson, "A Library Made More Lovely by a Tree," *USA Today,* 18 April 2003, D1.

113. Ibid.

114. NatureMaker, "Installations," http://www.naturemaker.com (accessed September 6, 2003).

115. Murphy, "Moving Beyond 'Shh,'" A20.

116. Public Library Association, *Public Library Data Service Statistical Report 2003* (Chicago: American Library Association 2003), 88.

117. Ibid., 88–89.

118. Carlson, "The Deserted Library," par. 41.

119. Murphy, "Moving Beyond 'Shh,'" A20.

120. Kimmelman, "Museums in a Quandary," 26.

121. Leslie Bjorncrantz, Jeffrey Garrett, and Harrie Hughes, "Northwestern's Art of the Story: Public Relations on a Grand Scale," *American Libraries* 31 (December 2000): 52.

122. Ibid.

123. Ibid.

124. Ibid., 50.

125. Norman Morton, "Anatomy of a Community Relations Success," *American Libraries* 32 (February 2001): 40.

126. Ibid.

127. Ibid., 42.

128. Bjorncrantz, Garrett, and Hughes, "Northwestern's Art of the Story," 51.

129. Morton, "Anatomy," 41.

130. Ibid.

131. Karen Brown and Miriam Pollack, "Illinois Libraries and Museums: Connecting and Collaborating for the Future," *Illinois Libraries* 82 (summer 2000): 211–12.

132. Ibid., 211.

133. Weil, *Making Museums Matter,* 31.

134. Thompson, "History for Sale," par. 4.

135. Elaine Sciolino, "Smithsonian Is Promised $38 Million, with Strings," *New York Times,* 10 May 2001, A12.

136. David E. Rosenbaum, "Smithsonian Loses Millions After Dispute with Donor," *New York Times,* 6 February 2002, A14.

137. Stephen T. Asma, *Stuffed Animals and Pickled Heads: The Culture and Evolution of Natural History Museums* (Oxford: Oxford University Press, 2001), 270.

138. Perl, "Welcome to the Funhouse," 31.

139. Sciolino, "Smithsonian Is Promised $38 Million," A12.

140. Asma, *Stuffed Animals and Pickled Heads,* 269.

141. Ibid., 270.

142. Ibid.

143. Betsy Diamant-Cohen, "Role of Pratt's Exploration Center Clarified," *Baltimore Chronicle,* 27 June 2001, par. 2, http://baltimorechronicle.com/pratt_jul01.html (accessed June 21, 2003).

144. Jane Shipley, "A Tale of Two Libraries: Clifton and Port Discovery," *Baltimore Chronicle,* 30 May 2001, par. 2, http://baltimorechronicle.com/library_jun01.html (accessed June 21, 2003).

145. Ibid., par. 14.

146. Ibid., par. 24.

147. Jane Shipley, "Role of Pratt's Exploration Center Clarified: Jane Shipley Responds," *Baltimore Chronicle,* 27 June 2001, par. 21, http://baltimorechronicle.com/pratt_jul01.html (accessed June 21, 2003).

148. Diamant-Cohen, "Role of Pratt's Exploration Center," par. 16.

3 LIBRARY-MUSEUM PARTNERSHIPS AS LEARNING COMMUNITIES

We saw in the previous chapter that many museums and libraries, as separate entities, responded to the growing competition from diverse entertainment-based sources by taking on some of the characteristics of those entertainment sources. Various marketing techniques were used to attract patrons, often with ambiguous results. In addition, the idea of partnerships between libraries and museums was proposed as the culmination of these competitive efforts. These partnerships, it was argued, would form the basis of a new conceptual model for the development and perpetuation of seamlessly integrated and dynamic learning communities that would make extensive use of the rich complementary heritage resources of both types of institutions. Access to museum and library collections would be enhanced, and new audiences would be attracted to these institutions, often through digital means.

One of the most important ways in which the concept of library-museum partnerships was manifested at the beginning of the twenty-first century was a series of projects funded by the Institute of Museum and Library Services (IMLS). Established in 1996 "to improve museum, library and information services" under the aegis of the Museum and Library Services Act, a part of Public Law 104–208 (the Omnibus Consolidated Appropriations Act of 1997), IMLS is an independent agency within the National Foundation on the Arts and the Humanities funded through the offices of the secretary of education.[1] IMLS has two main divisions: the Office of Museum Services (OMS) and the Office of Library Services (OLS). OMS "encourage[s] and assist[s] museums in modernizing their methods and facilities so that they may be better able to conserve our cultural, historic, and scientific heritage; and to ease the financial burden borne by museums as a result of their increasing use by the public."[2] OMS also "encourage[s] and assist[s] museums in their educational role, in conjunction with formal systems of elementary, secondary, and postsecondary education and with programs of nonformal education for all age groups."[3] Several key goals of OLS are to "promote access to resources in all types of libraries for individuals of all ages, to promote library services that provide access to information through electronic networks, to provide linkages among and between libraries and to promote targeted library services to people of diverse backgrounds and abilities."[4] OLS thus "stimulate[s] excellence" and facilitates learning opportunities for all individuals, with special attention given to promoting "targeted library services to people of diverse geographic, cultural, and socioeconomic backgrounds, to individuals with disabilities, and to people with limited functional literacy of information skills."[5] In 2003 the Museum and Library Services Act was reauthorized, and the connection between museums and education, on the one hand, and museums and libraries, on the other, was made even more explicit.[6] Section 271 (2) of the reauthorized act called museums "core providers of learning in conjunction with schools, families, and communities," and section 271 (6) suggested that a central way that this core provider function can be achieved is through "resource sharing and partnerships among museums, libraries, schools, and other community organizations."

In addition to working on the state level with libraries through such entities as State Library Administrative Agencies and working at the federal level with Native American tribes (including organizations that represent native Hawaiians) to improve library services in their communities, IMLS sponsors three national competitions: the National Leadership Grants for Libraries Program; the National Leadership Grants for Museums Program; and the National Leadership Grants for Library and Museum Collaborations Program. The purpose of these competitions is to identify projects that have the "potential for national impact" insofar as "they creatively address issues of concern to libraries [and museums] across the country and provide potential solutions to common problems."[7] The mandate for these programs, especially the National Leadership Grants for Library and Museum Collaborations Program, is enshrined in section 262 of the Museum and Library Services Act, which obliges the director of IMLS to "establish and carry out a program of awarding grants or entering into contracts or cooperative agreements to enhance the quality of library services nationwide and to provide coordination between libraries and museums," including "model programs demonstrating cooperative efforts between libraries and museums."[8] And, as per section 221 (a) (1) (b) "Reservations and Allotments," 3.75 percent of the amounts appropriated to IMLS by Congress for any given fiscal year are designated for section 262 programs.

In other words, library and museum collaboration became a broadly defined national goal with legal force. And, to judge from some of the additions and changes in the reauthorized 2003 Museum and Library Services Act, museums were viewed as the lead agents in this collaborative process. While their mandate was to be "core providers of learning...connecting the whole of society to the cultural, artistic, historical, natural, and scientific understandings that constitute our heritage," libraries were defined as entities that "facilitate access to resources . . . for the purpose of cultivating an educated and informed citizenry" and that share resources among themselves in order to "achiev[e] economical and efficient delivery of library services to the public."[9] Although no one would dispute that libraries contribute to learning, it is nevertheless telling that libraries were not designated as "core providers of learning," but rather as delivery mechanisms.

LIBRARIES, MUSEUMS, AND OUTCOME MEASURES

Two intertwined elements contributed to making library and museum partnerships a highly desired undertaking worthy of government support. First, the Government Performance and Results Act (GPRA) was passed in 1993, with an effective date of 2000. GPRA may seem like an odd factor in the growth of library and museum partnerships in the United States, but it is nevertheless a crucial one. GPRA stated that each government agency was responsible "for establishing—preferably in objective, quantifiable and measurable terms—specific performance goals for every one of its programs and . . . thereafter reporting annually to the Congress on its success or lack of success in meeting those goals."[10] The implication was that, if an agency could not produce quantifiable measures attesting to the efficacy of a given program in terms of intended outcomes, then Congress had a duty to ask hard questions about whether that program was giving good value to taxpayers. If the program was not effective in meeting goals and producing outcomes, either it would have to be reconceptualized so that it would henceforward be effective, or it would be allowed to wither (i.e., its funding would be reduced) and eventually die. A new era of "positive accountability" had begun—an era in which governmental programs were required to achieve demonstrable results that were worthy of continued financial support.[11]

GPRA can be seen as part of the movement to conceptually understand nonprofit organizations in the same way as for-profit organizations from the perspective of operational objectives. As explained by J. Gregory Dees, both types of organizations pursue bottom-line results "by adding value to the resources which they acquire and process."[12] In the case of for-profit companies, the bottom line is a "positive economic outcome, i.e., a profit"; in the case of nonprofits, the bottom line is "a positive social outcome."[13] If the for-profit company is successful in making a profit, it will have the financial capacity to acquire replacement resources to ensure continued productivity and profitability. On the other hand, the nonprofit organization is "dependent in whole or in part upon contributed goods, funds, or services" for its continued existence.[14] If it fails to produce a positive social outcome, such funding may be in jeopardy. Accordingly, nonprofits should be managed just like for-profits, with a clear emphasis on measurable results and outcomes. When results and outcomes remain steady or improve in a for-profit company, more and more people are willing to invest in that company. Similarly, the extent to which a nonprofit generates positive social outcomes is reflected in the willingness of legislators, taxpayers, and donors to financially support that nonprofit. All this, of course, takes place against the background of a market economy. After all, individuals can choose among a large number of for-profit companies in which to invest their money; obviously, they will choose those companies that have a good track record of, or the greatest potential for, delivering the highest profits. For-profit companies therefore compete against one another to attract new investment capital on the basis of past results, defined as profits, dividends, and stock prices. In the same way, nonprofits compete for financial resources from donors and funding agencies on the basis of their past results, defined as positive social outcomes.

A good example of how this works in practice is the method adopted by the United Way to determine which applicants it will fund. The United Way, an umbrella charitable organization that dispenses funds to various petitioning agencies who have proposed diverse fundable programs to address specific community needs, no longer bases its funding evaluations on the merits of the providers of the programs nor on the intrinsic nature and quality of the program itself, but rather on "program performance"—the degree to which the program in question positively affected "the recipients of [those] services."[15] In other words, the United Way wants to know whether the program accomplishes what it claims to accomplish—that is, whether a program can point to tangible outcomes, defined as "benefits or changes for individuals or populations during or after participating in program activities." More specifically, they can be quantified as the difference in "knowledge, attitudes, values, skills, behavior, condition, or other attributes" that a program participant has before and after participating in a program.[16]

For all intents and purposes, government agencies and departments can be equated with umbrella nonprofit organizations such as the United Way. Government agencies can only fund a small percentage of programs and proposals presented to them, so they must use certain criteria to distinguish among all applicant programs and proposals. Whether they like it or not, programs are thus placed in a position of having to compete against each other on the basis of past or projected outcomes. And the more tangible the outcomes, the better the chance that a program or proposal gains funding. The move to outcome-based evaluation thus constitutes the first element facilitating the creation of library and museum partnerships. Certainly, this type of evaluation does not directly lead to library and museum partnerships, but it provides an enabling structure in which the rise of such partnerships can more easily occur.

The second important element is the gradual evolution of the museum, over the course of the last century, from a purely collecting and curating institution— that is, an institution that was "oriented primarily inward on the growth, care, study, and display of its collection"—to a postobject institution "engaged primarily in providing a range of educational and other services to its visitors and . . . to its community."[17] In broad terms, the library underwent a similar transformation, offering a range of services and activities—from ready reference to story times to adult literacy classes—designed to benefit as many community members as possible, not just serious readers and scholars. Yet, as we saw in chapter 2, the educative function of libraries and museums, beginning in the last decades of the twentieth century, was often made subservient to an entertainment function. That is, libraries and museums felt that they had to compete with other entertainment venues to attract visitors who, when all was said and done, could choose from a wealth of exciting, fun, and stimulating leisure-time options.

As outcome-based evaluation began to be adopted as the standard by which to judge nonprofit programs and proposals, and as libraries and museums were increasingly compelled to justify their share of municipal, state, and federal funds against a background of shrinking tax receipts and declining government budgets, defining a series of measurable and quantifiable outcomes—outcomes that would justify tax dollars received—assumed a primary importance for these institutions. Libraries and museums could no longer say they ought to exist qua libraries and museums. Rather, they had to show that they should exist, given all the other competing priorities and programs that governmental departments and agencies were interested in funding (i.e., parks, health care, and roads). As Peggy D. Rudd summarizes, "while it would be much more convenient if the worth of libraries was simply accepted on faith by university presidents, county commissioners, city managers, and school boards, that is frequently not the case [so] outcome measurement has the potential to be a powerful tool to help us substantiate the claims we know to be true about the impact of libraries in our institutions and in our society."[18] Stephen Weil says much the same thing about museum funding: "If our museums are not being operated with the ultimate goal of improving the quality of people's lives, on what [other] basis might we possibly ask for public support?... It [is not] likely that we could successfully argue that museums...deserve to be supported simply as an established tradition, as a kind of ongoing habit."[19] Libraries and museums must therefore have, and clearly articulate, a purpose—a purpose that should provide necessary, visible, and ongoing value to their communities in readily measurable terms.

LIFE-LONG LEARNING COMMUNITIES

In its role as an umbrella organization that identifies societal needs and envisions how best to meet those needs, IMLS chose to focus on lifelong learning and the development of learning communities as its central purpose, implicitly recognizing that the process of learning (and, by extension, teaching) as constituted in the United States at the end of the twentieth century was beset with numerous problems. As summarized by Reed Larson, children in their early and middle teens report being bored, disconnected, and unmotivated in general. These are unhealthy psychological emotions, Larson states, and he attributes such emotions to the collective failure of the existing education system to "keep their fires lit."[20] Given these problems, learning needs to be redefined for the twenty-first century such that it becomes both lifelong and "free choice"; that is, individuals of all ages should be motivated to learn independent of external forces such as parents, schools, and job requirements. Learning should be something that individuals of all ages truly want to do at all stages of their lives; it should be seen neither as a burden nor as a chore, but something that is to be undertaken willingly as a pleasant and satisfying experience that is indeed so pleasant and satisfying that the individual looks forward to repeating that experience again and again. For this to occur, learning should become an endeavor that takes place within a community and is guided by the community.

To help with the challenging and arduous task of redefining learning as lifelong and free choice, IMLS created the 21st Century Learner Initiative. Starting from the premise that "we are a nation of learners continuously pursuing learning, independently and collectively, throughout our lives," the initiative seeks to encourage learners "to use and become accustomed to using library and museum resources to explore issues that they value, to gain understanding of the world and to take part in their communities." In addition, learning is made all the more relevant to learners because libraries and museums develop programs "to support needs identified by learners." This, then, is one way that a learning community is formed. Because "learning in the future will increasingly take place within networks [consisting] of people, of information, and of ideas," libraries and museums can become cornerstones of such learning communities insofar as they are "dynamic partners in providing learning resources and expertise that support formal and informal lifelong learning." Certainly, other partners—for example, Head Start, Elderhostel, churches, newspapers, and public broadcasting—contribute to lifelong learning, but libraries and museums are ideally positioned to "take a leadership role in building community partnerships that will support the development of learning communities" consisting of institutions that are sufficiently "responsive and flexible...to identify common missions, goals and constituencies and collaborate to benefit the learner."[21]

The establishment of government-mandated, outcome-based evaluation criteria, together with the perceived need, articulated by IMLS and others, to reposition learning as a lifelong and free-choice activity, created a propitious situation for individual libraries and museums as they struggled—some more than others—to define and justify their value to the general public. A duly constituted and authorized government agency was encouraging—through grant monies—libraries and museums, both separately and together, to embark on model programs for the purpose of creating—and perpetuating—learning communities. If libraries and museums could argue that they positively—and quantifiably—affected learning outcomes through their programs, then they would be viewed as important—perhaps the most important—parts of the solution to the documented problems swirling around current models of learning. In essence, outcome-based evaluation could be used to show that libraries and museums keep the fires of interest lit, in both children and adults. And if this were true for libraries and museums considered separately, then library-museum partnerships—as well as partnerships involving libraries, museums, and other community social and cultural agencies—would be an even more powerful force for learning.

Of course, museums and libraries, as discrete entities, have always been involved in educational activities. Most everyone can recall taking a field trip to a local museum during his or her high school years, for instance, and most everyone has an intuitive sense that public library story times are an engaging way to develop a love of reading in young children. Statistics bear this out. According to the IMLS report *True Needs True Partners 2002: Museums Serving Schools*, based on survey responses from 376 museums in the United States, "nearly 70% of responding museums said [in 2000–2001] that the number of schools, students, and teachers they serve had grown in the past five years."[22] This figure translates into an estimate that some 11,000 museums provided "more than 18,337,800 instructional hours" for K–12 educational programs in 2000–2001, with a median museum cost of $22,500, which "represents 12% of the median museum annual operating budget, four times the 3% reported in 1995." Overall, "expenditures in support of K–12 education have grown to exceed a billion dollars annually." Museums are especially strong in serving the middle elementary grades. Single-day museum visits remain the most popular kind of educational activity, but an increasing number of museums offer traveling exhibits, sequenced or multiple visits, print and electronic educational materials, hands-on workshops, and overnight programs. In addition, 72 percent of surveyed museums use Web sites as an educational tool in their interactions with students, with 58 percent and 24 percent of them communicating by e-mail with teachers and students, respectively. Given the high levels of expenditure, it is perhaps not surprising that 50 percent of museums "evaluate enhanced understanding of target subjects," with 10 percent and 13 percent measuring "improved classroom behavior or academic performance," respectively.

As examples of education programs in museums, *True Needs True Partners 2002* highlights the work done by, among others, the Pittsburgh Center for the Arts, which offers an Arts-in-Education program in which people with mental or physical disabilities can earn certificates in illustration and decorative painting after taking a 12- to 15-month vocational training program taught by professional artists; the Lindsay Wildlife Museum in Walnut Creek, California, which conducts a year-long science education program for troubled teenagers, who then present "environmental education activities for local third-grade classes"; and the Roswell Museum and Art Center in New Mexico, which provides outreach programs to rural schools through portable Discovery Boxes based on "the themes of masks of the world, art basics, and architecture of the past and present." Equally noteworthy are Old Sturbridge Village in Worcester, Massachusetts, which gives fifth-grade students the opportunity to "take a field trip to [a] recreated 1830's community, study primary source documents, and explore the diverse society of early New England Life through [its] *Reading and Writing About History Curriculum Unit*"; the project Reclaiming Latino History, conducted by the Oakland Museum of California, in which Mexican American and Latino teenagers, working in internships with professional historians in after-school and summer sessions, collect, preserve, and exhibit the rich history of their community, a history that was in danger of slipping away because it existed "mainly in the memories of community elders, in private family collections, and in the informal archives of local Latino organizations"; and the Madison Children's Museum's Cultural Exchange Through Mobile Museums program, which allowed students in Wisconsin to collaborate with "musicians, artists, and scholars to create exhibits on immigration, pop culture, village life…, the Latin American marketplace," and the Mayan codex to learn about Meso-America and Mexico.[23]

While the six above-mentioned programs do not emphasize Web-based technology, two other museum educational projects make extensive use of online tools. The Minnesota Historical Society, through its Online Access to Primary Source Learning project, created a series of Web sites "to tell the story of industrial development at the Falls of St. Anthony." Not only can students link to images of historical items, they can also participate in such activities as History Mystery, in which they "sleuth through primary source 'evidence' and form conclusions about items related to an historical event or entity." And in the Bronx, New York, the Lehman College Art Gallery "developed an online reference guide to public art in the Bronx [containing]…biographical information about 111 artists, descriptions of 87 sites where art can be viewed, and the histories of 35 neighborhoods" so that elementary schoolteachers can create lesson plans in a wide variety of disciplines, including history and civics.[24]

Libraries too have formed partnerships with educational facilities, especially Head Start programs, embracing findings from childhood experts who have shown that "exposing infants and toddlers to early learning activities is critical for later language acquisition, learning, and literacy."[25] For instance, the Geneva Free Library in New York worked with Head Start and the local housing authority "to provide reading-related programs and training and even open a mini-library in a low-income apartment complex."[26] And the Idaho State Library implemented the Read to Me and First Book projects, which allowed participating public libraries in the state to work with preschools and daycare centers "to distribute books as well as educational activities and handouts for families to nurture children's early literacy skills, [thus] helping them become independent readers and lifelong learners."[27] In one such activity, a librarian typically visits Head Start centers, giving each family "a canvas bag with puppets, writing materials and books. She showed them how to use the puppets and read to their children. It very directly affected the parents. You could see the lights going on with them."[28]

Within the array of facts and figures we've quoted, particular attention should be given to the finding that some 70 percent of museums report that their educational activities have "grown in the past five years" and that 50 percent of museums evaluate whether students derive an "enhanced understanding of the target subjects." In other words, the increase in the breadth and scope of educational activities in museums seems to be correlated with the establishment of IMLS and outcome-based evaluation measures. To be sure, no cause-and-effect relationship can be traced, yet it is intriguing to note this juxtaposition. Accordingly, the clear success of museum-school partnerships, on the one hand,

and library-school partnerships, on the other, was a good reason to suppose that library-museum-school partnerships or library-museum partnerships would be just as efficacious, if not more so, in creating the conditions for and encouraging lifelong learning.

EXAMINING IMLS LIBRARY-MUSEUM PARTNERSHIPS

But what, exactly, is the nature of the library-museum partnerships funded by IMLS? Are the partnerships implemented in such a way that their intended audiences actually use the resources of both partners? Or does one partner (or the resources of one partner) take center stage and relegate the other partner to a secondary role? Are they collaborations in name alone, not in deed, such that the partners continue to exist and develop along parallel tracks, coming together only on a contingent and convenient basis? Are some library-museum partnerships more robust than others in merging the strengths of one institution with the riches of the other so that there is a chance that a new institutional model will arise? What are some of the strengths and weaknesses of these partnership projects? To what extent are these partnerships conducive to developing knowledge in users, as opposed to providing them with informational snippets? Is there a growing dedifferentiation of services in libraries and museums, as discussed in chapter 2?

To answer these questions, we examined the 80 library-museum partnership projects to which IMLS awarded collaborative grants under section 262 (a) between 1998 and 2003. Our analysis relies on two sources of information. First, under the auspices of the Freedom of Information Act (FOIA), we requested copies of selected portions of all 80 successful National Leadership Grants for Library and Museum Collaborations (1998–2003). Elements of the grant applications included in our request were the face sheet (basic identifying information about the applicants), abstract, narrative, and partnership statement.[29] The narrative is the main element in the IMLS grant application since it contains detailed information about the nature, scope, anticipated results, and sustainability of the project for which funding is requested.[30] Second, information derived from grant applications was supplemented, where possible, by Web-based materials about the partners involved in the project and the project itself. When project information was not available on the Web, successful grant applicants were contacted by e-mail and asked to send any information—brochures, flyers, reports, and so on—about their funded project.[31]

Some overall statistics are in order before we begin our analysis of individual projects. From 1998 to 2003, IMLS granted just over $19.8 million to 80 library-museum collaborative projects; on average, this was $247,652 per project (see table 3.1). When projects were funded, the vast majority of them (71.3 percent, representing 57 projects) were funded at or above the requested amount; only 11 projects (13.8 percent) were funded at a rate below 90 percent of requested funds (see table 3.2). Successful projects encompassed a wide variety of subject areas, audiences, and approaches. As shown in table 3.3, 17 projects were intended mainly for children and teenagers (K–12); 28 mainly for adults; and 26 for chil-

Table 3.1
Grants Awarded by IMLS for Library-Museum Collaborative Projects (1998–2003)

Year	Number of Grants	Total Amount of All Grants ($)	Average Grant Amount ($)
1998	12	2,371,937	197,661.42
1999	12	3,306,904	275,575.33
2000	14	3,204,735	228,909.64
2001	15	3,675,861	245,057.40
2002	11	2,764,022	251,274.73
2003	16	4,488,671	280,541.94
Total	80	19,812,130	247,651.63

Table 3.2
Degree to Which Successful IMLS Library-Museum Collaborative Applications Are Funded (1998–2003)

Degree of Funding	Number of Grants ($N = 80$) Funded at This Level (%)*
100.01% to 125% of request	18 (22.5)
100% of request	39 (48.8)
90% to 99.99% of request	12 (15)
80% to 89.99% of request	4 (5)
70% to 79.99% of request	3 (3.8)
50% to 69.99% of request	3 (3.8)
49.99% or less	1 (1.3)

* Percentages do not add to 100 because of rounding.

dren, teenagers, and adults. Nine grants (11.3 percent of the total) were given to professional groups or organizations (i.e., librarians, educators, archivists, and museum personnel) for organizing conferences to discuss the possibility of establishing and extending partnerships, forging relationships and networks, or training various personnel to work with tools that enable digital collaborations.[32] Although these nine grants funded important initiatives, they were not library-museum collaborations per se, and so we do not discuss them further.

The central subject or content area of 29 projects could be broadly classed within the field of history; 23 within arts and literature; and 19 within science and environment.[33] Nine grants were awarded to partnerships whose project dealt, for the most part, with the preservation and valorization of various aspects of Native American history and culture.[34] Four grants supported projects memorializing the heritage and contribution of African Americans,[35] while two grants supported a project whose primary audience was the Hispanic American community.[36] Another two grants targeted remote geographical locations among the territorial possessions of the United States.[37] Based on these figures alone, IMLS

Table 3.3
IMLS Library-Museum Collaborative Projects by Intended Audience and Subject Area (1998–2003)

Subject	Mostly Children and Teenagers (K-12)	Mostly College and Adult	Children, Teenagers, and Adults
History (27/29)	6/7*	11	10/11*
Arts and Literature (22/23)	4	9/10*	9
Science and Environment (19)	6	7	6
Totals (68/71)	16/17	27/28	25/26

*Denotes a category in which one of the projects received two separate IMLS library-museum collaboration grants.

distributed funds on an equitable basis among major subject areas and audience groups. In the sections below, we examine each of the nine main categories of IMLS library-museum collaboration grants as per the grid in table 3.3, in which each of the three identified subject areas (history; art and literature; science and environment) are cross-categorized by intended audience (children and teenagers; adults; children, teenagers, and adults). Each of the sections begins with an overview of individual projects and concludes with an analysis of the extent to which the partnerships create viable and sustained models for knowledge acquisition and lifelong learning. The chapter concludes with an overall assessment of these collaborations—an assessment that includes an analysis of the first successful grant applications under the Museums in the Community program, an IMLS granting category established in 2003.

HISTORY PROJECTS INTENDED MOSTLY FOR CHILDREN AND TEENAGERS: DESCRIPTION

Of the six projects (receiving seven grants) in this category (see table 3.4), Making Cultural Connections in Education, spearheaded by the Birmingham Civil Rights Institute, is the only one that does not emphasize digital collaboration. Instead, it brings together seven partners to create an after-school program for grades six through eight in an Alabama district that is 95 percent African American. The task of each partner in the Birmingham Culture Alliance Partnership (BCAP) was to "develop a culturally sensitive curriculum" focusing "on the African-American experience in Alabama" by including "relevant history of African-Americans consistent with the mission and purpose of that institution," thus not only helping students in their formal academic work, but also "build[ing] self-esteem" by giving them "awareness of their cultural and artistic heritage."[38] Students were bussed to each partner's site four days per week and spent "up to 4 weeks" at each site in groups of no more than 30 students.

At the Birmingham Civil Rights Institute, students were introduced to the Oral History Project of the Richard Arrington Jr. Resource Gallery, an "ongoing

Table 3.4
IMLS Library-Museum Collaborative History Projects Intended Mostly for Children and Teenagers (K-12) (1998–2003)

Year	Title of Project	Selected Major Applicants	Grant Amount ($)
1998/ 2000	Building a Digital Cultural Heritage Community and Teaching with Digital Content	University of Illinois Libraries; Early American Museum; Illinois Heritage Association	157,981 and 249,583
1999	Rochester Images	Rochester Public Library (New York); Rochester Museum and Science Center	279,346
1999	Territorial Kansas Online	Kansas State Historical Society; Spencer Research Library at the University of Kansas	224,076
2000	Beyond the Turns of the Centuries	Memorial Hall Museum (Deerfield, Massachusetts); Frontier Regional Union #38 School District	249,100
2000	Making Cultural Connections in Education	Birmingham Civil Rights Institute (Alabama); Birmingham Botanical Gardens; Birmingham Historical Society	216,580
2003	Windows on Maine	University of Maine Libraries (Orono); Maine State Museum (Augusta); Maine Public Broadcasting Corporation	470,305

accumulation of interviews with individuals who discuss how the Civil Rights Movement affected their lives." They heard and saw segments taken from 201 conversations, all enhanced with "archival footage and still images."[39] At the Botanical Gardens, they learned about the plants and vegetables "made famous by George Washington Carver" and partook in hands-on projects to "understand the science of horticulture." At the Historical Society, they participated in My History Hunt, "a walking tour to view historically significant architecture in Birmingham," and learned photography skills. At the Museum of Art, students undertook their own Story Quilt project after being introduced to the rich history of quilt making and its role in the African American community. At the Public Library, they completed a Genealogy and Oral History Research project.

Birmingham, of course, was known as a major center for iron and steel production throughout the twentieth century. To commemorate this role, a statute of the Greek god Vulcan soars above the city skyline, and the Sloss Furnaces National Historic Landmark "preserve[s] and interpret[s]...iron-making and iron-working structures and artifacts" through a "near complete 17-acre blast furnace plant, worker housing, blast furnace tools, [and] foundry." The Sloss historic site also serves as a "center for [the] study, creation, and exhibition of metal art." Much of Birmingham's wealth and prestige was built on the backs of skilled

African American foundry workers, so it is appropriate that students in the BCAP program traveled to Sloss not only to learn how "African-American labor advanced and strengthened Birmingham's industrial and economic development," but also to understand "how iron is made through participatory activities." Finally, at the Southern Museum of Flight, they were informed about the African American contribution to aviation through the story of the Tuskegee Airmen.

As mentioned earlier, the majority of projects in this category are digital collaborations. One of these is Beyond the Turns of the Centuries, a partnership between a rural school district and its libraries, on the one hand, and the Memorial Hall Museum, a history museum in western Massachusetts, on the other, to "develop curriculum that uses the collections of the Museum to enrich the teachings of history, with the ultimate goal of making the curricula and related collections accessible on a website."[40] Four themes—Native Americans, Newcomers (settlers, African Americans, and immigrants), Family Life, and the Land—were highlighted across the Colonial Period (1680–1720), the Federal Period (1780–1820), and the Progressive and Colonial Revival Period (1880–1920) in a way that "tie[d] collections directly to curriculum and activities that conform to mandated educational standards." The completed digital library contained about 1,800 objects, manuscripts, and photographs from the museum's collection and a "full array of classroom lessons" for all grade levels. Each of the items was accompanied by two levels of "age-appropriate interpretive text" written by museum education staff, here termed "in-school humanists-in-residence," and reviewed by school librarians, who also served as liaisons with teachers by bringing "the resources on the website to the attention of teachers and work[ing] with them to create activities specifically designed for their classrooms that incorporate the pedagogy and content of current education standards." Searchable, browsable, and containing a thesaurus, the database also allows librarians to "request specific digitized items, ask for research on a topic, or request further background information [from the museum] on a resource already included." In sum, the resources of the Memorial Hall Museum were "permanently integrated into the offerings of the school library" and became "a central feature of the museum's education offerings," thus cementing the school library–museum relationship. Because the museum pledged to assume "responsibility for responding to ongoing educator requests including the addition of primary resources and curricular materials as well as website maintenance," it agreed to draw budgetary and staff support from its curatorial, library, and education departments, investing $17 per item (without interpretive text) for "the cost of scanning and creating the image for display on the website."

The standards-based Web site facilitates a wide range of curriculum activities, including thematic overviews for students on selected topics and background essays for teachers, as well as lesson plans and interactive files depicting such topics as men's and women's clothing from different eras.[41] For example, digitized probate inventories allow students to "deduce what can be learned about the [deceased] person's life and the community [and to undertake] comparisons between inventories of different [time] periods [to] illustrate changes in community life," to say nothing of answering the question, What did children get when their parents died? Because the collection also includes digitized images of local newspapers and photographs of immigrants by Frances and Mary Allen, students can unravel "myths of the melting pot...by contrasting the Allen Sisters' soft-focused photographic images of Polish immigrants to anti-Polish sentiments in the local newspaper." Under the section Children: School Books: Smith's Geography, students could read a descriptive caption informing them that "although Massachusetts towns provided free public education from the seventeenth century on, students and their families bought their own school books [and] teachers taught the subjects from the books each child brought."[42] Children from richer homes would likely have more books and thus more opportunity to read, study, and continue their education—something that may have contributed to a lack of upward mobility and inequality of chances later in life. Given that the students for whom Beyond the Turns of the Centuries was originally intended come from Franklin County, the poorest and most rural of Massachusetts counties—where 27 percent of adults do not have a high school diploma and where 28 percent of the students in the town of Sunderland qualify for a free/reduced lunch—the descriptive caption affixed to Smith's Geography may give them ironic insight about how times have, or have not, changed. And, although social studies and history students and teachers would be the primary users of the Web site, it could also be beneficial in mathematics classes, in which students could "use historic photographs to calculate heights through measurement of the shadows."

Territorial Kansas Online was, in many ways, similar to Beyond the Turns of the Centuries.[43] A collaboration between the Kansas State Historical Society and the Kansas Collection of the Spencer Research Library at the University of Kansas, the project created a "virtual repository" of "government documents, diaries, letters, photographs, maps, newspapers, rare secondary sources and historical artifacts" dating from 1854 to 1861 and related to the highly charged and polemical question of whether the Kansas Territory would enter the Union as a free or slave state. Relevant images were also included to give a sense of the reality of historic events. For example, an electronic copy of John Brown's pamphlet *Parallels* could be linked to a photograph of Brown and "to the desk on display at the Adair Cabin in Osawatomie where he wrote *Parallels* and to digitized images of the Adair Cabin." Printer's type "from the infamous sacking of free-state stronghold Lawrence, which resulted in printing press and type being dumped into the Kansas River in an attempt to silence the press" could be linked to relevant articles from 1850 newspapers. Correspondence from Senator James Lane, Senator John J. Ingalls, and Governor Charles Robinson was also included, as were the records of the New England Emigrant Aid Company, "which was instrumental in bringing anti-slavery settlers to Kansas." On the whole, the selected materials represented "a balanced approach...and convey[ed] the sentiments and emotions of the people participating in and experiencing" these fraught events.

The historical materials making up the Territorial Kansas Online project "may be used for research papers, History Day projects, and by teachers developing their own lesson plans," as well as by "Civil War buffs and re-enactors endeavoring to understand and articulate the motivations of individual soldiers who participated in the Civil War." In addition, "curriculum units based on selected digitized items" were developed "to enhance the teaching of U.S. history at the middle school, high school, and college levels," with Kansas State Historical Society staff preparing "contextual essays for each of the [curriculum] units that provide the necessary historical context for using the materials in the classroom." Some of the instructional objectives included "comparing the view[s] of the free-state and pro-slavery supporters, appraising the impact of the Kansas territorial conflict on national politics and on tensions between the North and the South, and analyzing the role of partisans, politicians and newspapers in establishing the reputation of 'Bleeding Kansas.'"

Rochester Images, a project of the Rochester Public Library and the Rochester Museum and Science Center (RMSC), was a somewhat more sophisticated iteration of the two previous projects, but, essentially, it too concerned itself with "the development of digitized products for the support of educational use."[44] Building on an existing collaboration with the City Hall Photo Lab, the Municipal Archives, and the Historian's Offices of Monroe County, Brighton, and Perinton that had produced an electronic collection of about 15,000 photographs and maps, Rochester Images focused on digitizing and cataloging an additional 7,500 photographs from the Albert R. Stone Negative Collection, housed at RMSC. Albert and Daniel Stone were photographers for the *Rochester Herald* and *Democrat and Chronicle* during the first four decades of the 1900s; their cameras not only captured the vicissitudes of daily life in Upstate New York, but also recorded such "important figures and topics as Frederick Douglass and abolitionism, Susan B. Anthony and the women's rights movement, and the Erie Canal." Among the items featured on the project's Web site were guided online history tours about the role of a small town (Hilton) fire department (which included The Department and the Village: Social Connections, and Then and Now: Fire Changes Downtown Hilton Through the Years), the pomp, glory, and tangled contradictions of patriotism in Rochester between 1892 and 1922, and the complexity of the Erie Canal, including Changing Transportation on the Erie Canal, and The Influx of Cultures and Service Industries along the Canal.[45]

Taken together, the collection allowed for the development of new curricula in local schools, thus addressing state educational standards that required students to be competent in the interpretation of primary source materials. In effect, an "electronic thematic anthology" was created, supplemented by "electronic pathfinders and usage guides linking the image database to Library, Museum, and community resources." And, because museum objects were integrated into the library catalog through the addition of "subject descriptors and other data necessary for [conversion to] MARC records," patrons of the Rochester Public Library who, for example, performed a search for *bridges* were presented not only with books and journal articles about bridges, but also with thumbnail images of any bridges that happened to reside in the Rochester Images database, along with "direct access to additional resources about bridges." Finally, RMSC, "which provides an extensive series of adult and youth education programs…, including consistently oversubscribed courses on local history and interpreting photographs," offered a new course about ways to use the Rochester Images database.

Bringing together the Maine Public Broadcasting Corporation as well numerous state museums and historical societies, Windows on Maine was one of the most elaborate examples of education-oriented digitization projects in the area of history.[46] Taking advantage of the fact that Maine has a broadband Asynchronous Transfer Mode (ATM) network linking over 80 high schools, the Bangor Public Library, and the Maine State Library and that, in 2002, Governor Angus King established the Learning Technology Initiative to provide wireless laptops to all students and teachers at or above the grade seven level, Windows on Maine not only worked toward creating "a [centralized] digital archive and interactive information system" about Maine history and science for students in grades seven and eight, but also developed a corollary program for teachers "designed to advance an understanding of how to interactively use digital resources" in their classrooms. At the heart of the project was a series of thematic learning modules (HOME: The Story of Maine, and QUEST: Investigating our World) that integrated 13 half-hour television programs about the history of Maine, between 18 and 24 television programs about the natural and environmental history of Maine, and a vast array of "exemplary multimedia materials" such as historical film footage, facsimile full-text documents, photographs, oral history audio files, and maps. Overall themes and content requirements of the learning modules were defined by the Maine Department of Education and an Education Advisory Board, by which participating libraries, museums, archives, and historical societies were represented. Once the themes were identified, each cultural institution selected and digitized resources from its collections that it felt would enhance and support "multidisciplinary and interactive educational approaches." These resources were then centrally archived in a digital repository that "organize[d] the multiplicity and volume of resources in a coherent way" on a Web portal so that "multiple target audiences" in all parts of the state could have convenient access to all instructional materials through the ATM network. Training sessions were offered to teachers so that they could become comfortable with "an interactive teaching methodology in which video and telecommunications merge with hands-on activities to enhance critical thinking, motivate student learning, and sharpen students' perceptual skills" so that they can "make the connection between history and science and [their] own lives and futures."

While the four previously mentioned digital partnerships propose exciting opportunities, they nevertheless raise a host of thorny issues—issues that are clearly visible in the project Building a Digital Cultural Heritage Community: The East Central Illinois Framework and its continuation, Teaching with Digital Content: Describing, Finding and Using Digital Cultural Heritage Materials,[47] as well as in conference papers and other documents that are an outgrowth of these two projects. From one perspective, the fact that the project was renewed is testimony to its ongoing success and vitality; from another perspective, it could be argued that the second grant application (as well as the project's ulti-mate renewal) was a recognition that the original project not only was incom-plete, but also raised more questions than it answered about the wisdom and efficacy of succumbing to unbridled enthusiasm for the creation of what the Rochester Public Library called, in its grant application, "digitized products for the support of educational use."

One of the tasks of Building a Digital Cultural Heritage Community was to "identify materials (text, images, video) within museum, library and archival collections that have already been digitized or that will need to be digitized for inclusion in a digital repository in order to meet curriculum goals" as well as "teaching goals for Social Science in the Illinois Learning Standards." As the project developers stated, the use of primary source materials in classrooms re-duces boredom and leads students to "higher-level thinking [because such mate-rials]…offer the experience of collecting, organizing, interpreting, and weighing the significance of factual evidence," a precursor of "systematic analysis" that at-tempts to differentiate fact from opinion so that "justifiable inferences and con-clusions" can be made.[48] For instance, because one of the goals of the Illinois learning standards is to "understand world geography and the effects of geogra-phy on society, with an emphasis on the United States [and to] understand the historical significance of geography [by] identify[ing] different settlement pat-terns in Illinois…and relate them to physical features and resources," digitized information could be developed about how central Illinois attracted many "East Frisian settlers, who were experienced at draining swampy areas because the land was similar to their homeland."[49] Or, to take a more concrete example, a digitized image of a contraption known as a bed key—together with the contex-tual information that "in the 19th century many bed frames used ropes to hold up mattresses which were often filled with corn husks. It was hard to sleep well on a saggy mattress, so periodically people had to tighten the ropes [with the bed key] in order to sleep well," which gave rise to the phrase *sleep tight*—could be used "as a springboard to discuss the cycle of a pioneer's day, sleeping habits, no-tions of privacy, [or] the importance of corn in pioneer life."[50]

As the Illinois project progressed, however, many hurdles appeared—hur-dles that likely were experienced by other education-oriented digitization proj-ects. Because the Illinois Learning Standards (ILS) were broad and vague, it was difficult to determine which artifacts from the collection of the Early American Museum (EAM) "could serve each particular learning goal"; the cu-rator of EAM "could…think of several hundred other artifacts that might serve equally well" for each goal.[51] Also problematic was the fact that, while the ILS focus on "state and national history and only infrequently mak[e] use of local examples," EAM concentrates, for the most part, on local history, "con-sciously work[ing] to interpret the lives of ordinary people who do not often show up in history textbooks."[52] In addition, teachers had difficulty under-standing the nature of the project; they were "seeking not simply images of arti-facts, but rather entire educational components which could be used to expand their curriculum," so much so that "in the end a substantial number of artifacts were chosen not because the teachers originally requested them, but because the museum curators and librarians suggested items to the teachers who in turn agreed that they would be useful."[53]

Questions and concerns of a more philosophical nature also arose. As Barbara Jones noted, are students *really* learning to do research when they use image databases? After all, "the images are pre-selected, so that students are not getting the experience of selecting and discarding. Also, the selection is already 'framing' a particular subject or theme."[54] In effect, how is a set of images in a database any different from a set of images in a textbook, a handout, or a slide display? Certainly, electronic database images may be more visually appealing and can be rotated, enlarged, or otherwise manipulated according to individual specifications, but, at the end of the day, such capabilities may not substantially contribute to knowledge acquisition in the way that touching, or being in the presence of the original artifact, can. This is particularly true when "most of the information entered into the [Dublin Core] interpretation field [of the image database] remains superficial," perpetuating a situation "where the majority of the artifacts...are still expected to 'speak' for themselves."[55] Indeed, many of the project participants—for the most part, librarians—were reticent about the idea of having an interpretation field in the first place.[56] Yet, as Jones points out, "many schools and colleges do not have good rare book and special collections to draw upon," and so they welcome the opportunity to access digital collections, especially since the digital images "may whet the appetite for visiting a repository." But, again, how is that any different from a textbook, a handout, or a slide display—all of which, too, can whet the appetite for visiting museums or other cultural institutions?[57] In other words, digital collections may be a visual feast, but they may not be an intellectual feast. Aimed more at stimulating—and bringing enjoyment to—the sensual eye than activating the mind's eye, they may give the illusion of satiety without, however, providing any underlying substance or value.

Implicitly recognizing that their initial approach to digitizing images consisted of little more than "worrying about getting it on the Web," project participants in Building a Digital Cultural Heritage Community applied for a second grant, with the express purpose of being "truly more interested in assisting educators do a better job teaching American history."[58] In many ways, this is a startling admission, suggesting that the first iteration of the project really did not help educators very much because technological concerns were allowed to define the direction of the project. This admission is encapsulated—unintentionally, to be sure, yet tellingly—in the two following sentences, the first of which ends a paragraph and the second of which begins the next paragraph: "The developed database was robust enough to enable very different participant institutions [to] deposit metadata records conforming to the Dublin Core format. The teachers argued that the quality as opposed to the quantity of the resources was important."[59] On the one hand, institutions did not experience any problems in depositing as many records as they wanted; on the other hand, teachers were adamant that the high rate of such deposits had little, if any, bearing on educational imperatives.

The sense of failure is further solidified in the first paragraph of the abstract of the grant application Teaching with Digital Content: Describing, Finding and Using Digital Cultural Heritage Materials, in which the applicants request supplementary funds to develop a "successful model program" that would "identify reliable methods" of integrating digital content into K–12 curricula. In other words, they are signaling that their previous efforts were neither successful nor reliable. Yet, the guiding principle of their second grant application narrative still remains a form of technological determinism. The logic of their argument is informative. They have admitted that, in their first project, they spent too much time "worrying about getting it on the Web" and that this worrying was a major contributing factor in the project's lack of success. Thus, to ensure success and reliability, a second project was needed, but this project nonetheless proposed to use the digital content that proved so worrisome in the first place. In light of this, perhaps it is not surprising that one of the central components of the Teaching with Digital Content project is a Microsoft-sponsored,[60] one-week summer institute, held at various statewide locations, emphasizing the integration of technology with defined educational standards.[61] Thus, a company with vested interests in the creation and proliferation of image databases was closely involved in efforts to ensure that teachers become convinced that such proliferation had real benefits.

Another main component of this second grant application is a focus on "visual thinking strategies." And it is here that the project participants—whether inadvertently or not—touch upon what could be called the superfluity of undue fascination with image databases. Developed by Abigail Housen and Philip Yenawine, visual thinking strategies (VTS) promote "the use of interpretation and evidence gathering to describe visual artifacts and content." Originally used in art education, VTS is transferable to nonart domains insofar as it is based on the "careful observation of objects and images; the ability to articulate an idea and present a logical argument for it, using visual evidence; the ability to listen to others, value their ideas, sometimes changing one's own mind in light of new evidence; critical and creative thinking; greater awareness of one's own learning process; [and] the ability to use expert sources effectively and confidently." No doubt VTS is a valuable learning tool; the problem does not lie there. Instead, the difficulty lies in the circumstance that, as the Teaching with Digital Content application states, only a select few images from the project database are "especially appropriate for VTS discussions." In fact, an expert in VTS is needed to select these appropriate images. Moreover, classroom discussions following VTS protocols can equally make use of Web images, CD-ROM–based images, slides, print illustrations, or, as the applicants themselves conclude, "they may use actual objects in a museum gallery." There seems to be some tacit awareness here that digital images may be neither especially useful nor unique; other media—even in-person visits to a museum—can lead to successful learning with VTS. And, given the drawbacks that digital images have been shown to possess—lack of tactility; loss of important details; preselection; preframing; and scant contextual information—overmuch reliance on them for educative purposes may be counterproductive.

HISTORY PROJECTS INTENDED MOSTLY FOR CHILDREN AND TEENAGERS: ANALYSIS

Collaborations between museums and libraries that concentrate on creating digital-image databases for curricular goals therefore risk coming up against the philosophical divide separating libraries from museums: while museums "have a mandate to interpret," librarians "traditionally place a high value on making information accessible without mediation."[62] Institutional prerogatives and concerns thus bring about a situation in which interpretation of digital artifacts is likely to be minimal, but it is this act of interpretation that gives richness and meaning to the artifact in question. Rather than trying to yoke libraries and museums into partnership agreements, one solution might be to consider refashioning libraries into institutions with a strong—that is, not ancillary—museum function, and museums into institutions with an equally strong—again, not ancillary—library function in such a way that museum artifacts juxtapose and inform, in the same physical location, explanatory library collections, and vice versa. Libraries would be museums, and museums would be libraries, with all the attendant benefits of a newly created institution rather than the residual friction and endless discussion that invariably results from attempting to establish linkages between two existing institutions with settled professional practices and approaches that may ultimately turn out to be linkages in name alone, or linkages without real purpose other than edutainment. Instead of libraries and museums coming together in order to compete with other entertainment venues—George Ritzer's notion of the dedifferentiation of consumption—and in the process becoming just another site for edutainment, they would merge into a new construct whose purpose would be a serious exploration of a wide range of issues through in-depth and interconnected analysis of objects and texts.

Otherwise, the result is—for want of a better phrase—a kind of silo effect, as found in the Birmingham Cultural Alliance Partnership (BCAP) project or in Beyond the Turns of the Centuries. Although the after-school visits to seven cultural institutions that were the heart of the BCAP plan are intrinsically valuable in and of themselves, they cannot, theoretically, be distinguished from discrete visits to a series of museums and libraries undertaken thousands upon thousands of times by children and teenagers of all ages in the normal course of a school year. Even the sustainability section of the BCAP grant application alludes to this dilemma: "It will be the primary duty of the project coordinator to explore ways to sustain the project. However, each team member and partner will seek ways to maintain services provided through the project....For example, the Birmingham Botanical Gardens has stated that the George Washington Carver Trail will be a permanent addition to its tours. The Birmingham Public

Library will continue to provide opportunities for genealogical [re]search."[63] In addition, the project coordinator will become a marketer, "advocat[ing] and act[ing] as ambassador for BCAP [by] prepar[ing] and disseminat[ing] information packets about the project." There is no indication of any interaction between and among the seven cultural institutions—no indication, for example, that the Birmingham Public Library will, as a follow-up, make available resources about the African American contribution to ironmaking or the Tuskegee Airmen. Instead, despite the ambitious concluding statement that "the excitement of partners generated by this project will forever change the way libraries and museums do business and deliver programs [so that] collaboration will be the order of the day," the institutions moved forward on their own as stand-alone entities, adding a program here or there to enrich their offerings, but essentially not supporting and supplementing each other's (or their own) resources with ongoing contributions that reinforced what had already been learned or that actively caused students to want to explore more about a specific area. They remained on parallel tracks. To be sure, the project may have generated excitement among the seven participating institutions, but it cannot be said to have generated a thoughtfully conceived plan about how libraries and museums can permanently integrate—that is, have omnidirectional connections among—their visual, print, and electronic resources for educational purposes.

This same problem arises in Beyond the Turns of the Centuries. In that project, participants stated that their database will place an "emphasis on visuals" and will contain a "limited amount of printed material"; much of their efforts were devoted to developing "a highly sophisticated search tool" and such features as "a special magic lens feature" on selected items.[64] And, as we saw above, any existing interpretive material was written by museum staff; the role of librarians was, for the most part, limited to requesting "specific digitized items, ask[ing] for research on a topic, or request[ing] further background information" about an already-included resource. While the grant application does mention that the school library collections support the curriculum, there was little indication that librarians worked to enhance and supplement the database "visuals" with creative initiatives of their own. Rather, they sent messages requesting that museum staff take action of some kind, in effect becoming mechanical order takers and order placers. In addition, we are told that the school library media center contains a state-of-the-art "21st century classroom" with access to a satellite dish, television studio, and a networked computer system with 28 terminals. In all likelihood, students come to the media center, access the Beyond the Turns of the Centuries database, look at the visuals using the magic-lens feature, undertake a lesson of some kind with or without their teacher, and then leave. Again, there is little indication that the school library media center is taking steps to offer comprehensive material about the visuals such that students have the desire to use related (print) materials to make in-depth explorations of specific subject matter. In short, there is little indication of omnidirectional integration of resources. Yet the grant application hints at a possible solution, observing that a "remarkable feature of the collection [of the Memorial Hall Museum] is the depth of the documentation of its objects within the curatorial files as well as interrelation to the journals, newspapers, and schoolbooks in the museum library." Faced with this obviously extensive and rich documentation, school librarians, instead of being order takers and placers, should be proactively working to ensure that such interrelation is comprehensively available in the school library in print or digital form and that it is complemented by material that the museum may not have—perhaps books, articles, and videos that place the museum's objects into a broad and comparative social and cultural framework.

On the other hand, we can see a step toward such omnidirectional integration in Rochester Images. In this project, recall that a person searching for *bridges* in the library catalog not only would find a typical list of books and articles about that topic held by the library, but would also be informed, through a thumbnail photo linked to further explanatory information, about any photographs, maps, or other artifacts dealing with bridges from the Rochester Images digital database. Here, the integration of source materials, each with the potential to enhance and explicate the other, creates the possibility for a well-rounded learning experience for children and adults. Juxtaposing the resources of libraries and museums so that individuals are made aware of, encouraged to use, and benefit from both sets of institutional resources to the extent that they no longer conceive of themselves as using libraries or museums, but rather a single locus of cultural memory—this might be the ideal to which museum and library collaborations should aspire.

In Windows on Maine, the fact that the numerous state libraries, museums, archives, and historical societies have a strong voice in defining the themes and content of learning modules—as well as selecting the objects to be digitized—meant that the end result of the project could, theoretically, be a digital environment that does not assume that a complete understanding of diverse historical phenomena can be accomplished through visual and audio resources alone or through visual and audio resources that are merely supplemented by extracts from textual materials. Instead, the project could result in a digital environment that literally forces students and their teachers to realize that they can only make sense of visual and audio resources through a necessary and rigorous act of reading and exploration of a rich assemblage of textual material from which they then could derive their own (often unique) conclusions through "critical thinking" about given historical, environmental, or social issues. The emphasis on half-hour and hour-long television programs as cornerstones of Windows on Maine suggests, however, that the project is more about "leveraging the delivery power of broadband technology [and] statewide digital broadcasting"[65] and about edutainment than about creating a single locus of cultural memory in which resources of libraries and museums inform one another and symbolically interact to encourage self-forged paths of discovery and creative juxtapositions. While digital libraries/museums ostensibly and theoretically claim to be such a locus of cultural memory, it is very often the case that the lack of interpretive context in these organizations makes them more akin to dedifferentiated entertainment centers in which it is an open question as to how much real educative value visitors receive.

ART AND LITERATURE PROJECTS INTENDED MOSTLY FOR CHILDREN AND TEENAGERS: DESCRIPTION

To varying degrees, an attempt to create a single locus of cultural memory can be seen in all four of the collaborative projects categorized in the areas of art and literature intended mostly for children and teenagers (see table 3.5). But, as we shall see, not all such loci are equal: while some go to great lengths to establish learning communities based on rich collections, others tend more toward the "tourist attraction" direction of the Enoch Pratt Exploration Center. Info-Zone, a project bringing together the Indianapolis Marion County Public Library and The Children's Museum of Indianapolis (TCM) and building upon the success of Rex's Lending Center, is particularly compelling.[66] Indeed, Rex's Lending Center (RLC) is one of those rare ideas that deserves to be called visionary. It exemplifies what museum and library cooperation, in the best sense of the word, can produce: an institution of a new kind that is neither called library nor museum, but that serves as a place of discovery.

The basic facts about RLC are elegant in their simplicity; there is even a dash of historical resonance because TCM "stands physically on the site where a library branch once stood."[67] In 1989, TCM, as part of a two-month exhibition about space exploration, decided to "create an information lending facility within its exhibitions," with a total of 100 titles made available to exhibition attendees.[68] Over the next five years, the initial concept was refined and expanded. Each of TCM's 10 galleries would have 100 different titles—70 percent books and 30 percent periodicals, audio and video cassettes, computer software, and objects—available for lending. Each of those 100 titles would be available in 10 copies, for a grand total of 10,000 items. All 1,000 unique titles were carefully chosen, with each gallery collection containing a regularly updated and "representative, concentrated selection" of materials that had been judged as being the best at "relating to the visions, concepts, goals and objectives" of that particular gallery.[69]

How would all this work in practice? A child walking through the museum's galleries would find objects or exhibits that intrigued her, say, for example, a coral reef, a dinosaur, African folk tales, a nineteenth-century locomotive, or a mummy's tomb.[70] Wanting more information about the topic of the exhibit, the child would select a book or video from nearby shelves and place a reservation for that item—using the barcodes on her museum card and on the item—at a "reservation station" in each gallery. A maximum of three items could be reserved per museum card, and as the child wends her way through the museum, she can remove previously reserved items from her account and add new choices. Children are not the only ones who can make reservations. Indeed, a "child's father might use his own card to reserve both a picture book for little brother and an adult book about children's emotional development for himself."[71] At the end of a family's visit to TCM, they would find themselves at RLC, "exactly in the core of the museum's main spiral ramp at the base of five exhibit levels,"[72] where a staff member would take their bar-coded cards, print off the list of reserved items, and retrieve them from shelves. After using the items at home or at school, borrowers could return them to any public library location in Indiana, from which the items "will be picked up by a courier for return to TCM."[73]

From a theoretical perspective, RLC can be placed within the framework of Klaus Krippendorff's "emancipatory" theory of communication.[74] Arguing that most cultural institutions are "closed systems of reality constructions" that offer patrons and beholders "coherent explanations, selectively [admit] experiences consistent with it, and suppress feelings that do not fit,"[75] Krippendorff urges the creation of open systems, which work toward "advanc[ing] the horizons of possibility accessible to its users by constructing a situation for unpredictable, inventive, critical thinking."[76] RLC aims to become just such an open system by creating a "responsive setting" that encourages users "to juxtapose and compare" and that connects the user "to other information, so a user can design knowledge independent of the collection or the curator."[77] In short, it recognizes that, to "sustain interest and satisfy questions" over the medium term and to continue nourishing that interest over the long term, deeper levels of information must be provided that "can be taken in hand beyond the museum, and beyond the [short-term] moment of inspiration."[78] And, when the child returns RLC material to her local public library, it is hoped that she will borrow other material on that topic—or a cognate topic—from her branch, thus perpetuating and intensifying the nourishing process.[79] While the museum "stimulates ideas with objects," libraries "nourish ideas with information," with the result that information itself becomes an "artifact."[80] But, if "*the information given*" is to rise to the status of an artifact, it must be "deeply influenced by *the quality of the giving* that

Table 3.5

IMLS Library-Museum Collaborative Art and Literature Projects Intended Mostly for Children and Teenagers (K-12) (1998–2003)

Year	Title of Project	Selected Major Applicants	Grant Amount ($)
1998	Down Under and Over Here	Leigh Yawkey Woodson Art Museum (Wausau, Wisconsin); Marathon County Public Library (Wisconsin)	95,542
1998	Brooklyn Expedition	Brooklyn Children's Museum (New York); Brooklyn Museum of Art	297,900
1999	Discovery to Go	Madison Children's Museum (Wisconsin); Madison Public Library (Wisconsin)	154,741
1999	InfoZone	Indianapolis Marion County Public Library; Children's Museum of Indianapolis	410,931

surrounds it," that is, the institution providing such information must "antici-pat[e] the interests and needs of the learner" by becoming a "cognitive environ-ment constructed by the questions and interactions of its users" (original emphasis).[81] According to the developers of the RLC idea, museums can thus be reinvented to become "information disseminators, under the control of their users"—which, by implication, is something that they have not heretofore been.[82]

Throughout the 1990s, RLC met with much success, and an expansion of the original idea was a natural next step. The result was the InfoZone project. Not only would InfoZone more than triple the physical size of RLC, it would move it to TCM's main level, where it would become part of TCM's "free zone." Up to 75 individuals can use InfoZone at any one time, reading books, using electronic resources, or simply sitting. The RLC reservation system was also eliminated, and the materials—with the exception of kits and CD-ROMs—were "placed on the shelves available to the public to simply pick up and check out" in a more direct and streamlined fashion. In addition, each gallery was out-fitted with "exhibit specific Internet access," where the sites were "pre-selected by [a] librarian working with the programmer-educator for the gallery." As with the RLC plan, the idea was that "at the moment a child becomes engaged in dis-covery, the young visitor will be 'pulled' into a corresponding program available on personal computers in the gallery that, through a series of engaging activities, will bring the visitor to new information resources provided by the library" on adjacent shelves. In total, 10 new galleries were developed, including the Cen-ter for Arts Exploration as well as five traveling exhibits and a planetarium. To extend the reach of the program, bookmobiles were employed to bring ex-hibits—as well as accompanying material—"to city parks and other youth ser-vice agencies"; branch libraries throughout Marion County were also recipients of exhibits.

The outreach aspects of InfoZone constituted the heart of the Discovery to Go project of the Madison Children's Museum and Madison Public Library.[83] Aiming to overcome geographic, physical, cultural, and language and literacy barriers—as well as to "encourage the development of the joy of reading and in-dependent learning"—Discovery to Go brought "integrated, flexible sets of book-based library/museum materials and programs" to various convenient, fa-miliar, and trusted "neighborhood hosts" in community centers or other com-mon gathering places. Participants entered into a museumlike setting with themed exhibits where their interest was held by "intriguing library books and media" relating to the exhibits. A variety of "attention-centering" educational programs of about 45 minutes in length were presented to small groups, after which children had an extended period "for open-ended play in a purposefully-designed, literacy rich setting, and plenty of time for browsing through and se-lecting library materials."

Two examples of programs were Bridges and The Shoes We Use. The out-reach version of Bridges, adopted from and based on a featured exhibit at Madi-son Children's Museum, started from the premise that physical, cultural, and metaphoric "bridges are ubiquitous, essential, and easily overlooked as integral elements of our physical and social landscape." Because individuals have become "increasingly sophisticated in [their] efforts to be completely connected with as many people and places as possible," the concept of bridges also taps into "ideas of linking the isolated and reaching the remote." The traveling museum miniexhibits therefore stressed this diversity, focusing on "replicated settings and components" of "architectural bridges, natural bridges, bridge types and uses, physics of bridges, musical/artistic bridges, biological bridges, [and] communication and technology bridges," while related books included titles by such authors as Christen Asbjornsen, Lee Sullivan Hill, Ken Robbins, and Sheila Hamanaka. The Shoes We Use, a traveling exhibit developed by Kohl Children's Museum in Illinois, not only "explores how shoes help...feet...accomplish various things, shows how shoes differ across cultures, and provides opportunities for foot art," but also introduced children to books by Laurie Lawson, Ann Morris, Ann Schreiber, and others.

Combining some of the elements of InfoZone and Discovery to Go, the Down Under and Over Here project of the Leigh Yawkey Woodson Art Museum (LYWAM), best known for its annual Birds in Art exhibitions,[84] builds on the Down Under and Over Here exhibit organized by the Cedar Rapids [Iowa] Museum of Art, which featured "55 illustrations by 22 Australian and 26 American artists," by adding a wide range of hands-on activities, curricular materials, and educational programming.[85] In expectation of visits to the exhibition from area schools, museum staff created "a comprehensive pre-visit education packet that helps teachers directly link their classroom curriculum" with the illustrators and authors appearing in the exhibit. Teachers themselves were given "small-group training sessions" at the museum so that they could better understand and answer questions from their students about the exhibit. Marathon County Public Library staff developed "Stories-To-Go-Boxes featuring books represented in the exhibition as well as books related by theme, culture, or artist to those in the exhibition; videos; flannel boards; biographical materials; and props that encourage story telling." The museum and library also committed to buying "an extensive array of other books illustrated and authored by the [exhibition] artists and writers." These newly purchased materials would be placed in the Stories-To-Go-Boxes, highlighted in the museum's family reading area, or made generally available through the various branches of the library system.

Emphasis on developing the museum's family reading area was especially important, since LYWAM had learned, from a previous exhibition, that it was "beneficial" to "creat[e] a place for families to slow down, read, and respond" instead of just hurrying through the museum galleries. To reach the growing Southeast Asian population in Wisconsin, there were plans to translate four of the exhibition books into Hmong, donate these translations to relevant community centers, and have them available for circulation at area libraries. In addition, there were visits from the authors and illustrators of the exhibited books as well as numerous activities grouped under the rubric of Toddler Tuesdays or Art Quest for Adults.[86] Finally, a family activity guide was created so that children, together with their parents, would read the books featured in the exhibition and apply the lessons therein learned to their own local circumstances. For example, after reading *The Sign of the Seahorse* by Graeme Base—a book in which the characters gather "at the Seahorse Café to solve the mystery of who and what is destroying the Australian coastal reef"—children were encouraged to "make a list of places you know that could be harmed by pollution" and to draw pictures of those places.[87] In a similar vein, after reading *Possum Magic* by Mem Fox and Julie Vivas—a whimsical book in which an adult possum makes a baby possum invisible to protect him from snakes and then travels "throughout Australia in search of the foods that will make the possum visible again"—children were asked to make a list of characteristic foods of Wisconsin.

While the three aforementioned art and literature projects took place—whether on a permanent basis or for limited periods—in a physical location, Brooklyn Expedition, under the direction of the Brooklyn Children's Museum, was, ostensibly, situated in the digital realm. Yet a number of steps were taken by its creators to encourage a palpable sense of physical community so that the digital experience could be understood as being only a precursor to in-person exploration of museum and library resources that are conveniently linked by the Brooklyn Trolley, which connects the Brooklyn Museum of Art, the Brooklyn Children's Museum, and the Brooklyn Public Library. In addition, the project included a significant element of career training for underprivileged teenagers.[88]

In some ways, Brooklyn Expedition resembles the digital education projects described in the previous section; in other ways, it does not. Users have a choice of four "thematic trails": Latin America, which "focuses on the arts and cultures of Mexico and South America"; Structures, which "explores the shared characteristics among animal skeletons and homes, architecture, art forms, and information cataloging systems"; Brooklyn, which emphasizes the richness and diversity of art and culture in this New York City borough; and Africa, which "uses art to introduce users to the diverse cultures of the continent."[89] The "thematic principle of website management" thus allows many different types of users—not just students in formal education settings—to interact with the site "in accordance with their own interests." Since the project strove "to attract and train young people from diverse backgrounds" as both volunteers and interns "in information technology, library science, and museum programming," it is these young people who will not only "enhance existing trails," but also develop "a youth-generated theme." Accordingly, Brooklyn Expedition constantly evolved, with "multiple themes that can grow and change over time with input from new generations of youth and content partners." And, unlike Beyond the Turns of the Centuries and Building a Digital Cultural Heritage Community, both of which worked from predefined curriculum standards and learning goals and then tried to find museum objects that would address those standards and goals, Brooklyn Expedition took the opposite approach. Its thematic trails were created independently of existing curricular requirements, but educators were subsequently invited "to create lesson plans…that focus on topics explored through the Expedition," an example of which is the teacher who developed

Eastern Parkway—Function and Culture, analyzing "one of Brooklyn's most fa-mous roads and its impact on the many communities that it intersects."[90]

The designs of the home pages of each "thematic trail" were particularly noteworthy. Stressing the equivalency of visual and print resources and, at the next hyperlink, providing site maps of locations for the displayed resources, the designs encourage users to undertake on-site visits to the institutions in question and to physically juxtapose the objects and books that they were shown virtu-ally. Books are not perceived as afterthoughts; they are not merely listed in a link containing bibliographies for "further reading" or "further information." Rather, books are displayed with their own thumbnail image that is the same size and shape as the thumbnail images of artworks and objects from museums. For instance, on the Latin America home page, under the category Converging Cultures, we find, aligned vertically, thumbnail images of the "Atahuallpa Por-trait, Brooklyn Museum of Art," the "Cortes Mural, Brooklyn Children's Mu-seum," and the cover of a book entitled "*Montezuma and the Aztecs*, Brooklyn Public Library." Under the subcategory Spinning Tales in Cloth, we find the "Paracas Textile, Brooklyn Museum of Art," a "Backstrap Loom, Brooklyn Chil-dren's Museum," and the book cover of "*Beneath the Stone: A Mexican Zapotec Tale*, Brooklyn Public Library." Books are thus presented as vital and indispensa-ble learning tools, every bit as interesting and colorful as the objects and art-works that they are grouped with. Indeed, when a user links to an indicated book, she is presented with not only a brief description of its contents, but also an exuberant testimonial from a previous reader such as "Matt, a fifth grader from P.S. 321," who comments in the following way about Philip Wilkinson's book *Super Structures:* "And, wow, did you know how many different types of bridges there are? From every screw to every nut, this book shows you every-thing."[91] Based on Matt's praise, who would not want to borrow Wilkinson's book—and perhaps others on the same shelf—from the library? Brooklyn Exhi-bition thus achieves an impressive feat: digital images are not seen as ends in themselves, but as avenues to a reality defined by a tangible assemblage of items from which individuals like Matt can shape, and come to understand, a world of their own making.

This idea is also present in the Journal function of the Web site, in which users are given "generous storage space for the collection of electronic informa-tion [so that they] can add, modify, or delete images and texts directly from the website, or they can work up their own copy to create a vast array of Journal types and subjects," as well as in the Camera function, which "allow[s] visitors to col-lect images and make notes and comments about their real or virtual visits to the three cultural institutions." But it is important to note that the Journal is not re-stricted to images from the Web site, since Brooklyn Expedition participants are strongly encouraged "to visit each institution to see exhibits, participate in edu-cational programs, and go to the multimedia education centers [where they] will receive specially-designed Journal folders (to hold print-outs and other Expedi-tion materials) and check out digital cameras to enhance documentation of their in-house visits." In a very grounded way, the expedition has turned into a journey, a journey in which one gathers and collects, from among all the offered possibilities, those things—books, printouts, programming handouts, and photographs that one takes oneself of whatever aspect of a museum object one is most interested in—that will be most germane for one's future purposes.

ART AND LITERATURE PROJECTS INTENDED MOSTLY FOR CHILDREN AND TEENAGERS: ANALYSIS

Of the four projects discussed in this category, Rex's Lending Center—as well as its successor, InfoZone—offers the most complete integration of and interconnection between library and museum resources. Because it is a permanent stand-alone venue, it gives a sense of inherent naturalness to the process of first viewing exhibits and objects, then immediately being able to borrow books and other materials about or related to the objects just viewed. Children and adults thus feel that what they are doing is an everyday occurrence, with nothing extraordinary about it. In a sense, the difference between libraries and museums is effaced in their minds, replaced by a new concept—"lending center," "infozone," or something else entirely—that is just beginning to crystallize. As we have seen, Discovery to Go and Down Under and Over Here have many of the components of InfoZone, juxtaposing exhibits and books in innovative ways. Yet, to state the obvious, these projects are not permanent, even though Down Under and Over Here is the fourth in a series of library-museum collaborations undertaken by LYWAM "based on exhibitions of original artworks that dealt with the words and images that make children's books memorable long after childhood is left behind." And because they are of a limited duration, the amalgamated library-museum structure that they have succeeded in forming for a short time quickly disappears—again to be subsumed, both physically and psychologically, by the existing and separate structures of a library and a museum. Of course, these two projects were not meant to be permanent, so it may seem moot to criticize them for something that they did not set out to do. But, while they certainly do have within them the seeds of a combined structure such as InfoZone, their impermanence raises questions about the extent to which they can be labeled as library-museum partnerships. Indeed, from one perspective, the Down Under and Over Here project can be seen as a skillfully developed, community-based, and smoothly deployed marketing campaign to attract new visitors to a museum long known for its Birds in Art exhibitions. LYWAM certainly *involves* the library in its efforts, but there is never the sense that the role and nature of the museum—nor of the library—will change so that contingent short-term interaction evolves into something more fundamental or structural. The exhibit remains on the level of sophisticated edutainment. Outreach efforts and one-time exhibits pairing libraries and museums are, without a doubt, worthy and exciting in their own right, but unless such events alter the daily cognitive habits of both sets of institutions—so that libraries recognize the value of having book and video collections always in the presence of objects; so that museums recognize the value of having their objects always in the presence of book and video collections—or work toward creating a new institution, they cannot be said to be more than transitory phenomena that do not change underlying suppositions about how to define, and understand, loci of cultural memory.

In this regard, the symbolism of the Brooklyn Trolley is both useful and powerful. As it shuttles among an art museum, a children's museum, and a public library, taking visitors from one venue of Brooklyn Expedition to another, the trolley is an apt reminder both of the spiritual proximity of these institutions and of ongoing efforts to physically link them. The act of passing from one to the next therefore becomes second nature, as patrons realize that the full meaning of resources held by one institution can only be grasped through extensive familiarity with the resources of the other two institutions. The design of the opening pages of each online thematic trail in Brooklyn Expedition reinforces this necessary affinity. The fact that for every two or three thumbnail images of artworks or objects from the Brooklyn Museum of Art and Brooklyn Children's Museum there is a thumbnail image of a relevant book from the Brooklyn Public Library gives a clear sign to users that, no matter which thematic trail or subtrail they follow, the experience of viewing objects and artworks will be immeasurably enriched by recourse to books in libraries, where further discoveries await.

SCIENCE AND ENVIRONMENT PROJECTS INTENDED MOSTLY FOR CHILDREN AND TEENAGERS: DESCRIPTION

Many of the same issues that arise with the history and art/literature projects discussed so far also appear in the six science and environment projects for children and teenagers (see table 3.6). We start with An Educational Collaborative for Rural Families, a joint effort of the Montshire Museum of Science, in Vermont, and the Howe Library, in New Hampshire, particularly because it is cited as being a determining influence on another project in this category—the Discovery in Motion project of the North Carolina Museum of Life and Science, itself an outgrowth of the same institution's Library Youth Partnership project. Recognizing the special challenges faced by small, rural libraries (e.g., insufficient financial resources and isolation from city-based cultural resources), the Montshire project brought together a network of eight such libraries to create "eight traveling interactive table-top science exhibits along with companion materials and activities…drawing on related library collections" to encourage and sustain "family learning."[92] Each of the eight libraries "sponsored" one exhibit, first collaborating with staff from the Montshire museum to select an appropriate theme and choose materials from the museum—"various interactive devices, objects, and/or natural history specimens"—to showcase that theme, then adding "companion activities suitable for a library setting, a bibliography of related books and electronic materials, and printed activity guides to encourage families to further their investigations at home." One such themed exhibit was Moving Air, which "explored how moving air affects us, how nature takes advantage of it, and how it can hold up objects like airplanes" by using "a small quiet, blower motor that…power[ed] several air streams coming out of vacuum cleaner–sized flexible hoses." In addition, bookshelves adjacent to the exhibits were stocked with "a great variety of related materials for parent-child sharing," including books purchased to complement themes of the exhibits. For the wind exhibit, accompanying books included *Catch the Wind, Jack and the Whoopee Wind, Windy Day Stories and Poems*, the video *Let Me Tell You About Planes*, and the CD-ROM *The Way Things Work*. As the exhibits rotated among the eight rural libraries at six-week intervals, the project as a whole provided the participating institutions with about a year's worth of "changing foci for programming and public relations," helping them to "build their images as dynamic and interesting places for families to gather for positive and non-threatening learning opportunities."

Discovery in Motion, together with Library Youth Partnership (LYP), combined "opportunities for high school teenagers...to learn, teach, volunteer and gain library and museum work skills" with a series of events that "[offer] thousands of elementary school children science-based programs using children's literature."[93] An extension of the Youth *ALIVE!* (Youth Achievement Through Learning, Involvement, Volunteering, and Employment) programs sponsored by the Dewitt-Wallace Readers Digest Fund, the LYP project presented an "opportunity ladder" for high school students—"50% of whom are African-American and/or from low-income families" and who, starting out as volunteers and then progressing to paid positions, devote "a minimum of 100 hours per year" to the project—to learn about science and storytelling techniques, mentor and serve as a role model for younger children, and work in a professional information-based environment, thus gaining valuable job-related skills that might lead them to consider library or museum science as a stimulating career.[94] Specifically, the LYP interns not only participated in the "design and construction of an Interactive-Museum Library Trailer," defined as a "custom-equipped 'science-on-wheels resource' bring[ing] science and literature to the community" that housed "12 portable museum exhibits," but also staffed it as it traveled through North Carolina to such venues as "festivals, schools, day-care centers, Durham Housing Authority Centers, library branches, [and] malls." The overall theme of the initial set of exhibits was Mathematics = Easy as Pi, and featured interactive displays about "measurement, logic, probability, spatial relationships, and estimation." Interns also selected "three to five books corresponding to each exhibit," with multiple copies of these books made available for circulation from the Discovery in Motion trailer. Finally, they presented "science-literature storytime programs" from the trailer stage "to elementary school children and their families."

The Florida Museum of Natural History project entitled Marvelous Explorations Through Science and Stories (MESS) was almost exactly the same as the three previously mentioned projects in the science and environment category, with the exception of the intended audience, which, in this case, was preschool children enrolled in a Head Start program.[95] To help meet federally mandated science objectives stating that children develop science literacy at a young age and to meet the requirements of the 1998 Congressional reauthorization of

Head Start, which stated that participants should "develop and demonstrate an appreciation of books," MESS produced 12 different kits containing "science books, materials, and inquiry-based activities," with each child receiving "a supplemental reading list to take home every time a new...kit comes to his/her classroom." Some of the topics covered were "reptiles, insects, dinosaurs, sound, water, and sea life," as well as "simple machines, weather, magnets, and light." Equipment included "microscopes, scales, and binoculars."[96] Children were not the only beneficiaries of MESS. Parents of Head Start children participated "in two workshops each year on ways to enrich language development, literacy, and science through books and everyday science activities," and both parents and children were invited to the Florida Museum of Natural History for a series of tours, exhibitions, and activities. While museum education staff members were responsible for designing the activities contained in the MESS kits, library staff selected the books. One positive outcome of library involvement was that staff became more proficient in selecting books for inclusion in the kits, thus improving collection development practices in general. Library staff paid greater attention to "really critically assessing the science books we buy now because of the education they've gotten through MESS."[97]

With the Eastern Iowa Community College District project Connected by a River[98] and the Discovery Center of Springfield (Missouri) project Virtual Technology and the Web,[99] we are back in the world of digital collaborations. Both projects approach the idea of library and museum partnerships from the same perspective as many of the digital education projects discussed in the history section

Table 3.6

IMLS Library-Museum Collaborative Science and Environment Projects Intended Mostly for Children and Teenagers (K-12) (1998–2003)

Year	Title of Project	Selected Major Applicants	Grant Amount ($)
1999	An Educational Collaborative for Rural Families	Montshire Museum of Science (Norwich, Vermont); Howe Library (Hanover, New Hampshire)	98,474
2000	Library Youth Partnership	North Carolina Museum of Life and Science (Durham); Durham County Library	243,386
2001	Marvelous Explorations Through Science and Stories	Florida Museum of Natural History (Gainesville); Alachua County Library District (Florida)	244,073
2001	Connected by A River	Eastern Iowa Community College District (Bettendorf); Putnam Museum (Davenport); Nahant Marsh Educational Center (Davenport)	229,972
2001	Virtual Technology and the Web	Discovery Center of Springfield (Missouri); Springfield-Greene County Library System	182,983
2002	Discovery in Motion	North Carolina Museum of Life and Science (Durham); Durham County Library	247,027

above. Connected by a River developed "five packaged 'turnkey' learning modules…for web-based or CD-ROM delivery" about various aspects of the Mississippi River. Based on Iowa education standards and benchmarks for K–12 students, the modules covered such topics as "life forms and habitat on the River; the role of wetlands in cleansing the River; pollution sources and their effects on the River; the impact of man-made structures on the River, i.e., locks and dams, construction on flood plains; and a case study [about] the creation, destruction, and eventual restoration of the Nahant Marsh." All modules were structured to include, among other features, a "listing of enhancement resources available through the library and inquiry-based projects to be completed either on-line, at the museum, or in the community." In other words, while the Putnam Museum and the Nahant Marsh Educational Center provided content for the modules, libraries involved in the project "locate[d] and organize[d] materials to enhance and extend student learning" and "provide[d] [a] web platform for [the] learning modules." Modules also made use of video conferencing and streaming, as well as simulations. Students not only took "video field trips to the [Putnam] Museum and Nahant Marsh [and] listen[ed] to museum staff and other on-site professionals [such as fish and wildlife officers] explaining various features of the river," but were also able to ask questions about the content of the modules. Simulations allowed students to see "a depiction of how chemicals dumped in the street reach the river and form a toxic plume [and] a comparison of water levels during flooding on a river bound by flood walls versus one surrounded by wetlands."

Virtual Technology and the Web was a two-part project. Taking as its guiding theme the "biodiversity and environmental sustainability" of the Ozark Mountain region in southern Missouri and northern Arkansas, it developed curricular material for K–12 schools about this topic, providing "age-appropriate reading lists, each containing incentives to encourage further reading, and extension activities beyond the core subjects." The project also resulted in Science Source, a tool for teachers that contained lesson plans, ideas for laboratory and online activities, and additional resources such as lists of "outreach programs, fieldtrip sites, library resources, and links of interest" on a variety of topics, including matter, the universe, living systems, force and motion, earth systems, and ecology.[100] On a more general level, it created an innovative "virtual library" at the Discovery Center of Springfield for about "10–15 hours per week during peak attendance" so that "visitors involved in exhibits and activities can immediately link to the [local public] library, interact with a live person in their reference department, and utilize the catalog system in the acquisition of reading materials and library resources." With this approach, the science center hoped that the "virtual librarian" would serve as "a personal and technologically-advanced extension of the library system into a museum setting," connecting "reading and research," on the one hand, with "inquiry-based and interactive learning," on the other. In addition, the virtual librarian was supplemented by the presence of the library's bookmobile at the Discovery Center on at least 10 occasions throughout the course of any one year. The bookmobile, "stocked with books, videos, CD-ROMs and other reference material that…correlate[d] to the theme" of a specific event or exhibit, "reinforced the interactive and inquiry-based learning that occurs at a science center…by providing the immediate opportunity to check-out related books and other resources" so that "the learning that has been stimulated will continue into the home."

SCIENCE AND ENVIRONMENT PROJECTS INTENDED MOSTLY FOR CHILDREN AND TEENAGERS: ANALYSIS

As we look back at the six science and environment projects for children and teenagers, we see that many of the library and museum partnerships have similar characteristics. To be sure, they strive to meet, often through different regional content, standards and guidelines set forth by various state and federal educational entities with regard to curricular and learning goals, so these projects represent a great boon to preschool, elementary, and high school teachers, as well as to home-schooling parents. Yet the emphasis on creating "national models" that can be replicated by others—mentioned as a goal in almost every grant application—is a double-edged sword. It can lead to a series of empirically tested and evaluated "best practices" that can be confidently adopted elsewhere, but it can also result in an ambient conformity—a range of ultimately limiting choices about what constitutes library-museum partnerships. In many of the science and environment examples, the core of the project is a series of interactive displays. And although library books and videos are indeed present and although they are presented as central components of these projects, they nonetheless seem peripheral in relation to the exciting "hands-on activities" that cannot but be the main attractions.

Consider also the temporary nature of the traveling science exhibits and the Discovery Center of Springfield's bookmobile or virtual librarian service. Again, it is as if library resources and services of any kind are articulated as being adjunct to the primary purpose of interacting with science demonstrations. The fact that the library and its resources are, for all intents and purposes, absent from the museum except for brief predetermined periods—or, in the case of traveling tabletop exhibits or kits, relegated to a secondary role—is not a very convincing argument that the library is a crucial element in the development of sustained learning. Metaphorically speaking, the library becomes an annex—a valuable annex, of course—but an annex nevertheless. The museum, science center, or traveling facsimile thereof—with all the attendant bells and whistles—is firmly entrenched as the magnet that draws users of all ages. As museums evolve into the defining forces of library-museum collaborations, the value of the library qua library is in danger of being etiolated, confined to museum "gift shop" status, in which books are artistically arranged and readily available but soon forgotten—or used only as coffee-table show items—after they are taken home.

HISTORY PROJECTS INTENDED MOSTLY FOR ADULTS: DESCRIPTION

Of the 11 history projects intended mostly for adults, 8 are primarily digital-based collaborations, 2 are exhibits (one traveling and the other nontraveling) with subsidiary digital components, and 1 is a literacy-oriented endeavor (see table 3.7). Four of the 11 projects focused on the social and cultural history of Native Americans in such diverse locales as Oklahoma, Colorado, and the Pacific Northwest. Another project involved cultural agencies and institutions in the Republic of Palau, located in the Micronesian Islands. While the digital-based projects necessarily differ in regard to the content of the images and objects to be digitized, they were nevertheless remarkably similar in their theoretical approach and guiding set of assumptions.

We begin with Travels Across Time,[101] a collaboration between the Greater Indianapolis Literacy League, an affiliate of the Indianapolis–Marion County Public Library, and Conner Prairie Living History Museum, founded by pharma-

Table 3.7
IMLS Library-Museum Collaborative History Projects Intended Mostly for Adults (1998–2003)

Year	Title of Project	Selected Major Applicants	Grant Amount ($)
2000	Image Archives Digitization and Access	Palau Community College (Republic of Palau); Belau National Museum (Republic of Palau)	137,546
2000	From Local to Global	Lee College (Baytown, Texas); Sterling Municipal Library; Baytown Historical Museum	258,290
2000	Voices of the Colorado Plateau	Sherratt Library at Southern Utah University (Cedar City); Museum of Northern Arizona (Flagstaff)	146,012
2001	Omaha Indian Cultural Artifacts and Images	University of Nebraska-Lincoln Libraries; University of Nebraska State Museum	168,688
2001	Crossing Organizational Boundaries	Museum of History and Industry (Seattle, Washington); University of Washington Libraries	334,400
2001	Cherokee Traveling Exhibits	Cherokee National Historical Society (Tahlequah, Oklahoma); Eastern Oklahoma District Library System	249,977
2002	Imaging Pittsburgh	University of Pittsburgh Libraries; Historical Society of Western Pennsylvania; Carnegie Museum of Art	242,157
2002	Travels Across Time	Greater Indianapolis Literacy League; Conner Prairie Living History Museum (Fishers, Indiana)	60,963
2002	Sharing Culture	Fort Lewis College Center of Southwest Studies (Durango, Colorado); Southern Ute Museum and Cultural Center	104,361
2003	Free Expression and American Democracy	Newberry Library (Chicago); Chicago Historical Society	152,913
2003	Community Museum Project	University of Washington Libraries (Seattle); Hoh, Makah, and Quileute Tribes	450,832

ceutical industrialist Eli Lilly on the original homestead of William Conner, "a fur trader, land speculator, entrepreneur, interpreter and legislator" who settled in Indiana in 1800–1801, "married a Delaware woman named Mekinges,... established a trading post along the White River," and "built a handsome brick residence for his second wife" in 1823.[102] Now administered by Earlham College, the Conner Prairie museum complex contains five historic areas that recreate, through restored buildings and costumed interpreters, small-town American village life in 1836 and in 1886, as well as the Lenape Indian Camp and McKinnen's Trading Post.

Relying on the principles of John Dewey, who stated that "interaction between the learner and the historical environment is critical in creating a meaningful learning experience," Travels Across Time developed a 15-month program in which approximately 200 adults (whose reading level was at or below the sixth-grade level) were presented with the opportunity to make numerous visits to Conner Prairie in the context of a wide-ranging educational effort combining "a non-threatening participative environment," "oral transfer of knowledge," and "multi-sensory" learning modules. Enrolled adults made seven formal visits to Conner Prairie built around carefully designed themes such as "religious celebrations, political issues, and everyday life." Each formal visit was preceded by classes based on an Educator's Kit containing "Indiana History of three different time periods written at [an] appropriate adult reading level" and "hands-on learning modules and reproduction artifacts representing those that will be seen on the actual visit." Students, their families, and instructors made seven additional less-formal visits to Conner Prairie for such events as the Military History Weekend, Hearthside Supper, and Follow the North Star, a program discussing prejudice in Indiana. There were also postvisit lesson plans, in which students filled out charts about what they had learned, participated in discussions about their visits with instructors, wrote essays about their experiences that, collectively, were published in a book at the end of the project, and received "take home kits containing a 'Hoosier Miscellany' booklet, a Conner Prairie coloring book for [their] children and a list of reading level appropriate resources in order to encourage the family unit to continue discussions and exploration of material learned." All phases of the project tried to create a "learning comfort zone" in which adult students would perceive themselves to be in a nonhumiliating and noncorrective environment such that "learning takes place conversationally" and becomes a shared process that acts to "[bond] participants in spite of educational or generational differences."

Exhibits were the focal point of Free Expression and American Democracy, a collaboration between the Newberry Library and the Chicago Historical Society (CHS),[103] and Cherokee Traveling Exhibits, a partnership between the Cherokee National Historical Society and the Eastern Oklahoma District Library System.[104] The Newberry-led project showcased "historical sources about Chicago's history of political, cultural, and artistic dissent and reform," with special emphasis on not only relatively well-known figures such as "civil libertarian Clarence Darrow, social workers Jane Addams and Graham Taylor, labor leader

Eugene Debs, [and] novelists and poets Sherwood Anderson, Gwendolyn Brooks, and Richard Wright," but also lesser-known "free speech activism" phenomena such as "contemporary independent magazines and the 'poetry slam' movement." Stressing that freedom of speech does not exist "in a social vacuum," the exhibit portion of the project, entitled Outspoken: Chicago's Free Speech Tradition and containing about "150 historical documents and objects," underscored "the organizational and institutional contexts for free speech" through an emphasis on the "social clubs, trade unions, churches, and reform organizations" that served as "vehicles and amplifiers of individual free expression." In addition to the exhibit itself, the Free Expression and American Democracy project included videotaped interviews with Chicago activists such as "author Studs Terkel and civil liberties lawyer Leon Despres," along with a series of "free public lectures [and] a workshop and educational materials for school teachers" dealing with "the historical and contemporary issues of freedom of speech, access to information, and the challenges of democratic societies." A Web site provided "a concise historical overview of Chicago's free speech tradition, . . . brief introductions to the four time-periods addressed in the exhibit, . . . a small sample of images drawn from the exhibit, . . . [and] links to other [relevant] educational resources provided by the Newberry and CHS." For example, exhibit sections on unionization and free speech activism were linked to "CHS interpretive and archival sites on the Haymarket incident." Perhaps the most significant element of the project was the circumstance that many of the Midwest Manuscripts collections (from which documents appearing in the exhibit were drawn) had "online finding aids," making it possible for exhibit visitors "to view an object . . . and then explore the contents of the entire collection for themselves."

Although smaller in scope, "Cherokee Traveling Exhibits" nonetheless covered an impressive amount of intellectual ground. Ten themed exhibits about the Cherokee nation and culture rotated through libraries in 14 small communities in rural northeastern Oklahoma. Themes included the Pre-Columbian period, Belief, Art, Warfare, Government, Daily Life, and the Trail of Tears.[105] While the Cherokee Heritage Center was responsible for supplying the objects, artifacts, and bibliographies that would be the core of each exhibit and for the overall design of the exhibits, the 14 rural libraries recommended "which adult/children's books and videos" would accompany each exhibit and determined, with the help of a "resource coordinator," the nature of "any special events" to be held at the library in conjunction with the exhibits. Once the exhibits had rotated through the designated libraries, they were "transferred to the Oklahoma Museum Association" for subsequent statewide dissemination in schools, museums, and other libraries.

Three other Native American projects had digitally based outcomes. Omaha Indian Cultural Artifacts and Images, a collaboration involving the University of Nebraska–Lincoln libraries, state museums and historical societies, and members of the Omaha tribe, "created an online catalog of tribal resources drawn from international sources."[106] Artifacts and photographic images of the Omahas, a small and little-known "earthlodge-dwelling plains people who reside in northeastern Nebraska," are not only rare, but have been scattered among numerous world museums and private collections. Many of them are contained in the Francis LaFlesche collection at the University of Nebraska State Museum, but the Smithsonian Institution has "only thirteen catalog entries for Omaha [and] the Buffalo Bill Historical Center in Cody, Wyoming, has just six." In overall terms, "the number of pre-1940 artifacts and images" does not exceed 1,000. After ascertaining the location of relevant artifacts through an international and national survey and "critically evaluat[ing] cultural attribution and [museum] collection records," selected artifacts were "digitally photographed or scanned for archival purposes" and for subsequent inclusion on a searchable Web site, which also contained explanatory text and links with other sites "that feature the Omaha Indians and the ethnography of other prairie or Plains tribes." As additional artifacts were located and digitized, the Web site was updated with newer images, thus allowing tribal members to have a comprehensive inventory of their culture and history. All digital images were cataloged for inclusion on the Online Computer Library Center (OCLC) bibliographic database, and the University of Nebraska library system committed "to warehousing the web site on [its] servers" and undertaking data migration at regular intervals.

In much the same way, Sharing Culture, a project bringing together the Center of Southwest Studies (CSWS) at Fort Lewis College in Durango, Colorado, and the Southern Ute Museum and Cultural Center (SUMCC), developed a Web-accessible digital-image database of many of the important artifacts, audio tapes, text, and photographic collections pertaining to the Southern Ute peoples housed at CSWS and SUMCC.[107] Bibliographic records were enhanced by "refining cultural affiliation information" and "adding native language terms" to facilitate "the goal of many Indian communities to preserve and teach Indian language[s]." Computer interfaces taking into account the needs of various audiences with different learning styles were created, and "project assistants and student teachers [took] CD based versions of the database and interface program to local and remote schools and community centers." Finally, the collections database was used as the basis for a series of K–12 "virtual trunk programs" about selected cultural topics.

By far the most impressive Native American library-museum collaboration was the Community Museum Project, a joint effort of, among others, the University of Washington Libraries, the Clallam County Historical Society Museum, and the Hoh, Makah, and Quileute tribes.[108] Of particular interest in this project was its strong community-involvement component. Focusing on the west end of the Olympic Peninsula in Washington State, a remote, rural community where 17 percent of the population is Native American and 11.2 percent is Latino, the project started from the premise that vital cultural information is not only contained in institutions, it is also "cloistered inside the scrapbooks, barns, living rooms, and memories of community members." While project partners formally committed to "surfac[ing], select[ing], digitiz[ing], and creat[ing] metadata for 12,000 images, oral histories, objects and other cultural artifacts from a multitude of public and private collections," they also realized the importance of establishing a "community documentation team" whose task it was to interview and videotape "community members to record their reflections and memories of the events and people depicted in the [gathered] materials." The result was a comprehensive digital database from which a series of six online and on-site (physical) exhibitions was drawn. Topics included the culture and history of the Quileute, Hoh, and Makah tribes, timber and forest history, fishing and maritime history, the history of early pioneers and farmers, and the history of recent immigrants to the Olympic Peninsula. Each exhibit was accompanied by "curriculum materials and teacher workshops" and supplemented by appropriate documents and images drawn from the collections of the libraries and archives of the University of Washington. Taken as a whole, the exhibits became an electronic "community museum" that provided "differentiated [levels] of access" insofar as some tribal cultural materials could only be shared among limited groups, whether family, clan, or tribe. Perhaps most important, the project was conceptualized as a living museum: because numerous Community Museum Development Kits were distributed to partner organizations, it was hoped that the number of images residing in the digital collection would continue to grow, allowing for the development of future online exhibitions.

The Image Archives Digitization and Access project, undertaken by Palau Community College (PCC) and the Belau National Museum (BNM) in the Republic of Palau, was conceived "to promote and improve the use of visual information as an enhancement to a traditional library catalog through resource sharing and networking."[109] While the BNM has an artifacts collection and a document library, the focus of the project was on its media holdings, which include "over 25,000 slides, photographs [beginning in 1800 and continuing through the German colonial period to the present], 5,500 photo prints (including rare etchings of Palau and Micronesia from the 1700s), 450 negatives, twelve motion picture films, as well as 574 hours of unedited video documentary films,... [and] 365 audio tapes." The photographs "depicting natural settings, geology, land formations, and vegetation patterns" are particularly valuable, given the "dramatic changes in the landscape of Palau brought about by recent development activity." Images to be digitized were selected according to "previous user requests," placed on the BNM Web site, and integrated into the PCC online catalog such that each image had a complete bibliographic record and a link back to the BNM Web site, which itself was linked "to a variety of other relevant web sites [that contained]...more information about related collections" and "subjects relevant to research and learning interests."

In From Local to Global, Lee College in Baytown, Texas, the Baytown Historical Museum, and Sterling Municipal Library joined forces to develop a digitization project about the birth of the oil industry in Texas and the growth of a prototypical company town (Baytown) associated with that industry.[110] After oil was first discovered at Goose Creek, east of Houston, in 1908, the Humble Oil and Refining Company (a forerunner of Exxon), in conjunction with Standard Oil, built what was to become known as the Baytown Refinery in 1920. The town of Baytown subsequently grew up around, and dependent upon, the refinery, and, as the From Local to Global narrative states, the town and the refinery are typically viewed as "the nursery for...developments that were later applied to the whole company." While the Baytown Historical Museum has a large collection of photographs "from the earliest years of the...refinery and the development of Baytown," the Sterling Municipal Library owns many of the in-house publications associated with the refinery: *Humble Bee*, 1921–58; *Humble Way*, 1945–71, *Humble News*, 1962–65, *Baytown Briefs*, 1953–92; union contracts; personnel policies; telephone directories; accident-prevention manuals; and minutes from the Joint Conference, described as a "unique partnership between management and labor." Working from these collections, From Local to Global scanned some 3,000 photographs and 2,000 print documents, added subject descriptors and other metadata to each scanned item, created a Web site, and, recognizing the importance of the oil industry throughout Texas, developed a series of college-level courses about digital imaging technology in the hopes of encouraging other small libraries and museums to digitize and interlink their holdings about the early days of the oil industry in the state.

Much like From Local to Global, Imaging Pittsburgh, a collaboration among the University of Pittsburgh Libraries, the Historical Society of Western Pennsylvania, and the Carnegie Museum of Art, created an online resource of about 7,000 photographs—mostly "monochrome prints and negatives"—depicting the "cultural, educational, and social development" of Pittsburgh, as well as the "vast infrastructure and industry of the region."[111] Indeed, Imaging Pittsburgh was planned as an extension and amplification of Historic Pittsburgh, a project that includes full-text access to over 500 books from the nineteenth and early twentieth centuries, an updated chronology of important events in the life of the city and region based on a respected reference book, census schedules for Pittsburgh and Allegheny City for 1850, 1860, 1870, and 1880, and an extensive collection of real estate atlases and plat maps that show names of property owners, lot and block numbers, dimensions, street widths, churches, schools, roads, lakes, ponds, rivers, and cemeteries for numerous Pittsburgh-area neighborhoods from the early 1870s to the 1930s.[112] Grouped into such themes as Business and Industry, the Immigrant Experience, and Culture, photographs were selected according to whether they were "repeatedly requested by researchers" or whether they had "significant scholarly value, but [were] underutilized by researchers." Of particular importance in this project was the Charles "Teenie" Harris Archives at the Carnegie Museum of Art, which is regarded as one of the "most complete visual record[s] of twentieth-century African-American urban life" insofar as it contains over 75,000 negatives of "community life in Pittsburgh's black neighborhoods from ca. 1935–1970" drawn from the collection of Harris, who was a news photographer for the *Pittsburgh Courier*, an internationally renowned African American newspaper. Equally prominent were the collections of the Historical Society of Western Pennsylvania, which contributed photographs about Pittsburgh's large immigrant workforce, especially the "social customs, living conditions, trade association, and educational opportunities of these communities." As with many other digital projects, the photographs were encoded with descriptive information using commonly accepted metadata standards and indexed to allow for "cross-collection searching from a single interface and access to images with consistent cataloging information."

Taking as its subject Seattle and surrounding King County, Crossing Organizational Boundaries—a partnership spearheaded by the University of Washington Libraries and the Museum of History and Industry (MOHAI) that also included 10 smaller museums and historical societies such as the Puget Sound Maritime Historical Society, the White River Valley Museum, the Black Heritage Society of Washington, and the Wing Luke Asian Museum—also developed an online searchable research collection of photographs for a single metropolitan area.[113] Stressing that "many of the collections held by smaller [cultural and historical] groups are stored in private buildings and are accessible to only the most determined scholars [because of] short hours [and] insufficient collection display space," collaborators brought together, on a central Web gateway officially called King County Snapshots, over 12,000 images chronicling both urban and rural life.[114] Especially noteworthy were the inclusion of "rarely seen images of African-Americans in early twentieth-century Seattle," photographs of "railroad expansion of the 1890s," an extensive Seattle postcard collection, and early photographs of vegetable, dairy, and hops farming in Auburn and Kent, former agricultural communities south of Seattle in the White River Valley and the home of a large number of Japanese families. The creation of substantial metadata for each image meant that the collection could be searched not only by such fields as *creator*, *source*, and *format*, but also by such categories as Eating and Drinking, which was further subdivided into 10 categories, including Bakeries, Cooks and Cooking, and Grocery Stores.

The developers of Voices of the Colorado Plateau—a group led by the library systems of Southern Utah University, Northern Arizona University, and the University of Nevada–Las Vegas, as well as the Utah Historical Society and the Edge of Cedars Museum—took a slightly different approach, concentrating on weaving a rich multimedia tapestry of 48 interpretive exhibits, each of which consisted of short oral history interviews, 20 historic photographs illustrating the interview, and a "short narrative" describing its historical and cultural context.[115] Frequently making use of *Flash 5 Player*® animation software, which allows "fade and pan images in a manner reminiscent of documentary films," the designers of Voices of the Colorado Plateau created "short, captivating presentations"—accessible through three umbrella categories called People, Places, and Topics—that would "stand alone as interpretive exhibits but at the same time could serve as introductions or gateways to the larger interviews and collections from which the exhibits were drawn."[116] As described by Yahoo! Picks, "old-timers share memories of life on the range, on the reservation, and in town [and you can] listen to accounts from denizens of the young city of Page, Arizona, a town built by workers on the Glen Canyon Dam, or from residents of Flagstaff, the trading hub of the timber-rich high country of Northern Arizona, [or] interviews with Georgie Clark, famed rafting pioneer and Crazy Woman of the River, and Paul Begay, a Navajo storyteller."[117] Among the other voices included are those of Dorothy Hunt, who "waited on customers in the Bright Angel Lodge's dining room and tended bar at the Fred Harvey House in Winslow, Arizona"; Dilworth Wooley, whose "family promoted the railroad and highway system in Southern Utah and led some of the first sightseeing trips to the Grand Canyon"; Margarita Martinez de Gomez, who migrated from Spain to Arizona to "join her father who had established himself as a lumberman and sheep herder"; and Heber Hall, who describes how a homestead could be purchased for $14.90."[118] In general, the idea was to create a virtual museum that moved "beyond a collection of digital surrogates by supplying valuable context and telling wonderful stories" so that the "individual experience (voice)" of typically overlooked individuals could be privileged "within the larger tide of history."[119] As visitors to the site listened to the interviews, it was hoped that there would be "less clicking, more watching," thus giving additional intellectual substance to the digital museum experience.[120]

HISTORY PROJECTS INTENDED MOSTLY FOR ADULTS: ANALYSIS

Many of these projects make innovative and far-reaching use of both library and museum resources. Travels Across Time is a particularly good model, since it is based not only on repeated formal and informal visits to the Conner Prairie museum over a 15-month period, but also on supplemental reading, writing, and other learning activities at libraries and in the home between museum visits. Adult students enrolled in this literacy program thus developed the habit of seeing museum and library visits as integral aspects of a holistic educational program—one that constantly encouraged them to pursue and deepen their initial discoveries with further explorations and to impart these discoveries to their children. And, as the project creators recognized, their model can be expanded to serve other target populations such as "adults preparing to take the GED, or higher level English as a Second Language students."[121] But, because the Conner Prairie museum is about 20 miles north of downtown Indianapolis and its central library facilities, special transportation arrangements had to be made to link these two institutions. Unlike Brooklyn Expedition, in which a permanent trolley shuttles back and forth among area museums and libraries, the Conner Prairie shuttle was temporary—an inhibiting (although by no means an unsolvable) factor in forging a long-term intellectual nexus between the Indianapolis library system and Conner Prairie.

Free Expression and American Democracy had no such transportation problems as the Newberry Library and the Chicago Historical Society are separated by only a few city blocks and thus within easy walking distance. And, since this project was conceived so that visitors "will...be able to view an object in the exhibit and then explore the contents of entire collections for themselves," geographic proximity was a great facilitator in creating what amounts to a single locus of cultural memory that makes extensive use of both visual objects and textual documents. To a certain degree, the same positive assessment could be made about Cherokee Traveling Exhibits, especially if the participating 14 libraries made efforts to institute permanent minidisplays about the topics show-cased by the traveling exhibits and created new displays—and new bibliogra-phies—dealing with other aspects of Native American culture. After all, the goals of the project are to sustain "interest and enthusiasm for indigenous cul-tures around the world" by developing "active centers for learning" in numerous local communities. The Oklahoma traveling exhibits should thus be seen not as the culmination of a library-museum partnership, but as the first steps to visibly entrenching such a partnership on a daily basis through ongoing events and activities.

Of the digital projects, four stand out because of their commitment to a well-rounded educational experience in which individuals have the possibility of doing more than just moving through accumulated images with minimal contex-tualizing information. As its name implies, the Community Museum Project not only involved entire communities in the act of digital accumulation, but, most important, it involved entire communities in the act of contextualizing that which has been accumulated, thus suggesting that these two activities should be viewed as inseparable. Recall that the project members did not simply gather ma-terials for inclusion in the digital collection; they also established a "community documentation team" whose task it was to conduct interviews about the gathered objects and images. Accordingly, the materials included in this project are under-stood not just as objects qua objects or images qua images. Rather, their meaning has to be filled in and fleshed out through recourse to the memories and reflec-tions of individuals for whom the objects and images were important events and milestones. This is true for each object or image taken as a single entity, but it is also true for a series or groups of objects or images, in which additional meaning may lie in the relationship of objects and images between and among each other. "Community documentation"—the act of giving meaning to gathered materials, whether orally or in written form—can therefore be seen as a necessary part of the accumulation process for digital images and objects.

From Local to Global, Voices of the Colorado Plateau, and Imaging Pitts-burgh also participate in this dynamic. As we have seen, Voices of the Colorado Plateau distinguished itself by juxtaposing oral interviews with images to create a sense of both geographic and emotional space as the words of ordinary people resonated against and informed a photographic background that is often simul-taneously harsh, beautiful, and stark. Although there is no explicit provision in the From Local to Global narrative for juxtaposing and intellectually linking, for example, individual articles from issues of the *Humble Bee* or *Humble Way* and sections of accident-prevention manuals or union contracts with relevant photographs of oil workers and refinery conditions, the potential to do so exists. In Imaging Pittsburgh (when paired with Historic Pittsburgh), someone inter-ested in the demographics of a specific area neighborhood at a defined moment in history can find a detailed plat map of, census information about, and photo-graphs from that neighborhood. One can also see how the addition of interlinked explanatory background text or documentary evidence (in the case of Voices of the Colorado Plateau) and oral interviews (in the case of From Local to Global or Imaging Pittsburgh) would enhance the educational experience available at these Web sites to an even greater extent, thus creating a body of unparalleled evidence about a given subject or issue. In the language of research methodology, the knowledge gained about a given topic or question would be all the more reliable and valid because such knowledge is based on triangulated evidence—visual, aural, and written.

From a philosophical viewpoint, the Republic of Palau project Image Archives Digitization and Access provides some of the most intriguing hints about the larger issues at stake in what can be described as a wholesale stampede toward digitization collaborations that, for the most part, confine themselves to accumulation. Because of its integration of images into a library catalog, the Palau project has many parallels with the Rochester Images project described in the previous section. Thus, many of the same benefits accruing to Rochester Images also accrue to Image Archives Digitization and Access. Yet, unlike Rochester Images, one gets the sense from the Palau narrative that images replace explanatory textual documents, not complement them. Emphasis is placed on "the importance of visual learning in Micronesian cultures," and explicit reference is made to how "much easier" it would have been to produce, for example, a high school history textbook entitled *History of Palau: Heritage of an Emerging Nation*, which "includes BNM Media Collection images on almost every page," had the BNM collection been digitized at that time.[122] Here, the writers of the Palau project narrative may have inadvertently put their finger on the crux of the matter. To be sure, it would have been easier to create the aforementioned textbook had digital images been available, but the more salient issue may be whether the textbook would have been created in the first place if digital images had been easily accessible. Convenient access to digital images may have rendered the very idea of a textbook moot and superfluous because it could have been argued that the images themselves—possibly with brief captions and a cursory timeline—would suffice for understanding history. Students would thus have been deprived of a rich written contextual account about the visual images.

Of course, this is mere speculation. The textbook, after all, could still have been written, and it could have been written in a much shorter time, thus making it available for earlier generations of students. Yet, if we reexamine the Palau narrative, we are given another clue about the learning process and the issues at stake in digitization projects of all kinds. It was, we are told, a "monumental task for the BNM Media Manager to provide [the] images" for the textbook, and it is implied that it was unfortunate that the BNM media manager had to embark upon such a monumental task. In other words, if only the images had been digitized, the media manager would have had a much easier time of it. But the word *monumental*, with its connotations of *painstaking* and *difficult*, may be exactly the right term to use in describing the process that leads to in-depth understanding and knowledge about a given subject. For individuals of all ages, in-depth understanding is never easy and cannot be made much easier. Just as the BNM media manager was forced to perform a monumental task and just as the authors of *History of Palau* performed a monumental intellectual task of synthesis and analysis in writing their book, so the act of learning about and understanding a given subject is a difficult and painstaking process—a process that requires time to ponder, think, and muse about the interconnections between and among images, text, and spoken words. Digitization projects run the risk of short-circuiting this difficult process by the very ease with which they make available hundreds and thousands of images and objects. The sheer availability and number of the images renders each one less unique, less monumental, and somehow less precious, in effect causing individuals to quickly rush through each image in an attempt to see and consume them all. There is no longer a sense of awe about nor respect for the accumulated history hidden in an image, object, or document. There is little time to consider nuances and interstitial relationships. Instead of a monumental and arduous task that forces individuals to explore the multiple meanings of and stories told by, for example, a handful of images that have been painstakingly selected and contextualized in a textbook or monograph (or by the objects that one sees in a museum exhibition), the learning process is in danger of becoming an entertaining "point-and-click" race through thousands of Web images that, in the end, become undifferentiated—even mundane—because of ready availability. Accordingly, the educative process moves from the realm of serious endeavor into the world of disposable and commodified entertainment. Just as blockbuster museum exhibitions that gather together surefire audience-pleasing items—and for which there are timed entry and exit times—are very much removed from the world of serious contemplation and study of museum objects and documents, so Web sites and Web gateways that present a seemingly endless array of linked images that encourage facile browsing are not to be confused with an educational program whose mission is to engender detailed knowledge and critical analysis about a given topic. As digital images proliferate at a dizzying rate, each vies for our sustained attention, captures it for a fleeting moment, but is incapable of holding that attention for any length of time because there is always another more attractive, splendid, and entertaining image to which we feel compelled to turn. Library and museum collaborations that place overmuch trust in digital projects that accumulate images and objects without a strong interpretive component may find that, at the same time that they are providing a digital simulation of an object, image, or document, they are also providing a simulation of knowledge. In short, they are merely providing edutainment.

ART AND LITERATURE PROJECTS INTENDED MOSTLY FOR ADULTS: DESCRIPTION

Inventiveness is a hallmark of many of the 9 library-museum partnerships (10 total grants) in the art and literature category (see table 3.8), especially The Language of Conservation, which brought together Poets House (a poetry library and literary center founded in 1985 by Stanley Kunitz and Elizabeth Kray to provide "a place for poetry—library, meeting place, locus of discussion, research, writing and inspiration"), the Wildlife Conservation Society, and the Central Park Zoo.[123] Poets House, well known for its Poetry in the Branches program, a collaboration with selected branches of the New York Public Library that "tripled poetry circulation at target [locations], reached thousands of new poetry readers, and changed the way that local branch systems develop their poetry collections and provide poetry services," established "a six-month poet in residence program at the Central Park Zoo." The resident poet selected and created poems that would be "introduced and integrated into exhibitions and gardens" to form a "conservation language that bridges the connection between animal-inspired delight, education and conservation action." About 30 panels were placed throughout the zoo grounds and near major exhibits so that the broad educational goal of "communicat[ing] sensually, emotionally and intellectually the diversity, splendor and importance of the [displayed] animals and habitats" could be achieved. Using poetry as "an ecotone to translate the knowledge, urgency and spirit of conservation," the project hoped to leverage the increased popularity of poetry slams, spoken-word events, and poetry readings at the beginning of the twenty-first century to "draw the public into a richer conversation about the animals than simple facts can provide, with poetry as the tool and the poet as the master builder." To quote the internationally renowned poet Galway Kinnell, visitors would, through poetry, be able to "inhabit the life of an animal"—a process that would "create an intellectual path back to poetry" insofar as the "emotional response visitors naturally experience through visual interaction" would be transferred "to a mental connection that leads them to seek knowledge and become stewards of their environment."

English-language literacy was the centerpiece of Project Access, a partnership between the Frist Center for the Visual Arts (FCVA) and the Nashville Public Library (NPL).[124] Geared toward adults, especially Latin American immigrants, "who typically live in public housing or low-income neighborhoods with limited resources and few opportunities to visit cultural institutions," FCVA and NPL worked with the Metropolitan Nashville Public School Adult Education Program to develop a program that would not only teach about 200 adult students literacy skills by teaching them about art, but also allow them to create and display their own "personal narrative artworks," defined as a combination of visual art and writing. In addition to touring NPL and FCVA, adult learners were given the opportunity to digitize and post their personal narrative artworks on a Web site designed by Red Grooms, internationally known for his "exuberant pop renditions of urban life." In many ways, the Web site was the key element of the project insofar as it was conceived as a community space that resembled "a virtual gallery environment" in which the images and text created by participating students were shown. The Web site thus functioned as both tangible evidence of accomplishment and an incentive for others, since "lesson plans [were] available to instruct visitors how to create a similar personal narrative artwork at home, in their community center, or at school,"

Table 3.8

IMLS Library-Museum Collaborative Art and Literature Projects Intended Mostly for Adults (1998–2003)

Year	Title of Project	Selected Major Applicants	Grant Amount ($)
1999/ 2002	Museums and the Online Archive of California Project, Parts I and II	California Digital Library; Berkeley Art Museum and Pacific Film Archive	490,991 and 337,542
1999	The World from Here	Henry E. Huntington Library and Art Gallery (San Marino, California); William Andrews Clark Memorial Library (UCLA)	381,048
2000	Baltimore Art Resource Online Consortium	Milton S. Eisenhower Library at the Johns Hopkins University (Baltimore, Maryland); Baltimore Museum of Art	247,310
2000	The Sargent Murals Restoration Project	Boston Public Library; Harvard University Art Museum's Straus Center for Conservation	499,357
2002	Opening the Cultural Corridor	University of California–Merced Library; Ruth and Sherman Lee Institute for Japanese Art at the Clark Center (Hanford, California)	229,276
2003	Music of Social Change	Emory University Libraries (Atlanta)	52,160
2003	Project Access	Frist Center for the Visual Arts (Nashville); Nashville Public Library	244,750
2003	Digital Dress	Wayne State University Library System (Detroit); Detroit Historical Museums	249,433
2003	The Language of Conservation	Wildlife Conservation Society/Central Park Zoo (New York); Poets House (New York)	73,398

which could then be formally integrated into the project Web site if its creator visited FCVA.

In The World from Here: Treasures of the Great Libraries of Los Angeles, 32 eminent special collection libraries in Los Angeles, including the Henry E. Huntington Library and Art Gallery, the Getty Research Institute, Rancho Santa Ana Botanic Garden Library, and the Autry Museum of Western Heritage Research Center, joined forces to produce an on-site exhibit and Web site devoted to showcasing "the significance of books as cultural icons, spiritual symbols, and works of artistic, historical, or scientific importance."[125] As Ann Philbin and David Stuart Rodes write in their foreword to the exhibition catalog, the assembled treasures ranged "all the way from the precious, expected monuments of classical and European civilization...to Japanese obstetrical manuals and annotated Hollywood film scripts...and the subject matter can be as esoteric and otherworldly as an eighth-century Buddhist religious scroll or as quotidian as a nineteenth-century children's board game or the 1872 Los Angeles city directory."[126] Taking care to reflect "the constituent communities that make up the multicultural fabric of the city," the exhibit encompassed eight broad themes such as California history, science and medicine, engineering and architecture, and private life and entertainment. In order to entice visitors to further exploration beyond the selected objects, an accompanying Web site contained not only 32 objects represented by images and textual descriptions, but also a keyword-searchable database that could be used to "discover ideas that link objects...or themes—such as 'discovery,' 'dream,' or 'danger'—of possible interest to the student or casual reader."[127] A panoply of educational outreach efforts was directed at K–12 teachers so that they could teach their students to use primary source documents as "research tools and in their daily lives." Most important, English and Spanish family guides, printed as supplements in major area newspapers, offered "informative exercises relating to...familiar objects in daily life, such as journals, directories, children's books, maps, family photographs, and videos" that were highlighted in the exhibit.

Much as cultural institutions in Los Angeles drew attention to their extraordinary, though often hidden, collections through a large-scale exhibition, the Boston Public Library (BPL), through its Sargent Murals Restoration Project carried out in conjunction with the Harvard University Art Museum's Straus Center for Conservation, drew attention to a long-neglected and deteriorating resource—the murals of painter John Singer Sargent. Installed at BPL in 1919, the 16 murals that compose Sargent's *The Triumph of Religion* were, almost from the very beginning, "damaged by humidity, poor climate control, [and] decades of grime." Not only did the project partners clean and restore the murals, but they also documented the process using digital photography and then "used the documentation as source material for design and construction of an interactive" Web-based education program that featured multiple levels of content presented in a "layered format" so that users could choose their own level for "deeper or wider-ranging explorations of the subject." To say the least, there was a wide array of available information: an introduction to Sargent and his work; an overview of his mural techniques; a glossary of conservation and restoration terms; and in-depth background to the restoration, including Sargent's "original intentions...and the deleterious effects of previous restoration attempts." Interactivity was a key feature of the Web site, allowing viewers not only "to manipulate sections of an entire mural sequentially, in puzzle fashion, to see how restoration is accomplished over time" or "to vacuum layers of dust from mural surfaces to uncover paint abrasions that are the effect of earlier cleanings," but also to direct questions to experts who responded within specified time parameters. Indeed, the most frequently asked and most intriguing questions were collected and organized such that they became a further "resource for curriculum development or other educational collateral." Finally, numerous events and programs—colloquia, public lectures, tours, and special activities for children, young adults, municipal officials, and senior citizens—added another dimension to the project. Overall, the restoration of the Sargent murals was part of a plan to increase public awareness of the fact that the BPL was more than just a library, that it was, thanks to its collections of great art, a museum committed to regaining its image as a "palace of inspiration"—where "diverse cultural and learning styles include visual as well as verbal understanding and where "mosaics, statues, murals, paintings, prints, and photographs are as vital to the visitor's experience of the Library as the significant holdings in its collections."

One of the most extensive digitally based library-museum collaborations in this or any category was the Museums and the Online Archive of California (MOAC) Project, in which such institutions as the Japanese American National Museum, the Phoebe Hearst Museum of Anthropology, and the Berkeley Art Museum/Pacific Film Archive pledged participation, through MOAC, in the Online Archive of California (OAC), which itself was a part of the California Digital Library, founded by the University of California.[128] In essence, MOAC became a "virtual archive" or "virtual museum" of 27 thematic collections that, in late 2003, contained about 75,000 images from 11 cultural institutions, with each image linked to encoded archival description (EAD) finding aids to provide both item-level ("well-structured, authoritative, and unmediated information about objects and makers") and collection-level descriptions ("richly illustrated, engaging explanations of objects and their relationships to people and events"). Included in MOAC were, for example, the Helen Nestor Free Speech Movement Photographs, the Alfred L. Kroeber Ethnographic Photographs of California Indian and Sonora Indian Subjects (1901–30), and the Hisako Hibi Collection, a series of 63 oil paintings depicting the daily activities and landscapes of incarceration centers and concentration camps in California and Utah in which Hibi, a Japanese American who studied at the California School of Fine Arts, was forced to reside during World War II.[129]

When all is said and done, MOAC cannot be separated from OAC, especially since many of the collections are complementary. One can easily see how such OAC collections as the Free Speech Movement (FSM) Digital Archive, which thoroughly documents the role of Mario Sovo and others in the Berkeley FSM through newspapers, journals, oral histories, pamphlets, minutes of meetings, newsletters, and legal defense papers and the Japanese American Relocation Digital Archives (JARDA), which contain over 10,000 digital images and 20,000 pages of electronic transcriptions of text and oral histories about every aspect of the tragic internment saga, cannot be seen in isolation from MOAC collections dealing with identical themes.[130] Thus, the library-museum collaboration between the Ruth and Sherman Lee Institute for Japanese Art at the Clark Center and the library system at the University of California–Merced that resulted in Opening the Cultural Corridor: Japanese Art in the San Joaquin Valley should also be seen as a constituent part of both OAC and MOAC.[131] In this project, digital objects and EAD finding aids were created for 454 hanging scrolls and 46 folding screens—the first component of a long-term plan to digitize the complete holdings of the Lee Institute, including "13,000 photographs of artists' seals and signatures…, which are a unique authority file for identifying and validating Japanese artists" and "21,000 35mm slides of Literati painting photographed from original sources." To say the least, clear symbolic and intellectual linkages exist among the Hibi collection, JARDA, and Opening the

Cultural Corridor—linkages that form the basis of an integrated network of resources that allows for "a broader understanding of Japanese art, culture, and history and its intersection with American society."

Each in its own way, three other library-museum collaborations—Music of Social Change, Digital Dress: 200 Years of Urban Style, and the Baltimore Art Resource Online Consortium—also undertook a comprehensive overview of important aspects of social history through a focus on trends and achievements in the arts. Music of Social Change, a partnership among Emory University, the Center for the Study of Southern Culture, and the Georgia Music Hall of Fame,[132] started a digital collection about "the music and musicians associated with social change movements such as the civil rights struggle." Connecting relevant archival material from a variety of library, museum, and recording-label sites, employing the Open Archives Initiative for disseminating research metadata, and placing these "disparate resources with[in] a scholarly context through...study guides" and contextual essays, Music of Social Change was integrated, as a separate database, into AmericanSouth.org, "a comprehensive repository of materials and peer-reviewed sources related to the American South" consisting of background articles, archival collections of "more than three dozen universities, colleges, and museums," research guides, and online discussions.[133] As with the OAC and MOAC relationship, the value of the umbrella site AmericanSouth.org was enhanced each time that a subject-specific project such as Music of Social Change was added.

Just as social history can be traced through music, it can also be seen through the prism of fashion. This is the task that Digital Dress: 200 Years of Urban Style—a project drawing on the resources of, among others, the Wayne State University Library System, Detroit Historical Museums, and Meadow Brook Hall—set for itself as it produced a Web repository of about 5,000 digital images of historic costume collections housed in metropolitan Detroit cultural institutions.[134] Although many towns and cities can lay claim to being important loci of clothing and fashion trends, Detroit—and its various symbolic incarnations as the Motor City and Motown—was particularly well placed in this regard because it was also a major center of industrial activity throughout the 1900s and thus attracted waves of immigrants from all parts of the United States and the world. Each group of immigrants—whether African Americans, white tenant farmers from the Mississippi Delta region, Germans, Irish, Poles, or Hungarians—and their descendants had unique styles of occupational, formal, recreational, and everyday dress that, collectively, illuminate the history of "popular culture, industrialization, inventions, labor organization" and urban transformation in the United States. And, because Detroit was also the home of automobile barons Henry Ford and John Dodge, custom-made domestic and imported couture fashion from such designers as Callot Soeurs, Paul Poiret, Peggy Hoyt, and Sally Milgrim was also an important part of the city's clothing history, as was the prevalence of fur coats, tippets, and muffs because of Detroit's role as "a major processor of furs throughout the 19th and early 20th centuries." Of interest to both social historians and art historians as a vivid testimony of social change, Digital Dress also aimed to be relevant to fashion design and merchandising programs in colleges and universities. After all, contemporary fashions are often based on newly discovered historical precedents—both recent and not so recent. Thus, instead of providing rotational digital images, the project created "multiple images" of individual artifacts "from a variety of angles," allowing users to pan and zoom in on relevant details—the very kind of details that design students and professional designers focus on in their work.

The Baltimore Art Resource Online Consortium, later renamed the Baltimore Art Research and Outreach Consortium (BAROC), created a multidimensional Web portal called Maryland ArtSource featuring a database of about 300 to 500 artists—both historic and contemporary—that had an affiliation with Maryland, whether through birth, residency, or depiction of Maryland subjects.[135] A collaboration among Johns Hopkins University, the Baltimore Museum of Art, Walters Art Museum, the Maryland Historical Society, and the Enoch Pratt Free Library, BAROC, in its final iteration, was searchable by medium or discipline (e.g., sculpture, architecture, decorative arts, photography, etc.), gender, race/ethnicity, and time period.[136] Resources available for each artist often included full-text "exhibition information, news clippings, art sales, critiques of works, and digitized images of artwork," as well as links to external sources. In addition to housing a wide range of digital images of paintings from participating institutions—all browsable by subject, title, artist, or date—and online catalogs of their entire collections, BAROC also provided extensive information about "grants, commercial gallery contacts, organizations that provide group health information and other benefits to self-employed artists, and career development assistance." To facilitate communication among area artists, "interactive bulletin boards and chat rooms" were implemented, and, for those interested in art education, "a database of art course syllabi" was provided. Finally, anticipating that continued existence of its Web presence would need to be subsidized by advertising, BAROC included "online museum shops...to promote sales for museum stores, university book stores and regional art galleries." As a result, BAROC saw itself both as an essential source of scholarly and historical information as well as a vibrant gateway that could be used by working artists, gallery owners, and the general public.

ART AND LITERATURE PROJECTS INTENDED MOSTLY FOR ADULTS: ANALYSIS

The contrast between digital and on-site library-museum collaborations is particularly stark among the nine arts-based projects (receiving ten grants) discussed above. On the one hand, although the Sargent murals restoration project at the Boston Public Library (BPL) has a significant digital component, it is inscribed within an overarching vision in which the type of art that would typically be found in museums is comfortably (and naturally) located in a library as a matter of course. The fact that an individual may enter into a single building, stroll among and gaze at art objects such as murals, statues, paintings, photographs, and then have the possibility of exploring in greater depth—whether in linear fashion or through serendipitous browsing—any discovered aspect of the viewed art through the multiple print-based resources also contained in that single building creates a world of rich, exciting, and almost limitless possibilities. In effect, that building then becomes the "palace of inspiration" that BPL aspires to be insofar as it has created the conditions for "communicat[ing] sensually, emotionally and intellectually the diversity, splendor and importance" of any given object or idea.[137] That quoted phrase, of course, is drawn from the narrative for The Language of Conservation: Poet in Residence at the Central Park Zoo. We refer to it again here because it captures the necessity of juxtaposing visual and intellectual experiences in order to forge a mental connection that leads individuals to seek knowledge—a step that, ideally, allows them to become "stewards of their environment" in a very broad and general sense (i.e., they form a better understanding of the connections between and among diverse elements of their world). As visitors to the Central Park Zoo walk through the grounds, they see not only animals and explanatory information about the animals, but also poetry that addresses "a wide range of processes that involve destruction and degradation of nature, the efforts to conserve natural resources and life, descriptions of the affected animals and finally the impact on human quality of life."[138]

In much the same way, when visitors to BPL become fascinated or awed with the Sargent murals, they can, to be sure, find out more about the murals and their restoration through the project Web site, but they are not just restricted to the Web site for additional information. If they so desire, they can borrow books about Sargent's contemporaries, the historical sweep of American painting in the late nineteenth and early twentieth century, the tradition of religious art in different countries, the founding of New England libraries, the architectural and spatial nuances of public buildings, or a host of other topics. Because no one can precisely tell in which direction the interests of a given individual will travel, part of the virtue of the physical library lies in the fact that it functions as an in-depth provider of information and knowledge about as many possible interconnections and juxtapositions as the human mind can imagine. Simply put, all those possibilities—and the secondary and tertiary avenues raised by the initial set of possibilities—reside on the shelves of the library, ready to be concretely explored, ready to be juxtaposed with the viewed art (or museum) object in an intellectual symbiosis made all the more visceral and immediate because that art (or museum) object exists in a very tangible way in close proximity.

While digital libraries and museums aspire to that type of productive symbiosis, it is often the case, as Michael Buckland writes, that the digital program has been "data-centric, focusing on how to create a database and how to enable individuals to search a database [and] then to do the same with another dataset."[139] Most digital libraries, he continues, have "adopted the approach of a publisher—producing one book after another—rather than of a librarian whose task it is to form a coherent collection of resources for library users," with the result that "this phenomenon reflects the difference between use of a single reference *work* and using a reference *collection*" (original emphasis).[140] Focusing on the example of places—"users want to know about hiking in the Himalayas, the castles of Quercy, the birds of the Pacific Northwest, and so on"—he suggests that the ideal digital library would be one in which catalogs, gazetteers, encyclopedias, bibliographies, biographical dictionaries, socioeconomic data series, and other resources would be interlinked so that a user could search "eclectically" among them all "as one could do in an *old-fashioned* reference library" (emphasis added).[141] But, as he has already pointed out, present versions of digital libraries do not live up to this vision.

Unfortunately, this seems to be the case with many of the digital projects mentioned so far. While there are links within the databases comprising individual projects, there are very few, if any, explicit links to substantive external sources and projects. In the Digital Dress narrative, for example, there is no provision for links of the kind proposed by Buckland—no links, for instance, to detailed sources describing the social conditions in which (and why) specific types of clothing and dress flourished; no links to discussions about the economics of the fashion industry, marketing, and distribution; no links to the way in which culture tastes affected clothing choices. In the Music of Social Change narrative, there is no provision for visitors to discover how a song or musician fits into the complex social and historical currents of the region, perhaps through an entry in the *Encyclopedia of Southern Culture*; listen to the song and/or the artist's comments about the song, perhaps through audio provided by the record label; examine digital images of various versions of the music or the words in order to trace the song's evolution; or see video clips of the song being performed. Likewise, in Opening the Cultural Corridor, users who want to find out how hanging scrolls and folding screens fit into Japanese art history, cultural history, and social history or Japanese American history would not be well served. To learn about such connections in any great depth, it is ironic that individuals would have to physically visit a library and use a variety of print sources. This goes to the heart of Buckland's criticism because, in many grant applications, the role of the library and its staff is not to contribute to the formation of a coherent digital library (or museum) through intellectually based collection development decisions—decisions of the kind that might be based on theorizing an "eclectic" user who wants wide-ranging information about a viewed object. Rather, it is confined to computer and database services departments with their emphasis on technological skills, database algorithms, and prowess with interface "look and feel" issues. Instead of providing content and intellectual leadership about how to conceptualize that content, libraries are often relegated to creating the database, digitizing the data, and loading the images.

Indeed, Buckland's notion that digital projects have failed "to form a coherent collection of resources for library users" is given further credence when some of the assumptions and guiding principles underlying grant application narratives are examined. Consider, for example, these three sentences from Opening the Cultural Corridor: "The primary purpose of this project is to establish a model for digital exploration and exploitation of the cultural corridor. Digitization of a scholarly set of Japanese paintings is an outcome, but it is not the primary motive.... The primary result will be infrastructure, trained staff, and equipment that can be used for additional digitization projects."[142] Or this statement from Digital Dress: "the proposal evolved from the overall digital library strategic directions of Wayne State University and the needs of the other collaborating partners."[143] What is strangely missing from these formulations is any sign of what may be good for the "eclectic" user. Instead, institutional imperatives dominate. The feeling could be summed up as if we build it, they will come, and they must be convinced to come because we have spent so much money on it. But where is the money to come from? Large-scale digitization projects require great initial expenditures and even greater continuing expenditures for newer, better, and faster technological hardware, middleware, and software if initial costs are to be justified. Indeed, many of the project narratives foresee subsequent phases of work beyond an initial stage, and it is in these subsequent phases that the project partners promise the most enticing and useful benefits for patrons. Many digitization projects have been seeded with grant money, but it is not apparent what will happen after grant funding runs out, or whether existing or new grant funding will allow projects to move onto their envisioned subsequent phases, or who will ultimately bear the burden of paying for and maintaining digital infrastructures. One worrisome answer is provided by BAROC, which bluntly states that, sometime in the future, maintenance of its Web site will be subsidized "through retail sales and advertising."[144] Advertising, of course, is inescapable in all spheres of contemporary life, but its association with library-museum partnerships dedicated to enhancing learning raises a host of thorny issues and hard questions about the real intellectual value—as opposed to entertainment value—of collaborations based on the accumulation of digital images. We saw in chapter 2 the extent to which reliance on corporate sponsors and advertising corrupts the educative function of museums and libraries. From many perspectives, the "old-fashioned" nature of the Boston Public Library, with its strong on-site museum component and extensive print collection acting as complements to one another, is much more conducive to the formation of coherent linkages among an untold number of topics for the eclectic user who wants to range widely across a large collection of resources, not just a single digital database.

SCIENCE AND ENVIRONMENT PROJECTS INTENDED MOSTLY FOR ADULTS: DESCRIPTION

Both utility and environmental stewardship characterize the seven library-museum projects in this category. Again, most of the projects (five) are digitally based (see table 3.9). The two exceptions are New Voices from the Upper Midwest: Writing for a Change[145] and The Jane Collaborative.[146] New Voices relied on the combined forces of the Cable Natural History Museum, three small public libraries, the Lac Courte Oreilles Ojibwa Community College (LCOOCC) Library, and tribally owned radio station WOJB-FM—all located in rural north-western Wisconsin in the Chequamegon National Forest. Although the partici-pating libraries were small, they had significant natural history collections. For instance, Forest Lodge Public Library was founded as a natural history library and is particularly strong in "field guides and historic natural history volumes"; the LCOOCC library has "a large natural history collection related to Native tradi-tions." The project selected 12 "low-income, unemployed or underemployed citi-zens"—mostly Native Americans—to participate in a "one-year paid internship in journalism and literary non-fiction" during which each person produced, using the resources of the museum and area libraries as starting points, four pieces of written work about diverse aspects of natural history and the environment. Working with an instructor and supported by the visits of four professional writ-ers who critiqued and analyzed their work in individual and group discussion ses-sions, the interns not only sought to publish their completed articles in local or regional newspapers and magazines, but discussed their work on WOJB-FM and at a public reading at a designated library. In addition, a booklet containing one article from each intern, together with a compilation CD of their readings, was published and made available to libraries in the Upper Midwest and tribal li-braries nationally. Their writings were also placed on the museum Web site and linked with other community-based writing sites. While interns gained expertise "in research, information-gathering and communication" and were eligible to re-ceive college credit at the local community college, the community as a whole gained "new voices" who could "thoughtfully engage the public in discourse" about such topics as the "export of Lake Superior's water; pollution within the Lake Superior watershed; loss of fresh-water fisheries through mercury contami-nation; and large-scale clearcutting of forests." The Cable Natural History Mu-seum also planned to call upon the interns when it needed freelance writers for special publications, exhibit research, copy writing, and newsletters. In addition, each visiting professional writer—the narrative mentioned Diane Ackerman, Sherman Alexie, Louise Erdrich, and Bill McKibben, among others, as possibili-ties—gave public readings and were interviewed on WOJB-FM as part of the sta-tion's series about environmental writing. Just as the books of the visiting established writers were given extensive exposure through displays in area li-braries, tapes of interviews and readings with interns and writers gained broad na-tional distribution through WOJB-FM's membership in American Indian Radio on Satellite, a consortium of some 50 Native American radio stations.

The Jane Collaborative, a partnership between the Burpee Museum of Nat-ural History (BMNH) and 61 rural libraries in northern Illinois and southern Wisconsin, used the controversy surrounding the discovery of the fossil skeleton of a dinosaur called Jane—"Is she a juvenile *T. rex*, a rare *Nanotyranus*, or a com-pletely new element in dinosaur evolution?"—as a catalyst to encourage people to view their local libraries as an important element in "a network of learning communities [providing]...experiential visits and educational programs." Ini-tially drawn to libraries to learn more about the issues behind the Jane debate, in-dividuals would subsequently recognize that the library was an excellent resource

Table 3.9
IMLS Library-Museum Collaborative Science and Environment Projects Intended Mostly for Adults (1998–2003)

Year	Title of Project	Selected Major Applicants	Grant Amount ($)
1998	Linking Florida's Natural Heritage	Florida Center for Library Automation (Gainesville); Florida Museum of Natural History (Gainesville)	235,803
1999	Smart Web Exhibits	Carnegie Mellon University Libraries (Pittsburgh); Carnegie Museum of Natural History	333,023
2000	Flora and Fauna of the Great Lakes Region	University of Michigan University Library (Ann Arbor); University of Michigan Natural History Museums	226,122
2000	National Collection of Endangered Plants Web Site	Chicago Horticultural Society/Chicago Botanic Garden; Library of the University of Illinois–Chicago	255,809
2001	Plant Evaluation Web Site	Chicago Horticultural Society/Chicago Botanic Garden; Library of the University of Illinois–Chicago	101,827
2001	New Voices from the Upper Midwest	Cable Natural History Museum (Cable, Wisconsin); Drummond Public Library (Wisconsin)	72,755
2003	The Jane Collaborative	Burpee Museum of Natural History (Rockford, Illinois); Rockford Public Library	246,600

for "popular information" of all kinds, thus allowing them to achieve "deeper levels of involvement and understanding" about crucial local and national issues. To this end, the project adopted a three-pronged approach: educating library staff; supplying libraries with the resources to develop topical displays; and educating the public. BMNH first established a Web-based Jane Discussion Board in which library employees could ask questions and participate in discussions with museum staff and scientists; then, two one-day professional development training conferences were held at BMNH so that two members from each participating library could be introduced to "dinosaur basics, geography, and the scientific method,… observe the Jane remains, learn about fossil preparation techniques, and get hands-on training in skeleton identification and the controversy surrounding the classification of Jane" from museum paleontologists and educators. The project also allotted each library $400 to purchase "dinosaur-related educational materials"—for example, "books, videos, CDs, [and] posters"—so that a Jane's Corner could be implemented at each library. Finally, a series of children's summer-reading programs revolving around the Jane theme was instituted at area libraries. Museum professionals made periodic visits to these reading groups and—together with well-known scholars and scientists—participated in a series of family workshops, adult lectures, and panel discussions at individual libraries.

While The Jane Collaborative focused on public outreach through on-site exhibits and events, Delivering Enhanced Library and Museum Collections Online, On Target and On Time did so through Smart Web Exhibits (SWEs).[147] Part of an ambitious effort to produce "an organizational paradigm and software tools for the low cost rapid production of SWEs on a national basis," this project was, in many respects, a prototype for Carnegie Mellon University's Universal Library Project, whose long-term vision included digitizing, preserving, and making accessible "the global multimedia history of human consciousness and culture" by constantly "migrating the collections to new technologies again and again over time, free searching and discovery of content (if not free viewing), eventually automated summaries of the items retrieved..., and ultimately machine translation of full text and discourse among many languages."

But what, exactly, is an SWE? Constructed "to accompany a museum or library exhibit," it invites Web users "to explore the topic of an exhibit more deeply" through a "video tutorial" in which a museum curator introduces and contextualizes the exhibit, a librarian describes where to look for related information, and an "automated reference assistant helps users find what they want, at the level and for the duration they want." In addition to digital images of exhibit artifacts, the SWE also contains links to library catalogs and preselected full-text books, chapters, and articles, as well as a fee-based print-request feature, images of related artifacts and information about where these objects are located, and a list of courses and other educational resources about the topic of the exhibit. As demonstrations of this concept, the project created two SWEs, one of which focused on the "text and images documenting the evolution of artificial intelligence" as seen through the archival collections—including photographs, correspondence, lecture notes, 32 hours of videotape, and published and unpublished papers—bequeathed by Herbert Simon and Allen Newell. Exhibit visitors not only could follow the early history of computer science, but could also interact with "a presentation on the development of a computer chess program that can beat a grand chess master." The other SWE documented the history of dinosaurs through field photographs, field notes, and other material pertinent to the dinosaur specimens housed at the Carnegie Museum of Natural History.

Plant Evaluation Web Site[148] and the National Collection of Endangered Plants Web Site,[149] both undertakings spearheaded by the Chicago Horticultural Society and Chicago Botanic Garden, were digital-based projects with a social purpose. Gardening, of course, is a popular leisure-time activity, and the demand for new ornamental plants is never ending, but gardening also has a strong connection to broad ecological principles. On the municipal level, city officials—together with horticulture students, green industry professionals, and park district staff—are increasingly interested in creating urban green space and community gardens that contribute to pronounced quantitative and qualitative increases in the realms of environmental, physical, spiritual, and emotional health. Against this background, Plant Evaluation positioned itself as an invaluable online resource that provided not only photographs and authoritative information about the ornamental aspects of about 1,000 herbaceous perennials, including flower color, bloom time, and foliage, but also information about their environmental and cultural adaptability, including such crucial factors as susceptibility to diseases, pests, extreme cold, drought, and herbicide damage. Because individuals and groups could select "the best plants for their specific climate and conditions" based on Plant Evaluation data, creating a sustainable environmental fabric was no longer just a theoretical notion. National Collection of Endangered Plants also aimed to raise environmental awareness by gathering extensive data about "570 globally rare plants," as defined by the Center for Plant Conservation, a consortium of 29 botanical gardens and arboreta in the United States. In addition to a photograph, description, and bibliographic information about each plant, the online database summarized scientific research about the plants and discussed their habitat, threats to survival, and management needs. The site thus functioned as an educational resource about the fragile and tenuous conditions in which plants exist and served as a clarion call for environmental stewardship.

If the endangered plants database was international in scope, two other library-museum collaborations—Linking Florida's Natural Heritage[150] and Flora and Fauna of the Great Lakes Region[151]—concentrated on specific regions of the United States. Building on the vast resources of the Florida Museum of Natural History (FMNH) and state academic libraries, Linking Florida's Natural Heritage developed a virtual ecological library connecting "museum specimen data to supporting scientific literature and digitized full texts." The online database featured a core collection of approximately 200 "Florida ecosystem/species texts," including the *Handbook of Common Freshwater Fish in Florida Lakes*, subject-specific bibliographies on such diverse topics as Florida ornithology, Florida herpetology, and Florida geology, and an environmental thesaurus that provided "searching continuity" among the newly digitized resources. The database was then linked with FMNH collection records, thus connecting scientific and common names. In sum, the project was a "critical resource in building a citizenry aware of the importance and intricacy of Florida's rich and unique natural heritage" and facilitated decision making that took into account environmental factors.

Flora and Fauna of the Great Lakes Region can, in many ways, be seen as an expanded version of the previous project. It digitized guidebooks, photographs, specimen data, DNA samples, and handwritten field notes from the collections of the University of Michigan Natural History Museums, enhanced existing descriptive records to simplify searching and "to promote better interoperability with other related collection databases and catalogs," and streamlined access to more than 20 online image collections of the museums through a "single unified access point." The project's central innovation, however, was the addition of geospatial coordinate information to its species data, which, by documenting "the location where a specimen was collected or where a species lives" through "user-friendly map-based database interfaces," allowed scholars and students "to see what flora and fauna exist in particular locations, to trace the history of land use [and] how species have moved over time, to study how climate relates to species location, or to develop environmental impact studies." And, by digitizing 100 "historical maps from the 1920s that summarized the distribution of mammals in the Great Lakes area as they were in the early 1800s," an important historical layer was added to the spatial data, thus permitting a detailed study of habitat change brought about by environmental degradation. Users were thus engaged in "new patterns of inquiry" as they viewed a "historical map detailing the fauna of the Michigan area, read field notes on the behavior of some of those fauna, and...look[ed] at images of skeletons."

SCIENCE AND ENVIRONMENT PROJECTS INTENDED MOSTLY FOR ADULTS: ANALYSIS

A particularly striking element of some of the science and environment projects discussed here is the degree to which library involvement was just as crucial as museum involvement. This is not always the case, even in the most worthy of projects. Consider the distribution of responsibilities in Plant Evaluation Web Site: "The Chicago Botanic Garden will provide data and images of all the plants to be included on the site. The Library at the University of Illinois at Chicago (UI-C) will create the database, digitize the data and load the images. Chicago Botanic Garden staff will provide direction in editing and design. The site will be housed on the Chicago Botanic Garden web site and maintained by Garden staff with annual updates to the data and images."[152] For all intents and purposes, the tasks allotted to the library could have been outsourced to any number of small- or medium-sized private businesses specializing in digital databases. As we saw in a previous section, the intellectual contribution—as opposed to technical contribution—of libraries to some library-museum partnerships is minimal. To be sure, it is convenient, in this collaboration, to use the expertise of the library systems department of the UI-C science library, but there could be a lively exchange of opinions about what such a collaboration— other than qualification for government funds—brings to the table that a contractual arrangement with a private entity could not.

Let us look at this situation from a related perspective. In a section entitled Management Plan, the Plant Evaluation Web Site narrative describes in great detail many of the wonderful resources available at the UI-C science library: in addition to approximately 70,000 books, 1,300 current serials, and 74,000 microforms, it offers access to Web of Science, U.S. Fish and Wildlife Service Bulletins, and much more. Yet these resources are not brought to bear in the project. One is left to wonder how much more valuable Plant Evaluation would have been if the digital images of the 1,000 or so herbaceous perennials therein contained could have been linked, for example, to relevant articles in full-text electronic journals available at UI-C, to Fish and Wildlife Service bulletins, or to newsletters published by environmental watchdog organizations. The lack of this kind of intellectual contribution from the library is all the more surprising in light of the description of National Collection of Endangered Plants Web Site, which is a collaboration between the same partners as in Plant Evaluation. In National Collection, library staff not only "verif[ied] and enhance[d]" bibliographic references, but also appended notes to each digital record, including "hyperlinks to scanned documents and files on each species, when this information is available for digitization from...agencies such as the U.S. Fish and Wildlife Service (and their *Endangered Species Technical Bulletin*)."[153] And in Linking Florida's Natural Heritage and Flora and Fauna of the Great Lakes Region, library contributions included thesaurus construction; creation of metadata; selection, cataloging, and indexing of texts; and the merging of bibliographies into federated databases.

In nondigital library-museum partnerships, there is a sense that the contributions of libraries and museums are mutually sustaining to a somewhat greater degree than in digital partnerships. Take The Jane Collaborative. While the Burpee Museum of Natural History supplied opportunities for the professional development of library staff members through discussion boards and conferences, funded the purchase of dinosaur materials for display in libraries, and made its personnel available for public lectures and workshops at libraries, librarians conducted extensive summer reading programs for children and young adults, thus initiating them into the world of science. As the summer reading programs progressed, it is easy to envision children not only making more and more use on their own of books and videos displayed at Jane's Corner, but asking library staff for additional information about cognate scientific topics—information that staff, thanks to the knowledge gained from their contacts with the Burpee Museum, could now supply, thus piquing the interest of their interlocutors for new reading and viewing material.

But perhaps the most reciprocally integrated library-museum partnership was New Voices from the Upper Midwest. Recall that, here, a dozen individuals underwent a year-long writing internship during which they made intensive use of the rich, natural history library and museum collections in a five-county area of northwestern Wisconsin to produce journalism articles and literary nonfiction about environmental topics—articles that would become part of weekly county newspapers, booklets, and larger-circulation magazines and that would eventually be found in the collections of local libraries, thus adding to the stock of natural history resources from which others could benefit. Moreover, these individuals could now become actively involved in shaping the legacy of the Cable Natural History Museum insofar as they could contribute to museum catalogs and newsletters, as well as disseminate information about museum activities in area newspapers. Establishing "community dialogue" and forging "a network of community leaders" capable of documenting changes in local and regional "environmental ethics," the project captured the very essence of fruitful library and museum interaction because it drew on existing library and museum resources, created new ones, and made visible the indelible bonds between informed and passionate literature, on the one hand, and the natural world as memorialized in museum collections, on the other.[154]

HISTORY PROJECTS INTENDED FOR CHILDREN/TEENAGERS AND ADULTS: DESCRIPTION

By now the conceptual shape of a large percentage of library-museum collaborations is clear: information of interest to local, state, or regional constituencies held in libraries and museums is being selected, organized, digitized, and made available online—in various permutations—through Web portals. Indeed, 8 of the 10 history projects (11 total grants) discussed in this section are primarily of this type (see table 3.10). One of the exceptions is Restoring the Past, Capturing the Present, Preserving the Future, a project undertaken by the Heritage Museum of Libby, Montana, a remote town in the extreme northwestern part of the state, and the local public and school library systems.[155] The central aim of Restoring the Past was to inventory, catalog, and index the museum's entire collection—tasks that were performed by community volunteers in conjunction with public library staff and an archival consultant, who provided a month-long training course about professional documentary practices and archival preservation issues. With input from area school libraries, traveling educational exhibits—which included "historical materials for enrichment activities" (e.g., thematic costumes, mineral samples, tools, maps, audio and video tapes of oral histories, etc.) and museum resource guides listing "available speakers, museum activities, and other local sites"—were developed. And, with input from the public library system, a Web presence for the museum was established.

The other exception was Worklore: Brooklyn Workers Speak, a partnership between the Brooklyn Public Library and the Brooklyn Historical Society.[156] Focusing on four themes—Newcomers: Immigrant Workforces, African Americans at Work in Brooklyn, Women at Work, and Unemployment: Confronting Job Displacement—the project created a major exhibit that was seen in its entirety at two central locations and then traveled "in sections to 16 branch libraries...where additional neighborhood-specific material" was presented "to help library patrons make connections between the exhibition themes and the rich histories of their local neighborhoods." As the exhibit traveled among branch locations, library patrons were encouraged to provide oral histories about their "memories and recollections of work in Brooklyn" and to "bring photographs and other...objects that [could] be scanned to add an extra dimension to the oral histories collected." Indeed, exhibit planners advertised widely for "items used in the workplace, such as uniforms, tools, production charts, lockers, safety posters; personal items such as identification badges, lunch pails,...labor union materials including banners, by-laws, minutes of meetings, [and] pamphlets."[157] Some of the narratives and images included in the exhibit included the story of "ropewalk workers in the 1830s organizing a strike to protest the mechanization of rope production," Brooklyn residents and their fight to prevent the Drakes Bakery factory—manufacturer of beloved cakes and pastries—from relocating, and "Navy Yard women assuming traditionally male jobs during World War II." An eight-part public lecture series—featuring such speakers as novelist Edwidge Danticat talking about "the role of women in Brooklyn immigrant households" and New York Times columnist Paul Krugman discussing "the relationship of Brooklyn's economy to that of the nation and the world"—complemented the exhibit, as did a Web site that housed many of the images, documents, lectures, oral histories, and curriculum guides associated with the exhibit cycle.

Table 3.10
IMLS Library-Museum Collaborative History Projects Intended for Children/
Teenagers and Adults (1998–2003)

Year	Title of Project	Selected Major Applicants	Grant Amount ($)
1998	Images of the Indian Peoples of the Northern Great Plains	Montana State University Libraries (Bozeman); Museum of the Rockies (Bozeman)	138,346
1999/ 2002	Connecticut History Online	University of Connecticut Libraries (Storrs); Connecticut Historical Society; Mystic Seaport Museum	335,101 and 498,770
2000	Restoring the Past, Capturing the Present, Preserving the Future	Libby (Montana) School District #4; Heritage Museum; Lincoln County Public Library (Montana)	175,042
2001	Engaging the Public with Digital Primary Sources	Washington State University Libraries (Pullman); Idaho State Historical Society; Oregon State Historical Society	197,371
2001	Western Trails	University of Denver Penrose Library; Kansas State Library; Wyoming State Library; Nebraska State Library	498,637
2001	WWII Richmond, California Home Front Digital Project	Richmond Public Library (California); Richmond Museum of History (California)	199,325
2001	Connections	Inter American University of Puerto Rico Virtual Library; Ponce Museum of History (Puerto Rico)	333,692
2001	Worklore	Brooklyn Public Library (New York); Brooklyn Historical Society	175,654
2003	The New Jersey Digital Highway	Rutgers University Libraries (New Brunswick, New Jersey); American Labor Museum (Haledon, New Jersey)	463,511
2003	The Civil Rights Movement	The Media Library of the WGBH Educational Foundation (Boston); Washington University (St. Louis, Missouri); Birmingham Civil Rights Institute (Alabama)	499,133

The eight projects that were exclusively—or almost exclusively—digitally based, varied only in the subject matter of their digitized content.[158] Connections: Linking Educational Institutions, Libraries, and Museums Through Technology, a partnership involving the Inter American University of Puerto Rico Virtual Library, the Ponce Museum of History, and the Ponce Historical Archives, planned an integrated virtual collection of historical resources about Puerto Rico to bring about "a significant increase in high school history assignments and class activities that require the use of primary documents."[159] The WWII Richmond, California Home Front Digital Project chronicled the effect that World War II and its aftermath had on Richmond, a city northeast of San Francisco that was a center of the defense industry, through a digital collection of about 10,000 photographs, textual documents, easel paintings, and objects.[160] As the project narrative relates, "one-fifth (747) of the large ships built for the war were fabricated at four shipyards" in Richmond. Overall, the city boasted more than 50 factories (employing more than 100,000 people, including many African Americans who had migrated from economically depressed areas in the South) that produced a wide assortment of goods for the war effort, and it is the home of the Rosie the Riveter Memorial that honors women defense workers.

Access to primary documents was also emphasized by Images of the Indian Peoples of the Northern Great Plains, a collaboration between the Montana State University library system, the Museum of the Rockies, and Little Big Horn College that generated a digital database of photographs, stereographs, sketches, and ledger drawings (with "some text to give context") of the Crow, Cheyenne, Blackfeet, Salish (Flathead), Kutenai, Chippewa-Cree, Gros Ventres (Atsina), and Assiniboine tribes.[161] Some of the included images provided rare visual evidence of "tribal dance ceremonies, tribal celebrations (Crow Fair), dwellings, children, reservation life, and portraits of significant tribal leaders." Especially compelling was a series of lantern slides and the "Montana Works Progress Administration (WPA) records [of] sketches produced in conjunction with legends…recorded by Native American WPA workers" at five reservations.

Two projects dealt specifically with the immigration experience and the contribution of diverse ethnic communities to the national fabric of the United States. Engaging the Public with Digital Primary Sources brought together Washington State University, as well as the historical societies of Idaho, Oregon, and Washington, to create a digital database—including government reports, maps, manuscripts, photographs, newspapers, museum objects, and oral history interviews—of the history of, among others, the Basque, Chinese, Japanese, Italian, and African American communities who settled the Columbia River Basin.[162] The project not only included online tutorials about "how to develop research questions, conduct ethnic history research, [and] evaluate sources," but also developed an online "threaded discussion program" that "linked historical research to contemporary issues" of interest in the region: "immigration policies, work and ethnicity, cultural legacies, [and] changing demographics." A particular strength of Engaging the Public was its extensive archives of oral history transcripts, which featured themes such as Women and Timber and the Columbia Rivers Dissenters Series.[163] A collection dedicated to the individuals who criticized the management of the Columbia River system, it included interviews with Kent Martin, "an outspoken critic of sports fishermen"; Wilbur Slockish, who "fought the storing of Hanford nuclear waste on the Yakama reservation"; and Walter Ericksen, an orchardist who "documented the effects of pollution emitted from the Harvey Aluminum Company for 21 years."[164] But the centerpiece of the project was a social and cultural history of Columbia River communities such Sandpoint, Idaho, and Umatilla, Oregon—histories that stand out for the way in which they interweave comprehensive background essays, photo archives, oral histories, and primary documents to "create tools and strategies for the online public to become their own historians."[165]

A consortium of institutions led by Rutgers University Libraries, working under the auspices of a project entitled The New Jersey Digital Highway: Where Culture, History and Learning Merge, implemented a "next generation" modular online database—one that supports "dynamic contextual portals providing [four] metadata schema [NJCore (8 elements), Dublin Core-Education (20 elements), IEEE Learning Object Metadata (more than 30 elements), and MPEG-7 Multimedia Content Description Interface (more than 30 elements)] and applications customized by user roles"—with the theme, The Changing Face of New Jersey: The Immigration Experience from Earliest Times to the Present.[166] Because of its proximity to Ellis Island, New Jersey has a rich immigrant culture and became "a permanent residence for many immigrants who worked in agriculture or local industries such as bog mining, canal building, and glass making." Portuguese settled in the Ironbound section of Newark, Swedes settled in Camden, and Japanese Americans were offered employment on Seabrook Farm, a large commercial operation that produces crops for frozen vegetables, in order "to effect their release from internment camps." Intended for both formal educational use and the general public, Changing Face digitized about 10,000 items, including "audio and video oral histories; photographs; household and industrial implements; sheepskin deeds; diaries; [and] annual reports of ethnic organizations." Another useful component of the project was the inclusion of maps that were "geo-referenced for use in GIS applications" so that "population distribution[s] for a specified number of ethnic populations" could be created based on national and state census information. These maps were, in turn, linked with survey and poll responses to questions about ethnic groups and attitudes of and about ethnic groups—a feature that allowed users to contextualize and frame the immigrant experience through statistical analyses. In addition to offering teachers a week-long seminar in which they would learn to "select and organize relevant content from the digital collection [and] refine their ability to use primary resources in classroom instruction," the project also helped teachers to navigate the database by linking metadata from objects to metadata for lesson plans. Thus, a teacher who came upon an interesting object in the collection could immediately know how to create a lesson and classroom activities around that object. And, so that the experiences of individual teachers with individual lesson plans could be known to others, teachers could "attach structured evaluations to the metadata...document[ing] student response to the lesson plan, the amount of time required, and any customization...added to the lesson plan."

Equally compelling was Western Trails, an ambitious digital initiative of the state libraries of Colorado, Wyoming, Kansas, and Nebraska in partnership with the University of Denver libraries and the Colorado Digitization Program (CDP).[167] The project's central theme of "trails" was a broad organizing principle encompassing "pre-historic trails through the current interstate highway system, including...the Santa Fe Trail and Overland Trail." Seeking to understand the social and cultural origins of trails, the factors that motivated people to follow them, the role of water in the development of the trails, and the ways in which trails were viewed in literature, the project included such thematic collections as Dodge City Cattle Trails and Tales, which examined the economic, social, and political impact of cattle drives on Dodge City through online access to articles from the Dodge City Times, and Early Omaha: Gateway to the West, a collection of 350 photographs, lantern slides, postcards, and maps "reflecting Omaha's importance as the site of the Union Pacific Headquarters and point of origin for the first transcontinental railway."[168] One of the most intriguing collections was In Search of Health: The Tuberculosis Trail in Colorado, which describes how, by 1920, approximately 60 percent of the population of Colorado—affectionately called the "World's Sanatorium"—could be attributed to the state's reputation as a salubrious place for the treatment of tuberculosis in such institutions as the Jewish Consumptives' Relief Society. Integrated into the CDP, Western Trails collections could therefore be juxtaposed with other CDP collections—such as Images of Pioneer Jewish Families in Colorado[169]—to form a richly nuanced portrait of some of the numerous hidden aspects of American frontier life.

Connecticut History Online (CHO) did for Connecticut what Western Trails did for Colorado, Wyoming, Nebraska, and Kansas.[170] Conceived by the University of Connecticut Libraries and involving such institutions as the New Haven Colony Historical Society and Mystic Seaport, the project—grouped according to five themes: diversity; livelihoods; lifestyles; environment; and infrastructure—began with a digital collection of about 15,000 black-and-white photographs, then expanded to include thousands of manuscripts, some 2,000 broadsides, over 500 maps, 450 artifacts, audio clips, and 200 journals and minute books.[171] As part of the state's "preeminent online historical database" connecting the holdings of both large and small institutions, CHO was well positioned to serve as a central research site for the exploration of the social, economic, and cultural history of the state. A panoramic sweep of the birth of American industry was one of the highlights of the project, since it included numerous images from the Southern New England Telephone Company, "one of America's first telephone companies and creator of the world's first telephone exchange"; Cheney Brothers Silk Manufacturing; the New York, New Haven, and Hartford Railroad; and Thermos Inc. Grouped into such thematic overviews as The Textile Industry in Connecticut, Moving Around: A Century of Transportation, and Women at Work: Work History of Women in America, CHO collections also included a wide array of textual documents such as railroad and trolley line maps, railroad station blueprints, military service questionnaires completed by returning soldiers after World War I, and extensive records and correspondence generated by members of Connecticut's congressional delegation over the course of the eighteenth and nineteenth centuries. Some of the most popular digitized material—nautical charts, model vessels, and oral histories of whaling families—came from the collections of Mystic Seaport, a world-renowned maritime museum.

But perhaps the most elaborate of the history-oriented projects was The Civil Rights Movement: 1950 to the Present, a partnership between the WGBH Educational Foundation, the Birmingham Civil Rights Institute (BCRI), and the library system of Washington University (WU), which set for itself the task of providing "broadband solutions to the challenge of matching rich media archives with educational needs" for K–12 students and their teachers.[172] In addition, it was used in undergraduate- and graduate-level classes at WU and was presented "in ongoing screening events hosted by the Film and Media Archive both on campus and in the community." It may, in fact, be an understatement to say that this project involved rich media archives, considering that it featured a wide array of oral histories recorded by BCRI, "the encyclopedic resources of the Henry Hampton Collection housed within the Film and Media Archive at WU, including the seminal *Eyes on The Prize* documentary films," and video programming from WGBH, including *The American Experience, Frontline,* and *Say Brother/Basic Black.* Using the Teachers' Domain, "an online digital library platform designed to harness public television's extensive broadcast, video, and interactive…resources to support standards-based education," the creators of The Civil Rights Movement: 1950 to the Present selected three major themes—Children of the Movement, Tactics for Justice, and Leaders and Organizers—that would structure the "representative set of fully contextualized assets" that each participating institution made available to the project from its collections. Not only did each organization supply about 20 such "assets" for inclusion in the digital library, but each institution was also responsible for supplementing each item by an annotation—"descriptions of what the user will see, the source of the asset, and the general concept portrayed"—and a "more extensive background essay" of "300 words in length [that] will anchor the event or person in its larger historical context." In addition, lesson plans that contain "specific ideas for the integration of the collection's resources within a coherent, inquiry-oriented" learning environment and that "suggested pathways through the subject matter while still allowing maximum flexibility for the teacher to adapt lesson strategies as appropriate" were also provided. "Tailored to the specific grade level and state location of the user," incorporating "local content and exchange of ideas," and allowing teachers and students to "organize and use resources as needed," the project engaged students of all ages "with the multidimensional issues, ideas and personalities that characterize the Civil Rights Movement."

HISTORY PROJECTS INTENDED FOR CHILDREN/TEENAGERS AND ADULTS: ANALYSIS

Many of the same statements that were made about Windows on Maine in a previous section could also be made about The Civil Rights Movement: 1950 to the Present: the fact that participating institutions—together with a "national advisory board of academics, teachers, and experts"—both select and contextualize the material augurs well for a well-rounded learning experience. On the other hand, much of the material consists of television programming, and it is difficult to see how a 300-word background essay appended to each digitized item can be considered to be "extensive" and provide anything more than a smidgen of historical understanding. But one of the most significant aspects of The Civil Rights Movement narrative is that it unintentionally lays bare one of the unexplored reasons why multimedia online resources have become so popular. "A distressingly high percentage of teachers," the narrative states, "have received little to no content training [because] the bulk of most teacher education programs concentrate on methodological issues rather than subject mastery," with the result that "too many teachers don't know the material in sufficient depth to assist their students in learning it."[173] One result of all this is that teachers are finding it increasingly difficult "to more actively engage their students." Thus, according to the logic of the argument, "today's classrooms demand visual materials characterized by relatively short length, limited use of lectures, and emphasis on interactivity, vivid graphics, and contemporary sound"—in other words, the type of "new media applications" that online digital resources can provide and which are explicitly associated with raised expectations and best practices in the twenty-first century. The goal of actively engaging students is, of course, eminently valuable, but the method(s) by which to do so is, ultimately, a choice. And all choices necessarily have long-term social and political implications.

Online digital resources are only *one* way to palliate the fundamental shortcoming of the lack of subject knowledge on the part of educators. Another equally valid way is for educators to simply take the time to gain a thorough subject mastery of the topics they teach through concerted, serious, long-term, and ongoing study of those topics. After all, the failure to actively engage students can be placed squarely in the lap of teacher education programs that do not teach subject mastery and on teachers who do not feel compelled to gain such subject mastery. Of course, relying on online digital resources is much easier than embarking upon in-depth study of one or more subjects or fields. But such reliance is a choice fraught with consequences; for example, it may actually inhibit educators from developing extensive subject knowledge on their own because they intuitively realize that an online digital resource will do the job for them. It may also suggest to the students of these educators that there is very little need to develop extensive subject knowledge through a concerted program of study that goes well beyond watching television programs and interactive media.

We thus enter into a vicious circle in which only a more powerful and entertaining battery of multimedia applications will permit students to become actively engaged. In other words, digital solutions are seen as the *only* solutions, with the result that little, if any, attention is accorded to other possible avenues—for instance, instituting a challenging process whereby teachers can actively engage their students by gaining sustained subject mastery. If teachers themselves do not feel any great urgency to give themselves a sound and detailed knowledge of diverse, content-based subject matter through painstaking study, it is little wonder that their students are not actively engaged and that digital resources are therefore viewed as a panacea. Instead of facilitating learning, digital resources may detract from a rigorous learning process insofar as they prepackage informational elements masquerading as knowledge. Libraries and museums that form exclusively digitally based partnerships may thus be complicit in creating an environment in which the learning process for students is made so easy and so visually attractive that no real knowledge is gained, in which the arduous task of juxtaposing detailed textual and visual sources in an attempt to develop a sound critical analysis of a given topic is rendered moot, and in which education has become edutainment.

Of course, the developers the digital projects discussed in both this section and elsewhere would all claim that their projects deliver untold educational value and democratize access to rare, fragile, and previously inaccessible material. And, to a certain extent, they do—especially those projects that involve community members in the gathering, selecting, contextualizing, and organizing of digital images and that allow community members to contribute their own memories, cultural history, or the products of newly developed skills to the creation (or improvement) of a library-museum entity (whether in the physical or online world) in which they can feel that they have a real stake. We have seen good examples of that kind of approach—recall, for instance, how Worklore: Brooklyn Workers Speak solicited memories and objects from exhibit attendees and then took pains to incorporate their contributions into subsequent iterations of the exhibit—and we will see additional examples in the next sections. And, although the Libby, Montana, project may not be as technologically sophisticated as many others discussed in this section, it nevertheless teaches a profound lesson—that the creation of "a living museum," defined as a "library-museum alliance,"[174] must call upon the competencies of the very people who will subsequently make use of it and for whom it will become an important part of their daily lives. After all, the Libby Heritage Museum was built by a community of volunteers from "the felling of the first tree, hauling of the logs, peeling, chinking, decking the room, pouring concrete and building exhibits."[175] This "surplus of volunteers" not only developed the "5.3-acre grounds and has surrounded the museum with numerous historical structures (such as the 1936 U.S. Forest Service 'cookhouse' from the Sylvanite Ranger Station which is used for community meetings and preparing meals for fund raising activities) and artifacts (such as the J. Neils Lumber Company Shay Locomotive, which is an original logging locomotive used in the Kootenai Country from 1906–1934)," but also planned to restore a "fifty year old Hyster Company Lumber Carrier [and]…a 1953 Buffalo fire engine," as well as establish "a working print shop" featuring "a 1887 Liberty Press used in the early Montana Territory."[176] After receiving archival training as part of the project, museum volunteers—assisted by local library staff and high school students—inventoried, indexed, cataloged, and professionally preserved "at least 75%" of museum materials, making the resources available for online searching. But much more significant than this list of accomplishments was the fact that these actions were instrumental in forming a "strong, multi-generational museum group" for whom local cultural and social history was not merely a point-and-click exercise, but something tangible—and all the more valuable because of that tangible nature.

All this is not to say that the project could not have been improved. As the narrative makes clear, Libby is a town that is struggling to survive, in part because of the closure of the nearby vermiculite mine and in part because of the asbestos-related illnesses connected with the operation of the mine. But, as the populations of the town and the surrounding county decrease—a common phenomenon in many rural areas of Nebraska, Oklahoma, the Dakotas, and Kansas that are some distance away from the interstate highway system—maintaining physically separate libraries and museums may represent an inopportune squandering of resources. Instead of two cultural institutions providing adequate, but not spectacular, services, the development of a single physical locus of cultural activity—informed by objects, photographs, archives, magazines, newspapers, and books—might constitute a workable and intellectually stimulating approach to a living exploration of the preserved and memorialized past. Certainly, the project mentions that the county library system "tie[d] its existing historical and genealogical projects to the Museum's programs,"[177] but it is not hard to see that such ties could have been made all the more firm in an amalgamated or hybrid institution where, to take one example, the physical collocation of personal documents of interest to genealogists—such as wills or photographs—could have been juxtaposed not only with the objects mentioned or represented in the wills or photographs, but also by books and articles explaining the social context of those objects.

Although the small neighborhood exhibits that formed such an essential part of Worklore were not permanent, their very presence at the branch library—as well as the fact that local residents were asked to make important contributions to them—provided evidence, at least for a brief time, of the myriad possibilities residing in an institutionalized and physical conjunction of library and museum. In some respects, what Worklore encouraged was a form of "Brautigan library"—so named after the novelist Richard Brautigan, who, in *The Abortion: An Historical Romance 1966*, envisioned a library "where anyone who writes a book can bring it to be added to the shelves that never attract dust," where children bring books "about their toys which they have illustrated with their crayons, adolescents bring the stories of the pains in their days, [and] old people write the book of their lives," and where the "author alone decides [on] which shelf the book is best at home."[178] Brautigan's idea is all about the necessity for community ownership and community self-definition, and whether the items brought to the library are books or objects is, ultimately, immaterial: the item qua item contains meaning in the eyes of the individual who brings it. Thus, the place to which the individual brings an item should welcome all items—books of poetry as well as tools, lunch pails, or reminiscences. In other words, it should be a library-museum hybrid where individuals can not only create their own juxtapositions—that is, where an "author alone decides [on] which shelf the book is best at home," or where a worker alone decides where the best location is for his lunch pail or first pay stub or fragmented memories—but also have the opportunity, by physically exploring the contributions of others (i.e., published books, other unpublished books, curated objects, and uncurated objects) to be imbued with the sense that her/his individual contribution has historical resonance and context.

ART AND LITERATURE PROJECTS INTENDED FOR CHILDREN/TEENAGERS AND ADULTS: DESCRIPTION

Many of the nine art and literature projects discussed in this section show a diversity of both form and spirit that distinguishes them from more typical—and less imaginative—digital collaborations (see table 3.11). Particularly noteworthy in this regard is Art ConText, a joint effort of the Museum of Art of the Rhode Island School of Design (RISD) and the Providence Public Library, which invited 11 artists to spend two- to three-month residencies based in Providence libraries working "on an art project in collaboration with a...community connected to...[a] library branch" and to exhibit the completed work at RISD or their chosen branch location.[179] Substantial emphasis was placed on giving 20 to 60 people—many of whom were RISD students—"an active role in the creation of [each] new work and its presentation in both the Museum and the public library system throughout the state." All residencies included one or more art workshops at branch libraries (held by either the visiting artist or the individuals who worked with the artist on his or her specific project), discussion groups at senior citizen centers, and family activity days at the installation site.[180] As part of the first residency, the library's bookmobile was converted into an Art and Text Mobile dubbed "Wheels of Wonder," which became not only the project's most visible icon, but also a reading and art activity center. Consider the following features of the bus, many of which were developed in conjunction with the John Hope Settlement House and Hasbro Children's Hospital:

> Along the driver's side of the bus is a slide projector peep hole. The artwork of bus visitors can be projected in the hole for viewing. The passenger side of the bus has a roll-down curtain that, when dropped, forms a booth for showing and taping videos. A giant wing...folds out from the bus. It represents the dream of flight and other dreams children have for the future. Two giant hands reach out from the back of the bus. Between them is a carnival-inspired wheel. Participants spin the wheel to get themes for books they create and illustrate.[181]

Other residencies were just as innovative. For example, Ernesto Pujol's installation *Memory of Surfaces*, developed with the help of high school students, consisted of items borrowed from "the reading rooms, attics, and basements" of various branches of the Providence library system, thus allowing Pujol to make a statement about the evolution of libraries from "sensual, poetic, formal environments" that "engaged all our senses" to places that, clothed in the new esthetic of the information revolution, are struggling to become "more organic through better industrial design."[182] Lynne Yamamoto fashioned a room called *This, and my Heart* that used "objects that are physical touchstones for passages in historical diaries from the collections of the Rhode Island Historical Society and Brown University's John Hay Library" and contemporary journals kept by female high school students.[183] Indira Freitas Johnson created *Freenotfree*, an installation based on Indian women's folk-art traditions that attempted to define the concept of *free* by contrasting "free offers" made to consumers with "the countless acts of love, kindness, and support that are freely given and freely taken." Giving pride of place to stories collected from, among others, literacy-center participants, library patrons, and clients of an African American–owned restaurant called Miss Fannie's Soul Food Kitchen, Johnson wove a tapestry of "stories

Table 3.11
IMLS Library-Museum Collaborative Art and Literature Projects Intended for Children/Teenagers and Adults (1998–2003)

Year	Title of Project	Selected Major Applicants	Grant Amount ($)
1998	Weaving a Tale of Craft	Public Library of Charlotte and Mecklenburg County (North Carolina); Mint Museum of Art (Charlotte)	309,484
1998	Art ConText	Museum of Art, Rhode Island School of Design (Providence); Providence Public Library	325,513
1998	Southwest Research Center of New Mexico	Kit Carson Historic Museums (Taos, New Mexico); Zimmerman Library at the University of New Mexico (Albuquerque)	103,833
1998	Library for Early Childhood Initiative	Children's Museum of Houston; Houston Public Library System	194,000
1998	Image Database Community Project	University Library of Indiana University–Purdue University–at Indianapolis (IUPUI); Indianapolis Museum of Art	290,000
1999	Education in Southern Maryland	Jefferson Patterson Park and Museum (St. Leonard, Maryland); Banneker-Douglass Museum (Annapolis, Maryland)	173,441
2002	On with the Show	Cornell University Library (Ithaca, New York); Museum of the City of New York; San Francisco Performing Arts Library and Museum	471,724
2003	Para los Niños—For the Children	Children's Museum of Houston; Houston Public Library System	249,844
2003	Cultural Connections	Public Library of Charlotte and Mecklenburg County; Mint Museum of Art (Charlotte)	161,970

about the people who had made a difference in their lives . . . and small daily actions that added up to a vast accumulation of love."[184] Of course, the list of artists and their unique artworks could go on—David McGee, for example, replaced nine paintings in the RISD Museum of Art's permanent collection with portraits of people "he met during his residency at the Olneyville branch," thus giving them the chance "to see themselves as part of a global history"[185]—but one common thread remained: each installation project was meant to convey that the library is not only a significant locus of "educational programs focusing on the process of creativity," but also a "living, evolving [site] of public discourse" in which all can participate.

Exhibits and community involvement were also the hallmarks of Education in Southern Maryland: From Segregation to Integration, an initiative of the Jefferson Patterson Park and Museum in St. Leonard, Maryland, and the Charles County Community College (CCCC) Library.[186] An outgrowth of "extensive interviews . . . document[ing] the experience of educators at African-American public schools, 1865–1965" and grounded in a philosophical approach that ensured that multicultural voices "reflective of the community's interest" would not be drowned out by the "authoritative voice" of cultural institutions, the project created a traveling modular exhibit that included "a partial reproduction of a one-room school house typical of Southern Maryland up until the 1940s," a wood stove, student desks, a water bucket, and slates. Visitors not only met "retired school teachers and administrators [serving as docents] and learned [about]…the complexities and demands of public education in a one-room school house"—for instance, how "nearly depleted materials" and textbooks that had outlived their usefulness were "handed down from white schools to black schools"—but they could also "browse through a range of stories and storytellers" on touch-screen computers in an adjacent area. Interactive CDs containing educational curricula and a Web site (mounted by the CCCC library) "extend[ing] the interpretive themes" of the physical exhibit facilitated wide dissemination of the project throughout area schools and libraries.

Drawing ideas from the integration of library and museum services at the Children's Museum of Indianapolis, the Children's Museum of Houston (CMH) developed two projects. The first, in 1998, was the Library for Early Childhood Initiative.[187] Five years later, CMH built on its initial success with Para los Niños—For the Children, a program designed for the rapidly growing population of monolingual Spanish-speaking parents in Houston that was later expanded to libraries and museums in Las Vegas, Nevada, and St. Paul, Minnesota.[188] As a result of CMH's efforts, a small Parent Resource Library (PRL)— located near the entrance and gift shop—was placed in the museum.[189] Viewed as an integral component of CMH's overall commitment to early childhood development, care giving, parenting, and family learning, PRL became the physical manifestation of the broadly based Tot*Spot Redevelopment Project, whose goal, in partnership with area hospitals, was to provide information about "recent understandings about the learning and developmental needs of children and how these needs can best be provided in the home, through child care settings, in school activities, and through other informal learning activities and environments." Described as a "resource niche" with an innovative shelving arrangement (adult books at eye level for adults and children's books at eye level for children), PRL quickly gained a reputation for offering parents an accessible and joyous place to learn about both practical and theoretical aspects of early childhood development through a wealth of "book, video, article, lecture, exhibit, Internet, and workshop resources" while their children read books and played in the same physical area. While PRL did contain Spanish-language materials, the Para los Niños project made PRL a truly welcoming bilingual space by developing a suite of lectures, discussion groups, hands-on workshops, and written guides that "recogniz[ed] and support[ed] the cultural and intercultural variations in parenting that are unique to the Latino community."

A project to establish the Southwest Research Center of New Mexico (SRCNM) had many parallels with the creation of PRL within the Children's Museum of Houston.[190] Put forward by the Kit Carson Historic Museums, the plan amalgamated approximately 8,000 publications and original manuscripts about the history, archaeology, art, and literature of the Southwest from three area museums into a research center housed within the Harwood Museum of Art in Taos. After this initial phase, the partner museums hoped to expand both the intellectual and physical ambit of SRCNM through the addition of "historic photographs, study slides, vertical files and periodical collections." Because the Harwood Museum has an extensive collection of paintings, drawings, prints, sculpture, and photography—including nineteenth-century religious paintings on wood, wood sculptures, and twentieth-century works by such influential Taos-associated artists as Victor Higgins, Oscar Berninghaus, Larry Bell, Bea Mandelman, and Agnes Martin—the placement of SRCNM in the museum opened up tantalizing possibilities with regard to the interplay of textual study and visual display.

As in previous sections, digital library-museum collaborations were an inescapable part of the landscape. In partnership with the Indianapolis Museum of Art, the library system of Indiana University–Purdue University at Indianapolis, under the auspices of the Image Database Community Project, provided cultural heritage resources—for example, digitized versions of the works of such well-known Hoosier artists as William Forsyth, Maxine Lain, and Cecil Head; Indiana Post Office murals created as part of the Works Progress Administration; the AMICO Library; CORBIS Images; and the *Grove Dictionary of Art*—and "instructional strategies for educational activities"[191] to K–12 schools, colleges, and universities.[192] Somewhat similar was On with the Show: Access to the World's Performing Arts Through Museums and Libraries, a far-reaching collaboration among members of the Global Performing Arts Consortium (GloPAC), including Cornell University Libraries, the San Francisco Performing Arts Library and Museum, the St. Petersburg State Museum of Theatre and Music, and the Gertrude Stein Repertory Theatre.[193] Starting from the premise that existing metadata standards "fail to provide a satisfactory framework for describing performance [which] is a complex event that often has multiple creators and participants," GloPAC members implemented a 5,000-image performing arts database along with a prototype metadata structure to capture "the ephemeral nature" of their subject matter. Thus, a student or amateur director of a community center production who wants to research, for example, George Bernard Shaw's *Arms and the Man,* could search the GloPAC database "and find images from many different productions, including pictures of performances, costumes, and set designs, as well as play scripts and promptbooks." Or a painting of a scene from a production of Shakespeare's *A Midsummer Night's Dream* that features the character Bottom might be important for what it reveals about Bottom's "costume, his posture and gestures, and the depiction of the performance space he occupies." As the GloPAC database became more sophisticated by adding "virtual tours of theatres [and] 3D models," it evolved into an indispensable resource with which researchers could perform cross-cultural studies about the characteristics of different national theatrical, music, and dance traditions, with which educators could easily integrate performing arts modules into humanities and social science classes, and with which practitioners could find "inspiration and practical information for creating new works of art."

Two projects—Weaving a Tale of Craft[194] and Cultural Connections[195]—drew upon the combined resources of the Public Library of Charlotte and Mecklenburg County, the Mint Museum of Art (MMA), and the Mint Museum of Craft and Design (MMCD). In Weaving, an extensive interactive Web site was created about the rich heritage of North Carolina arts and crafts. Making use of approximately 1,200 digital images from the MMA collection, as well as audio and video clips of craftspeople discussing North Carolina crafts history, crafts techniques, and their own work, the Web site aimed to develop and expand a "base of knowledge" about ceramic and fiber arts by allowing visitors to "[play] around in online studios."[196] In the ceramics module, visitors could "become a virtual artist and throw a pot, then glaze and fire it," or, if they so chose, they could learn about the history of ceramics, view artists at work, have "opportunities for real-time conversations with artists and/or demonstrations," and be provided with a list of additional print resources. In the fibers module, visitors "explore[d] stories found in quilts…, or create[d] their own virtual quilt block which may be added to a large virtual quilt gradually composed by users of the site"; they could also see presentations about the way in which various fabrics are transformed into consumer goods. Recognizing that "to truly explore art and the creative process children must become physically involved in making art themselves," the project also included hands-on opportunities through four family day events, during which children and families could visit with artists, listen to storytellers, and spend time making various crafts. One of these four days was to be held in the context of the Charlotte library's week-long Festival of Reading that features "authors, illustrators, and storytellers in more than 100 programs for children and adults."

From one perspective, the purpose of Cultural Connections was to extend and amplify the interest in arts and crafts developed by Weaving. In conjunction with relevant full-scale exhibits at both MMA and MMCD—for example, The Artful Teapot: 20th Century Expressions from the Kamm Collection, or Woven Worlds: Basketry from the Clark Field Collection—Cultural Connections developed a Web portal, which was available at kiosks throughout the museums and also accessible from the Web site of the Charlotte library, containing exhibit-related information about specific artists and genres and book lists for children, teens, and adults about themes and topics pertinent to each exhibit. In addition, a series of public programs—art workshops at library branches and literacy classes and storytelling at museums—was instituted in an attempt to cross-pollinate venues with nontraditional activities.

ART AND LITERATURE PROJECTS INTENDED FOR CHILDREN/TEENAGERS AND ADULTS: ANALYSIS

Although it may seem overly pedantic to criticize collaborations that, when all is said and done, are eminently worthy in one or two of their individual aspects, it is instructive, from a conceptual standpoint, to compare Art ConText with Weaving a Tale of Craft to catch a glimpse of two very different ideas—undergirded by different philosophical bases—about the way in which libraries and museums could work together. The first thing to notice about Art ConText is that the artist's residency took place over a prolonged period of time: the artists conducted research at libraries, spoke extensively to library patrons, and created large-scale artworks with the concrete help of the entire local library community over the course of two or three months. And since artists typically displayed their artworks at branch libraries, these libraries metaphorically became museums—museums that contained art that was at once a reflection of the live library community and a point of departure for new explorations about topics and ideas generated by the art. Art could be illuminated by, and enter into new conversations with, library resources. Recall how Pujol scoured the built environment of libraries for materials that would be included in his installation; how Yamamoto delved into the intellectual legacy of libraries for materials that would become central to her installation; and how Johnson gathered stories from library patrons—stories that would be the central thematic axis of her installation. Recall, too, how library and art museum literally merged in the "Wheels of Wonder" bookmobile and how McGee's decision to replace existing portraits on the walls of the RISD art museum with the portraits of individuals that he and RISD students met either at the Olneyville branch library or within a two-block radius of it could be construed as a statement about the necessity to import the social and cultural world of the library into the museum—or the museum into the library. Indeed, McGee was agnostic about whether the library should move to the museum, or vice versa.

As part of his residency, McGee worked with 18 RISD students, each of whom created a photographic portrait. Before he installed nine of the portraits at the RISD museum, all 18 portraits were placed in the front windows of the Olneyville library and were backlit. In addition, the students created artworks in their preferred media "in response to the people they met," and these works too were displayed in the branch. As with many Art ConText projects, McGee's work was therefore an inspired vision of a new type of cultural institution blending the best of libraries and museums. As he observes, "the Library show informs the Museum's installation, and the Museum is part of the Library exhibition. It is all one big gig."[197] Equally important was the notion of physicality—the fact that artists, students, and other community members created their artworks through face-to-face and long-term interaction, conversation, and proximity. In a sense, the finished installation was an artwork created by the entire community, and its placement within the walls of a small branch library signified the extent to which that library is the sum of its cultural and social milieu. The community not only physically enters the doors of the library, but it does so artistically as well, contributing intellectual capital through art of its own making so that, in the end, the library is inexorably transformed into a new type of entity.

Contrast this with Weaving, in which, although the project developers ostensibly recognized that a true exploration of art only occurs through the physical act of making art, they allot only four days for such creation, devoting the majority of the project to digital interaction on a Web site. To be sure, one of the days designated for physically making art and meeting artists was within the parameters of the library's Festival of Reading, but there is never the sense that this day—or any of the three other days—are anything but ephemeral adjuncts to the Weaving Web site. The gaining of knowledge here is not understood as a long-term process requiring considered attention to nuance, detail, and background as it is in Art ConText. Rather, it is positioned as a piece of entertainment, one among the many available at the festival. And while the Web site certainly provides visitors with snippets of interesting information about North Carolina crafts, it does not immerse them into a world of creation in quite the same way that Art ConText immersed its participants in an act of artistic creation that was made all the more meaningful and significant because it had recourse to numerous gathered texts (e.g., oral histories and published works) over a prolonged period of time. Indeed, the atypical capitalization of the project's title invokes the Italian word con—"with" in English—thereby suggesting that art must necessarily be linked with text in a new amalgam. By extension—and given the fact that art (traditionally associated with museums) was created and displayed in libraries—the project also suggests that museums must necessarily be linked with libraries in a similarly new amalgam. Read in a more traditional manner, the title also suggests that art must be seen in context—perhaps the type of context provided by a library milieu that was the basis for the creation of the art in the first place.

In other words, while the Weaving Web site had many of the characteristics of an edutainment resource—short video clips, short audio clips, virtual demonstrations—whose lessons would likely be forgotten because they were not grounded in lived experience, Art ConText took the more difficult path of lovingly elaborating the principle that libraries and museums are, both physically and spiritually, "one big gig" that should no longer be seen as separate institutions because all aspects of human endeavor demand the type of context that only art con text provides. Certainly, Weaving could be a step in the right direction. But, just as the creation of a Parent Resource Library (PRL) within the Children's Museum of Houston (CMH) is only a step in the right direction—after all, unlike Rex's Lending Center/InfoZone at the Children's Museum of Indianapolis, there is very little integration of the functions of PRL with CMH—so Weaving, on its own, must ultimately be seen as a flawed instantiation of a library-museum partnership that failed to appreciate the extent to which the gaining of context—indispensable for knowledge—demands the possibility of juxtaposing, and being physically in the presence of, a wide array of art and text-based resources.

SCIENCE AND ENVIRONMENT PROJECTS INTENDED FOR CHILDREN/TEENAGERS AND ADULTS: DESCRIPTION

Some of the six science and environment projects (see table 3.12) have what by now are familiar forms. This is especially the case with ABC's of Science[198] and Satellite Science.[199] ABC's of Science, a partnership between the Museum of Science and Industry (MOSI), its science library, and the Tampa Public Library (TPL) system, conducted a series of "outreach training workshop sessions for teachers, teacher's aides, and parents/significant adults" in Tampa-area Head Start centers so that they could use science to spur learning in young children. Librarians from both MOSI and TPL created curriculum packets, each of which included background material on a chosen topic, suggestions for games and activities "requiring supplies of limited complexity that can be done in the classroom or at home," a list of related children's books, and conversational ideas. MOSI also brought its bookmobile to each workshop session, thus encouraging the use of resources (e.g., reference books, CDs, fiction books with scientific themes) beyond those contained in the curriculum packet. As parents and teachers were presented with new ideas and concepts to stimulate early childhood learning, any accompanying children were cared for by members of the MOSI YES! team (Youth Enriched by Science: "a tiered mentoring and employment program for at-risk teens"), who, while engaging them in reading and storytelling activities, served as "model[s] [of] positive behavior for the children."

Although targeted, for the most part, to middle school and high school students and their families, Satellite Science, a collaboration between Arizona Science Center (ASC) and the Phoenix Public Library, was remarkably similar to the MOSI project and, in other ways, echoed the North Carolina Museum of Life and Science's Library Youth Partnership discussed in a previous section. Supplementing "the efforts of existing library programming by focusing on science liter-

Table 3.12

IMLS Library-Museum Collaborative Science and Environment Projects Intended for Children/Teenagers and Adults (1998–2003)

Year	Title of Project	Selected Major Applicants	Grant Amount ($)
1999	Partners in Extended Learning for the Mars Millennium and Beyond	Triton College Library (River Grove, Illinois); Cernan Earth and Space Center Planetarium/Museum (River Grove)	107,835
2000	ABC's of Science	Museum of Science and Industry (Tampa, Florida); Tampa-Hillsborough County Public Library System	202,418
2000	Satellite Science	Arizona Science Center (Phoenix); Phoenix Public Library	384,200
2002	Desert Connections	Tucson Botanical Gardens (Arizona); Tucson-Pima Public Library	220,536
2003	Keeping Oregon Memories Alive	University of Oregon Museum of Natural History (Eugene); University of Oregon Libraries	240,894
2003	Ephemeral Cities	University of Florida Libraries (Gainesville)	184,609

acy activities among participants with otherwise limited access to high-quality science enrichment activities," Satellite Science trained inner-city high school students—guided by adult mentors—to present hands-on science workshops to middle school students and their families at local libraries. While high school students selected the presentation topics, staff at ASC designed the workshops and, working with area librarians, developed supplementary science resource collections, bibliographies, activity sheets, take-home kits, and a Web site—all of which served as an extension of and follow-up to the workshop sessions.[200]

Part of a White House Millennium Council youth initiative called The Mars Millennium Project launched in 2000, the Mars Millennium Project and Beyond of Triton College Library and the Cernan Earth and Space Center Planetarium/Museum allowed 50 academically disadvantaged K–12 students and 25 adults to use the online and print resources of both partner institutions "to research topics to aid them in designing a new community on Mars that is scientifically sound and offers a high quality of life and in which the developers would be proud to live."[201] Participants were given instruction about researching topics in libraries and museums, visited relevant institutions to gather materials, kept journals and portfolios of their work, and videoconferenced with Cernan scientists and other experts about topics related to space exploration—all the while developing "problem solving and decision making skills" that were reinforced by a series of career and adult re-entry workshops. As a capstone of their efforts, they presented the final version of their Mars project to the Triton College and Cernan Earth and Space Center communities through cable TV programs.

While the three projects so far mentioned in this section relied heavily on formal, in-person instructional elements, the three other science and environment projects—although educational in nature—relied on a less didactic approach. Consider, for example, Desert Connections, a project drawing on the resources of the Tucson Botanical Gardens and Tucson-Pima Public Library.[202] Realizing that the explosive population growth in the Tucson metroplex likely could not be stopped, that "many of the newer neighborhoods are close to natural areas," and that "many new residents lack knowledge of and appreciation for the delicate relationships between plants and wildlife in the desert" because they bring with them gardening preferences and habits (from less arid regions) that "lead to horticultural failure and subsequent reduction of wildlife in the garden," Desert Connections produced a wide range of print and online resources "to effect positive change in how...residents view and create their landscapes and gardens." The centerpiece of the project was an illustrated and interactive digital database—available from the Web sites of both institutions—containing detailed information about the interconnections among wildflowers, butterflies, and birds. Users could easily find, for example, names of "spring blooming perennials that attract goldfinches like desert marigold or flowering vines that...attract hummingbirds like cape honeysuckle, or a drought tolerant hardy shrub that attracts butterflies." In addition to developing a 16-page *Backyard Nature and Gardening Guide*, coloring books and downloadable coloring pages, and annotated bibliographies, project partners also conducted classes and demonstrations about selected natural history subjects, trained docents to deliver lectures about such topics as desert ecology and ethnobotany to the general public, held story times, organized conservation conferences and symposia, and created "Welcome to the Desert" informational sheets about environmental and ecosystem issues for local realtors to pass on to home buyers. In combination, these efforts articulated "a grassroots conservation message" that not only promoted awareness of the "nature-gardening connection," but also helped "to compensate for lost habitat and wild areas."[203]

Keeping Oregon Memories Alive for 21st Century Learners, an undertaking spearheaded by the University of Oregon Museum of Natural History, preserved the work of Don Hunter, a legendary Oregon photographer and audio archivist who, in the 1950s and 1960s, "recorded and collected sounds, matched the sounds to his photography," and developed an array of multimedia shows using "slide screens closely cued to music and [his] narrative" on such topics as "anthropological discoveries ('The Sandal and the Cave'), volcanic activity ('Mt. St. Helens and the Volcanic Cascades'), and the steam engines of the Northwest ('The Last of Steam')."[204] As Hunter toured the shows throughout the Pacific Northwest, he gained a large and enthusiastic following, not the least because his archives contained invaluable and unique photographs about Oregon's natural history and anthropology. As Hunter grew older, he could no longer perform the shows in person, so Keeping Oregon Memories Alive digitized a selection of his presentations on DVDs; distributed the DVDs to schools, local groups, and community organizations throughout Oregon; supplemented them with Web-based curricular resources (i.e., "streaming versions of the presentations...and additional Hunter documentation including [a] documentary,...audio interviews, and biographical materials"); and created a Don Hunter exhibit space at the museum and a stand-alone kiosk system in which digitized versions of the performances were accessible.

Reminiscent of the Flora and Fauna of the Great Lakes Region project in its use of geospatial data, Ephemeral Cities, a project initiated by the libraries of the University of Florida and involving public libraries and historical societies in Gainesville, Tampa, and Key West, developed digital city atlases with the aid of geographic information system (GIS) technology.[205] At the center of this project were nineteenth-century Sanborn maps—maps of streets and buildings drawn at one inch = 50 feet used by the insurance industry to assess risk—that, because of their rich structural details, are invaluable to architectural historians, urban planners and urban restoration specialists, economists, and historians for their glimpse into the "changing character of American cities." In an attempt to raise disturbingly low levels of geographic literacy and to engage children, teenagers, and adults to explore "the historic geographies of cities and compar[e] them to modern metropolitan areas," Ephemeral Cities georectified late nineteenth- and early twentieth-century Sanborn maps of Gainesville, Tampa, and Key West—two for each city—"to provide historic base layers"; referenced digitized images of historical objects and buildings to the maps; and then added "modern thematic layers of roads, county boundaries, [and] rivers" to form "comparative layers of modern city geographies." As users accessed the project Web site, they could manipulate layers to see, for example, how "prominent thoroughfares were renamed, redirected, relocated and/or obliterated and [how] major features such as foundries, grist mills, and stables were replaced by schools and hospitals." Adopting an approach similar to the Community Museum Project discussed previously, citizen involvement was an important element of Ephemeral Cities. Individuals were strongly encouraged by My Town events to bring photographs, postcards, brochures, and letters that could be digitized and added to the approximately 2,500 items—including city directories and newspapers drawn from the archives and special collections of participating libraries and museums—that constituted the historic layers of the atlas for each city. Well beyond the 15 educational modules that were one result of this project—10 geared toward mandated state of Florida instructional standards and 5 designed for the general public—Ephemeral Cities conveyed how "geography intersects with life," how cities "reflect the mosaic of cultural backgrounds of their inhabitants," and how "place identity" affects individual identity.

SCIENCE AND ENVIRONMENT PROJECTS INTENDED FOR CHILDREN/TEENAGERS AND ADULTS: ANALYSIS

As we look back at these six projects, it is evident that—as in previous sections—there is a continuum along which library-museum projects fall. On one end of this continuum there are collaborations—such as ABC's of Science and Mars Millennium Project and Beyond—that show very little integration of library and museum resources. The individuals who are envisioned as the intended audience for these projects attend workshops or training sessions at a museum or library or both, are informed about the resources available at each, and then go their separate ways. By analogy, after briefly—and contingently—coming together, the library and museum go their separate ways as well. To be sure, individuals have gained new information along the way—as have libraries and museums, and they likely will return to each separate institution on one or more occasions—just as libraries and museums will work together when another profitable opportunity presents itself. But, conceptually, these library-museum interactions remain tenuous, event driven, and, despite optimistic rhetoric about the formation of sustainable models and enduring professional relationships, operational only for the grant period.

In some projects, the end product is such that it seems it could have been generated without the help of libraries or museums and delivered anywhere. Consider these statements in the sustainability section of ABC's of Science: "Additional funding sources will be sought on the local, state and federal level to perpetuate the program at the close of this grant period." And if future grants are not forthcoming, "the workshop curriculum can continue to be useful in subsequent years [since] Head Start Education Managers and/or Social Workers…will share the information and the intent of the original workshops with parents in future years at Parent Night meetings."[206] Certainly, there is nothing wrong with social workers or Head Start personnel making use of the developed materials, but the real issue lies in the elision of libraries and museums from the equation. It is very much as if they are no longer necessary. And if that is the case, it is an open question whether, in this project, they were truly necessary in the first place. After all, the curriculum could have been developed by teachers or other professionals independently. And while Parent Night meetings could take place at libraries or museums, it is likely that they do not, thus eliminating libraries and museums—as central and indispensable content contributors and/or venues—to an even greater extent.

Much the same could be said of Triton College's Mars Millennium Project and Beyond. Recall that the project was part of the nationwide Mars Millennium Project (MMP) sponsored by, among others, the U.S. Department of Education, the National Endowment for the Arts, the National Aeronautics and Space Administration, and the White House Millennium Council. "Challenging students across America to imagine establishing a village for 100 transplanted earthlings on the planet Mars in the year 2030," MMP implemented "a national website [that] connects student teams of 'mission specialists' to a universe of resources that can help them develop new knowledge and skills." Students had access to "artists, scientists, engineers, architects—even astronauts—through on-line chats…and participation guides geared for use in classrooms from kindergarten through high school, libraries, museums, clubs and community centers, [were] downloadable from the website,"[207] all in the interest of exploring "the culture, history, and traditions of their communities, along with local artistic, cultural, scientific and social characteristics that might be exported to another planet."[208] In other words, while the resources of libraries and museums might be useful, they were not necessary because students could take part in MMP activities in classrooms, clubs, or community centers by means of the resources available from the MMP Web site. Libraries and museums were tangential players, and even if they did undertake some kind of partnership with MMP, that partnership was temporary: witness the nonfunctionality of the MMP link, which, although "once available from the White House Web Site," has not been maintained because it is now "an historical record and is no longer being updated."[209] Triton College's project replicated and extended MMP at a local level, but its focus was not so much on library-museum cooperation in support of MMP. Instead, the focus was on using MMP as a means to conduct remediation and career workshops for academically disadvantaged participants. There is nothing wrong with career workshops, of course, but as in ABC's of Science, the chief purpose of Triton College's project could just as easily have been accomplished by other social organizations. Libraries and museums may have contributed something to the project, but they were not central to the realization of project goals.

In the middle of the continuum are projects such as Satellite Science and Keeping Oregon Memories Alive. In addition to the activities already described, Satellite Science recognized the need to establish tangible links between the Phoenix Public Library (PPL) and the Arizona Science Center (ASC). Just as PPL established an affiliate branch library at the Phoenix Art Museum—thus creating, in theory, a juxtaposition of print and visual resources in a single location—so it worked toward a similar affiliate branch arrangement with ASC.[210] Keeping Oregon Memories Alive not only preserved the unique narrative presentations of a local photographer and audio archivist, but also added supplementary materials including documentaries, interviews, and biographical materials about Hunter. While the potential for these two projects is large, there are also numerous questions. Will the PPL branch library follow the model of Rex's Lending Center/InfoZone (RLC) in Indianapolis—a positive occurrence—or will it be more like the Parent Resource Library at the Children's Museum of Houston—a less positive occurrence? Recall that RLC integrated its gallery exhibits with regularly updated and a "representative, concentrated selection" of print materials that had been judged as being the best at "relating to the visions, concepts, goals and objectives of [that particular] galler[y]."[211] And while Keeping Oregon Memories Alive promised to include additional biographical information about Hunter himself, what will it do about the subjects, scenes, and personalities mentioned in his shows? Will there exist the possibility of discovering detailed print or online information about the subjects touched upon in Hunter's shows—subjects such as the growth of the city of Eugene or the role of steam engines in the Northwest? In short, both the Satellite Science and the Keeping Oregon Memories Alive projects have the opportunity to become examples of a new type of educational hybrid—one that recognizes that the healthy interplay of enticing visual, audio, and richly detailed textual resources is a sine qua non of knowledge acquisition.

On the opposite end of the continuum from ABC's of Science we find Desert Connections and Ephemeral Cities, both of which were concerted attempts to fashion a multidimensional learning experience in which the contributions of libraries and museums (or botanical gardens) were highly relevant and indispensable. In Ephemeral Cities, contemporary and historical maps—together with newspaper accounts and photographs, as well as the accumulated memories of, and objects collected by, community members—fashioned a living laboratory for the exploration of place and time. In Desert Connections, the combination of interactive educational Web pages describing the environmental issues pertinent to desert gardening, enhanced collections of gardening and natural history books at all library branches, trained docents, informational sheets and guidebooks, and an extensive series of discussion periods and lectures for children and adults created, in principle, the conditions for understanding the library and the botanical gardens as an extension of each other. Having identified a significant theme, desert environmentalism, both institutions set out to establish themselves as the focal point for anyone interested in this subject by intertwining themselves in such a way that they became—at least symbolically—a single institution.

CONCLUSION

As shown in table 3.13, 56.4 percent of all IMLS library-museum partnerships and collaborations are of an exclusively or primarily digital nature; 32.4

Table 3.13

Nature of Library-Museum Collaborative Projects by Subject Area (1998–2003)

Subject	Exclusively digital	Primarily digital with on-site components	Approximately equal digital and on-site components	Exclusively on-site	Primarily on-site with digital components
History (29)	19	4	1	3	2
Arts and Literature (23)	8	1	4	8	2
Science and Environment (19)	7	1	3	7	1
Total (71)	34 (47.9%)*	6 (8.5%)*	8 (11.3%)*	18 (25.4%)*	5 (7%)*

*Percentages do not add to 100 because of rounding.

percent are exclusively or primarily on-site; and 11.3 percent have approximately equal digital and on-site components. Digital partnerships are in the majority, although the number of on-site partnerships is not negligible. When the subject matter of the collaboration is taken into account, starker differences emerge. Of the 29 history projects, 23 are exclusively or primarily digital (79.3 percent), while only 39.1 percent of art and literature (9 out of 23) and 42.1 percent of science and environment (8 out of 19) projects are exclusively or primarily digital. When the intended audience of IMLS library-museum projects is taken into consideration, a similar differentiation emerges (see table 3.14). On the one hand, of the 28 projects intended for adults, 20 are exclusively or primarily digital (71.4 percent); on the other hand, only 46.5 percent of the projects in which children and teenagers are either exclusively or partially the intended audience (20 out of 43) are exclusively or primarily digital. One conclusion to be drawn from these data is that the subject matter forming the substrata of the collaboration—as well as its intended audience—affects the nature of the collaboration. If it is a library-museum partnership focused on history and intended for adults, it is more than likely that it will be a digitally based partnership. Conversely, if the library-museum partnership is oriented toward some aspect of the arts, literature, or science, there is a strong chance that on-site collaborations will be favored. One explanation for these divergences may be the different learning styles of intended audiences when faced with different subject matter.

Over and above such considerations, it is interesting to note that, in many of the library-museum partnerships discussed above, libraries were often confined to an ancillary role while museums supplied much, if not all, of the content-based materials that were the cornerstones of the respective projects. Beyond the Turns of the Centuries, Plant Evaluation Web Site, and Digital Dress were three such projects. Accordingly, it is not surprising that, in the 2003 reauthorization of the Museum and Library Services Act, museums were called "core providers of learning in conjunction with schools, families, and communi-

Table 3.14
Nature of Library-Museum Collaborative Projects by Audience Type (1998–2003)

Type of audience	Exclusively digital	Primarily digital with on-site components	Approximately equal digital and on-site components	Exclusively on-site	Primarily on-site with digital components
Children and Teenagers (17)	4	3	2	8	0
Adults (28)	18	2	1	5	2
Children, Teenagers, and Adults (26)	12	1	5	5	3
Total (71)	34 (47.9%)*	6 (8.5%)*	8 (11.3%)*	18 (25.4%)*	5 (7%)*

*Percentages do not add to 100 because of rounding.

ties," while libraries were, tellingly, not considered as core providers, but rather as delivery mechanisms that "facilitate access to resources...for the purpose of cultivating an educated and informed citizenry."

The downplaying—at least rhetorically—of the role of libraries as core providers of content and subject matter may be viewed as a marker of the shift from a print-based to a visual-based culture. Far-reaching and ubiquitous as a societal trend—though nonetheless poignant as a sign of the evolution of value systems across the generations—this shift, by now firmly ensconced as a reigning paradigm, is given dramatic immediacy in the relationship between text and objects in the Steven F. Udvar-Hazy Center, a cavernous building on the outskirts of Washington, D.C., that houses some 90 percent of the Smithsonian's National Air and Space Museum aviation collections—"more than 200 aircraft and 135 space artifacts."[212] Opened in late 2003, the center was the focus of controversy from the very beginning as antinuclear activists—including six Japanese survivors of the Hiroshima bombing—protested the way in which the Enola Gay, the B-29 that carried the first atomic bomb dropped on Japan, was described. More precisely, they were protesting what was *not* said in the description, which called the Enola Gay "the most sophisticated propeller-driven bomber of World War II" and noted that "it dropped the bomb but tells little more." In other words, they were protesting a lack of historical context.

The contention—vociferously articulated by protestors—that the display of the Enola Gay "builds cultural and political forces in this country for the use of nuclear weapons again" may or may not be accurate, but what was especially intriguing in this incident are some of the comments of General John R. Dailey, a retired marine pilot and director of the Air and Space Museum. Speaking about the overall mandate of the museum and the dearth of textual information alongside individual exhibits, he observed that the purpose of his institution was "to stimulate interest in technology and science [and that] 'the political aspects are more difficult to cover in three paragraphs.'" Indeed, while the museum is praised as offering "a vicarious pleasure to visitors, who can contemplate flying the craft on display," the plaque adjacent to the Enola Gay has only "14 lines of text, similar in length to the descriptions of other historic craft." Any opportunity to gain contextual information that might illuminate the social and cultural issues represented by the Enola Gay—or any other aircraft on display—is lost as the sweep of history is reduced to self-referential comments such as those of Alison Tokar, who, on viewing the tiny and claustrophobic *Gemini VII* capsule in which Frank Borman and James A. Lovell were sent aloft "to demonstrate that astronauts could endure in space long enough to get to the moon and back" observed, "I can't spend an hour in the car....And they eat like, toothpaste, right?"

As museums are enshrined as "core providers of learning," the real question should be about the nature of the learning that takes place at museums. To judge by the above example, the museum can be viewed as a synecdoche of the shift to a visual-based culture—a culture in which historical and social context is reduced to 14 lines of text and in which edutainment seems to be the order of the day. The library—as the traditional central locus of rich, contextualizing information—is all but absent. Just as children, teenagers, and adults stroll among the 300 or so air and space artifacts in the Udvar-Hazy Center marveling at the assembled planes and being exposed to fragmentary information about each one, so also do many digitally based library-museum partnerships offer the same type of visually rich and context-poor experience as online visitors click through a vast array of images that, to be sure, offer stimulation, but, for the most part, offer very little chance to reach a meaningful understanding about the myriad tangled issues lying behind those images. As individuals click through images—lingering at the ones that interest them the most, quickly passing by the ones that hold no interest—what has happened, from a structural perspective, is very much akin to what has happened to the multitrack album as single-song downloads threaten to eradicate "the very concept of songs integrated into a whole."[213] Certainly, music lovers feel empowered since they can now "make" their own albums to suit their individual tastes, but the ability to cherry-pick songs has created a culture of disposability in which often crucial information—in the form of other tracks on an album—about the meaning of the cherry-picked single is missing. As they move from cherry-picked song to cherry-picked song, they resemble visitors to those digital library-museum partnerships that, in the cascade of digitized objects and artifacts unfurling before the eyes of online visitors, offer only 14 lines of text by way of background explanation for each image. In other words, they are edutained, not informed. Each online visitor can certainly pick and choose to view only those objects that interest him or her, but the level of detailed knowledge about any subject that can result from that kind of learning experience may not be as much as could be hoped.

Still, the argument could be made that "three minutes of good music is better than 30 minutes of drivel," and because "each generation gets the music it deserves," it may well be the case that "three good minutes is about all anyone really wants...in the mad pace of the 21st century."[214] In much the same way as a culture of single-song downloads (a culture that excises valuable supplementary background information in its quest for self-referential empowerment) is well on its way to being established, a culture that privileges the visual edutainment-type stimulation of (digital or on-site) museums—"core providers of learning"—without providing significant intellectual space to a range of text-based documents (the preserve of libraries and archives) may also be looming. Of course, we have seen examples in this chapter of a deep awareness, on the part of IMLS library-museum partnerships, of the necessity to make full and complete use of the resources of both libraries and museums in their collaborative efforts. We have only to think of Rex's Lending Center/InfoZone, Brooklyn Expedition, or the Sargent Murals Restoration Project. These projects—and others like them—are admirable in their scope and philosophical underpinnings. At the same time, it is also true that an increasing number of IMLS-sponsored projects both intellectually and concretely bypass libraries completely. In this respect, the establishment of the Museums in the Community program in 2003 by IMLS can be viewed as a two-edged sword. To be sure, the six inaugural projects funded in this program's first year of operation were eminently worthy in and of themselves (see table 3.15). But, in reading the successful grant applications for these projects, one is struck by the fact that museums alone often provide the type of contribution that was provided by libraries in the library-museum partnerships discussed extensively in previous sections of this chapter. That is to say, libraries and their rich, text-based contextualizing resources are—metaphorically at least—deemed superfluous in these projects.

Table 3.15
IMLS Museum-Community Collaborative Projects (2003)

Year	Title of Project	Selected Major Applicants	Grant Amount ($)
2003	Making Connections for School Readiness	Boston Children's Museum; Countdown to Kindergarten (Boston)	499,840
2003	La Primera Ciencia	Chicago Botanic Garden; Gads Hill Center (Chicago)	222,988
2003	From the Source to the Sea	Florida Aquarium (Tampa Bay); Lowry Park Zoological Society of Tampa	121,022
2003	Proyecto Futuro Bilingual Partnership	New Mexico Museum of Natural History and Science (Albuquerque); Albuquerque Public Schools	249,923
2003	Re-presenting Race in the Digital Age	New Museum of Contemporary Art (New York); Heritage School (New York)	94,398
2003	ArtREACH	Young at Art of Broward (Florida); School Board of Broward County, Florida	185,902

Consider Re-presenting Race in the Digital Age, a collaboration between the New Museum of Contemporary Art (NMCA) and two high schools.[215] Here, NMCA pledged to provide humanities teachers with "visual and media literacy guidelines, curriculum frameworks, distillations of current race theory, and an image-bank of photographic and media-based images depicting race" so that the teachers could "skillfully incorporate the discussion of race into their humanities instruction." Or La Primera Ciencia: An Urban Environmental Science Camp, a partnership between the Chicago Botanic Garden and Gads Hill Center, a non-profit family resource center serving the Mexican American community, which allows middle school students "to explore environmental science and ecology topics with the Garden as their outdoor classroom."[216] The other four projects in the Museums in the Community program are similar: Proyecto Futuro Bilingual Partnership pairs the New Mexico Museum of Natural History and Science with Albuquerque public schools to engage parents and children in "bilingual math and science activities through family nights and…take-home kits";[217] From the Source to the Sea combines the forces of the Florida Aquarium, the Lowry Park Zoological Society, and Nature's Classroom to develop a wide-ranging home-school science curriculum "with an emphasis on marine science and zoology in the context of the Hillsborough River Watershed";[218] Making Connections for School Readiness commits the Boston Children's Museum "to build on Museum work, resources, and relationships to advance school readiness by creating unique opportunities for parents, kindergarten teachers, preschool educators, and children to work together";[219] and the Young at Art Children's Museum in Davie, Florida, pledged, through its ArtREACH project, to develop an "after school art and homework assistance center inside Providence Place, a homeless family transitional shelter for abused women and children."[220]

We want to stress that each of these six projects is, to say the least, a valuable undertaking that will benefit, to a great degree, its intended audience. But it is also true that libraries are conspicuous by their absence from these projects; museums take a lead role. And if we associate museums with visual culture—and libraries with text-based culture—then the absence of libraries from these projects is revealing. To be sure, the target audiences in the six Museum in the Community projects are mostly children and teenagers, so it may be more stimulating to partake in museum-based activities as opposed to library-based activities. But, as we look back over the 71 library-museum partnerships discussed in this chapter, the parameters of an edutainment culture centered on experiencing a vast array of museum objects—with only minimal opportunities (e.g., 14 lines of text) to contextualize and juxtapose the visual with textual documents—are very much apparent and becoming increasingly entrenched.

From the perspective of George Ritzer, the fact that museums are assuming library and other social functions would not be surprising. It is, after all, another example of the dedifferentiation of consumption: the same type of experience can be had at any undifferentiated location. As both libraries and museums gradually evolve into infotainment and edutainment centers, it nonetheless seems clear that museums are doing a more compelling job of entertainment. It is as if libraries—in their role as community providers of diverse and extensive sources of knowledge and information—can be taken out of the equation altogether. It could thus be argued that, because many libraries have abdicated their core purpose by trying to become edutainment centers, it is only fair that they are no longer seen as "core providers of learning." In this regard, the residents of Contra Costa, California—who, as we saw in chapter 2, rejected a tax increase to raise revenue for libraries because they did not think it was right that public money should be spent on an institution that had become an entertainment center—were, unlike their local librarians, very much aware of the difference between an edutainment-based social center masquerading as a library and a library with extensive collections of materials having the capacity to provide far-reaching interpretive detail about social, historical, and cultural phenomena.

NOTES

1. The law was first enacted on 30 September 1996. Revisions to the statute were made by the Museum and Library Services Technical and Conforming Amendments of 1997, Public Law 105–128, which was enacted on 1 December 1997. See especially sec. 203 and sec. 214 (2) of *The Museum and Library Services Act of 1996*. See also United States Code at 20 U.S.C. 9101.

2. Institute of Museum and Library Services (IMLS). *2003 National Leadership Grants for Libraries and Museums*, http://www.imls.gov (accessed June 15, 2003).

3. *The Museum and Library Services Act of 1996*, sec. 271.

4. IMLS. *2003 National Leadership Grants for Libraries and Museums*, http://www.imls.gov (accessed June 15, 2003).

5. *The Museum and Library Services Act of 1996*, sec. 212 (1) and 212 (5).

6. The Museum and Library Services Act was reauthorized in 2003. The reauthorization was passed in the House of Representatives (HR 13) by a vote of 416–2 on 6 March 2003. Two different versions of the reauthorization were introduced in the Senate by Senator Jack Reed (D-Rhode Island) and Senator Judd Gregg (R-New Hampshire). According to a press release on the IMLS Web site documenting the history of the reauthorization, the "Senate Committee on Health, Education, Labor and Pensions and the House Committee on Education and the Workforce reached a consensus measure that was unanimously approved by the Senate on August 1, 2003." The House of Representatives then passed the consensus measure on 16 September 2003, and it was signed into law by President George W. Bush on 25 September 2003. In addition, President Bush requested a total of $242,024,000 for the Institute of Museum and Library Services in Fiscal Year 2004, a 15 percent increase over Fiscal Year 2003. Of this total, $8,700,000 was requested for the National Leadership Grants program, which includes grants for museum and library partnerships.

7. Ibid., sec. 2.2 and 2.6.

8. *The Museum and Library Services Act of 1996*, sec. 262 (a) and 262 (a) (4).

9. *The Museum and Library Services Act of 2003* (Enrolled as Agreed to or Passed by Both House and Senate); Title II—Library Services and Technology, sec. 201 (Purpose); Title III—Museum Services, sec. 271 (Purpose), HR 13, 108th Cong., 1st sess. This bill is now Public Law 108-81, http://thomas.loc.gov (accessed October 8, 2003).

10. Stephen E. Weil, "Transformed from a Cemetery of Bric-a-Brac...," in *Perspectives on Outcome Based Evaluation for Libraries and Museums* (Washington, DC: IMLS, 2000), 9.

11. Ibid. As explained by Weil, the notion of "positive accountability" comes from Peter Swords of the Columbia University Law School. Negative accountability refers to "making sure that nobody [is] doing anything wrong." Positive accountability refers to "making sure that government programs actually work to achieve their intended outcomes, making sure that federal money is not only being spent honestly but also that it is being spent effectively."

12. Ibid., 7. Weil discusses the work of Dees in this section.

13. Ibid. Weil draws on the work of Dees in this section.

14. Ibid.

15. Ibid., 9.

16. Ibid., 8–9. Weil quotes from a 1996 United Way handbook.

17. Ibid., 6.

18. Peggy D. Rudd, "Documenting the Difference: Demonstrating the Value of Libraries Through Outcome Measurement," in *Perspectives on Outcome Based Evaluation for Libraries and Museums* (Washington, D.C.: IMLS, 2000), 23, http://www.imls.gov (accessed June 15, 2003).

19. Weil, "Transformed from a Cemetery," 10.

20. Reed W. Larson, "Toward a Psychology of Positive Youth Development," *American Psychologist* 55 (January 2000): 170–83.

21. Quotes in this section are from IMLS, *2003 National Leadership Grants for Libraries and Museums,* sec. 2.10.

22. All quotations and statistics contained in this paragraph are drawn from IMLS, *True Needs True Partners: Museums Serving Schools: 2002 Survey Highlights* (Washington, DC: IMLS, 2003), 1–7, http://www.imls.gov (accessed June 15, 2003).

23. All information and quotations contained in this paragraph are drawn from IMLS, *True Needs True Partners: Museums Serving Schools: 2002 Survey Highlights* (Washington, DC: IMLS, 2003), 2–9, http://www.imls.gov (accessed June 15, 2003).

24. Ibid., 10–11.

25. IMLS. *Libraries and Museums Give Kids a Head Start,* par. 2, http://www.imls.gov/closer/archive/hlt_c0503.htm (accessed June 14, 2003).

26. Ibid., par. 5.

27. Ibid., par. 6, 8.

28. Ibid., par. 13.

29. The requests were made on 30 April 2003 and 23 September 2003. These requests were processed under the *Freedom of Information Act* (FOIA), 5 U.S.C. § 552. IMLS determined that "the requested documents are appropriate for release with the exception of that portion of the Face Sheet which pertains to the employer/federal tax identification number. This information is withheld pursuant to FOIA exemption 4,5 U.S.S. § (b) (4), which protects commercial or financial information that is privileged or confidential." Information contained in this footnote is based on a letter to the authors dated 5 June 2003 from Mamie Bittner, director of public and legislative affairs, IMLS. We would like to thank IMLS staff members, especially Mae Patten, for complying with our FOIA request in a professional, courteous, and prompt manner.

30. Grant applications have positive and negative features. On the negative side, they typically make far-reaching claims for their proposed projects in language that often becomes jargon ridden, smug, and empty. All projects are described as being innovative, unique, bold, and seminal, to list only a few of the self-laudatory terms used. On the positive side, grant applications capture the ideal vision of the project as conceived by each applicant. Because one of our purposes is to explore various manifestations of library-museum interactions and partnerships, we thought that an examination of various ideal visions of such interactions and partnerships would be germane.

31. Three institutions were contacted by e-mail. We would like to thank the director of the Leigh Yawkey Woodson Art Museum, Kathy Kelsey Foley, and Jane Hetrick of the Connor Prairie Living History Museum, coauthor of the Travels Across Time grant proposal, for sending print and CD-based information about their respective projects to us. Staff members from the Baytown Historical Museum indicated that they did not have any information to send.

32. In chronological order, these nine projects are (1) Selecting for Digitization: A Conference for Library and Museum Leaders (major applicants: Council on Library and Information Resources and the Chicago Historical Society; grant amount: $72,990; 1998 IMLS National Leadership Grants Application LL-80026; the applicants hosted a conference for representatives of museums, libraries, and archives "on content development in the digital environment" in which participants developed "a set of principles for selecting works to be disseminated in digital collections"); (2), (3), and (4) Five State American Indian Project and Preserving Our Language, Memory, and Lifeways (three grants, with major applicants: Arizona State Library, Archives and Public Records, Nevada State Library, Utah State Library, and the Museum of Indian Arts and Culture and Laboratory of Anthropology (New Mexico); grant amounts: $150,545, $317,897, and $248,819; 1998, 1999, and 2003 IMLS National Leadership Grants Applications LL-80062, LL-90079, and LG 30-03-0272; in order to "increase library and curatorial services to American Indian tribal communities," the applicants convened a series of conferences, workshops, and discussion groups to produce a "regional action plan to address the needs identified by tribes; establish a regional network among tribes and state library agencies; create a plan for ongoing education and information sharing and identify content for a web site about the project, based on the needs and preferences of tribes; encourage local collaborative projects and increase communication among tribal cultural organizations and state library agencies, museums, or archives"); (5) Preservation Training Initiative for Small Libraries and Museums in South Carolina (major applicants: Thomas Cooper Library at the University of South Carolina and the McKissick Museum; grant amount: $213,337; 2000 IMLS National Leadership Grants Application NL-00038; the applicants aimed "to help small local libraries, museums, and related organizations learn proper preservation and collection care techniques," including environmental control, disaster prevention, and recovery techniques); (6) Archival Basics Continuing Education (major applicants: American Association for State and Local History, Ohio Historical Society, Michigan Historical Center, and the New York State Archives; grant amount: $187,150; 2001 IMLS National Leadership Grants Application NL-10001; the applicants developed a "core curriculum for non-archivists in the basic principles and practices necessary to effectively manage archival records held by their institutions" and

delivered this curriculum in an online course and through on-site workshops); (7) The Basics and Beyond: Digitization Training Program for Illinois (major applicants: University of Illinois Libraries, Illinois Heritage Association, and the Illinois State Library; grant amount: $241,348; 2002 IMLS National Leadership Grants Application LG-30-02-0254; the applicants developed "a multi-track digitization training program for museums and libraries of all sizes throughout Illinois and neighboring states"); (8) The 21st Century Learner: The Continuum Begins with Early Learning (major applicants: Association of Children's Museums and the Association for Library Services to Children of the American Library Association; grant amount: $110,318; 2002 IMLS National Leadership Grants Application LG-30-02-0249; as a follow-up to an earlier conference, the applicants held another conference whose aim was "to position museums and libraries as integral players in the early learning community at the national and local levels" and to "model how community-wide partnerships can take advantage of cultural resources to offer early-learning programming"); and (9) NMC Museum/Library Collaboration in Online Authoring and Publishing (major applicants: New Media Consortium and the San Francisco Museum of Modern Art; grant amount: $499,500; 2003 IMLS National Leadership Grants Application LG-30-03-0214; the applicants created "a new, open source authoring environment based on *Pachyderm*, the multimedia online authoring and publishing tool" that can be used in conjunction with "current and emerging collections of digital materials found in libraries and museums" to increase the number of "pedagogical templates" allowing for the implementation of "new interactive experiences that can be delivered online, via kiosk, or CD-ROM in support of formal or informal learning"). All quotations in this footnote are taken from the abstracts of the nine relevant grant applications.

33. Many of these projects are interdisciplinary, so any categorization of the subject area of a specific project is open to dispute. Moreover, many of the projects have components that could appeal to all ages, from children in the early grades to senior citizens. However, we have made a good-faith effort to create mutually exclusive categories of the type presented in table 3.3.

34. These nine projects are Omaha Indian Cultural Artifacts and Images (see table 3.7); Cherokee Traveling Exhibits (see table 3.7); Sharing Culture (see table 3.7); Community Museum Project: A Library/Museum Cultural Collaboration (see table 3.7); New Voices from the Upper Midwest: Writing for a Change (see table 3.9); Images of the Indian Peoples of the Northern Great Plains (see table 3.10); and Five State American Indian Project and Preserving Our Language, Memory, and Lifeways (a series of three grants categorized among the nine training grants for professionals).

35. These four projects are Making Cultural Connections in Education (see table 3.4); Music of Social Change (see table 3.8); The Civil Rights Movement: 1950 to the Present (see table 3.10); and Education in Southern Maryland: From Segregation to Integration (see table 3.11).

36. These projects are Project Access (see table 3.8) and Para Los Niños—For the Children (see table 3.11).

37. These two projects are Image Archives Digitization and Access (see table 3.7) and Connections: Linking Educational Institutions, Libraries and Museums Through Technology (see table 3.10).

38. Unless otherwise indicated, all information about and quotations describing the Birmingham Cultural Alliance Partnership project entitled "Making Cultural Connections in Education" are drawn from its 2000 IMLS National Leadership Grants Application (NL-00055), narrative, 1–10.

39. Birmingham Civil Rights Institute, "The Richard Arrington Jr. Resource Gallery," par. 2, http://bcri.bham.al.us/multimedia.htm (accessed May 11, 2003).

40. Unless otherwise indicated, all information about and quotations describing the Memorial Hall Museum and Frontier Regional Union #38 School District project entitled "Beyond the Turns of the Centuries" are drawn from their 2000 IMLS National Leadership Grants Application (NL-00019), narrative, 1–10.

41. Memorial Hall Museum, "American Centuries: Views from New England," http://www.memorialhall.mass.edu/site_intro.html (accessed May 11, 2003).

42. Memorial Hall Museum, "American Centuries: Views from New England." http://www.memorialhall.mass.edu/collection/itempage.jsp?itemid=5868 (accessed May 11, 2003).

43. Unless otherwise indicated, all information about and quotations describing the Kansas State Historical Society project entitled "Territorial Kansas Online" are drawn from its 1999 IMLS National Leadership Grants Application (LL-90069), narrative, 1–10.

44. Unless otherwise indicated, all information about and quotations describing the Rochester Public Library project entitled "Rochester Images" are drawn from its 1999 IMLS National Leadership Grants Application (LL-90067), narrative, 1–10.

45. Central Library of Rochester and Monroe County, New York, "Rochester Images," http://www.libraryweb.org/rochimag (accessed June 6, 2003).

46. Unless otherwise indicated, all information about and quotations describing the University of Maine Libraries project entitled "Windows on Maine: Using Technology to Learn" are drawn from its 2003 IMLS National Leadership Grants Application (LG-30-03-0320), narrative, 1–10.

47. Unless otherwise indicated, all information about and quotations describing the University of Illinois Libraries and Early American Museum projects entitled "Building a Digital Cultural Heritage Community: The East Central Illinois Framework" and "Teaching with Digital Content: Describing, Finding and Using Digital Cultural Heritage Materials" are drawn from their 1998 IMLS National Leadership Grants Application (LL-80113), narrative, 1–10, and their 2000 IMLS National Leadership Grants Application (NL-00003), narrative, 1–10.

48. Nuala A. Bennett, Beth Sandore, Amanda M. Grunden, and Patricia L. Miller, "Integration of Primary Resource Materials into Elementary School Curricula," in *Papers: Museums and the Web 2000*, http://www.archimuse.com/mw2000/papers/bennett/bennett.html (accessed June 10, 2003).

49. For other examples, see University of Illinois Libraries, "Teaching with Digital Content: Describing, Finding and Using Digital Cultural Heritage Materials," http://images.library.uiuc.edu.projects/tdc (accessed June 10, 2003).

50. Nuala A. Bennett, "Building a Web-Based Collaborative Database: Does It Work?" in *Papers: Museums and the Web 2001*, http://www.archimuse.com/mw2001/papers/bennett/bennett.html (accessed June 10, 2003).

51. Ibid., section entitled "Illinois Learning Standards."

52. Ibid., section entitled "Curriculum Units."

53. Ibid.

54. Barbara M. Jones, "Providing Virtual Archives for the Classroom: The Librarian's Perspective," abstract in *SHARP 2001: 9th Annual Conference*, par. 4, http://www.wm.edu/CAS/ASP/SHARP/abstract.php?author=bjones-session11 (accessed June 10, 2003).

55. Bennett, "Building a Web-Based Collaborative Database," section entitled "Interpretation of Artifacts."

56. Ibid.

57. Jones, "Providing Virtual Archives for the Classroom," par. 2.

58. Bennett, "Building a Web-Based Collaborative Database," section entitled "Interpretation of Artifacts."

59. Nuala A. Bennett and Brenda Trofanenko, "Digital Primary Source Materials in the Classroom," in *Papers: Museums and the Web 2002*, section entitled "Background," http://www.archimuse.com/mw2002/papers/bennett/bennett.html (accessed June 10, 2003).

60. University of Illinois Libraries, "Teaching with Digital Content: Describing, Finding and Using Digital Cultural Heritage Materials," grant application NL-00003, abstract, bullet point 2.

61. The exact phrasing used in the application to describe the purpose of these sessions is "tailored to meet the needs of training teaching in technology."

62. Bennett, "Building a Web-Based Collaborative Database," section entitled "Interpretation of Artifacts." Bennett quotes Abby Smith from the Council of Library and Information Resources.

63. Birmingham Cultural Alliance Partnership, "Making Cultural Connections in Education Program," 2000 IMLS National Leadership Grants Application (NL-00055), narrative, 9–10.

64. Memorial Hall Museum and Frontier Regional Union #38 School District, "Beyond the Turns of the Centuries," 2000 IMLS National Leadership Grants Application (NL-00019), narrative, 1–10.

65. University of Maine, "Windows on Maine: Using Technology to Learn," 2003 IMLS National Leadership Grants Application (LG-30-03-0320), narrative, 2.

66. Unless otherwise indicated, all information about and quotations describing the Indianapolis Marion County Public Library and The Children's Museum of Indianapolis project entitled "InfoZone" are drawn from their 1999 IMLS National Leadership Grants Application (LL-90102), narrative, 1–10.

67. Information about Rex's Lending Center is taken from David Carr, "Rex's Lending Center and the Information Life of the Child at the Children's Museum of Indianapolis," http://www.scils.rutgers.edu/~kvander/books/CARR.pdf (accessed May 15, 2003). The PDF file contains 28 unnumbered pages. Page numbers are cited as if the article were numbered starting at page 1. This article also appears in Kay E. Vandergrift, ed. *Ways of Knowing* (Lanham, MD: Scarecrow Press, 1996), 89–118.

68. Carr, "Rex's Lending Center," 9.

69. Ibid., 12. Carr quotes from the TCM *Collection Statement* (1991).

70. Ibid., 1–3.

71. Ibid., 3.

72. Ibid.

73. Ibid.

74. Ibid., 6–8. Carr discusses Krippendorff's work in detail on these pages.

75. Ibid., 6. Carr quotes Krippendorff, "The Power of Communication and the Communication of Power: Toward an Emancipatory Theory of Communication," *Communication* 12 (1989): 177.

76. Carr, "Rex's Lending Center," 6.

77. Ibid., 7.

78. Ibid.

79. Ibid. Carr draws some of these phrases from the TCM *Materials Selection Policy* (1991), which he quotes here.

80. Ibid., 7, 20.

81. Ibid., 26, 27.

82. Ibid., 26.

83. Unless otherwise indicated, all information about and quotations describing the Madison Children's Museum and the Madison Public Library project entitled "Discovery to Go" are drawn from their 1999 IMLS National Leadership Grants Application (LL-90084), narrative, 1–10.

84. For more information about the Leigh Yawkey Woodson Art Museum and its diverse range of exhibits and programs, see http://www.lywam.org (accessed June 7, 2003). For more information about the annual Birds in Art exhibits, see http://www.lywam.org/birdsinart (accessed June 7, 2003).

85. Unless otherwise indicated, all information about and quotations describing the Leigh Yawkey Woodson Art Museum project entitled "Down Under and Over Here" are drawn from its 1998 IMLS National Leadership Grants Application (LL-80208), narrative, 1–10.

86. Leigh Yawkey Woodson Art Museum, *Calendar of Events. Down Under and Over Here: Children's Book Illustration from Australia and America.* We thank Kathy Kelsey Foley, director of LYWAM, for sending us this publication.

87. Leigh Yawkey Woodson Art Museum, *Family Activity Guide. Down Under and Over Here: Children's Book Illustration from Australia and America.* We thank Kathy Kelsey Foley, director of LYWAM, for sending us this publication.

88. Unless otherwise indicated, all information about and quotations describing the Brooklyn Children's Museum project entitled "Brooklyn Expedition" are drawn from its 1998 IMLS National Leadership Grants Application (LL-80072), narrative, 1–10.

89. For more information about "Brooklyn Expedition," see http://www.brooklynexpedition.org (accessed June 6, 2003).

90. Brooklyn Children's Museum, "Brooklyn Expedition Lesson Plans," http://www.brooklynexpedition.org/lessonplans.html (accessed June 6, 2003).

91. See http://www.brooklynexpedition.org/structures/buildings/bui_index_4.html (accessed June 6, 2003).

92. Unless otherwise indicated, all information about and quotations describing the Montshire Museum of Science and Howe Library project entitled "An Educational Collaborative for Rural Families" are drawn from their 1998 IMLS National Leadership Grants Application (LL-90100), narrative, 1–9.

93. Unless otherwise indicated, all information about and quotations describing the North Carolina Museum of Life and Science project entitled "Discovery in Motion" are drawn from its 2002 IMLS National Leadership Grants Application (LG-30-02-0233), narrative, 1–10.

94. Unless otherwise indicated, all information about and quotations describing the North Carolina Museum of Life and Science project entitled "Library Youth Partnership" are drawn from its 2000 IMLS National Leadership Grants Application (NL-00045), narrative, 1–10.

95. Unless otherwise indicated, all information about and quotations describing the Florida Museum of Natural History project entitled "Marvelous Explorations Through Science and Stories (MESS)" are drawn from its 2001 IMLS National Leadership Grants Application (NL-10011), narrative, 1–10.

96. IMLS, "What's the Buzz?" http://www.imls.gov/closer/archive/hlt_m0902.htm (accessed May 10, 2003).

97. Ibid., section entitled "What's New at the Library and Museum."

98. Unless otherwise indicated, all information about and quotations describing the Eastern Iowa Community College District project entitled "Connected by a River: A Collaboration of Museums, Libraries, and Schools to Create Community Based Learning Spaces" are drawn from its 2001 IMLS National Leadership Grants Application (NL-10010), narrative, 1–36.

99. Unless otherwise indicated, all information about and quotations describing the Discovery Center of Springfield (Missouri) project entitled "Virtual Technology and the Web" are drawn from its 2001 IMLS National Leadership Grants Application (NL-10040), narrative, 1–10.

100. The quotations are from Discovery Center of Springfield, Science Source, http://www.discoverycenter.org/sciencesource.asp (accessed May 10, 2003).

101. Unless otherwise indicated, all information about and quotations describing the Greater Indianapolis Literacy League project entitled "Travels Across Time" are drawn from its 2002 IMLS National Leadership Grants Application (LG-30-02-0241), narrative, 1–10.

102. Conner Prairie Living History Museum, "The Conner Estate," http://www.connerprairie.org (accessed May 9, 2003).

103. Unless otherwise indicated, all information about and quotations describing the Newberry Library and Chicago Historical Society project entitled "Free Expression and American Democracy" are drawn from their 2003 IMLS National Leadership Grants Application (LG-30-03-0205), narrative, 1–10.

104. Unless otherwise indicated, all information about and quotations describing the Cherokee National Historical Society and Eastern Oklahoma District Library System project entitled "Cherokee Traveling Exhibits" are drawn from their 2001 IMLS National Leadership Grants Application (NL-10008), narrative, 1–10.

105. For a complete list of themes, see Cherokee Heritage Center, Cherokee Traveling Exhibits, http://www.cherokeeheritage.org/coe/ov_imls.html (accessed May 10, 2003).

106. Unless otherwise indicated, all information about and quotations describing the University of Nebraska–Lincoln Libraries project entitled "Omaha Indian Artifacts and Images: Online Inventory and Web Site" are drawn from its 2001 IMLS National Leadership Grants Application (NL-10025), narrative, 1–10.

107. Unless otherwise indicated, all information about and quotations describing the Fort Lewis College Center of Southwest Studies and Southern Ute Cultural Center project entitled "Sharing Culture" are drawn from their 2002 IMLS National Leadership Grants Application (LG-30-02-0284), narrative, 1–10.

108. Unless otherwise indicated, all information about and quotations describing the University of Washington Libraries project entitled "Community Museum Project: A Library/Museum Cultural Collaboration" are drawn from its 2003 IMLS National Leadership Grants Application (LG-30-03-0209-03), narrative, 1–10.

109. Unless otherwise indicated, all information about and quotations describing the Palau Community College and Belau National Museum project entitled "Image Archives Digitization and Access" are drawn from their 2000 IMLS National Leadership Grants Application (NL-00041), narrative, 1–10.

110. Unless otherwise indicated, all information about and quotations describing the Lee College and Baytown Historical Museum project entitled "From Local to Global: An IMLS Library/Museum Collaboration" are drawn from their 2000 IMLS National Leadership Grants Application (NL-00028), narrative, 1–10.

111. Unless otherwise indicated, all information about and quotations describing the University of Pittsburgh Libraries project entitled "Imaging Pittsburgh: Creating a Shared Gateway to Digital Image Collections of Pittsburgh" are drawn from its 2002 IMLS National Leadership Grants Application (LG-30-02-0251), narrative, 1–10.

112. University of Pittsburgh, Historic Pittsburgh, http://digital.library.pitt.edu (accessed November 7, 2003).

113. Unless otherwise indicated, all information about and quotations describing the Museum of History and Industry (Seattle, Washington) project entitled "Crossing Organizational Boundaries" are drawn from its 2001 IMLS National Leadership Grants Application (NL-10016), narrative, 1–10.

114. For more information, see Museum of History and Industry, "King County Snapshots," http://content.lib.washington.edu/imls/kcsnapshots/explore.html (accessed November 7, 2003).

115. Unless otherwise indicated, all information about and quotations describing the Southern Utah University Library System (Cedar City) project entitled "Voices of the Colorado Plateau" are drawn from its 2000 IMLS National Leadership Grants Application (NL-00011), narrative, 1–10.

116. Matthew Nickerson, "Voices: Bringing Multimedia Museum Exhibits to the World Wide Web," *First Monday* 7 (May 2002). See the section entitled "Multimedia Exhibits," http://www.firstmonday.dk (accessed May 11, 2003).

117. Yahoo! "Yahoo! Picks: May 26, 2002," http://picks.yahoo.com/picks/i/20020526.html (accessed May 11, 2003).

118. See the Web site for Southern Utah University, "Voices of the Colorado Plateau," http://archive.li.suu.edu/voices (accessed November 8, 2003).

119. Nickerson, "Voices." See the section entitled "Multimedia Exhibits."

120. John Vergo and others, "Less Clicking, More Watching: Results from the User-Centered Design of a Multi-Institutional Web Site for Art and Culture," in *Papers from Museums and the Web 2002*, http://www.archimuse.com (accessed November 8, 2003). Nickerson refers to this paper.

121. Greater Indianapolis Literacy League, "Travels Across Time," 2002 IMLS National Leadership Grants Application (LG-30-02-0241), narrative, 4.

122. Palau Community College and Belau National Museum, "Image Archives and Digitization Access," 2000 IMLS National Leadership Grants Application (NL-00041), narrative, 5.

123. Unless otherwise indicated, all information about and quotations describing the Wildlife Conservation Society/Central Park Zoo and Poets House project entitled "The Language of Conservation: Poet in Residence at the Central Park Zoo" are drawn from their 2003 IMLS National Leadership Grants Application (LG-30-03-0255), narrative, 1–10.

124. Unless otherwise indicated, all information about and quotations describing the Frist Center for the Visual Arts and the Nashville Public Library project entitled "Project Access" are drawn from their 2003 IMLS National Leadership Grants Application (LG-30-03-0252), narrative, 1–10.

125. Unless otherwise indicated, all information about and quotations describing the Henry E. Huntington Library and Art Gallery project entitled "The World from Here: Treasures of the Great Libraries of Los Angeles" are drawn from its 1999 IMLS National Leadership Grants Application (LL-90110), narrative, 1–10.

126. Ann Philbin and David Stuart Rodes, "Foreword," in *The World from Here: Treasures of the Great Libraries of Los Angeles*, ed. Cynthia Burlingham and Bruce Whiteman (Los Angeles, CA: UCLA Grunwald Center for the Graphic Arts and the Armand Hammer Museum of Art and Cultural Center, 2001), 7.

127. Henry E. Huntington Library and Art Gallery, "The World from Here: Introduction to the Website," http://www.calbook.org (accessed November 15, 2003).

128. Unless otherwise indicated, all information about and quotations describing the University of California (California Digital Library) project entitled "Museums and the Online Archive of California" and "Museums and the Online Archive of California II: User Evaluation" are drawn from its 1999 and 2002 IMLS National Leadership Grants Applications (LL-90130 and LG-30-02-0258), narratives, 1–10.

129. For more information and a complete list of collections contained in MOAC, see the MOAC Web site at California Digital Library, http://www.bampfa.berkeley.edu/moac (accessed November 19, 2003).

130. For more information about the "Free Speech Movement Digital Archive" and the "Japanese American Relocation Digital Archives," see California Digital Library, http://bancroft.berkeley.edu/FSM (accessed November 19, 2003) and http://jarda.cdlib. org (accessed November 19, 2003).

131. Unless otherwise indicated, all information about and quotations describing the University of California–Merced Library and the Ruth and Sherman Lee Institute for Japanese Art at the Clark Center project entitled "Opening the Cultural Corridor: Japanese Art in the San Joaquin Valley" are drawn from their 2002 IMLS National Leadership Grants Application (LG-30-02-0260), narrative, 1–10.

132. Unless otherwise indicated, all information about and quotations describing the Emory University Libraries project entitled "Music of Social Change: Library-Museum Collaboration Through Open Archives Metadata" are drawn from its 2003 IMLS National Leadership Grants Application (LG-30-03-0229), narrative, 1–10.

133. For more information about this Web portal, see Emory University Digital Library, http://www.americansouth.org (accessed November 19, 2003).

134. Unless otherwise indicated, all information about and quotations describing the Wayne State University Library System and Detroit Historical Museums project entitled "Digital Dress: 200 Years of Urban Style, A Model Web Portal for Library/Museum Collaboration" are drawn from their 2003 IMLS National Leadership Grants Application (LG-30-03-0218), narrative, 1–10.

135. Unless otherwise indicated, all information about and quotations describing the Johns Hopkins University–Milton S. Eisenhower Library and Baltimore Museum of Art project entitled "Baltimore Art Resource Online Consortium" are drawn from their 2000 IMLS National Leadership Grants Application (NL-00039), narrative, 1–10.

136. For more information about BAROC, see Maryland ArtSource, http://www.marylandartsource.org (accessed May 11, 2003).

137. Wildlife Conservation Society/Central Park Zoo and Poets House, "The Language of Conservation: Poet in Residence at the Central Park Zoo," 2003 IMLS National Leadership Grants Application (LG-30-03-0255), narrative, 6.

138. Ibid., 4.

139. Michael K. Buckland, "Five Grand Challenges for Library Research," *Library Trends* 51 (spring 2003): 680.

140. Ibid.

141. Ibid., 681.

142. University of California–Merced Library and the Ruth and Sherman Lee Institute for Japanese Art at the Clark Center, "Opening the Cultural Corridor: Japanese Art in the San Joaquin Valley," 2002 IMLS National Leadership Grants Application (LG-30-02-0260), narrative, 2, 7–8.

143. Wayne State University Library System and Detroit Historical Museums, "Digital Dress: 200 Years of Urban Style, A Model Web Portal for Library/Museum Collaboration," 2003 IMLS National Leadership Grants Application (LG-30-03-0218), narrative, 5.

144. Johns Hopkins University–Milton S. Eisenhower Library and Baltimore Museum of Art, "Baltimore Art Resource Online Consortium," 2000 IMLS National Leadership Grants Application (NL-00039), narrative, 3.

145. Unless otherwise indicated, all information about and quotations describing the Cable Natural History Museum (Wisconsin) project entitled "New Voices from the Upper Midwest: Writing for a Change" are drawn from its 2001 IMLS National Leadership Grants Application (NL-10007), narrative, 1–10.

146. Unless otherwise indicated, all information about and quotations describing the Burpee Museum of Natural History and Rockford Public Library project entitled "The Jane Collaborative" are drawn from their 2003 IMLS National Leadership Grants Application (LG-30-03-0233), narrative, 1–10.

147. Unless otherwise indicated, all information about and quotations describing the Carnegie Mellon University and Carnegie Museum of Natural History project entitled "Smart Web Exhibits: Delivering Enhanced Library and Museum Collections Online, On Target and On Time" are drawn from their 1999 IMLS National Leadership Grants Application (LL-90080), narrative, 1–10.

148. Unless otherwise indicated, all information about and quotations describing the Chicago Horticultural Society and Chicago Botanic Garden project entitled "Plant Evaluation Web Site" are drawn from their 2001 IMLS National Leadership Grants Application (NL-10009), narrative, 1–10.

149. Unless otherwise indicated, all information about and quotations describing the Chicago Horticultural Society and Chicago Botanic Garden project entitled "National Collection of Endangered Plants Web Site" are drawn from their 2000 IMLS National Leadership Grants Application (NL-10072), narrative, 1–10.

150. Unless otherwise indicated, all information about and quotations describing the Florida Center for Library Automation and Florida Museum of Natural History project entitled "Linking Florida's Natural Heritage: Science and Citizenry" are drawn from their 1998 IMLS National Leadership Grants Application (LL-80016), narrative, 1–10.

151. Unless otherwise indicated, all information about and quotations describing the University of Michigan Library System and University of Michigan Natural History Museums project entitled "Flora and Fauna of the Great Lakes Region: A Multimedia Digital Collection" are drawn from their 2000 IMLS National Leadership Grants Application (NL-00034), narrative, 1–10.

152. Chicago Horticultural Society and Chicago Botanic Garden, "Plant Evaluation Web Site," 2001 IMLS National Leadership Grants Application (NL-10009), abstract.

153. Chicago Horticultural Society and Chicago Botanic Garden, "National Collection of Endangered Plants Web Site," 2000 IMLS National Leadership Grants Application (NL-10072), abstract; narrative, 3.

154. Cable Natural History Museum, "New Voices from the Upper Midwest: Writing for a Change," 2001 IMLS National Leadership Grants Application (NL-10007), narrative, 2–3.

155. Unless otherwise indicated, all information about and quotations describing the Libby (Montana) School District #4 project entitled "Restoring the Past, Capturing the Present, Preserving the Future" are drawn from its 2000 IMLS National Leadership Grants Application (NL-00067), narrative, 1–10.

156. Unless otherwise indicated, all information about and quotations describing the Brooklyn Public Library project entitled "Worklore: Brooklyn Workers Speak" are drawn from its 2001 IMLS National Leadership Grants Application (NL-10006), narrative, 1–10.

157. Brooklyn Historical Society, "Brooklyn Works: 400 Years of Making a Living in Brooklyn," www.brooklynhistory.org/main/brooklyn_works4.html (accessed December 5, 2003).

158. Some project narratives provided a great deal of specific information about the content of their digital collections; others did not.

159. Unless otherwise indicated, all information about and quotations describing the Inter American University of Puerto Rico Virtual Library project entitled "Connections: Linking Educational Institutions, Libraries, and Museums Through Technology" are drawn from its 2001 IMLS National Leadership Grants Application (NL-10035), narrative, 1–10.

160. Unless otherwise indicated, all information about and quotations describing the Richmond Public Library project entitled "WWII Richmond, California Home Front

Digital Project" are drawn from its 2001 IMLS National Leadership Grants Application (NL-10030), narrative, 1–10.

161. Unless otherwise indicated, all information about and quotations describing the Montana State University Libraries project entitled "Images of the Indian Peoples of the Northern Great Plains" are drawn from its 1998 IMLS National Leadership Grants Application (LL-80101), narrative, 1–10.

162. Unless otherwise indicated, all information about and quotations describing the Washington State University Libraries project entitled "Engaging the Public with Digital Primary Sources: A Tri-State Online History Database and Learning Center" are drawn from its 2001 IMLS National Leadership Grants Application (NL-10032), narrative, 1–10.

163. For more information, see Center for Columbia River History, http://www.ccrh.org/oral/index.htm (accessed December 4, 2003).

164. Quotes are taken from http://www.ccrh/org/oral/ohsoh/contents.htm (accessed December 4, 2003).

165. See, for example, http://www.ccrh/org/comm/sand/begin/htm (accessed December 2, 2003).

166. Unless otherwise indicated, all information about and quotations describing the Rutgers University Libraries project entitled "The New Jersey Digital Highway: Where Culture, History and Learning Merge" are drawn from its 2003 IMLS National Leadership Grants Application (LG-30-03-0269), narrative, 1–10.

167. Unless otherwise indicated, all information about and quotations describing the University of Denver (Colorado Seminary) Penrose Library project entitled "Western Trails: A Museum/Library Collaborative in Western States" are drawn from its 2001 IMLS National Leadership Grants Application (NL-10024), narrative, 1–10.

168. Colorado Digitization Program, "Western Trails Collections," http://www.cdpheritage.org (accessed December 6, 2003).

169. Penrose Library, University of Denver, "Images of Pioneer Jewish Families," http://www.library.du.edu/specoll/beck/images.cfm (accessed December 6, 2003).

170. Unless otherwise indicated, all information about and quotations describing the Connecticut Historical Society and University of Connecticut Libraries project entitled "Connecticut History Online" are drawn from their 1999 IMLS National Leadership Grants Application (LL-90087) and their 2002 IMLS National Leadership Grants Application (LG-30-02-0256), narratives, 1–10.

171. See their Web site at http://www.cthistoryonline.org (accessed May 9, 2003).

172. Unless otherwise indicated, all information about and quotations describing the WGBH Educational Foundation, Birmingham Civil Rights Institute, and Washington University Library System project entitled "The Civil Rights Movement: 1950 to the Present, A Digital Library Collection" are drawn from their 2003 IMLS National Leadership Grants Application (LG-30-03-0318), narrative, 1–10.

173. WGBH Educational Foundation, "The Civil Rights Movement: 1950 to the Present, A Digital Library Collection," 2003 IMLS National Leadership Grants Application (LG-30-03-0318), narrative, 2.

174. Libby (Montana) School District #4, "Restoring the Past, Capturing the Present, Preserving the Future," 2000 IMLS National Leadership Grants Application (NL-00067), narrative, 2.

175. The Heritage Museum, "Museum History," http://www.lincolncountylibraries.com/museum/museum_history.htm (accessed May 11, 2003).

176. Libby (Montana) School District #4, "Restoring the Past, Capturing the Present, Preserving the Future," 2000 IMLS National Leadership Grants Application (NL-00067), narrative, 6.

177. Ibid., abstract.

178. AHA Books, "Put Your Books in the Brautigan Virtual Library," http://www.ahapoetry.com/braushlf.htm (accessed December 6, 2003). For a complete description of this concept, see Richard Brautigan, *The Abortion: An Historical Romance 1996* (New York: Simon and Schuster, 1970), 11–36.

179. Unless otherwise indicated, all information about and quotations describing the Museum of Art, Rhode Island School of Design project entitled "Art ConText" are drawn from its 1998 IMLS National Leadership Grants Application (LL-80095), narrative, 1–10.

180. For detailed information about each residency, see http://www.risd.edu/artcontext (accessed June 10, 2003).

181. Rhode Island School of Design, "Artist Residencies: Jerry Beck, Wheel of Wonder," http://www.risd.edu/artcontext/artists/jerry/jerry_artwork.htm (accessed June 10, 2003).

182. Rhode Island School of Design, "Interview with the Artist: Ernesto Pujol, Memory of Surfaces," http://www.risd.edu/artcontext/artists/ernesto/ernesto_interview.htm (accessed June 10, 2003).

183. Rhode Island School of Design, "Artist Residencies: Lynne Yamamoto, This, and my Heart," http://www.risd.edu/artcontext/artists/lynne/lynne_artwork.htm (accessed June 10, 2003).

184. Rhode Island School of Design, "Interview with the Artist: Indira Freitas Johnson, Freenotfree," http://www.risd.edu/artcontext/artists/indira/indira_interview.htm (accessed June 10, 2003).

185. Rhode Island School of Design, "Artist Residencies: David McGee, 15 Minutes: The Ballad of Then and Now," http://www.risd.edu/artcontext/artists/david/david_mcgee.htm (accessed June 10, 2003).

186. Unless otherwise indicated, all information about and quotations describing the Jefferson Patterson Park and Museum project entitled "Education in Southern Maryland: From Segregation to Integration" are drawn from its 1999 IMLS National Leadership Grants Application (LL-90096), narrative, 1–10.

187. Unless otherwise indicated, all information about and quotations describing the Children's Museum of Houston project entitled "Library for Early Childhood Initiative" are drawn from its 1998 IMLS National Leadership Grants Application (LL-80071), narrative, 1–10.

188. Unless otherwise indicated, all information about and quotations describing the Children's Museum of Houston project entitled "Para los Niños—For the Children" are drawn from its 2003 IMLS National Leadership Grants Application (LG-30-03-0244), narrative, 1–10.

189. See the map of the Children's Museum of Houston at http://www.cmhouston.org/map/map.htm (accessed June 10, 2003).

190. Unless otherwise indicated, all information about and quotations describing the Kit Carson Historic Museums project entitled "Southwest Research Center of New Mexico" are drawn from its 1998 IMLS National Leadership Grants Application (LL-80139), narrative, 1–10.

191. Unless otherwise indicated, all information about and quotations describing the University Library of Indiana University–Purdue University at Indianapolis (IUPUI) and Indianapolis Museum of Art project entitled "Image Database Community Project" are drawn from their 1998 IMLS National Leadership Grants Application (LL-80198), narrative, 1–10.

192. A complete list of artists and educational activities associated with this project is available at Indiana University–Purdue University at Indianapolis Library, http://www.ulib.iupui.edu/imls (accessed June 7, 2003).

193. Unless otherwise indicated, all information about and quotations describing the Cornell University Library project entitled "On with the Show: Access to the World's Performing Arts Through Museums and Libraries" are drawn from its 2002 IMLS National Leadership Grants Application (LG-30-02-0235), narrative, 1–10.

194. Unless otherwise indicated, all information about and quotations describing the Public Library of Charlotte and Mecklenburg County and Mint Museum of Art project entitled "Weaving a Tale of Craft" are drawn from their 1998 IMLS National Leadership Grants Application (LG-80153), narrative, 1–10.

195. Unless otherwise indicated, all information about and quotations describing the Public Library of Charlotte and Mecklenburg County and Mint Museum of Art project entitled "Cultural Connections" are drawn from their 2003 IMLS National Leadership Grants Application (LG-30-03-0265), narrative, 1–10.

196. Public Library of Charlotte and Mecklenburg County, "Weaving a Tale of Craft: About this Project," http://www.handsoncrafts.org (accessed June 10, 2003).

197. Rhode Island School of Design, "Interview with the Artist: David McGee, 15 Minutes: The Ballad of Then and Now," http://www.risd.edu/artcontext/splash_frame.htm (accessed December 12, 2003).

198. Unless otherwise indicated, all information about and quotations describing the Tampa Museum of Science and Industry project entitled "ABC's of Science: A Collaboration for Head Start Preschoolers" are drawn from its 2000 IMLS National Leadership Grants Application (NL-00054), narrative, 1–10.

199. Unless otherwise indicated, all information about and quotations describing the Arizona Science Center project entitled "Satellite Science" are drawn from its 2000 IMLS National Leadership Grants Application (NL-00044), narrative, 1–10.

200. For more information, see Arizona Science Center, http://www.satellitescience.org (accessed May 11, 2003).

201. Unless otherwise indicated, all information about and quotations describing the Triton College Library and Cernan Earth and Space Center Planetarium/Museum project entitled "Partners in Extended Learning for the Mars Millennium and Beyond" are drawn from their 1999 IMLS National Leadership Grants Application (LL-90103), narrative, 1–10.

202. Unless otherwise indicated, all information about and quotations describing the Tucson Botanical Gardens and Tucson-Pima Public Library project entitled are drawn from their 2002 National Leadership Grants Application (LG-30-02-0296), abstract and narrative, 1–10.

203. For more information, please see Tuscon Botanical Gardens, http://www.tucson botanical.org/desert_connections (accessed May 9, 2003).

204. Unless otherwise indicated, all information about and quotations describing the University of Oregon Museum of Natural History project entitled "Keeping Oregon Memories Alive for 21st Century Learners: A University of Oregon Museum and Library Collaboration" are drawn from its 2003 IMLS National Leadership Grants Application (LG-30-03-0268), narrative, 1–10.

205. Unless otherwise indicated, all information about and quotations describing the University of Florida Libraries project entitled "Ephemeral Cities" are drawn from its 2003 IMLS National Leadership Grants Application (LG-30-03-0285), narrative, 1–10.

206. Tampa Museum of Science and Industry, "ABC's of Science: A Collaboration for Head Start Preschoolers," 2000 IMLS National Leadership Grants Application (NL-00054), narrative, 10.

207. White House Millennium Council 2000, "The Mars Millennium Project," http://www.clinton4.nara.gov/initiatives/millennium/mars.html (accessed December 21, 2003).

208. Getty Museum, "Getty to Partner with U.S. Department of Education, NEA, NASA, and the White House on Mars Millennium Project," http://www.getty.edu/news/press/la/marsmill.html (accessed December 21, 2003).

209. National Archives and Records Administration, "Exit Nara Notice," http://clinton4.nara.gov/cgi_bin/good_bye_cgi?url (accessed December 21, 2003).

210. Arizona Science Center, "Satellite Science," 2000 IMLS National Leadership Grants Application (NL-00044), narrative, 10.

211. Carr, "Rex's Lending Center," 12. Carr quotes from the Children's Museum's *Collection Statement* (1991).

212. All quotations about the Steven F. Udvar-Hazy Center are taken from Matthew L. Wald, "A Big Museum Opens, to Jeers as Well as Cheers," *New York Times,* 16 December 2003, A28.

213. Edna Gundersen, "Downloading Squeezes the Art out of the Album," *USA Today,* 5–7 December 2003, A1–2.

214. Ibid. Gundersen quotes Ray Manzarek, former keyboardist for The Doors.

215. Unless otherwise indicated, all information about and quotations describing the New Museum of Contemporary Art project entitled "Re-presenting Race in the Digital Age" are drawn from its 2003 IMLS National Leadership Grants Application (LG-21-03-0155), narrative, 1–10.

216. Unless otherwise indicated, all information about and quotations describing the Chicago Botanic Garden project entitled "La Primera Ciencia: An Urban Environmental Science Camp" are drawn from its 2003 IMLS National Leadership Grants Application (LG-21-03-0134), narrative, 1–10.

217. Unless otherwise indicated, all information about and quotations describing the New Mexico Museum of Natural History and Science project entitled "Proyecto Futuro Bilingual Partnership" are drawn from its 2003 IMLS National Leadership Grants Application (LG-21-03-0159), narrative, 1–10.

218. Unless otherwise indicated, all information about and quotations describing the Florida Aquarium project entitled "From the Source to the Sea: An Innovative Program

for Homeschool Families" are drawn from its 2003 IMLS National Leadership Grants Application (LG-21-03-0161), narrative, 1–10.

219. Unless otherwise indicated, all information about and quotations describing the Boston Children's Museum project entitled "Making Connections for School Readiness" are drawn from its 2003 IMLS National Leadership Grants Application (LG-21-03-0153), narrative, 1–10.

220. Unless otherwise indicated, all information about and quotations describing the Young at Art of Broward project entitled "ArtREACH" are drawn from its 2003 IMLS National Leadership Grants Application (LG-21-03-0141), narrative, 1–10.

4 THE MUSEUM-LIBRARY
HYBRID INSTITUTION

Museum-library partnerships are, for the most part, a marketing-based relationship driven by outcome measures that have been conceived in such a manner as to generate the highest possible attendance figures or, in the case of digital partnerships, the highest possible number of online visits. The intent of these ventures is to increase the visibility of both institutions by producing and then successfully selling a product. The product itself can assume different forms, as demonstrated by the examples of IMLS partnerships in chapter 3. And as we have seen in such cases as Opening the Cultural Corridor and Digital Dress, the final product of the museum-library partnership matters less than the ability to demonstrate that there is cooperation between these institutions. In this sense, a conference to discuss future endeavors carries as much weight in the realm of partnerships as the endeavors themselves. The situation is reminiscent of the plot of the film *Lover Come Back,* in which Rock Hudson and Doris Day play warring advertising executives. In the battle to out-maneuver each other, Hudson's character achieves the ultimate coup: he develops an enormously successful advertising campaign for a product that does not exist.

To be sure, most museum-library partnerships do provide a "product." And, because it is often the case that these partnerships involve digitization projects, the "product" is made available online. The proliferation of Web-based initiatives raises the question of how successfully the partnership product meets the needs of museums, libraries, and their users. Certainly, there is a demand for "remote access to resources via the Web" and "speedy delivery of services via the Internet."[1] Yet museums and libraries are also brick-and-mortar (or, more likely, glass-and-steel) structures with a physical presence in their communities. As we discussed in chapter 2, museums and libraries have been struggling to reconnect with their communities and have therefore turned to various postobject roles to increase attendance and circulation statistics. Just as many of these postobject roles are misguided attempts to create edutainment spectacles, much to the detriment of the institutions' mandate, one questions how Web-based projects will reestablish the library as a physical space and presence in the community. The need to address this issue takes on particular urgency considering that, as Ray Lester writes, "the notion that from now on museums and libraries are all about, and just about, using IT [information technology] has been vigorously promoted."[2]

There is also the issue of autonomy. In chapter 2 we described how postobject roles and the emphasis on providing edutainment-based experiences tend to deemphasize museum and library collections. This deemphasis means that there is little to differentiate museums and libraries and the services they provide from other leisure-time attractions and venues. The fact that museums, libraries, restaurants, bookstores, and theme parks are blending into one undifferentiated mass results in a loss of autonomy for traditional cultural institutions. This problem is compounded by the fact that creating edutainment spectacles often depends on funding from corporate partners, which, in turn, weakens the museum's or library's control over the direction and content of their projects. Library professionals have voiced similar concerns regarding the loss of autonomy in museum-library partnerships, expressing uncertainty as to whether partnerships would afford libraries the opportunity to demonstrate the distinct role they play in their communities—a role defined by their collections and by what Niedzviecki calls "their position as free storehouses of information and places where we can learn how to interpret and dispense information in a way that empowers us as a citizenry" in a world dominated by a corporately controlled "media system."[3]

Of course, the entire notion of museum and library autonomy is being redefined by organizations that support collaborative ventures, including IMLS. In comments made to the Natural Science Collections Alliance, Robert Martin, director of IMLS, observes that

> the distinction between library and museum that we now accept as common is really a matter of convention, a convention that has evolved over time. That convention is predicated on a perception that libraries and museums collect very different kinds of things. In fact, however, from one perspective or frame of reference, libraries and museums collect precisely the same kind of things.... When we move from the physical to the digital world, it seems to me, the distinctions between text and image, object and artifact appear to diminish.... This leads...to the inescapable conclusion that, in the digital environment, the distinctions between libraries, museums and archives that we take for granted are in fact artificial.[4]

While we have argued that the autonomy of museums and libraries is weakened by postobject roles that deemphasize collections, Martin concludes that, in the

144

digital world, the distinctions among the collections themselves are blurred. Martin's comments also suggest that this lack of distinction, rather than cause for concern, can be seen as a raison d'être for museum-library partnerships: "Large numbers of individuals who heretofore made little or no use of [museum and library] materials—who perhaps were even unaware of their existence—are now frequent users of digital collections. And these new users do not care, and may not even be aware, whether the original materials are in a library or a museum."[5]

The idea that "the distinctions between text and image, object and artifact appear to diminish"[6] in digitized formats has significant repercussions for libraries. Ironically, these repercussions hinge on a point of divergence between museums and libraries that becomes apparent in the digital realm. Lester points out that "conventional museums of physical cultural artefacts have an inherent value in themselves which will not be superseded once all their artefacts are digitized."[7] Consider the example of Leonardo da Vinci's *Mona Lisa*. Despite the availability of countless reproductions of this image, people still flock to the Louvre to see the original painting, whether to study da Vinci's artistry first hand or simply to be able to say that they viewed the original masterpiece. The same principle of being able to see an authentic object also applies to less-renowned examples. Dinosaur skeletons are collected by numerous natural history museums across the United States, with digitized images of the specimens available on these institutions' Web sites. But no two skeletons are exactly the same, a fact that differentiates both the objects themselves and the museums that collect them. And downloading an image of a prehistoric skeleton does not have the same impact as coming face-to-face with, say, a 45-foot-long *Tyrannosaurus rex*. With the obvious exception of rare books and manuscripts, library collections do not have this advantage. If a book or article is available online, there is little difference between a downloaded version and the original print version. Likewise, one library's copy of a book or journal is basically identical to that at another library. As Lester points out, the frequent response of the library community to these arguments is a) "digital versions as 'good' as the comparable physical versions of the artefacts just do not exist," and b) "the prospective users of those physical versions actually need to handle and peruse the physical items themselves (cf. browsing)."[8] Despite the validity of these points, Lester concludes that this reasoning is "very flimsy...for planning a longer-term future for the physical collections of information artefacts that we call 'libraries'"—a conclusion that leads him to suggest "that we are not facing the 'convergence' of libraries and museums; we are instead facing the 'takeover' of libraries by museums!"[9]

Takeover is generally not a term associated with partnerships. In corporate parlance, takeovers entail the consumption of a weaker entity by a stronger one, while partnerships theoretically involve the interaction of separate but equal parties. Yet, with their failure to outline a clear role for library collections and to restore libraries as viable non-edutainment-oriented physical presences in their communities, museum-library partnerships are moving in a direction not unlike the scenario predicted by Lester. Considering the specific problems that libraries face today—and the inadequacy of museum-library partnerships as a solution to these problems—what if libraries abandoned the role of museum partner? What if, instead, libraries "took over" the role of the museum?

This proposal is not as far fetched as it might sound. Martin was correct in his observation that "the distinction between library and museum that we now accept as common is really a matter of convention, a convention that has evolved over time."[10] While Martin emphasizes the blurred distinction between library and museum collections in a digital environment, there is an inherent link between the two in the physical realm as well. Libraries and museums were often housed in a single edifice, and "it was largely the need for roof lighting of museum exhibits" that caused them to split apart.[11] In other words, "the technical problems of lighting galleries and libraries were so different that the impetus for functional separation was more practical than cultural."[12] But the connection between the printed artifacts of library collections and the object-based artifacts of museum collections has less to do with erasing the boundary between the collected materials themselves than with deconstructing the roles of museums and libraries in collecting, displaying, and providing access to objects and documents.

A good place to begin tracing the link between museums and libraries, on the one hand, and objects and documents, on the other, is the "cabinet of curiosities." Scholars have long recognized the cabinet of curiosities as the precursor to the modern museum. These private collections of miscellaneous manmade objects and natural specimens emerged in sixteenth-century Europe and, in many cases, formed the core around which public-access museums expanded. In their introduction to *The Origins of Museums*, Oliver Impey and Arthur MacGregor identify the evolutionary thread linking cabinets of curiosities to the mandate of museums today: "With due allowance for the passage of years, no difficulty will be found in recognizing that, in terms of function, little has changed; along with libraries, botanical and zoological gardens, and research laboratories, museums are still in the business of 'keeping and sorting' the products of Man and Nature and in promoting understanding of their significance."[13] Their comments highlight the relationship not only between cabinets of curiosities and museums, but also between museums and libraries. In fact, the connection between libraries and museums extends beyond the shared organizational and educative function that cabinets of curiosities embodied. Books, librarians, and libraries all played a part in the development of the cabinets themselves and their eventual metamorphosis into publicly accessible museum collections. This historical role blurs the distinction between what constitutes the domain of library versus museum collections, in the process challenging contemporary constructs of these institutions. In pursuit of the goal of preserving and organizing "the products of Man and Nature," museums and libraries have not always traveled on parallel courses. These courses have frequently intersected, producing institutions that functioned, for all intents and purposes, as a museum-library hybrid and that offered a collection of books and objects that had "wonder, broadly conceived, [as] its unifying theme."[14]

Wonder was the theme of an exhibit at the New York Public Library in the summer of 2002 entitled The Public's Treasures: A Cabinet of Curiosities. The exhibit was composed of objects—treasures—from the library's holdings, which the curators "examined through the window of a cabinet of curiosities, with the hope of edifying, delighting, and perhaps even surprising modern-day viewers."[15] In addition to presenting visitors with a brief history of cabinets of curiosities, the New York Public Library itself assumed the role of a cabinet of curiosities, displaying objects from its own collection such as Elizabeth Barrett Browning's shoes and a lock of Walt Whitman's hair.[16] Although demonstrating the inherent connection between museums and libraries, the New York Public Library's exhibit does not qualify as a museum-library partnership. As the IMLS literature indicates, "Neither a library that had an exhibition function as part of its internal operations, [nor] a museum with a library function would constitute a partnership."[17]

Our purpose in this chapter is to examine the relationship between museums and libraries and the materials they collect in terms of specific historical models for museum-library hybrid institutions. We suggest that, rather than partnering with museums, libraries build on their "exhibition function" by assuming the role—and spirit—of the cabinet of curiosities. We present an overview of the relationship between museum collections and libraries, beginning with the origins of the modern museum—the European cabinets of the sixteenth and seventeenth centuries—and culminating with the American Progressive Era in the early twentieth century. We do not claim that this is a comprehensive history of museum-library interaction. Rather, we focus on museums or libraries that have assumed a hybridized role through collections that defy conventional categorization and expectations. Chapter 5 will then explore ways in which contemporary libraries can utilize these historical precedents to reconnect with their communities, "edifying, delighting, and perhaps even surprising" their patrons.[18]

WONDERS OF THE WORLD

The various terms synonymous with the phrase *cabinets of curiosities* are as diverse as the contents of the cabinets themselves. Words such as *Wunderkammern*, *Kunstkammern*, *studioli*, *repository*, and *museum* are interchangeable with *cabinet of curiosities*; the application of a particular term to a specific collection is generally a reflection of where the owner lived and the range of objects collected. Susan Pearce points out that the "notion of 'cabinet' in English could mean the small room in which the whole collection was housed, or the cupboards which held it, or the collection itself....The usage overall is very loose, benefiting the many-faceted and individualistic character of the whole enterprise."[19]

The incarnation of a cabinet of curiosities as a small room echoes the literal translation of the German word *Kammer* and the Italian word *studiolo*. It also best imparts the visual impact of these collections, as captured in engravings of prominent European cabinets. This is certainly the case with a 1599 engraving of the collection of Ferrante Imperato (1550–1631), a naturalist and pharmacy owner from Naples.[20] The image depicts four gentlemen gathered in a small room teeming with natural and man-made objects. Three of these individuals are grouped in front of floor-to-ceiling shelves, gesticulating in the direction of the preserved crustaceans, fish, and reptiles that ornament the room's ceiling. The fourth individual stands close to the room's only window and gazes in the direction of the cabinets positioned opposite the shelves. The cabinets themselves are divided horizontally into thirds, with stuffed birds standing guard in the recessed alcoves of the uppermost compartments. The contents of the lower two compartments reside behind cupboard doors. The engraving shows some of these doors opened, providing the four gentlemen (and the viewer) a glimpse of the intricate interior structure of the cabinets and the treasures housed within them. While these cabinet doors have a subdued decorative pattern, in other contemporary *studioli* the doors often served as a visual record of the curiosities they protected. In the *studiolo* of grand duke Francesco I de Medici (1541–87), "the cupboards are concealed by panels depicting various subjects symbolically related to their contents."[21]

The fact that a grand duke such as Francesco I de Medici and a pharmacist such as Ferrante Imperato both had *studioli* points to the demographics of these collections in sixteenth- and seventeenth-century Europe. On the one hand, there were "the princely collections"[22] of royalty—those of the Medicis, of Rudolf II (1552–1612) at Prague, Elector Augustus (1553–86) at Saxony, and, a century later, Peter I (1672–1725) at St. Petersburg, to name but a few. These princely collections were encyclopedic efforts to collocate diverse man-made and natural specimens "within a program aiming at nothing less than universality."[23] The idea that these specimens could express universality can be traced to "the belief that by using the devices of symbolism and allegory inherited from the Middle Ages, creation could be replicated in miniature and represented by the careful and deliberate assemblage of signifying objects."[24] The juxtaposition of objects in princely *Wunderkammern* was intended not only to replicate the workings of the universe, but also to convey the collector's position and prestige: "the collection itself stood as a huge allegory for the prince's absolute power."[25] The *studiolo* of Francesco I de Medici exemplifies this type of allegorical collection. Giuseppe Olmi suggests that it can be read "as an attempt to reappropriate and reassemble all reality in miniature, to constitute a place from the centre of which the prince could symbolically reclaim dominion over the entire natural and artificial world."[26] Pearce similarly acknowledges that the Medici cabinet was "intended to hold artefacts which represented the hierarchical order of the world as a microcosm of art and nature, in which the prince could appear symbolically as ruler."[27] At the same time, the ability to appear symbolically as a ruler had concrete foundations in the collector's access to the objects needed to create the microcosm. By assembling a miniature world of diverse man-made and natural artifacts, a princely *Wunderkammer* also "testified to material possession and far-reaching trade links"[28]—concrete signs of power outside the realm of allegory.

On the other hand, there were the "study collections"[29] of the professional classes. Some of the earliest and most renowned of these collections belonged to Ferrante Imperato in Naples, Antonio Giganti (1535–98) in Bologna, and his

peer and neighbor Ulisse Aldrovandi (1522–1605), who was referred to "by contemporaries as a 'second Pliny' and a 'Bolognese Aristotle.'"[30] Like princely collections, study collections were created with encyclopedic aspirations, though
the underlying impetus was not a straightforward symbolic display of the collector's power. As their name suggests, study collections served a didactic function
that corresponded to both the professional background and temperament of the
collector. These collectors had in common an inquisitive nature, and Matthew
Simpson points out that "a collection of curiosities was, first of all, the product
of a curious mind, essentially a personal effect rather than the creation of an institution or science."[31] The concept of an encyclopedic collection was therefore
applied within a narrower, more specialized framework in study collections than
was the case with aristocratic *Wunderkammern*. Describing the collections of Imperato and Aldrovandi, Olmi notes that the "essentially practical purpose behind these scientists' museums and botanic gardens was that of providing
opportunities for the first-hand observation of natural objects."[32] Indeed,
sixteenth-century study collections generally focused on natural specimens rather
than on man-made artifacts. Another description of the botanist Aldrovandi's
studiolo points to the fact that, "although not ignoring antiquarian items—sculptures, paintings, plaster models of statuettes, clocks, burning glasses, distorting
mirrors—his greatest interest was in animals, plants, fossils and rocks."[33]

Although study collections like Aldrovandi's emphasized natural specimens,
his display of flora and fauna with plaster models and distorting mirrors reveals
an overarching theme that links princely and study collections: the interaction
of art and nature as manifested by the display of objects representing these two
realms. The combination of natural and man-made artifacts worked on both
symbolic and didactic levels. With aristocratic *Wunderkammern*, the display of
objects from both *naturalia* and *artificialia*, as the two categories were known, was
intended to signify the collector's intellectual mastery of both domains. For example, Archduke Ferdinand II of Austria (1529–95), while not a naturalist by
training, nonetheless staged elaborate displays of *naturalia* meant to evoke realis-
tic scenes. In one case he grouped "corals together with sponges in a recreation
of their environment," thereby bestowing upon the display "a didactic value."[34]
Although this display suggests "a certain interest in nature, it would be a mis-
take to ascribe to Archduke Ferdinand any pronounced ambition to document
the environment in the sea [because] the exploration of nature was for the
Archduke a matter of representation, a facet of the normal activities of a
princely collector, testifying to his universal interest."[35]

While *artificialia* and *naturalia* together conferred an air of scholarly interest
upon aristocratic collectors, artworks in study collections served a didactic role
by complementing natural objects. For the botanist Aldrovandi, the "desire to
possess a complete documentation of nature led him not only to collect concrete
objects but also to undertake an enormous programme for the systematic illustration of the entire nature world."[36] In a description of his collection from
1595, Aldrovandi writes, "Today in my microcosm, you can see more than
18,000 things, among which 7000 plants in fifteen volumes, dried and pasted,

3000 of which I had painted as if alive....I have had paintings made of a further 5000 natural objects—such as plants, various sorts of animals, and stones—some of which have been made into woodcuts."[37] The reference to his collection as "my microcosm" reflects similar encyclopedic aspirations of princely collections—aspirations, which, if not to affirm the collector's power and position in the universe, were geared toward producing a microcosm of how the universe operates. While focusing on *naturalia* rather than *artificialia*, this type of study collection nonetheless demonstrates the intrinsic relationship between the two categories. The cleric and naturalist Antonio Giganti, for instance, arranged his natural and man-made artifacts together thematically to create "a harmonious vision which enabled a simultaneous evocation, or *ars memoriae*, of the whole of art and nature."[38]

Wunderkammern not only embodied a vision of art and nature as a harmonious whole, but also challenged the distinction between the two categories because "cabinets of curiosities juxtaposed the natural with the artificial, not least with the intention of remarking how nature was herself ingenious and artful, and art was the ape of the actual world."[39] More to the point, many of the objects displayed in the cabinets could not be assigned exclusively to one or the other category. As Lorraine Daston and Katharine Park comment, "not only did the *Wunderkammern* display *artificialia* and *naturalia* side by side; they featured objects that combined art and nature in form and matter, or that subverted the distinction by making art and nature indistinguishable."[40] John Dixon Hunt's description of art as "the ape of the actual world" rings true in many examples of cabinet objects that defied simple classification. While Archduke Ferdinand II created seascape vignettes by displaying corals and sponges in their original forms, Elisabeth Scheicher points out that these objects held his interest more "as material for carvings," especially the corals, which were "carved as mythological figures or beasts and mounted in cabinets."[41] Daston and Park, citing similar carvings in other collections (e.g., "a goblet formed from a nautilus shell"), question whether "these *Wunderkammer* showpieces" were *naturalia* or *artificialia* because "these hybrid objects undermined the nature-art opposition not only by transforming natural materials by craftsmanship (the simplest piece of furniture or clothing did as much); they additionally exploited an analogy of form...between the lip of a nautilus shell and the lip of a pitcher. Nature had, as it were, already begun the work of art."[42]

By blurring the line between *naturalia* and *artificialia*, "hybrid objects" simultaneously gained admittance to the overarching category that defined *Wunderkammern*—that of "wonders" or "curiosities." Indeed, the majority of the diverse objects that comprised both aristocratic and study collections reflected collectors' pursuit of the wondrous. As Daston and Park explain, "To count as one of the 'curious' was hence to combine a thirst to know with an appetite for marvels, which also came to be known as 'curiosities' in this period.... The new community of the curious was nearly as socially diverse as it was geographically far-flung, embracing aristocrats and merchants, physicians and apothecaries, lawyers and clergymen of all denominations; but it was united in its preoccupation with the marvels of art and nature."[43] They argue that the use of the term *universality* is somewhat misleading in the context of *Wunderkammern* because the collections "excluded 99.9 percent of the known universe, both natural and artificial—namely, all that was ordinary, regular, or common."[44] Rather, collectors attempted to achieve a sense of universality as defined by a set of distinct yet overlapping categories of wondrous objects. In addition to *artificialia* and *naturalia*, categories of curiosities included *antiquitas* ("mementos of the past");[45] ethnographical materials often referred to as *exotica* ("things from exotic, foreign lands");[46] and *mirabilia* ("everything beyond the normal and commonplace—the particularly large, the particularly small, and the misshaped—as well as the miraculous").[47] To be considered wondrous in the context of one or more of these categories depended upon a number of criteria: the rarity of an object's occurrence in the natural world, the exoticness of its provenance, the quality or level of skill evident in its craftsmanship, its monstrousness or freakishness, or even its ability to amuse—what Hans-Olof Boström refers to as the "'Aha!' experience" conferred by objects such as "halves of nuts with illusionistic wire insects" and "pairs of vexing gloves one cannot put on since they are sewn together."[48]

Inventories from both aristocratic and study *Wunderkammern* indicate that objects collected for their wondrous qualities transcended the various categories that defined these collections. Both the breadth and protean nature of this world of wonders can be seen in the category of *exotica*. Exotic curiosities were prized foremost for their origins—most often, Africa, America, Asia, and India—and were considered "tokens or emblems of societies whose very existence was a source of astonishment to the intensely parochial European public."[49] *Exotica* varied greatly in both form and function in cabinet displays. Cleric and naturalist Antonio Giganti collected *exotica* that simultaneously showcased the natural resources of foreign locales and "the utilization of such raw materials by non-European cultures."[50] Much like his penchant for arranging *naturalia* and *artificialia* together thematically "to achieve an effect of harmonious symmetry," Giganti's displays of ethnographic objects such as "feather head-dresses from Florida" and "a stone axe, a series of bows and arrows, and an obsidian razor" explored the relationship between indigenous materials and the man-made artifacts fashioned from them.[51]

The *exotica* category encompassed not only *artificialia* such as ethnographic materials, but also *naturalia*. Collectors valued the exotic origins—and therefore novelty—of flora and fauna in the same way they did man-made artifacts from foreign lands. In some cases, the novelty of natural specimens had less to do with geography than with perceived mystical associations. The cabinet of Englishman John Tradescant contained a collection of stuffed birds that was "impressively widespread in geographical origin, ranging from a penguin, through Brazilian, Virginian, and other New World species."[52] Alongside these various New World species was a display of "barnacle geese," which "attracted the curiosity of collectors on account of the tradition, enshrined in their name, that they sprang from barnacle shells adhering to driftwood and trees rather than from eggs."[53] Rather than representing the *exotica* of a foreign land, contemporary sources claim that this species was "a sorte of Geese sayd to grow in Scotland on trees."[54] Many of the objects classified as *naturalia* were also examples of *mirabilia*. What made the barnacle geese miraculous in the eyes of collectors was the perception of the birds as a manifestation of the perfection of nature. This notion is exemplified by one collector's description of the shells from which the geese supposedly emerged as "having within them little birds perfectly shap'd…making up a perfect Sea Fowl."[55]

There is another connection between *naturalia* and the category of *mirabilia*, defined as "everything beyond the normal and commonplace…as well as the miraculous."[56] Rather than producing a sense of wonder through their perfection, natural history specimens also were thought to be miraculous based on their freakish imperfections. Thus *Wunderkammern* in the sixteenth and seventeenth centuries boasted such specimens as a "chicken with two beaks" and "a deer with four ears."[57] The interpretation of deformity as both wondrous and curious—as well as the characterization of anything outsized as being miraculous—also applied to human subjects. Peter the Great's fascination with deformity led him to create a living display built around a boy named Foma. Foma had what is known as "'lobster claw' deformity," in which the "index finger and thumb fuse together, as do the fourth and fifth finger. These 'blended' digits are oriented in opposition to each other and function like a lobster claw."[58] Foma spent the rest of life, and beyond, in the display. In addition to serving as a living exhibit, he "died young, and Peter had him stuffed for permanent display at the museum."[59]

Regardless of whether objects belonged to the categories of *naturalia* or *artificialia*, *mirabilia* or *exotica*, there were numerous reasons for collectors during the sixteenth and seventeenth centuries to focus their efforts on acquiring "the new, the rare, and the unusual."[60] These motivations reveal the dynamic role that cabinets of curiosities played as tools for acquiring knowledge and proof of that knowledge: "Collected material…stands at the heart of modernist knowledge, both as evidence of particular truths, and as demonstrating what constitutes evidence.…Collections, therefore, do not merely demonstrate knowledge; they are knowledge."[61] Given that objects represent concrete evidence of knowledge, the new and rare materials displayed in a cabinet of curiosities would not only expand the knowledge of the inquisitive collector into previously uncharted areas, but also provide proof of this knowledge to the world. Indeed, collections of rare objects played a symbolic role such that both the knowledge and sense of wonder conferred by curiosities reflected favorably on their owners. Describing the role of study collections, Daston and Park explain that "the aim of the naturalist's collection of marvels, like the collections of princes from the dukes of Burgundy to Rudolf II, was to transfer the emotion of wonder from the objects themselves to their erudite and discriminating owner."[62]

More specifically, this emotion of wonder translated into social standing and power for the cabinet owners: "Objects of curiosity were widely exchanged within the nobility. Gifts made between such families were a means of reinforcing the sense of self-worth they enjoyed as a class, just as the degree of comprehensiveness of a collection could be reflected in the degree of esteem a collector enjoyed among his peers."[63] Yet collections of rarities were not simply a means of maintaining the social status quo. Since "the rare, outlandish piece…immediately conferred status on a collection and spread its fame beyond the scientific world,"[64] the owners of study collections used their novel specimens not only to garner the esteem of their peers, but also to curry favor with members of higher social strata. Marvels could also be "a vehicle for social mobility, bridging university and court for the natural philosopher on the make," as in the case of botanist Ulisse Aldrovandi, who "hoped to parlay an anatomy of a dragon whose appearance had coincided with the investment of Pope Gregory XIII into papal favors."[65]

Since cabinets filled with noteworthy curiosities could reinforce a collector's social standing or help him climb the social ladder, there was an obvious need for collectors to make these curiosities known. Of what benefit was a princely or study *Wunderkammer* if nobody knew about it? The response of collectors to this dilemma was to grant public access to their cabinets. Instances in which private collections served as public exhibitions were, with a few exceptions, extremely rare prior to the sixteenth century.[66] But the popularity of cabinets of curiosities ushered in a new era in which the strategic marketing of collections was a viable tool for social mobility and public recognition. By making their collections available for public viewing, both aristocratic and scholarly collectors were able to establish themselves as serious members of the "new community of the curious."[67] Olmi describes the effect of opening cabinets to members of both the aristocracy and the general public:

> Not only did the creation and enrichment of a museum constitute an occupation worthy of a nobleman; they were also a means of acquiring renown and prestige and of turning the owner's home into an almost obligatory sight for everyone. Nor was it just a question of attracting "cavaliers and curious ladies" or countless travellers from England, Germany and France. The popularity of the cabinet of curiosities had for a time the effect of overturning rigid social hierarchies, giving the collector the unique opportunity of attracting important personages of royal blood to his own home and of guiding them through his museum.[68]

One of the most prominent examples of the cabinet of curiosities as a means of social mobility is the collection that John Tradescant assembled at his home in 1628—a "house in which his collection was to develop into a nationally and internationally known spectacle and which was ultimately to give the house itself a new name—The Ark."[69] Tradescant, often referred to as John the Elder to differentiate him from his son, namesake, and fellow collector, began his career as head gardener to a series of noblemen. It was in this capacity that he was sent to track down *naturalia* for his employers' collections. At the same time, "he showed little reticence about using his position to procure items for his own garden and museum, often from duplicates or unwanted remainders of gifts or bribes initially intended for loftier hands."[70] This collection of "leftovers from the excesses of courtly consumption" around which Tradescant created the Ark was quickly enshrined as "a popular resort for visits by the mighty and wealthy."[71]

With the proliferation of collections accessible to the public in the seventeenth century—MacGregor points out that Italy alone had "some 250 *musei naturali*"[72]—collectors developed marketing campaigns to attract visitors. One component of these campaigns was the publication of catalogs that would draw attention to the wonders on display. Ulisse Aldrovandi published such a catalog in 1595 in which he emphasized both the range and quantity of marvels in his collection. "You can see more than 15,000 different things," he informs his reader, painting a captivating picture of "sixty-six armoires, divided into 4500 pigeonholes, where there are 7000 things from beneath the earth, together with various fruits, gums, and other very beautiful things from the Indies, marked with their names, so that they can be found" and stressing that there are many visitors who consider his collection to be "like an eighth wonder of the world."[73] For cabinet visitors who wanted less subjective descriptions of collections, there were also guides not unlike Frommer's and Zagat's of the early twenty-first century. Some guides "even lectured readers on cabinet etiquette: make sure your hands are clean, follow the guide obediently, don't admire things that aren't particularly rare—you'll make yourself ridiculous."[74] Reviews and recommendations of collections also appeared in contemporary publications. One visitor to the Ark in 1676 waxed rhapsodic in *The Universal Angler* about the various species of fish he encountered: "You may there see the Hogfish, the Dog-fish, the Dolphin, the Cony-fish, the Parrot-fish, the Shark, the poison fish, sword-fish, and not only other incredible fish! but you may there see the Salamander, several sorts of Barnacles…and such birds-nests, and of so various forms, and so wonderfully made, as may beget wonder and amusement."[75]

Another component of collectors' marketing campaigns involved how the curiosities were displayed. Aldrovandi makes a point of informing his reader and prospective visitor that the objects in his collection are "marked with their names, so that they can be found"[76]—a realization on his part that the arrangement of items played an important role in guaranteeing a pleasurable visit to his museum. People not only wanted to see the curiosities, but also wanted to identify and learn something about them. Collectors therefore made a concerted effort to enhance visitors' experiences through both aesthetic and didactic elements. Olmi indicates that the *studioli* of sixteenth- and seventeenth-century Italian naturalists such as Aldrovandi "were frequented for recreation and pleasure as well as instruction, because of the unusual and wonderful objects on display. This explains the fact that the arrangement of the products of nature within this setting was often determined by the desire for symmetry and a pleasing appearance.…The imposed order was not one believed to exist in nature itself, but one calculated to appeal to the eye of the visitor."[77] The English collector Robert Hubert developed specially coordinated, theme-based displays of certain types of rarities, which he advertised in his catalog as distinct exhibitions: "on

Mondays & Thursdayes things of the sea; Tuesdays and Fridays things of the land; Wednesdays and Saturdays things of sea land and air."[78] Hubert also boasted that group tours could be accommodated "in three or four tongues," revealing yet another technique for attracting and catering to visitors.[79]

Members of the aristocracy also arranged their princely collections into displays intended to please visitors, as in the *Wunderkammer* of Archduke Ferdinand II. He first selected raw material as the basis for grouping together various *artificialia* in his collection so that "the first cupboard contained the works in gold, the second silver, another bronze, and so on."[80] To further enhance this arrangement, Ferdinand had the interiors of the cabinets painted in colors that would both highlight and complement the objects on display: "the inventory of 1596 specifies colours for eight of the eighteen cupboards—blue being used for those containing gold, for example, and green for those housing silver—so that the background harmonizes the pieces displayed against it. In addition to aesthetic considerations, the row of cupboards was assured of the best possible light by its position in the middle of the room in front of the windows."[81]

BOOKS AND THE DIDACTIC FUNCTION OF CABINETS OF CURIOSITIES

The new emphasis on both attracting and pleasing *Wunderkammern* visitors affected not only how objects were displayed, but also the range of materials found in the cabinets. In addition to their careful labelling and display of objects, collectors included items that would help create an environment conducive to "recreation and pleasure as well as instruction."[82] Collectors thus began to exhibit local ethnographic materials to develop a comparative context for their *exotica*. As Impey and MacGregor observe, "Perhaps in response to a growing awareness of the value of these exotic exhibits as representatives of the societies which produced them, collectors began to take an interest in the formerly unconsidered elements of their own surroundings. Obsolete tools, peasant costumes and other items of local produce began to appear in collections as if in comparison with objects of antique or exotic origin."[83] They note that the same motivation led to the display of local *naturalia*: "Scholars began to consider their own local natural history...and to describe and collect items where possible. Fossils, incomprehensible as yet, and stone implements, which were still regarded as of natural origin, were actively sought, along with dried flowers, beetles and bones."[84] In the case of objects prized for their "technical virtuosity," such as a "nest of 52 wooden-cups turned within each other as thin as paper" and "Halfe a Hasle-nut with 70 pieces of housholdstuffe in it,"[85] collectors developed displays that stressed the aesthetic qualities of the items while explicating how they were created. Elector Augustus of Saxony (1553–86) was renowned for his appreciation of minute and intricately carved objects, stemming from the skills he himself possessed as "a highly trained ivory turner,"[86] and so "the lathes, tools, and magnifying glasses associated with the production of these objects were equally venerated in the collection and frequently were themselves provided with ornately worked mounts."[87]

Along with local specimens and tools, books played a significant role in the transformation of cabinets of curiosities into a source of both diversion and instruction for collector and visitor alike. In study collections, the combination of books and objects in displays reflected "the new scientific spirit which gave impetus to enquiry in the natural world."[88] Laura Laurencich-Minelli explains how Antonio Giganti—a man firmly grounded in the Renaissance—conceived of his collection, including the library, as a unity: "His museum and his library, while occupying two different though intercommunicating spaces, were unified to such an extent that the ceiling of the latter formed an exhibition space, and the former contained a table which formed a physical base for research, whether with books or with museum items."[89] Like Giganti, owners of princely collections generally housed their books in self-contained royal libraries. In numerous cases, these individuals also maintained distinct cabinets within their *Wunderkammern* for carefully selected books. Duke Albrecht V (1528–79) commissioned a building in 1568 that housed what came to be known as the Munich *Kunstkammer* and his court library on separate floors,[90] but the *Kunstkammer* itself included "a grey-painted case where certain books were stored, that is, valuable volumes often containing drawings or engraved illustrations. These were not kept in the court library since in the first place they were regarded as works of art, and secondly their artistic, antiquarian and numismatic content was relevant to the objects in the *Kunstkammer.*"[91]

In Britain, examples of books in cabinets of curiosities can be found from the sixteenth to the eighteenth century. One compelling example is the private library of Sir James Balfour (1600–57), which he subsequently expanded into a cabinet. Balfour, "having compiled a library of some distinction and of antiquarian flavour, and appreciating 'that things and events involved in obscurity are often illustrated by ancient coins, rings, seals and other remains of a former age,'...carefully collected this precious antiquarian material and arranged it in cabinets to supplement his library."[92] A century later, another prominent collector, Sir Hans Sloane, whose cabinets became the foundation for the British Museum, reserved an area of his cabinet specifically for books. A description of his cabinet is preserved in a visitor's account from 1710. The visitor's tour began with Sloane guiding him "into a room of moderate size, which was quite full. Above are three or four rows of books, while all the lower part is furnished with cabinets and natural curiosities."[93]

But visits to private collections "involved far more than just observing specimens in glass cabinets"; they were also "'interactive' encounters with exhibits."[94] The addition of books to cabinets of curiosities contributed to this sense of interactivity, providing relevant information that made the objects on display more immediate to the visitor. Books in cabinets of curiosities were not treated simply as another form of rarity to be shelved and admired, but rather as a resource to be used—one that would complement the other materials in the collection. Three cabinets in the *Kunstkammer* of Rudolf II contained books.[95]

Considering his intense interest in the fine arts, it is tempting to connect these volumes to the art treatises that were consulted by the artists who regularly visited his *Kunstkammer*. As Eliška Fučiková writes, "The Emperor's collection was a source of learning and inspiration and it represented an important resource for court artists. Landscape painters studied here the work of Dürer, Bruegel, Clerck and Bols. Painters of religious and mythological pictures scrutinized drawings and prints of famous masters of the Italian Renaissance and of Mannerism. They studied the compendia of classical art and various iconographical handbooks."[96] Even more detail about the functional relationship between books and objects can be discerned from accounts of Elector Augustus's *Kunstkammer*, also known as the Dresden *Kunstkammer*. As noted earlier, Augustus was a skilled ivory carver and had great appreciation for this branch of the arts. This interest and appreciation becomes apparent in a 1587 inventory of his collection, which indicates that Augustus possessed 7,353 tools, making up 75 percent of the total number of objects in the *Kunstkammer*.[97] The inventory also lists 288 books, representing 3 percent of the *Kunstkammer* collection.[98] These books provided a resource in support of the *Kunstkammer*'s didactic role of art instruction, and it was in this capacity that the books were lent to collection visitors. As Joachim Menzhausen recounts, "From the very beginning, it was not a museum in the sense of an exclusive exhibition; it was a working collection. Not only were there places to work practically everywhere, but there were numerous products, especially turned items, by the Elector himself and his son. Moreover,...artists and craftsmen were loaned tools, instruments and books especially for works ordered by the prince."[99]

Given these connections between books and objects in aristocratic *Wunderkammern*, it is not surprising that court librarians in the seventeenth and eighteenth centuries were responsible for acquiring both of these materials. References can be found to at least three court librarians who played an administrative or collection development role in their employers' cabinets of curiosities. Adam Olearius (1603–1671) was "appointed keeper of the Library and Kunstkammer at Gottorp" (the Royal Danish *Kunstkammer*) in 1649.[100] Lorenz Beger (1653–1705), employed as "Counsellor and Librarian to the Elector" (Elector Friedrich III of Brandenburg), was responsible for not only the library but also the *Kunstkammer*; he played "the most important role for Friedrich III's collections," overseeing the addition of "coins, medals and antiquities numbering more than 12,000."[101] Details are also known of the purchasing expeditions on which Peter the Great sent his "Librarian and Keeper of Rarities," Johann Schumacher, in 1711. As Oleg Neverov relates, Schumacher was instructed "to visit the museums of learned men, both public and private, and there to observe how Your Majesty's museum differs from theirs; and if there is anything lacking in Your Majesty's museum, to strive to fill this gap."[102] In keeping with his instructions, Schumacher acquired, among other objects, "ancient lamps, gems and engraved shells which he purchased at Utrecht."[103] Implicit in this description is the level of competition that existed among collectors who "vied with one another in the collection of marvels of art and nature that would impress visitors and trumpet their fame abroad."[104] It also suggests the trust placed in the competency of librarians to recognize not only the lacunae in cabinet collections, but also which rarities were worthy of consideration. This knowledge, in turn, would depend upon the librarians' familiarity with the cabinets themselves.

CABINETS OF CURIOSITIES AND THE UNIVERSITY LIBRARY

By the eighteenth century, European cabinets of curiosities had completed a gradual metamorphosis, emerging from the chrysalis of private ownership to become the cornerstones of nascent public museums. In some cases, royal *Wunder-* and *Kunstkammern* were converted into public institutions under the patronage of their aristocratic owners. Peter I opened the St. Petersburg *Kunstkammer,* the first public museum in Russia, in 1719. While it originally featured German and Dutch collections acquired during a massive buying spree in 1716, by 1728 the museum collection included the rarities previously on display in Peter's own personal cabinet.[105] In other cases, study collections were donated or bequeathed to institutions that had expressed interest in founding a publicly accessible museum. These institutions courted donors by emphasizing the care and accommodation of collections after the collector had passed away: "Whereas cabinets accumulated and owned by individuals were vulnerable to dispersal after that person's death, institutions had a corporate life beyond that of their members, thus offering a potential guarantee of indefinite continuity and growth for collections vested in them."[106] The incipient Royal Society of London sought "potential benefactors" in 1666 "with the assurance that their gifts would there be preserved for posterity 'probably much better and safer, than in their own private cabinets.'"[107]

One of most prominent examples of a public museum based on a private collection is the transformation of the Tradescants' collection at the Ark into the Ashmolean Museum at Oxford University in 1683. Widely recognized as Britain's first public museum, the Ashmolean was the creation of Elias Ashmole (1617–92), who had come to inherit the Tradescant family collection through his friendship with John Tradescant the Younger and subsequent legal wrangling with John's widow, Hester. An alumnus of Oxford, Ashmole deemed the university to be a proper venue for a public museum "devoted solely to the study of the natural sciences," and he made clear that his donation of the Tradescants' collection was contingent upon "the construction of a suitable new building by the university to house it."[108] This was not an insubstantial request. Construction expenditures "exceeded £4,500; an enormous sum, which so exhausted the university finances that for some years afterwards the Bodleian Library was unable to buy books."[109] Yet once it opened, the new museum had no difficulty attracting visitors, who "paid admission upon leaving the building, the fee calculated by the length of time the patron had spent looking at the exhibits."[110] A report from one visitor in August 1686 mentions that "when he and his brother attempted to visit...the upper room [the top floor of the museum building, where the objects were displayed] was so crowded with country folk, as it was market day, that they thought it better to come another day."[111]

While the Tradescants' curiosities, like many contemporary cabinet collections, were "gathered partly for reasons of family aggrandisement and partly for the sake of learning and the accumulations of knowledge about the material world,"[112] Elias Ashmole positioned his museum solely as an educational resource—one that would demonstrate firsthand to its visitors the workings of the natural sciences. He formulated his vision of the institution in the "Statutes, Orders and Rules, For The Ashmolean Museum in The University of Oxford" (1686): "Because the knowledge of Nature is very necessarie to humaine life, health & the conveniences thereof, & because that knowledge cannot be soe well & usefully attain'd, except the history of Nature be knowne & considered; and to this [end], is requisite the inspection of Particulars, especially those as are extraordinary in their Fabrick, or usefull in Medicine, or applied to Manufacture or Trade."[113] In addition to "the inspection of Particulars," or objects, Ashmole believed books to be a crucial part of "the knowledge of Nature," a point that he addresses in the museum's ninth statute. It stipulates that "all Manuscripts given to the Musaeum, shall be called the Library of the Musaeum, to the end the Curious, & such other as are desirous, may have the View of them; but noe person to use or transcribe them, or any part of them, but only such as the Keeper shall allow or appoint."[114] When the Ashmolean opened, it housed two libraries, one devoted to the topic of chemistry, the other to natural history and philosophy. While the focus of each library corresponded to the objects on display in the museum and to Elias Ashmole's vision of providing instruction in the natural sciences to the public, the libraries and the rarities were housed in discrete areas.

While the Ashmolean Museum at Oxford kept separate the museum libraries and display areas, Oxford's Bodleian library already had its own cabinet of curiosities. Foremost among the Bodleian's rarities was a collection of antiquarian coins that had been cataloged by none other than Elias Ashmole.[115] Along with numismatics, the Bodleian collection presented its visitors with "a miscellany of curiosities, mainly ethnographic items but also including such memorabilia as Guy Fawkes lantern"—donations from both alumni and merchants who "regarded the Bodleian as an appropriate repository for rarities acquired during their voyages."[116] As was the case with nascent museums, donors recognized that universities would provide a safe and permanent venue for their collections.[117] They also appreciated the fact that the rarities "would serve a direct didactic function" in their new educational setting.[118] One can also surmise that collectors enjoyed the prestige granted to themselves and their collections from an association with academic institutions. Indeed, the act of donating rarities for public exhibition is analogous to the public display of princely and study collections in the previous century—a process in which the "transfer to the public gallery of sumptuous private property...consecrated collecting as an expression of the worthiness of an individual life."[119]

Similarly, by recognizing both the monetary and symbolic value of the collections, the universities themselves—and their libraries—solidified their position in society through the acquisition and display of curiosities. Perhaps the most concrete example of this process is the library at St. Andrew's University, Scotland, between 1795 and 1838. Matthew Simpson paints a vivid picture of eighteenth-century St. Andrew's as "a visibly declining town" that "appear[ed] as if it had been ravaged by pestilence."[120] The university itself was in similarly dire straits, "short of money and, at times, of students," yet it could boast from the 1760s onward the "one public building which could be (and thereafter commonly was) recommended to visitors for other than antiquarian interest: the University's Library."[121] From a historical vantage point, "the Library was much more than a library; it was a depository for all kinds of artefacts, including paintings and objects normally associated with museums. It was a 'cabinet of curiosities.'"[122] As the university library accrued rare objects, it also accrued the symbolic significance imparted by these items. Like the earlier privately owned study and princely collections, the university library's cabinet was a means of transferring the wonder and significance of its contents to its proprietor—in this case, to both the university collectively and the library specifically.

Like the Bodleian Library cabinet, the St. Andrew's Library cabinet was eclectic, a result of being assembled from multiple donations. Simpson characterizes the majority of gifts from alumni and university associates as "ethnological," and an inventory of the collection from 1838 includes such *exotica* as "Pair of Snow Shoes from Canada," "One Burmese Idol," "Cloth (Africa)," and "Parasol from the leaf of Talipot tree (Ceylon)."[123] Since the collection was essentially a grouping together of donations from disparate sources, it is difficult to draw conclusive links between the objects on display and any specific course of learning undertaken by the students. But there nevertheless were affinities between the collection's *exotica* and particular volumes in the library: "the Sandwich Islands spear, for instance, and…the antipodean maps in the Library's gallery, were externalities of Cook's Voyages, which the Library had on its shelves." In much the same way, the numerous "accounts of voyages and travels" in the library, such as Philip von Strahlenberg's *Description of the North and Eastern Parts of Europe and Asia* and George Anson's *Voyage Round the World,* limned the very places that were the sources of the objects now found in the library.[124]

Just as these books situated the objects on display in the library, the rarities themselves situated the university within a broader cultural realm: the culture of the elite collecting community. The importance of the library cabinet extended beyond its identity as a collection of rarities to what the rarities collectively represented in that specific setting: "The library became a mission statement for the university, publicly committing it to an established metropolitan tradition of polite learning, and to the newer but related culture of British imperialism."[125] The display of curiosities in the library presented an image of how the university itself wanted to be viewed, much as it did for private collectors in the previous centuries. Indeed, the motivating factors behind the collections were the same: a means of satisfying an intellectual curiosity concerning the wonders of the material and natural world and of establishing and possibly furthering one's reputation. In the case of St. Andrew's Library, this entailed "rather a conscious effort to promote the purpose and elegance of the university within the eighteenth-century tradition of polite learning" by symbolically connecting the curiosities in the library—materials collected through British trade or exploration—to the trajectory of the British Empire in the nineteenth century: "the curiosities and maps were charting not simply British trade but also the British empire promoted by that trade and the successes of the British forces which were winning and securing the empire against other European states."[126]

The sphere of influence resulting from this connection can be visualized as a series of three concentric circles. The outermost circle represents the success of the British Empire, which is reflected upon St. Andrew's University (the second circle) by dint of its display of wonders gleaned from Britain's territorial ties and trade links. The connection between empire and university forged through these rare objects establishes the institution's reputation as a prominent academic and culturally refined institution. Finally, the innermost circle represents the university library, which houses the wonders and provides them with a specific intellectual context. While the cabinets of curiosities served as symbols of the position of the university in intellectual, social, and international spheres, the development and housing of these cabinets established the library as the center—the heart and spirit—of St. Andrew's. By the time the St. Andrew's collection was deaccessioned in 1838, the library was considered to be "the University's most demonstrable asset" and "the focus of the University."[127]

AMERICAN CURIOSITIES

As European *Wunderkammern* were evolving into publicly accessible museums or bolstering the prominence of universities and university libraries, cabinets of curiosities were just emerging in eighteenth-century America. Like their European counterparts, American cabinets strove to create a microcosm of the world through the display of natural and man-made artifacts. And, as was the case with earlier *Wunderkammern*, this replication of the world in miniature was not only a tool for scholarly inquiry, but also a flattering portrait of the collector. This was certainly true of Thomas Jefferson, whose "entrance hall at Monticello [was] a veritable cabinet of curiosities that included fine arts, natural wonders, ethnographical artifacts, and marvellous curios of human contrivance [that]... functioned as a public reception space where guests could entertain themselves, and...visitors were quick to associate the wide variety of objects displayed with the diverse interests of their owner."[128] Although Jefferson's collection mirrored European *Wunderkammern* in its breadth and completeness, it "was not a courtly expression of imperial magnificence or hegemonic power. Jefferson's more egalitarian intention, rather, was to create an *American* museum; that is, a display celebrating the indigenous puissance and incipient potential of the New World."[129]

As this description of Jefferson's collection suggests, American cabinets of curiosities differed from their European predecessors in both their focus and underlying purpose. The emphasis that Jefferson placed on American artifacts also characterized his compatriots' efforts to collect and display these materials. Moreover, these individuals shared a similar utopian vision in which their collections would edify and inform the public, rather than bolster their own reputations. Yet the most striking—and unlikely—distinction between American and European cabinets has less to do with what was collected and to what purpose than the fate of these collections. Despite the ideal of an American museum, American cabinets of curiosities did not metamorphose into public museums in the manner of European *Wunderkammern*. None of the first publicly endowed museums in America—the Smithsonian Institution (1846), the Metropolitan Museum of Art (1870), the American Museum of Natural History (1870) in New York, and the Museum of Fine Arts (1870) in Boston—can be linked to the curiosity cabinet phenomenon. Instead, the historical roles of American cabinets of curiosities were informed by the fact that these collections were "most often amassed in conjunction with libraries or historical societies, or by enterprising private collectors."[130]

While there is a disconnection between the American cabinets of curiosities of the late eighteenth century and the public museums founded a century later, "enterprising private collectors" did attempt to create an American museum from their collections. Twenty years before Thomas Jefferson displayed wondrous objects in his entrance hall, Pierre Du Simitière of Philadelphia opened his private collection of "flora and fauna, Indian and African artifacts, prints, drawings and books" to the public.[131] His enterprise lasted from 1782 to 1784; its relatively short existence can be attributed to Du Simitière's dual intent that the museum "broaden the artistic taste and attitude of the average citizen" while supplying him with supplemental income from the admission fee.[132] The museum's "fifty-cent admission charge was extremely steep," especially considering that Du Simitière's goal of edifying the public meant that the museum "maintained a high level of integrity, apparently never integrating popular amusements into the exhibitions, and never catering to cultural tastes at their lowest."[133] Two years after Du Simitière's museum closed, Charles Willson Peale opened his own museum in Philadelphia. An artist by training, Peale combined *artificialia* and *naturalia* in the creation of what he referred to as "a World in Miniature."[134] While the combination of art and natural specimens recalls European *Wunderkammern*, Peale's microcosm had a distinctly American focus, with displays that included portraits of luminous figures from the Revolutionary War, a complete mastodon skeleton, "nearly seven hundred specimens of birds exhibited in lifelike habitats, and cases of insects, minerals, and fossils."[135] Peale's museum, which operated from 1786 to 1845, "provided in miniature a synopsis of the New World, linking recent historical events to the grand context of nature and providing evidence of a natural providence legitimating those events."[136]

Like Du Simitière, Peale anticipated that his Philadelphia museum could simultaneously legitimate a nascent society, establish its cultural values, and furnish him with additional income. Unlike Du Simitière, Peale was successful in applying the formula of both entertaining and informing the public. While offering "authentic scientific displays, experiments, and lectures to an audience comprising both scholars and ordinary citizens," Peale also recognized that he had "to incorporate elements of popular entertainment" to appeal to these ordinary citizens.[137] This meant displaying the type of freakish *mirabilia* popular in European cabinets, such as "a chicken with four legs and four wings, an 80-pound turnip, [and] the trigger-finger of a convicted murderer."[138] Foreshadowing the edutainment model of today, the Philadelphia museum also attracted visitors by providing "live performers and light amusements" such as musicians and magicians.[139] Peale himself was reluctant to add these live amusements; however, his son Rubens, who took over the management of the museum in 1810, felt that "the museum's heavy didactic and moralistic tone repelled those Philadelphians who wanted to attend the place for relaxation and enjoyment."[140]

In addition to these privately owned and operated ventures, Philadelphia was also home to learned societies whose libraries incorporated cabinets of curiosities. One of these was the Library Company, founded in 1731 by Benjamin Franklin. While operating primarily as a subscription library, the Library Company not only made available books for a small annual fee, but also served "as an all-embracing cultural institution" for its members.[141] Accordingly, displays of objects were interspersed throughout the library—a juxtaposition recalling the combination of books and curiosities in European cabinets. Members of the Library Company "deposited in its rooms antique coins, fossils, fauna pickled in spirits, unusual geological specimens, tanned skins, and other oddities."[142] An influx of objects donated during the 1750s and 1760s, including "Roman coins," "Eskimo parkas," and "the hand of a mummified Egyptian Princess,"[143] resulted in the library having a cabinet of curiosities in the sense of both a collection of objects and a separate room for displaying these objects. A visitor in 1787 commented that "from the Library we were conducted into the Cabinet, which is a large room on the opposite side of the entry....Here we had the pleasure of viewing a most excellent collection of natural curiosities from all parts of the globe."[144]

The connection among books, objects, and intellectual inquiry also characterized the development of another prominent cabinet of curiosities in Philadelphia. The American Philosophical Society for Promoting Useful Knowledge was instituted in 1769, and its members included such collecting aficionados as Benjamin Franklin, Thomas Jefferson, and Pierre Du Simitière. As the name of the organization suggests, the members of the society "were interested in every sort of human knowledge and in everything that might improve American methods in agriculture, mechanics, manufacturing, and shipping," and, toward that end, they "felt a special responsibility to observe and record facts of nature and of man in America."[145] As with the library society, furthering human knowledge meant collecting and utilizing both print sources and natural and man-made artifacts. These artifacts were assembled in a cabinet of curiosities more by chance than by plan: "members and friends of the Society presented anything they thought significant, interesting, or merely strange."[146] In an interesting parallel to the cabinet of curiosities at the St. Andrew's University Library, the fact that the collection evolved randomly—rather than according to a prescribed plan—did not adversely affect its usefulness. For all intents and purposes, the society "serve[d] as a kind of national museum, library, and scientific academy," and during its early years of operation, members borrowed both books and artifacts "for study and examination at home."[147] And, as with the university library at St. Andrew's, the cabinet at the American Philosophical Society established the institution within the larger sphere of historically significant world events. The society's cabinet held numerous objects that, rather than representing the wonders of rare natural specimens or of fine craftsmanship, "were doubtless expected to inspire reverent thoughts and patriotic impulses in those who held or beheld them."[148] These items included "a fragment of Plymouth Rock," a clear glass bottle filled with "tea gathered at Dorchester Neck after the Boston Tea Party," "the chair with a writing arm on which Jefferson was said to have composed the Declaration of Independence," donated by his daughter, and "a square of marble from the Capitol 'conflagrated' by the British in 1814."[149]

By the 1850s, both the Library Company and the American Philosophical Society had dispersed most of the objects in their cabinets. By 1840, the American Philosophical Society's collection "was demonstrably an old-fashioned eighteenth-century cabinet of undifferentiated curiosities. It could not equal in extent or depth the more specialized collections of other institutions" in Philadelphia. The haphazard nature of the collection—what one uncharitable visitor called "meaningless and useless clutter"—was no doubt accentuated by the society's limited display space and a lack of personnel "with time, interest, and, in many cases, competence to study, arrange, and evaluate the various specimens." These factors led to the decision by society members in 1849 to donate the majority of their artifacts to institutions "where they might more appropriately be exhibited and studied."[150]

While the connection between cabinets of curiosities and libraries in America began with privately owned and operated enterprises, in the second half of the nineteenth century this relationship moved into the public realm. Around the time that private institutions were deaccessioning objects from their collections, public libraries in America were developing artifact collections. Unlike the more random nature of donated objects on display in learned societies, artifacts in public libraries were collected and displayed within a more specific framework, one in accordance with the American Public Library Movement. Not unlike the intent of Charles Willson Peale and Pierre Du Simitière to create museums that would edify the public, the core principle of the American Public Library Movement in the second half of the nineteenth century was the notion that public institutions such as museums and libraries could somehow affect the "betterment" of society. For libraries, this goal was articulated in the concept that "good reading led to good social behaviour."[151] Museums were similarly viewed as a means of dispensing what Tony Bennett calls the "the civilising influence of culture"—an influence "expected to give rise to social benefits" for those exposed to it.[152] The founding fathers of public libraries—and the librarians who implemented their visions—shared the goal of providing the public with the means for self-improvement, but only if they, in their capacity as moral guardians, could guide the process of improvement according to their views of appropriate public tastes. Indeed, library benefactors and librarians alike recognized the benefit of accomplishing this goal by combining the "civilising influence" of libraries and museums within one institution.

The development of the public library in Woburn, Massachusetts, is an example of how museums were incorporated into both the physical and intellectual plans of public libraries. The funding for the Woburn library, which opened in 1879, came from a bequest from Charles Bowers Winn. In addition to funding, Winn, who died in 1875, provided a vision for the components of the library. According to his specifications, it was to include "a book room and delivery area, at least two reading rooms, an art gallery, and a natural history museum, which was to house a collection of fossils, minerals, and birds that belonged to Winn's uncle."[153] Architect Henry Hobson Richardson thus designed a structure anchored at one end by what Woburn librarian George M. Champney referred to as "the Circulating department of the Library" and at the other by an octagonally shaped museum.[154] Period photographs show that the walls of the museum were lined with glass-fronted cabinets—a visual reminder of the cabinet of curiosities precedent that is also echoed in Champney's reference to the museum as "a Cabinet Room."[155]

The placement of the museum and library at separate ends of the building's primary axis is open to a number of interpretations. It imparts a visual equality between the two components of the library, but it also physically separates the book room from the museum. The impression is that the museum and book room are separate but equal entities, performing distinct functions within the institution. This interpretation overlooks the iconography of the ornamentation incorporated by Richardson throughout the building. Richardson, using the Oxford Museum of the Physical Sciences as a model, created a decorative, botanically accurate bower that spanned the entire building: "a diverse local flora has been carved into the capitals and cornices of the delivery and book rooms and wreathes the art gallery and natural history museum. In the book room, realistically portrayed specimens of horse chestnut, oak, butternut, and elm leaves, as well as a variety of fruits and flowers...replaced the more abstract and figural capitals of the Romanesque basilica."[156] The use of flora-inspired motifs extends beyond Richardson's personal aesthetic sensibility because the ornamentation "was also likely to have been intended to reflect the institution's lofty purpose—to prepare its visitors for the contemplation of its collections, which included specimens of art and natural history as well as literature."[157] The use of natural iconography in the building's decoration bridges not only the physical distance between the museum and book room, but also any conceptual distinction between the function of these components of the library. In this sense the design recalls the museum and library of the sixteenth-century collector Antonio Giganti, who considered these two facilities as "intercommunicating spaces"—a belief that manifested itself in the use of the library ceiling as a display area.[158] In the case of the Woburn library, images of flora and fauna serve the same role as the natural specimens that adorned Giganti's library.

The design of the Woburn building echoed the mission of the Woburn library it-self: to produce a public cultural institution with a broad educational scope.

The benefactors of the Woburn Public Library were not the only individuals contemplating the potential "civilising influence" that would result from merg-ing museum and library within a single public institution. In 1876, the U.S. Bu-reau of Education issued the multivolume work *Public Libraries in the United States of America: Their History, Condition and Management.* This report, which Champney studied during the planning stages of the Woburn Public Library,[159] consisted of numerous essays about library planning, including one written by Henry Simmons Frieze (1817–89) entitled "Art Museums and Their Connec-tion With Public Libraries." A classics professor, Frieze spent the majority of his career at the University of Michigan, where he served as president of the univer-sity and chair of its Latin department. He also had a deep interest in art, and he produced a biography of the nineteenth-century Italian sculptor Giovanni Dupré in 1887. It is perhaps not surprising, then, that he urges the amalgama-tion of art museums and public libraries into a single facility so that the merged institution would serve as both "innocent and improving recreation" and an "educational and refining influence" for the public.[160]

The arguments Frieze makes in support of the merging of art museums and libraries combine the often exalted rhetoric of the American Public Library Movement with practical considerations. Frieze argues that these institutions' "aims are kindred, indeed identical" insofar as both "promote the intellectual culture of the people" by elevating their collective taste.[161] At the same time, he observed that, while public libraries received funding through taxes, this type of financial support was less forthcoming for public art museums: "Now, can any just reason be given why the aesthetic faculty should be left out of our plans for public and popular education? why money should be expended for in-structive books, and not also for instructive and elevating works of art?"[162] To Frieze, the combination of art museum and library was a practical way of ad-dressing this oversight and of promoting the beneficial influence of both insti-tutions. In presenting his case, Frieze used a basic form-follows-function line of reasoning. Since public libraries and museums share similar goals, "their associa-tion under one roof would naturally follow from their internal relation." Again merging theoretical and practical considerations, he noted that public libraries and museums within a communal space would not only give physical form to their shared cultural mission, but would also boost attendance. Commenting on the "economy of connecting museums and libraries," he suggests that "the placing of the museum and library in one building would subserve the public convenience by saving time and trouble to visitors; and that thus both would be much more frequented than if they were situated in separate localities; and so both would accomplish much more effectually the purposes of their institu-tion."[163]

While Frieze discusses the economy of connecting museums and libraries in terms of public convenience, he also broaches the issue of economy in a differ-ent sense. His special interest in the relationship between libraries and art museums—as opposed to, say, natural history or anthropological institutions—reflects his belief in the importance of art education in an economic, as well as cultural, context. Observing that England "has opened museums of industrial and fine art in connection with free libraries as a new and legitimate instrumentality for educating and elevating the people," Frieze bluntly states that "already the beneficial effects of this movement are perceptible, not only in the improved tastes and manners of the large numbers who visit the museums and libraries for the purposes of study, reading, and recreation, but also in the improved training of young persons for the arts and trades."[164] In describing England's gains in this area, Frieze spoke to his audience's nationalistic impulses, raising the spectre of future generations of Americans left behind in art training and appreciation. His emphasis on training young persons for the arts and trades recalls Elias Ashmole's belief that the Ashmolean Museum at Oxford should collect not only wondrous objects, but also those that are "applied to manufacture or trade."[165] Frieze also suggests that art education has "an economical aspect," concluding that "a due regard even to the material interests of the nation, and to the successful prosecution of our national industries, should awaken in every community a lively interest on this subject. We should not rest contented with a state of culture in this direction inferior to that which has been attained by England, and far inferior to that enjoyed by some of the nations of the Continent."[166]

While Frieze's reference to Britain highlights that country's lead in connecting art museums and free libraries, it may also be a nod to its role as the foremost producer and distributor of plaster casts. Britain's "plaster shops made mass-production sculpture, from varieties of plaster treated superficially in various ways to resemble bronze, gold, and marble."[167] The sculptures themselves were reproductions of "great works" that travelers to Europe would have viewed on their grand tours and that were marketed as souvenirs for tourists. The casts were also sold for use in art schools, and these institutions were thus able to assemble "great art" from around the world for their students. One of the most comprehensive of these collections was in Edinburgh, begun in 1798 by the Board of Trustees for Manufactures in Scotland for their drawing school.[168] This collection of over 250 plaster casts came to be known as the Sculpture Gallery and was in existence until 1904.[169] Frieze, who had traveled abroad in 1855 and 1871,[170] was aware of the benefits of plaster-cast collections: "Some of the most interesting museums in the world, some of those most valuable at once for the artist, the scholar, and the tourist, consist mainly of copies; copies, made in plaster or of other material, of the great masterpieces of statuary, and well executed copies of the great painters."[171] Frieze describes how the new American museums/public libraries that he envisioned could likewise collect original artworks and "copies." Citing as a model the collection of plaster casts at the library of the Boston Athenæum, he fondly recollected that he "owe[d] his first impressions of the power of painting and sculpture to his occasional visits in early life to this gallery; where the Apollo, the Laocoön, and the Diana first opened his mind to the wonders of ancient sculpture."[172]

THE PUBLIC LIBRARY AND "THE NEW MUSEUM"

Despite enthusiastic plans for combining museums and libraries in the second half of the nineteenth century, the idea of such a hybrid cultural institution gave way, in practice, to a more subsidiary role for museums in libraries. Chicago's Newberry Library, founded in 1887, demonstrates how the museum-library concept evolved. Ten years after its opening, the Newberry established an in-house museum based on the Henry Probasco Collection, purchased in 1890, which consisted of 2,500 volumes, including "incunabula, Shakespeare folios, Grolier bindings, rare Bibles, ten early editions of Homer, nine of Dante, and eight of Horace."[173] Although the Newberry does include objects among its various collections—for instance, a history of the library mentions a donation of "the magnificent Walters collection of Oriental Ceramic Art" in 1898[174]—the museum itself served mainly as a type of exhibition hall for the library's print collections. A chronology of the library shows that, by 1923, "the 'Museum' [had] become the Ayer collection room,"[175] dedicated specifically to holdings related to "the discovery and exploration of the New World,"[176] while a separate space was created to display specially mounted exhibitions of the library's print artifacts. Rather than a museum as envisioned in the public library movement, the Newberry's exhibition space became "an afterthought, stuck in a corridor someplace, ill conceived."[177] At the same time, the Newberry's development of specialized programming suggests the historical precedent of an athenaeum, rather than of an integrated museum-library collection.

While the American Public Library Movement of the nineteenth century first gave voice to the idea of a museum-library as an institution dedicated to cultivating public tastes, a very different conception of the museum-library emerged during the American Progressive Era in the opening decades of the twentieth century. As Kevin Mattson suggests, between 1890 and 1917 "many Americans challenged the nineteenth-century romantic conception of a lone individual genius as being the sole creator of art; rather, communities could create works of beauty collectively and for themselves, not just for a genteel elite."[178] Mattson contends that the work of librarian and museum-founder John Cotton Dana must be viewed against this contextual backdrop. During his tenure from 1902 to 1929 as director of the Newark Free Public Library in New Jersey, Dana used the concept of community involvement and democratic ideals to establish the library as "a cultural center for the local community" and to connect library and community "in innovative ways."[179] One of Dana's innovations was to establish a museum within the Newark library, where, over a period of 15 years, he and his staff "did in the library many of the things that are done in modern museums," including the development of 74 exhibitions "visited by 300,000 persons."[180]

Although the idea of forming a cultural institution by linking the public museum and library echoes the designs put forward a generation earlier during the American Public Library Movement, Dana innovated by involving the community in forming this institution. While past models were intended to elevate public tastes according to an imposed standard, Dana, in keeping with the ideals of the American Progressive Era, wanted the institution to reflect the tastes and interests of the community itself. This required a new configuration of the museum, or what Dana termed "the new museum." Acerbic in his criticism of the museums of his day, Dana contends that "museums came to be so deadly dull" because they "are not made to fill a present need," but instead "are made in obedience to an ancient fashion."[181] This older approach treats the museum as a temple or palace to be filled with objects "first collected…by wealthy and powerful individuals."[182] Such objects, moreover, were valued for the qualities of age, rarity, and monetary value, rather than for their aesthetic or practical qualities, as in the following example: "The necklace found on an Egyptian mummy is unique, old, and costly. But even if presented to a museum by someone of wealth and influence, it still may be hideous and it may have no suggestion whatever for the modern designer."[183] Although he acknowledges the archaeological importance of such objects, Dana's primary objection is that their placement in the museum signifies the exclusion of materials that have a more direct bearing on the institution's user community. Because Dana's notion of community encompassed a diverse population with equally diverse interests, his solution was to create a new museum as diverse and eclectic as its surrounding community. The new museum, he wrote, "wishes to be useful to its community from the very first day of its existence."[184] Central to the implementation of this new model is the collecting and display of "that community's output"[185]—materials both produced and used by the museum's own patrons.

It is precisely the idea of collecting and displaying materials that serve the needs of a community that recommended to Dana the expanded role of the library as a new museum. Noting that "a good librarian is eminently well fitted to be a museum founder," he was firmly convinced that, "just as a librarian selects for purchase for a library for the public the books that will be to that public most acceptable and most useful and most used, so the director of a museum of the new type collects for his community not what convention and fashion say a museum should contain, but what a study of the tastes, industries, and pastimes of the community suggest as best fitted to fill that community's wishes."[186] Dana's image of the public library-museum was distinctive not only in its focus on community "tastes, industries, and pastimes," but also in its physical layout. Unlike the library at Woburn, his model does not house the library's nonliterary collection in a separate wing. Instead, books and objects were to be displayed together, a system that echoes the configuration of European cabinets of curiosities in the sixteenth through eighteenth centuries. Dana writes: "Connect the work the museum may do, its objects…with all the resources of the public library. In doing this, many books and journals will be displayed near objects on view, references to books and journals will be made on labels and leaflets of all kinds."[187] While the underlying objective of creating a seamless cultural institution echoes the earlier experiments in places such as Woburn, Dana's implementation is more radical. Instead of simply "subserv[ing] the public convenience" by placing both facilities in one building, as suggested by Frieze,[188] Dana creates a model in which the physical space and the function of the museum is subsumed by the library.

While the display of objects and books together is reminiscent of cabinets of curiosities, Dana's emphasis on community output in museum-library exhibitions marked a significant departure from what he referred to as museums' "mausoleums of curios."[189] He felt that the objects that belonged in "a living, active, and effective institution" for the community should be the materials most directly related to that community. In many cases, these objects represented the industrial arts. Mattson suggests that Dana was influenced by Progressive Era museums such as the Labor Museum that Jane Addams created in Hull House (Chicago), which displayed handicrafts and industrial arts "as if they too deserved aesthetic appreciation."[190] This influence can be detected in Dana's descriptions of an exhibit of porcelain mounted by the Newark library-museum: "In the pottery and porcelain exhibit of 1915, people in large groups, and especially the children, stood in fascination before a potter at work. They saw the relation between ancient and modern processes, traced through tools, designs, forms, and objects, the primitive bowl and jar, the modern teacup and bathtub. In this light the bathtub became to them an object of beauty and adventure."[191]

Dana used these materials not only "to show Newarkers that beauty and fitness are, and should be, basic elements in all the useful artefacts made by man, just as much as they are in the fine arts,"[192] but also to forge a link between historical processes and modern artifacts. While these artifacts represent objects that might be used by the community, Dana also highlighted the role that the citizens of Newark played in their production. In one example, Dana mounted a textile exhibit in Newark in 1916 in which, in addition to the handicrafts themselves, he showcased historical processes by having "a Greek woman spinning with a distaff and spindle" alongside "modern methods of spinning, weaving on Jacquard looms, and the more modern machine processes."[193] Dana thus used these exhibits not only to place industrial artifacts on equal footing with more traditional works of art, but also to show how these objects connected with the community's past and future in terms of both production and consumption. While the specific nature of the materials on exhibit represented one form of community outreach, so too did the role of the community in acquiring the objects on display. Dana relied heavily on and promoted the use of local collectors in gathering materials for these exhibitions. Accordingly, he admonished library/museum directors to "discover collectors and specialists and experts in the community and secure their cooperation in adding to the museum's collections."[194]

MUSEUM-LIBRARY HYBRID INSTITUTIONS TODAY

The concept of a cultural institution that combines the functions of museums and libraries, as envisioned by Frieze and Dana, has been reinterpreted in a contemporary context through museum-library partnerships. These reinterpretations vary considerably, ranging from the sharing of resources and expertise to the sharing of physical space. At one end of the spectrum, there is the collaboration between the Denver Public Library and the Denver Art Museum. Their close proximity to each other inspired the building in 1996 of "an underground concourse...to join the library and the museum."[195] Two years later, "a steel canopy...emerged from the museum's new entrance, symbolically reaching out to the library."[196] This reaching out assumes a more literal form as well, with the two institutions developing collaborative programs that incorporate "storytimes in the museum" and "art projects in the library."[197] Many of the IMLS partnerships discussed in chapter 3 are variations of the Denver model. In contrast to the symbolic reaching out of museum to library, partnerships at the opposite end of the spectrum involve merging the two institutions into one building. One manifestation is the satellite branch, exemplified by the Parent Resource Library in the Children's Museum of Houston, the Exploration Center at the Port Discovery children's museum in Baltimore, and Rex's Lending Center/InfoZone in Indianapolis. In addition to collaborating on programs, satellite branches entail a physical removal and relocation of resources, most often from the library to the museum. Another version of the museum-library hybrid institution can be found in the Sahara West Library and Fine Arts Museum in Las Vegas. The upper level of the Sahara West facility is the domain of the library and consists of a reading room, stacks, a children's/young adults' area, a story-hour reading room, and a meeting space.[198] The lower level houses the museum facilities, including a regional gallery, a main gallery, preparation, storage, workshop, and loading areas, a fine arts library, a gift shop, and a visiting artist's studio.[199] This is not the only museum-library hybrid building in the Las Vegas–Clark County library district. Seven years before the Sahara West Library and Fine Arts Museum branch opened in 1997, the central branch was reinvented as the Las Vegas Library and Children's Museum "to provide a central administrative location,...to bring back to the city a noteworthy public library; and...to provide a home for the Children's Museum."[200]

These experiments in contemporary museum-library hybrid institutions are not without controversy. As we mentioned in chapter 2, critics of the Exploration Center felt that the satellite branch used resources "to meet the needs of a museum created to attract tourists"[201] rather than the needs of regular library users. Charles Hunsberger, who, as director of the Las Vegas–Clark County library district proposed and implemented the city's museum-library hybrids, resigned "a year prior to his scheduled retirement...[because] the hybrid of library and museum caused an uproar in the local community for losing sight of its primary objective."[202] Clearly, the mere existence of museum-library hybrid institutions has engendered a great deal of controversy, not the least because there is much at stake in how cultural institutions position themselves in a twenty-first-century landscape marked by an increasing focus on outcome measures and edutainment.

In the next chapter we propose a variation on the museum-library hybrid institution, one that would avoid the problems of institutional autonomy and community roles that often characterize collaborative museum-library projects. Rather than partnering with museums, we suggest that academic and public libraries become library-museum hybrids by creating their own cabinets of curiosities. While partnerships can take resources and services away from a library's user community, the cabinet of curiosities model can augment the library's permanent text-based collections with objects and artifacts typically associated with museums.

NOTES

1. Karen Brown and Miriam Pollack, "Illinois Libraries and Museums: Connecting and Collaborating for the Future," *Illinois Libraries* 82 (summer 2000): 211.

2. Ray Lester, "The Convergence of Museums and Libraries?" *Alexandria* 13 (March 2001): 184.

3. Hal Niedzviecki, "Libraries Need to Mind Their Own Business," *The Globe and Mail*, 27 October 2003, R3.

4. Robert S. Martin, "Blurring the Boundaries of Cultural Institutions," (presented at the Natural Science Collections Alliance conference, Washington, D.C., 7 June 2002), par. 17, 28, 29, http://www.imls.gov/whatsnew/current/sp041902 (accessed September 9, 2003).

5. Ibid., par. 27.

6. Ibid., par. 28.

7. Lester, "The Convergence of Museums and Libraries?" 190.

8. Ibid.

9. Ibid.

10. Martin, "Blurring the Boundaries," par. 17.

11. Brian Edwards, with Biddy Fisher, *Libraries and Learning Resource Centres* (Oxford: Architectural Press, 2002), 19.

12. Ibid.

13. Oliver Impey and Arthur MacGregor, eds., "Introduction," in *The Origins of Museums: The Cabinet of Curiosities in Sixteenth- and Seventeenth-Century Europe* (Oxford: Clarendon Press, 1985), 1.

14. Lawrence Weschler, *Mr. Wilson's Cabinet of Wonder* (New York: Vintage, 1996), 60.

15. Jeanne Bornstein, Meg Maher, and Holland Goss, "The Public's Treasures: A Cabinet of Curiosities," par. 1, http://www.nypl.org/research/chss/events/images/curiosities brochure.pdf (accessed July 8, 2003).

16. Michael Frank, "Will Wonders Never Cease?" *New York Times*, 21 June 2002, B36.

17. Institute of Museum and Library Services, "2003 National Leadership Grants for Libraries and Museums," part 1.6, http://www.imls.gov (accessed March 19, 2003).

18. Bornstein, Maher, and Goss, "The Public's Treasures," par. 1.

19. Susan M. Pearce, *On Collecting: An Investigation into Collecting in the European Tradition* (London: Routledge, 1995), 109.

20. Lorraine Daston and Katharine Park note that this engraving by Costantino Vitale, which originally appeared as "the frontspiece of the treatise on natural history" written by Ferrante Imperato himself entitled *Dell'Historia Naturale di Ferrante Imperato Napolitano,* "is the first image of an early modern collection" in *Wonders and the Order of Nature, 1150–1750* (New York: Zone Books, 1998), 153. This engraving is reproduced in

a number of books on the subject of *Wunderkammern*, including Daston and Park, *Wonders and the Order of Nature* (figure 4.4.1), Impey and MacGregor, *The Origin of Museums* (figure 4), and Weschler, *Mr. Wilson's Cabinet of Wonder* (end pages).

21. Giuseppe Olmi, "Science-Honour-Metaphor: Italian Cabinets of the Sixteenth and Seventeenth Centuries," in *The Origins of Museums: The Cabinet of Curiosities in Sixteenth- and Seventeenth-Century Europe*, ed. Oliver Impey and Arthur MacGregor (Oxford: Clarendon Press, 1985), 7.

22. Arno Victor Nielsen, *Museum Europa: An Exhibition About the European Museum from the Renaissance to Our Time* (Copenhagen: The Danish National Museum, 1993), 16.

23. Ibid.

24. Anthony Alan Shelton, "Cabinets of Transgression: Renaissance Collections and the Incorporation of the New World," in *The Cultures of Collecting*, ed. John Elsner and Roger Cardinal (London: Reaktion Books, 1994), 184.

25. Nielsen, *Museum Europa*, 16.

26. Olmi, "Science-Honour-Metaphor," 5.

27. Pearce, *On Collecting*, 112.

28. Nielsen, *Museum Europa*, 16.

29. Ibid.

30. Daston and Park, *Wonders and the Order of Nature*, 154.

31. Matthew Simpson, " 'You Have Not Such a One in England': St Andrew's University Library as an Eighteenth-Century Mission Statement," *Library History* 17 (March 2001): 45–46.

32. Olmi, "Science-Honour-Metaphor," 6.

33. Laura Laurencich-Minelli, "Museology and Ethnographical Collections in Bologna During the Sixteenth and Seventeenth Centuries," in *The Origins of Museums: The Cabinet of Curiosities in Sixteenth- and Seventeenth-Century Europe*, ed. Oliver Impey and Arthur MacGregor (Oxford: Clarendon Press, 1985), 19–20.

34. Elisabeth Scheicher, "The Collection of Archduke Ferdinand II at Schloss Ambras: Its Purpose, Composition and Evolution," in *The Origins of Museums: The Cabinet of Curiosities in Sixteenth- and Seventeenth-Century Europe*, ed. Oliver Impey and Arthur MacGregor (Oxford: Clarendon Press, 1985), 32.

35. Ibid., 33.

36. Olmi, "Science-Honour-Metaphor," 7–8.

37. Daston and Park, *Wonders and the Order of Nature*, 154.

38. Laurencich-Minelli, "Museology and Ethnographical Collections in Bologna," 19.

39. John Dixon Hunt, "*Curiosities* to Adorn *Cabinets* and *Gardens*," in *The Origins of Museums: The Cabinet of Curiosities in Sixteenth- and Seventeenth-Century Europe*, ed. Oliver Impey and Arthur MacGregor (Oxford: Clarendon Press, 1985), 198.

40. Daston and Park, *Wonders and the Order of Nature*, 277.

41. Scheicher, "The Collection of Archduke Ferdinand II," 33.

42. Ibid.

43. Ibid., 218.

44. Ibid., 272.

45. Nielsen, *Museum Europa*, 13.

46. Scheicher, "The Collection of Archduke Ferdinand II," 34.

47. Ibid.

48. Hans-Olof Boström, "Philipp Hainhofer and Gustavus Adolphus's *Kunstschrank* in Uppsala," in *The Origins of Museums: The Cabinet of Curiosities in Sixteenth- and Seventeenth-Century Europe*, ed. Oliver Impey and Arthur MacGregor (Oxford: Clarendon Press, 1985), 97–98.

49. Impey and MacGregor, "Introduction," 2.

50. Laurencich-Minelli, "Museology and Ethnographical Collections in Bologna," 18.

51. Ibid, 18–19.

52. Arthur MacGregor, "Collectors and Collections of Rarities in the Sixteenth and Seventeenth Centuries," in *Tradescant's Rarities: Essays on the Foundation of the Ashmolean Museum 1683 with a Catalogue of the Surviving Early Collections* (Oxford: Clarendon Press, 1983), 91.

53. Ibid., 91–92.

54. Ibid., 92.

55. Ibid.

56. Scheicher, "The Collection of Archduke Ferdinand II," 34.

57. MacGregor, "Collectors and Collections of Rarities," 92.

58. Stephen T. Asma, *Stuffed Animals and Pickled Heads: The Culture and Evolution of Natural History Museums* (Oxford: Oxford University Press, 2001), 4.

59. Ibid., 5.

60. Daston and Park, *Wonders and the Order of Nature*, 310.

61. Pearce, *On Collecting*, 111.

62. Daston and Park, *Wonders and the Order of Nature*, 158.

63. Shelton, "Cabinets of Transgression," 187.

64. Olmi, "Science-Honour-Metaphor," 8.

65. Daston and Park, *Wonders and the Order of Nature*, 216.

66. MacGregor, "Collectors and Collections of Rarities," 70.

67. Daston and Park, *Wonders and the Order of Nature*, 218.

68. Olmi, "Science-Honour-Metaphor," 13.

69. Arthur MacGregor, ed., "The Tradescants as Collectors of Rarities," in *Tradescant's Rarities: Essays on the Foundation of the Ashmolean Museum 1683 with a Catalogue of the Surviving Early Collections* (Oxford: Clarendon Press, 1983), 20.

70. Susan Pearce and Ken Arnold, eds., "The Catalogue of the Tradescant Collection: England's First Substantial Museum," in *Early Voices*, vol. 2, *The Collector's Voice: Critical Readings in the Practice of Collecting* (Aldershot, England: Ashgate, 2000), 50.

71. Ibid.

72. MacGregor, "Collectors and Collections of Rarities," 73.

73. Daston and Park, *Wonders and the Order of Nature*, 154.

74. Ibid., 266.

75. Martin Welch, "The Foundation of the Ashmolean Museum," in *Tradescant's Rarities: Essays on the Foundation of the Ashmolean Museum 1683 with a Catalogue of the Surviving Early Collections*, ed. Arthur MacGregor (Oxford: Clarendon Press, 1983), 45–46.

76. Daston and Park, *Wonders and the Order of Nature*, 154.

77. Olmi, "Science-Honour-Metaphor," 8–9.

78. Arthur MacGregor, "The Cabinet of Curiosities in Seventeenth-Century Britain," in *The Origins of Museums: The Cabinet of Curiosities in Sixteenth- and Seventeenth-Century Europe*, ed. Oliver Impey and Arthur MacGregor (Oxford: Clarendon Press, 1985), 153.

79. Ibid.

80. Scheicher, "The Collection of Archduke Ferdinand II," 31.

81. Ibid.

82. Olmi, "Science-Honour-Metaphor," 8.

83. Impey and MacGregor, "Introduction," 2.

84. Ibid.

85. MacGregor, "Collectors and Collections of Rarities," 73.

86. Joachim Menzhausen, "Elector Augustus's *Kunstkammer*: An Analysis of the Inventory of 1587," in *The Origins of Museums: The Cabinet of Curiosities in Sixteenth- and Seventeenth-Century Europe*, ed. Oliver Impey and Arthur MacGregor (Oxford: Clarendon Press, 1985), 71.

87. MacGregor, "Collectors and Collections of Rarities," 73.

88. Olmi, "Science-Honour-Metaphor," 8.

89. Laurencich-Minelli, "Museology and Ethnographical Collections in Bologna," 18.

90. Lorenz Seelig, "The Munich Kunstkammer, 1565–1807," in *The Origins of Museums: The Cabinet of Curiosities in Sixteenth- and Seventeenth-Century Europe*, ed. Oliver Impey and Arthur MacGregor (Oxford: Clarendon Press, 1985), 77.

91. Ibid., 79.

92. MacGregor, "The Cabinet of Curiosities in Seventeenth-Century Britain," 154–55.

93. Susan Pearce and Ken Arnold, eds., "Zacharias Conrad von Uffenbach Describes Hans Sloane's Collection," in *Early Voices*, vol. 2, *The Collector's Voice: Critical Readings in the Practice of Collecting* (Aldershot, England: Ashgate, 2000), 111.

94. Ibid., 113.

95. Eliška Fučiková, "The Collection of Rudolf II at Prague: Cabinet of Curiosities or Scientific Museum?" in *The Origins of Museums: The Cabinet of Curiosities in Sixteenth- and Seventeenth-Century Europe*, ed. Oliver Impey and Arthur MacGregor (Oxford: Clarendon Press, 1985), 50.

96. Ibid., 53.

97. Menzhausen, "Elector Augustus's *Kunstkammer*," 72.

98. Ibid.

99. Ibid., 73.

100. Bente Gundestrup, "From the Royal *Kunstkammer* to the Modern Museums of Copenhagen," in *The Origins of Museums: The Cabinet of Curiosities in Sixteenth- and Seventeenth-Century Europe*, ed. Oliver Impey and Arthur MacGregor (Oxford: Clarendon Press, 1985), 129.

101. Christian Theuerkauff, "The Brandenburg *Kunstkammer* in Berlin," in *The Origins of Museums: The Cabinet of Curiosities in Sixteenth- and Seventeenth-Century Europe*, ed. Oliver Impey and Arthur MacGregor (Oxford: Clarendon Press, 1985), 111.

102. Oleg Neverov, "'His Majesty's Cabinet' and Peter I's *Kunstkammer*," trans. Gertrud Seidmann, in *The Origins of Museums: The Cabinet of Curiosities in Sixteenth- and*

Seventeenth-Century Europe, ed. Oliver Impey and Arthur MacGregor (Oxford: Clarendon Press, 1985), 55–56.

103. Ibid.

104. Daston and Park, *Wonders and the Order of Nature*, 266–67.

105. Neverov, "'His Majesty's Cabinet' and Peter I's *Kunstkammer*," 56.

106. Michael Hunter, "The Cabinet Institutionalized: The Royal Society's 'Repository' and Its Background," in *The Origins of Museums: The Cabinet of Curiosities in Sixteenth- and Seventeenth-Century Europe*, ed. Oliver Impey and Arthur MacGregor (Oxford: Clarendon Press, 1985), 159.

107. Ibid.

108. Welch, "The Foundation of the Ashmolean Museum," 40, 58.

109. Ibid., 49.

110. Stephen Mihm, "Museums: Firsts, Facts and Figures," *New York Times*, 19 April 2000, D20.

111. Martin Welch, "The Ashmolean as Described by Its Earliest Visitors," in *Tradescant's Rarities: Essays on the Foundation of the Ashmolean Museum 1683 with a Catalogue of the Surviving Early Collections*, ed. Arthur MacGregor (Oxford: Clarendon Press, 1983), 62.

112. Pearce and Arnold, "The Catalogue of the Tradescant Collection," 51.

113. Susan Pearce and Ken Arnold, eds., "Elias Ashmole Organises the Ashmolean Museum, Oxford," in *Early Voices*, vol. 2, *The Collector's Voice: Critical Readings in the Practice of Collecting* (Aldershot, England: Ashgate, 2000), 101.

114. Ibid., 102.

115. Ibid.

116. Hunter, "The Cabinet Institutionalized," 160–61.

117. Ibid., 160.

118. Ibid.

119. Shelton, "Cabinets of Transgression," 187.

120. Simpson, " 'You Have Not Such a One in England,' " 41–42.

121. Ibid., 42.

122. Ibid., 43.

123. Ibid., 52–53.

124. Ibid., 50.

125. Ibid., 51.

126. Ibid., 41, 49.

127. Ibid., 43.

128. Joyce Henri Robinson, "An American Cabinet of Curiosities: Thomas Jefferson's 'Indian Hall' at Monticello," in *Acts of Possession*, ed. Leah Dilworth (New Brunswick, NJ: Rutgers University Press, 2003), 17.

129. Ibid., 26.

130. Ibid., 21.

131. Andrea Stulman Dennett, *Weird and Wonderful: The Dime Museum in America* (New York: New York University Press, 1997), 10.

132. Ibid.

133. Ibid., 11–12.

134. Robinson, "An American Cabinet of Curiosities," 28.

135. Ibid., 28–29.

136. Susan Stewart, "Death and Life, in that Order, in the Works of Charles Willson Peale," in *The Cultures of Collecting*, ed. John Elsner and Roger Cardinal (London: Reaktion Books, 1994), 207.

137. Dennett, *Weird and Wonderful*, 12–13.

138. Ibid., 12.

139. Ibid., 13.

140. Ibid.

141. The Library Company, "At the Instance of Benjamin Franklin: A Brief History of the Library Company of Philadelphia," par. 6, http://www.librarycompany.org/instance.htm (accessed July 8, 2003).

142. Ibid.

143. Ibid., par. 13.

144. Ibid., par. 23.

145. Whitfield J. Bell Jr., ed., "The Cabinet of the American Philosophical Society," in *A Cabinet of Curiosities: Five Episodes in the Evolution of American Museums* (Charlottesville: University Press of Virginia, 1967), 1.

146. Ibid.

147. Ibid., 5, 8.

148. Ibid., 16.

149. Ibid., 16, 19.

150. All quotes in this paragraph are from Bell, "The Cabinet of the American Philosophical Society," 2–3, 16, 21.

151. Wayne A. Wiegand, "The Development of Librarianship in the United States," *Libraries and Culture* 24 (winter 1989): 102.

152. Tony Bennett, "The Multiplication of Culture's Utility," *Critical Inquiry* 21 (summer 1995): 877.

153. Kenneth A. Breisch, *Henry Hobson Richardson and the Small Public Library in America: A Study in Typology* (Cambridge, MA: MIT Press, 1997), 108.

154. Ibid., 110.

155. Ibid.

156. Ibid., 134.

157. Ibid., 137.

158. Laurencich-Minelli, "Museology and Ethnographical Collections in Bologna," 18.

159. Breisch, *Henry Hobson Richardson*, 111.

160. Henry Simmons Frieze, "Art Museums and Their Connection with Public Libraries," in *Public Libraries in the United States of America: Special Report: Part I,* by U.S. Bureau of Education (Washington, DC: Government Printing Office, 1876), 437–38.

161. Ibid., 440.

162. Ibid., 438.

163. Ibid., 440.

164. Ibid., 435.

165. Pearce and Arnold, "Elias Ashmole Organises the Ashmolean," 101.

166. Frieze, "Art Museums," 435–36.

167. Susan Pearce and Ken Arnold, eds., "Plaster Shops in Britain, 1760–1820," in *Early Voices*, vol. 2, *The Collector's Voice: Critical Readings in the Practice of Collecting* (Aldershot, England: Ashgate, 2000), 223.

168. Susan Pearce and Ken Arnold, eds., "The Edinburgh Trustees Buy Classical Plaster Casts for Their Academy," in *Early Voices*, vol. 2, *The Collector's Voice: Critical Readings in the Practice of Collecting* (Aldershot, England: Ashgate, 2000), 233.

169. Ibid.

170. Garance Worters, ed., *American Biographical Archive* (London: K.G. Saur, 1986), microfiche, sheet 577, frame 336.

171. Frieze, "Art Museums," 439.

172. Ibid., 434.

173. Lawrence W. Towner, "A History of the Newberry Library," in *Humanities' Mirror: Reading at the Newberry, 1887–1987*, ed. Rolf Achilles (Chicago: The Newberry Library, 1987), 19.

174. Rolf Achilles, ed., "The Newberry in Fact," in *Humanities' Mirror: Reading at the Newberry, 1887–1987* (Chicago: The Newberry Library, 1987), 68.

175. Ibid., 74.

176. James M. Well, "Building the Collection," in *Humanities' Mirror: Reading at the Newberry, 1887–1987*, ed. Rolf Achilles (Chicago: The Newberry Library, 1987), 30.

177. Lawrence W. Towner, *Past Imperfect: Essays on History, Libraries, and the Humanities* (Chicago: The University of Chicago Press, 1993), 166.

178. Kevin Mattson, "The Librarian as Secular Minister to Democracy: The Life and Ideas of John Cotton Dana," *Libraries and Culture* 35 (fall 2000): 517.

179. Ibid., 514.

180. John Cotton Dana, "The New Museum," in *The New Museum: Selected Writings by John Cotton Dana*, ed. William A. Penniston (Newark, NJ: The Newark Museum Association, 1999), 31. Originally published in John Cotton Dana, *The New Museum Series, no. 1* (Woodstock, VT: The Elm Tree Press, 1917).

181. John Cotton Dana, "Libraries and Museums: How Museums Came to Be So Deadly Dull," in *The New Museum: Selected Writings by John Cotton Dana*, ed. William A. Penniston (Newark, NJ: The Newark Museum Association, 1999), 118. Originally published in *The Library Journal* 46 (15 May 1921).

182. John Cotton Dana, "The Gloom of the Museum," in *The New Museum: Selected Writings by John Cotton Dana*, ed. William A. Penniston (Newark, NJ: The Newark Museum Association, 1999), 48. Originally published in John Cotton Dana, *The New Museum Series, no. 2* (Woodstock, VT: The Elm Tree Press, 1917).

183. Ibid., 56.

184. Dana, "Libraries and Museums," 123.

185. Dana, "The Gloom of the Museum," 56.

186. Dana, "Libraries and Museums," 123.

187. Dana, "The New Museum," 29.

188. Frieze, "Art Museums," 440.

189. Mattson, "The Librarian as Secular Minister," 523.

190. Ibid., 516.

191. John Cotton Dana, "A Museum of, for, and by Newark," in *The New Museum: Selected Writings by John Cotton Dana*, ed. William A. Penniston (Newark, NJ: The Newark Museum Association, 1999), 176. Originally published in *The Survey: Graphic Number 55*, no. 11 (1 March 1926).

192. Ibid.

193. Ibid., 175.

194. Dana, "The New Museum," 28.

195. Elizabeth Heilman Brooke, "Car Showrooms Give Way to Cultural Showcases," *New York Times*, 3 June 1999, B2.

196. Ibid.

197. Betsy Diamant-Cohen and Dina Sherman, "Hand in Hand: Museums and Libraries Working Together," *Public Libraries* 42 (March/April 2003): 104.

198. Karen Stein, "Meyer, Scherer and Rockcastle's Sahara West Library and Fine Arts Museum Is a World Apart from the Las Vegas Strip," *Architectural Record* 185 (March 1997): 58.

199. Ibid.

200. Joyce K. Dixon, "Experiencing Architecture: The Young People's Library Department in Las Vegas," *School Library Journal* 37 (February 1991): 30.

201. Jane Shipley, "Role of Pratt's Exploration Center Clarified: Jane Shipley Responds," *Baltimore Chronicle*, 27 June 2001, par. 22, http://baltimorechronicle.com/pratt_jul01.html (accessed June 21, 2003).

202. Stein, "Meyer, Scherer *and* Rockcastle," 55.

5   LESSONS FROM THE PAST AND MODELS FOR THE FUTURE

The evolution from privately owned *Wunderkammern* to publicly accessible, institution-based collections follows two trajectories, both of which illustrate how museums and libraries historically have faced the challenge of simultaneously educating and entertaining their patrons. Although both trajectories are essentially postobject-based, the first trajectory culminates in the edutainment phenomenon, while the second culminates in an educational approach that tries not to succumb to the easy temptations of edutainment.

Pierre Du Simitière, Charles Willson Peale, and his son Rubens Peale all navigated the edutainment course with varying degrees of success. At one end of the spectrum is Du Simitière's abbreviated attempt to convert his cabinet of curiosities into a public museum. Although many visitors did come to his museum, "it did not appeal to a broad spectrum of people"—a result of his reluctance to incorporate "popular amusements into the exhibitions."1 Du Simitière died of starvation in 1784—the same year that his museum closed—and his collection was dispersed through an auction.[2] At the other end of the edutainment spectrum are Rubens Peale's American museums. Fifteen years after he introduced live entertainment into his father's Philadelphia museum, Rubens opened a satellite museum in New York in 1825. To an even greater extent than the Philadelphia museum, the New York museum focused on attracting visitors with popular displays. Andrea Dennett explains that "Rubens knew that it was the outrageous curiosities that brought visitors; in early May 1828, Peale's New York museum exhibited 'a calf with two heads, six legs, two tails, two distinct hearts and backbones.' Rubens also placed on exhibition…a 'learned dog' named Romeo, who entertained by barking answers to questions."[3] Despite (or perhaps because of) this approach, Rubens ran into financial troubles in 1830, and P. T. Barnum of Barnum and Bailey Circus fame purchased the museum in the 1840s from Peale's creditors, converting "it into a full-fledged dime museum."[4] In contrast to Charles Willson Peale's vision of an American museum—what he referred to as an "'open book of nature' displayed for the leisurely perusal of the public"[5]—American dime museums existed solely to entertain visitors, using "dioramas, panoramas, georamas, cosmoramas, paintings, relics, freaks, stuffed animals, menageries, waxworks, and theatrical performances."[6]

Du Simitière's and Peale's very different responses to the issue of simultaneously edifying and entertaining the public serve as cautionary lessons for museums and libraries at the beginning of the twenty-first century. On the one hand, museums and libraries that do not conform to the edutainment model of emphasizing "authentic experiences" and spectacles rather than "authentic objects" become irrelevant: witness the fate of Du Simitière's museum. On the other hand, museums and libraries that embrace the edutainment model risk "degenerat[ing] into crass commercialism,"[7] as was the case with Rubens Peale's ventures. In fact, the dime museums that emerged from failed private museums in the mid-nineteenth century developed exhibition techniques associated with the current edutainment trend. Consider Dennett's description of how dime museums operated at the end of the nineteenth century:

> The process of uniting individual amusements and marketing them as a single, "walk-through" entertainment, suitable for the entire family, was what made the dime museum novel. In a sense it was a so-called environmental entertainment, among whose fixed exhibits mobile spectators could organize their own journey. The arrangement of space within a dime museum, with its display cabinets set around the periphery and grouped in the center of a room, created an environment in which customers were compelled to see each other as well as the exhibits themselves. In such a space the crowd became part of the performance, an important aspect of the experience.[8]

The fact that visitors could "organize their own journey" recalls the experiential museums and exhibitions that we described in chapter 2, such as the Sainsbury Gallery in London and the Newseum in Washington, where patrons were given control in designing their own museum experience. The contribution of visitors' interactions to the overall dime-museum experience likewise brings to mind the dependence of contemporary museums on patron-centered stories and activities in order to create authentic experiences.

This second—and more education-oriented—trajectory begins not with American cabinets of curiosities but with their European antecedents. Through concerted efforts to enhance visitors' experiences, collectors such as Ulisse Aldrovandi and Archduke Ferdinand II created displays that simultaneously entertained and instructed. They carefully labelled their exhibits, designed display areas that would highlight and complement their wondrous objects, and developed themed exhibitions, often by expanding the range of materials displayed to create a didactic context. Giuseppe Olmi's observation that the cabinets of private collectors "were frequented for recreation and pleasure as well as instruction"[9] echoes IMLS director Robert Martin's comments that museums and libraries at the beginning of the twenty-first century not only "support education" but also "provide extraordinary opportunities for recreation and enjoyment."[10] Just as cabinets of curiosities mirror the functions of contemporary museums and libraries, both the intent and result of early collectors' efforts to enhance visitors' experiences reflect the recent implementation of postobject roles in museums and libraries. The adjustments that owners of cabinets of curiosities made to their collections were part of strategic marketing plans to attract patrons. In the process of implementing these plans, collectors created what Susan Pearce and Ken Arnold refer to as "'interactive' encounters with exhibits,"[11] providing visitors with not only information, but also experiences in which they were active participants.

This same interactivity characterizes John Cotton Dana's plans for "a living, active, and effective institution"[12] in the opening decades of the twentieth century. While the exhibitions at the Newark Public Library displayed objects, they also created "authentic experiences" for visitors. In the textile exhibition Dana organized in 1916, patrons could watch a woman spin yarn and weave cloth, while the pottery and porcelain exhibit held in 1915 afforded an opportunity to view a potter at work. Dana argued that "the kind of museum best worth having in your community is the kind that is alive and active, is doing some rather definite work in the field of entertainment and of enlightenment and education."[13] At the same time that the Newark exhibits explored the boundary between education and entertainment, Dana's relentless focus on the needs of the community anticipated a patron-as-consumer model that typifies current postobject approaches. He favorably compared his concept for the new museum to first-class department stores, which classified their collections "according to the knowledge and needs of its patrons" and changed them "to meet daily changes in subjects of interest, changes of taste in art, and the progress of invention and discovery."[14] Both the content of the displays and the role of the community in providing exhibit materials produced an interactive experience for patrons that contemporary museums and libraries are striving to achieve.

We suggest that contemporary museums and libraries follow this second trajectory of the evolution of cabinets of curiosities—a path that culminates not in the edutainment phenomenon, but rather in a model of how museums and libraries can create "authentic experiences" for their patrons through the use of their collections. These cabinets—and, centuries later, the exhibitions developed by Dana in his hybrid museum-library in Newark—were, for all intents and purposes, the forerunners of the current generation of interactive displays that succeed in delineating a relationship between collection and patron. In fact, an analogy can be drawn between these early examples of interactive patron experiences and some of the current programs we described in chapter 2, such as the Denver Art Museum's Backpack Program or the San Francisco Museum of Modern Art's Learning Lounge—programs that are built around permanent museum collections.

This second trajectory also highlights the distinct role of libraries in developing collection-based, interactive experiences. As early cabinet owners recognized, the combination of objects, tools, and books created an intellectual context for their wondrous specimens that enhanced both the experiences of their visitors and the prestige of their collections. The juxtaposition of objects and books was similarly adopted in academic library cabinets, with the result that the library became the intellectual and cultural center of the university. In America, the idea of a hybrid collection of books and objects evolved into the concept of a hybrid institution that combined the functions of museum and library in one facility. While the developers of the Woburn library envisioned the museum and library as bookends of the same building, Henry Simmons Frieze—and, to an even greater extent, Dana—proposed a seamless cultural institution that would serve the public through a combined collection of books and objects. The fact that libraries, librarians, and literary societies are so intricately tied to the history of cabinets of curiosities and of proposed hybrid museum-library institutions points to the role that libraries, at the beginning of the twenty-first century, could play in reinterpreting the museum function within a library setting.

We turn now to an examination of how cabinets of curiosities and the hybrid museum-library institutions they inspired can serve as models for contemporary libraries, and to what advantage. Eschewing the present-day incarnation of a special exhibit area, we propose that public and academic libraries assume the function of museums by creating a series of in-house cabinets of curiosities. In this context, the term *cabinet of curiosities* would refer to both the materials collected and the physical space (e.g., a room) where these materials would be displayed for and utilized by the library's user community. Our proposed model would combine text-based materials (i.e., books, journals, etc.) with objects in a shared physical location. As we will describe in more detail later in this chapter, we envision this shared space as consisting of linked or closely proximate rooms (or designated areas/wings/floors) divided, for example, according to Dewey Decimal or Library of Congress classifications. Each of the rooms or designated areas/wings/floors—that is, each of the cabinets of curiosities—would contain an intermixture of museum objects arranged in so-called visible storage centers[15] and text-based materials arranged on shelving units. Taken together, the objects and text-based materials would constitute the collection of our proposed library-museum hybrid. The objects and text-based materials would reside in the rooms on a permanent basis, and "reintellectualized" collection development—again described in further detail later in the chapter—would, in conjunction with community members, have overall responsibility for forming and guiding the collections in the rooms.

In addition, each room would play host to a series of subject or thematic displays/exhibits to be determined in partnership with community interests in a public library or academic departments in a university library. From a historical standpoint, this is an approach that recalls the English collector Robert Hubert, who, as we saw in chapter 4, developed theme-based displays of certain types of rarities, which he advertised as distinct exhibitions: "on Mondays & Thursdayes things of the sea; Tuesdays and Fridays things of the land; Wednesdays and Saturdays things of sea land and air."[16] The displays/exhibits would be interdisciplinary in nature, that is, they would make use of objects and text-based materials housed in more than just one room. At the conclusion of a particular display/exhibit, objects and textual materials would be returned to their permanent visible storage center locations or shelving units. In sum, our library-museum hybrid consists of a series of cabinets of curiosities, each of which in turn consists of visible storage centers and text-based materials. Drawing on historical models, the implementation of modern-day cabinets of curiosities in libraries would redefine the current relationship between libraries and museums, and, ultimately, reestablish the relationship between libraries and their user communities.

MODERN WONDER

If a public or academic library were to create a cabinet of curiosities at the beginning of the twenty-first century, what types of objects would it include? Both private and institutional collectors from the sixteenth through eighteenth centuries satisfied their intellectual curiosity and attracted visitors with "wonders." Yet, as Daston and Park remark, what constituted wonder centuries ago is far removed from modern sensibilities: "Most objects that once adorned the *Wunderkammern* could now qualify for an exhibition of high kitsch. Once the cherished possessions of princes, the cherrystones carved in a hundred facets, the tableaux of seashells and coral, the ornamented ostrich eggs, and the delicate towers of turned ivory have sunk, at least in the view of art critics, to the cultural level of paintings on black velvet."[17] They suggest that only as part of an exhibit about the history of such collections would the *mirabilia* of cabinets of curiosities "command a place in large metropolitan museums."[18]

Indeed, the development of cabinets of curiosities in contemporary libraries would necessitate a rethinking of what the term *curiosities* should include. Certainly, we are not advocating that libraries begin collecting misshapen vegetables or trick drinking glasses in the mode of sixteenth- and seventeenth-century *Wunderkammern*. Rather, the aim of our proposed library-museum hybrids should be the *sense* of wonder that objects in cabinets of curiosities confer on their viewers. This sense of wonder still characterizes the collections of modern museums. Marc Pachter describes this wonder in terms of patrons' reaction to certain museum objects, such as the ruby slippers from the film *The Wizard of Oz*: "It's a touchstone to their childhood, a point of contact with the whole story of 'The Wizard of Oz' and how that came to be created. It's a way of getting them to think of history as including their own lives.... These objects are not simply illustrations. These are objects that had a life. And that's what people come here to connect with."[19] And this sense of wonder is even more palpable in James Cuno's lyrical account of ancient objects: "We have all had the experience before ancient objects—four-thousand-year-old Neolithic Chinese pots—

of a sudden jolt of recognition that people who lived so long ago and so far away...cared equally as we about beautiful things, and looked upon these pots as we look upon them now, in wonder and with a desire to hold and preserve them forever."[20]

The idea, then, would be for academic and public library-museum hybrids to collect and display objects that have this type of intrinsic relationship to their patrons—objects that would reflect these individuals' personal and community histories and that would simultaneously instil a sense of wonder through their illustration of the connection between artifact and viewer. We have seen that some of the IMLS projects—for example, Worklore: Brooklyn Workers Speak, Ephemeral Cities, and the Community Museum Project of the Hoh, Makah, and Quileute tribes—mentioned in chapter 3 do this, but many others do not. In the case of academic library-museum hybrids, objects could be selected based on their relevance to students' academic pursuits. Thus, instead of cabinets filled with curiosities valued according to their rarity, as was the case during the sixteenth and seventeenth centuries, the academic library-museum hybrid could collect and display objects that have a direct bearing on courses offered in various departments of the university. Although it would involve some coordination with, as well as cooperation from, academic departments, displays/exhibits could be designed with specific course syllabi in mind and could involve students and faculty in both the conceptual and implementation stages. In the same way that a cabinet in an academic library-museum hybrid could reestablish the role of that library-museum hybrid in fulfilling the university's educational mandate, a cabinet in a public library-museum hybrid could demonstrate that hybrid's role in reflecting and meeting the needs of its user community. The community itself would be an active participant in determining what materials to collect and display in the library-museum hybrid's cabinet of curiosities.

The suggestion that academic and public libraries collect and display objects normally found in museums raises the fundamental question, Why would libraries, already faced with budget constraints, want to add a responsibility that would appear to fall outside of its traditional mandate? As we saw in chapter 4, there are historical precedents that challenge contemporary notions of what constitutes library versus museum collections. Examples ranging from the library at St. Andrew's University to Frieze's plans for the merging of public art museums and libraries demonstrate that the permanent collections of hybrid institutions incorporated both texts and objects. Furthermore, these historical models do not simply call for the familiar implementation of "an exhibition function as part of [the library's] internal operations."[21] In contrast to the displays typically found in modern libraries, texts and objects were not simply part of a temporary special exhibit, but together composed the institution's permanent collection. These collections of text and object helped the institution, whether an academic library or public library/museum, to carry out its educative and cultural mandate.

Why would libraries need museum objects when many libraries already have artifact collections? This question is especially relevant, considering that libraries recognize the advantages of creating exhibits within designated display areas. As a librarian at Carleton College comments, "Exhibits have long been part of library programming. It provides a lively set of artifacts that tell a story that people can look at when they're taking a break."[22] And many libraries are using these displays to draw people back to the library. The library at Georgia College and State University recently added "computer labs, a cybercafe, and galleries to display the library's permanent collection, which includes artifacts and papers from Flannery O'Connor's estate."[23] The problem with this approach, however, is the notion of displaying artifacts. The objects collected and displayed by libraries are often special collections artifacts. The fact that these materials have significant scholarly and historical value does not guarantee that they will relate in a meaningful way to their intended audience. This problem is exacerbated by the fact that these displays are thought of as something for patrons to look at "when they're taking a break," rather than as a means of directly contributing to or connecting with patrons' interests or studies. In fact, libraries need not display rarities at all in their proposed cabinets of curiosities. Instead, they could adopt the approach taken by Dana, whose Newark library collected materials directly related to the surrounding community, including objects from the industrial arts and handicrafts, regardless of preconceived notions of aesthetic or monetary value.

While library-museum hybrids of the kind we propose need not collect the exact type of rare and wondrous material associated with early *Wunderkammern*, the inclusion of objects that fall outside the traditional domain of library collections could nonetheless produce similar benefits in a modern-day cabinet of curiosities. In the case of academic libraries, the combination of text and object could assist students with their scholarly pursuits while reflecting the mandate of the university as a whole. In much the same way that curiosities in nineteenth-century libraries symbolized the role of the university in scholarly society, the juxtaposition of media traditionally located in either the museum or library would mirror the current emphasis on multidisciplinary study in universities. As Roberta Shaffer explains, "Today's university is less concerned with maintaining the strict boundaries of traditional disciplines and instead encourages thinking that is transdisciplinary. Although this new model respects the uniqueness of various subject areas, it celebrates collaboration and interdisciplinary research and teaching."[24] Displays/exhibits that incorporate both object and text would provide a broad information context that would reflect and contribute to interdisciplinary education. Two goals would be met. First, the novelty—or "wonder factor"—of these mixed-media cabinets would attract patrons, thereby reasserting the library's presence as a physical space. Second, the integration of museum-type objects and traditional library materials would contribute to the work of the university and its students, thereby demonstrating the relevancy of the library and its collection. The heightened profile resulting from the implementation of a cabinet of curiosities would in turn increase circulation statistics as both faculty and students reacquaint themselves with the library's collection.

Displaying objects alongside of texts could bring similar benefits to public libraries. Following the lead of Dana, public libraries could create cabinets of curiosities filled with materials that have an intrinsic connection to the community—materials that are collected or produced by individual patrons or by the community collectively. Just as academic libraries could develop exhibits in conjunction with academic departments, public libraries could take Dana's advice and "discover collectors and specialists and experts in the community and secure their cooperation."[25] And, as with the academic library displays/exhibits, these exhibits could combine objects with texts from the library's collection. While patron involvement in creating exhibits would draw people back to the library, the cabinets themselves would demonstrate the unique role that libraries—and their collections—can play in the community. In the same way that a cabinet of curiosities creates an intellectual context for the objects on display, it also contextualizes the library's relationship to its community, presenting the library as a cultural institution that reflects community interests and connects these interests to the library collection.

NUTS AND BOLTS

In order to implement a cabinet of curiosities, where objects are collected and displayed in conjunction with print materials, academic and public libraries first need to obtain these objects. The fact that the objects could be either the type of artifact traditionally found in museums or materials associated with or produced by a user community suggests two sources, one of which is museums themselves. Despite the profusion of new building projects geared toward attracting visitors, many museums have acute shortages of display and storage space for their collections. Most display only a fraction of their total holdings. The American Museum of Natural History in New York has "a collection of 32 million specimens and artifacts," yet it is estimated that "as little as 1 percent" of this collection is on view.[26] In 2001, the Museum of Northern Arizona, "the official repository for Highway 89's archaeological bounty," stopped accepting artifacts from public excavation projects because of a dearth of storage space.[27] Some museums have responded to the problem of collection overcrowding by lending objects. The American Museum of Natural History "lends thousands of specimens to researchers and other institutions" each year,[28] as does the Cooper-Hewitt National Design Museum, whose "collection of 250,000 objects...spans 23 centuries."[29] The Museum Loan Network was developed in 1996 to facilitate the lending process; it is "a matchmaking program that encourages museums to dust off treasures they have buried in basements and storerooms and make them available to other museums."[30] The network is funded through charitable trusts and supplies museums not only with an "online directory of more than 6,000 objects" that can be borrowed, but also with funding for "shipping, insurance, staff time, cataloging and other costs at both the lending and borrowing museums."[31]

The problem of storage overcrowding—and museums' willingness to lend objects as a solution to this problem—opens avenues to libraries interested in developing a cabinet of curiosities. In the interest and spirit of cooperative ventures between museums and libraries, museums could make available to libraries online directories such as the one maintained by the Museum Loan Network. As peer collecting institutions with educative mandates, libraries would provide safe environments for museum objects. Libraries, in turn, would have access to a wealth of material with which they could develop long-term cabinet displays. The process of developing these displays would not constitute a partnership between museums and libraries per se, but rather a partnership between libraries and their own patron communities. Academic libraries could make use of, say, the American Museum of Natural History's 500,000 anthropology artifacts, only 5 percent of which are displayed at the museum itself.[32] With the assistance of faculty and students from the university's anthropology department, exhibits could be developed that correspond with the department's course offerings and that use both the borrowed specimens and resources from the library's own collection. Like the cabinets of curiosities that interspersed natural history specimens and man-made artifacts with informative texts, the resulting display would be interactive, granting library patrons an active role in the development of the project while demonstrating the use of library materials in the intellectual activities of the university.

Libraries can also generate ideas for the cabinets' physical design and layout from museums' responses to the problem of collection overflow. In 2003 the Basel Museum of Contemporary Art created "a new architectural category" in museum design: "the Schaulager, or show storage."[33] Separated from the museum itself, the Schaulager is a building dedicated to storage. Unlike typical museum storage areas, this new facility provides ready access to artworks that would otherwise be bundled and buried in some hidden area of the museum. The Schaulager, which caters to scholars and researchers, is part closet and part art gallery—a place where objects from the collection can be put away and yet where "every piece of art on its climate-controlled floors [is] easily visible."[34] According to Celestine Bohlen, other institutions are creating "visible storage centers" or "open study centers" that are geared toward the general public and housed within the museums themselves.[35] While visible storage centers consist of objects arranged in display cases, they share few features with traditional museum exhibits. Visible storage display areas consist of "unadorned cases...with a minimum of labeling," and therefore much of the material is left "uninterpreted" for the viewer.[36] Because the intent is to present as much of the museum collection as possible, a visible storage area "compresses the art object into a smaller area, [so that] hundreds and hundreds...can be seen at once, which means they can be shared, used, studied and enjoyed."[37] The result is that visitors are confronted not with a few carefully labelled specimens but with a profusion of a particular type of object, as in the case of the New-York Historical Society, which moved its collection of "several dozen" apple parers into a visible storage display in November 2001.[38]

Bohlen compares visible storage areas to both "Grandma's attic" and library open stacks.[39] Both images are useful in considering how libraries could utilize the concept of visible storage centers in creating modern-day cabinets of curiosities. The pleasant jumble of intriguing objects waiting to be discovered in

"Grandma's attic" and in visible storage areas is reminiscent of the random assemblage of intriguing objects collected in European *Wunderkammern*. Indeed, all are collections of objects conducive to exploration and discovery and that fuel curiosity by providing a glimpse of other cultures and eras. This shared trait relates to the other comparison made by Bohlen. The basic idea behind visible storage centers is "letting the public roam freely through what a library would call open stacks."[40] The idea of inviting patrons to freely explore within visible storage areas, much as they would with open library stacks, not only reinforces the image of these storage areas as a modern-day cabinet of curiosities, but also connects these areas to the environment of self-guided intellectual discovery that libraries provide.

The comparison to open library stacks also points to how libraries could develop a cabinet of curiosities based on the model of visible storage areas. Consider again the example of an anthropological display at an academic library. Instead of exhibiting museum objects in a typical library display area—one that is most likely physically removed from the library's permanent collection—a cabinet of curiosities could be created in close physical proximity to the library's holdings on the relevant subject matter. In other words, rather than having a selection of anthropological texts and artifacts displayed in an area of the library where visitors simply pass by on the way to other activities, why not display them in area where intellectual activity actually occurs—within the primary space occupied by the library collection itself? This approach recalls Dana's museum-library configuration, in which "books and journals will be displayed near objects on view, references to books and journals will be made on labels and leaflets of all kinds."[41] Instead of the sterility and remoteness of artifacts encased in plexiglass, libraries can create displays of texts and objects that patrons can explore, creating the atmosphere of intellectual discovery and unfettered access associated with open library stacks, cabinets of curiosities, and visible storage areas alike.

The way in which museums often acquired the inordinate quantities of objects displayed in visible storage areas suggests another approach libraries could take in collecting materials for a cabinet of curiosities. The New-York Historical Society acquired their dozens of apple parers in 1946 from Charles Larned Robinson, "a New York businessman who saw in the humble hand-held apple parer a symbol of an age that was soon to be swallowed up by mechanization."[42] In much the same way as the seventeenth, eighteenth, and nineteenth centuries saw a rise in the number of study and aristocratic collectors, the twentieth and twenty-first centuries have also produced a collecting culture. As Paul Martin recounts, "television teems with programmes on collectables and their values; price guides and collectors' reference books cram the shelves of bookshops; collectors' fairs…are held every week."[43] Rather than objects valued for their exoticness or rarity, many present-day collectors focus on what are termed "popular collectables"—"objects which are obtainable, affordable and appealing to the majority of people" and that are "inexpensive and unconsidered."[44] Just a few of the countless examples of popular collectibles include cow creamers, classic typewriters, lapel pins, snow globes, chess sets, Tupperware, beer labels, hand-bells, images of camels, and GI Joe action figures. Like Robinson's apple parers, many of these collections will be donated or lent to museums such as the New-York Historical Society or the Cooper-Hewitt National Design Museum, which collects objects "of both historic and contemporary design" ranging from buttons to blenders and electric mixers.[45] In some cases, enthusiastic collectors open their own specialty museums, such as the American Sanitary Plumbing Museum in Worcester, Massachusetts. Founded by plumber and plumbing-supplies distributor Charles Manoog, the museum grew out of a collection of materials intended to "illustrate how plumbing had evolved as a profession."[46]

As a form of community outreach, libraries could work in conjunction with patron collectors to develop cabinets of curiosities that include popular collectibles. Just as collectors in the seventeenth and eighteenth centuries sought institutions with educational mandates as repositories for their treasures, contemporary libraries could position themselves as suitable venues for popular collections, persuading collectors to make either long-term loans or donations of collected objects to our proposed library-museum hybrids. Bill Brown reminds us that the act of collecting is an exercise in identity formation, observing that "whether your collection serves as a public display or as a private preserve, it's a form of expression where you materialize that abstract thing called the self."[47] At the same time as forming one's own identity, collecting also serves to establish a relationship between an individual and a community: it "reassur[es] one-self of one's relationship to society by what we choose to see reflected back at us in the collected material."[48] This same process of identity is also carried out at an institutional level—for instance, in the idea that a library's collection is a reflection of the community it serves. The inclusion and exhibition of popular collections in a public library setting would be a new way for the community to see itself reflected in the library. When community members bring their collectibles to the library for storage and display, they also bring their extensive knowledge about their collections, thus strengthening both physical and intellectual relationships between the institution and the community. And when these popular collections are placed within an intellectual framework through the addition of other museum objects and text-based materials that identify and explore important thematic threads, then the groundwork for acquiring meaningful knowledge and developing habits of critical inquiry has been laid.

Museums have begun to recognize the value of local collectors in community outreach. The Anacostia Museum in Washington, D.C., established a "collector in residence scheme" that "encourages neighbourhood collectors to work in the museum for a few months, helping to strengthen community ties."[49] In Britain, museums sponsor People's Shows, defined as "essentially a collective display, in a museum environment, of a number of private collections ranging from pencil erasers to pulp fiction."[50] Despite such initiatives, many collectors remain wary of working with area museums, citing such factors as "the doorkeeping role of curators," "the social control over potential exhibitors" exerted by museum staff, and collectors' sense of simply being the "flavour of the month."[51] But a survey in Britain revealed that "amongst the qualitative comments made by collectors on mutual aid" between collectors and museums, one of the most common was that "libraries are more helpful than museums."[52] Accordingly, it is not so far fetched to believe that collectors would be willing to assist with libraries' endeavors to create cabinets of curiosities, where popular collectibles and materials from the libraries' own collections together would symbolically represent the symbiotic relationship between libraries and patrons.

A reconceptualization of libraries so as to create our proposed library-museum hybrid would require a number of changes in the physical space and configuration of a conventional library building. In this regard, it is important to remember that, as Brian Edwards observes, on those occasions when libraries and museums were housed in a single edifice, "it was largely the need for roof lighting of museum exhibits" that caused them to split apart.[53] In other words, "the technical problems of lighting galleries and libraries were so different that the impetus for functional separation was more practical than cultural."[54] Because such practical problems are no longer insurmountable, the paired cultural function of libraries and museums can reassert itself in bold visions manifested in a new type of shared and juxtaposed library-museum space that, on the one hand, does not renounce the principles of flexibility, modular design, and high-tech gateway functionality of libraries advocated, for example, by Richard Bazillion and Connie Braun, but that, on the other hand, does not follow the precept that book stacks, study spaces, and computer terminals should all be in their separate spheres.[55] In other words, we propose that our new library-museum hybrids develop a series of rooms or designated areas/wings/floors that would broadly correspond to and contain resources about a particular sphere of knowledge (i.e., social sciences, history, science, arts, geography, religion, psychology, etc.). Although the focus of each room or designated area/wing/floor would be on museum objects and text-based materials, users of each room or designated area/wing/floor would also have access to relevant digital resources. In addition, there would be a central space or lobby that would serve as an entrance/rotunda and contain circulation and reference services.

The important point to remember is that each of these rooms or designated areas/wings/floors, taken separately, would constitute a cabinet of curiosities. Thus our library-museum hybrid would consist of a series of cabinets of curiosities located in rooms or designated areas/wings/floors, and each cabinet of curiosities would, as we explain in more detail below, contain a mix of visible storage centers and text-based materials. The floor plans for our library-museum hybrids could be almost anything, limited only by the inventiveness and imagination of library-museum hybrid planners and architects. Hearkening back to historical antecedents, a large academic or public library-museum hybrid could, for instance, develop a series of contemporary improvisations on the classical library "with a central reading room about which were placed, normally on sub-axes, various subject libraries."[56] In smaller libraries, planners could resurrect a version of William Frederick Poole's idea of "multiple stories of small subject-oriented rooms grouped around a central courtyard."[57] Or, in still smaller libraries where separate rooms would be impossible, library architects could update the alcove system that characterized some American libraries in the second half of the nineteenth century.[58] This is not to say that the three foregoing architectural ideas are the only ones we are recommending; we mention them here simply because they are intriguing and relatively neglected. Other possibilities abound. But the common theme that would permeate all such architectural designs would be a central space (whether round, rectangular, or some other shape) around which would be grouped (in multifarious arrangements) a series of rooms or designated areas/wings/floors, each of which would be a cabinet of curiosities. In very large library-museum hybrids, a separate floor could be devoted to each cabinet of curiosities. And, in university settings in which various academic departments have their own departmental libraries, each such library could be transformed into a library-museum hybrid simply by the addition of visible storage centers containing objects relevant to that academic department.

The rooms or designated areas/wings/floors would broadly correspond to a classification system such as Dewey Decimal or Library of Congress. Each of the designated areas not only would contain text-based materials, but would house visible storage centers of carefully selected museum objects. Objects and text-based materials would thus constitute "the collection" of each of the rooms or designated areas. Juxtaposed and interspersed, objects and text-based materials would thus illuminate and deepen understanding of the myriad of topics and subjects pertaining to that area. For example, a library-museum hybrid could have nine areas divided according to the nine main Dewey classes (not counting the 000s class) or the nineteen main classes of Library of Congress (not counting "class A—General Works" or "class Z—Bibliography. Library Science. Information Resources [General]").[59] (Reference works—those works that would typically be classed in Dewey main class 000 or Library of Congress "class A" and "class Z"—would be centrally located in the circulation and reference rotunda.) But, depending on the space available or the strengths of various parts of its collections, a library-museum hybrid could choose to have a larger—or smaller—number of rooms than the number that corresponds to the main Dewey Decimal or Library of Congress classes. For example, a public library-museum hybrid that had particular strength in the 780s (music), or an academic library-museum hybrid that had particular strength in subclass "GC—Oceanography," could create a separate room or designated area for those subjects. Similarly, because of a lack of collecting strength in certain classes, public and academic library-museum hybrids could combine multiple classes in a single room or designated area.

We also propose that, on a regular basis, some of the objects and text-based materials would become the focus of a themed display or exhibit in the room itself. That is, each of the rooms would have a regular series of displays or exhibits; theoretically, we can envision anywhere from two to six displays per year in each room. These displays would be profoundly interdisciplinary, so the objects and text-based materials would be selected from the totality of objects in the visible storage centers and the totality of text-based materials of *all* rooms. For example, a display/exhibit about cranes would not just emphasize the biological sciences component of this subject, but would also touch upon various cultural, socioeconomic, environmental, and geographical aspects related to these birds: folk art depictions of cranes, their place in Greek and Roman mythologies or musical traditions, the effect of sandhill cranes on the economy of Nebraska as tourists follow the migratory path of these birds, maps of their migratory routes, and the movement to preserve wetlands and grasslands used by cranes as migratory staging grounds.[60] The display would appear in a single room or designated area—the Dewey class 500 area, since the focus is on cranes, and birds fall into subclass 598—but it would draw on objects and text-based materials from other Dewey subclasses such as 338 (tourism industry) and 745 (folk arts) that would be housed in other areas. On the other hand, if the focus of the display was folk art, it would appear in the Dewey class 700 area, with objects and text-based materials—for instance, folk art depicting a sandhill crane—contributed from other Dewey class areas.

Objects and text-based materials would not only be highlighted during the time period of the display, but they would also be intellectually framed and contextualized. In effect, these displays could be thought of as "nested" cabinets of curiosities, since they are organized and located within an area that is itself a cabinet of curiosities. Moreover, the displays could be mounted, for example, by students in an academic department (in the case of an academic library-museum hybrid) or by members of the general public (in the case of a public library-museum hybrid) working together with professional staff members from the library-museum hybrid in question. Once the allotted time period for the display had expired, the objects and text-based materials would be returned to the visible storage centers and shelving units of the particular area from whence they came.

The cabinet of curiosities model in library-museum hybrids could not come to fruition without the aid of museums and community members—whether in a public or academic setting. But a person (or persons) would also be needed to oversee the intellectual task of selecting, coordinating, and arranging the objects that would compose the visible storage center and integrating these objects with the circulating print collections of each area. We envision this person as a collection development librarian. Why? Simply put, the position of collection development librarian, in the early twenty-first century, is no longer what it once was; indeed, the idea of collection development—the task of selecting materials to shape a library's collection for present and future generations—has become a highly mechanical process that is less important than the idea of collection management.[61] Academic and public libraries "widely [employ]" various types of approval plans, defined as "business arrangements in which a wholesale dealer assumes responsibility for selecting and supplying, subject to return privileges [of 2 percent or less], all new publications that match a library's collecting profile."[62] Certainly, approval plans—or, less euphemistically, the library version of offshore outsourcing—"contain costs when library staffing has been reduced and [serve] as a way to release staff members for other responsibilities perceived as more important,"[63] but they also position collection development as an unimportant part of library work—something that is no longer to be considered as intellectual in nature, but rather managerial. And when "marketing-based selection policies and practices" of the type advocated by Sharon Baker and Karen Wallace are presented as worthy ideals to aim for in public libraries,[64] the decentering of the intellectual component—and the concomitant rise in the respect given to managerial adroitness—in collection development endeavors is complete. As collection development metamorphoses into collection management, librarians increasingly assume the role of purchasing agents, acquisitions and stock clerks, and vendor liaisons—deprofessionalized workers struggling to retain a vestige of professionalism. Given this phenomenon, it is little wonder that, as Kirsti Nelson and Lynne McKechnie discovered, only 34 percent of the public believes that library staff members are responsible for collection development.[65] And while Nelson and McKechnie attribute this to the fact that collection development is a hidden behind-the-scenes aspect of library work that does not fit the mental model of librarians as "organizers of preexisting collections" that exists in the public mind,[66] it may also be that members of the public, based on their perception of the materials appearing on library shelves, do not consider that the selection of such materials presents much of an intellectual challenge—and is hence not being done by a library professional—insofar as such materials are often a replication of the same titles that they see on various bestseller and award lists and in bookstores. It may also be a function of what could be termed the "Wal-Martization" of library collection work. Because Wal-Mart uses data-mining technology to track consumer buying preferences and then makes future orders based on analysis of that data, it has made an informed sales force obsolete because salespeople are no longer needed "to explain goods to customers."[67] As libraries increasingly rely on "market analysis" to stock their book shelves—a market analysis that is driven by using circulation statistics to collect detailed information on the borrowing patterns of customers and then, based on that information, ordering books, confident that customers will like them based on their past preferences—they also "eliminate some of the need for an informed" library collection development staff.[68]

On the other hand, were libraries to become library-museum hybrids of the kind we propose, the task of collection development could be reintellectualized because librarians would be asked to be sufficiently knowledgeable in specific subject areas to guide and shape the juxtapositions between text-based materials and museum objects in areas containing visible storage centers. Collection development librarians would have to be knowledgeable about the contents of the text-based materials that they purchase so that they could select those materials that would best inform any collected or displayed objects. And because collection development librarians, in conjunction with interested members of the community, would also be selecting objects, they would also have to know much about any selected objects so that they could make informed decisions about which collected or displayed objects would best inform the contents of text-based materials. In effect, they would become suitably updated versions of Adam Olearius, Lorenz Beger, and Johann Schumacher, mentioned in chapter 4, who

were responsible for acquiring both objects and text-based materials for the cabinets of curiosities of their respective employers.

To provide a more concrete idea of what our proposed library-museum hybrids would look like, we examine an exhibition about the first 100 years of the
New York City subway system entitled The Subway at 100: General William
Barclay Parsons and the Birth of the NYC Subway, presented in Sealy Hall, a
soaring lobby and reception area of the New York Public Library's (NYPL) Science, Industry and Business Library (SIBL).[69] We choose this exhibit (or display) not because it is an exact reflection of what we have in mind, but because
it contains some elements that we would wish to retain and some elements that
we would wish to alter. Providing a "succinct, well-edited look at the subway's
100-year sweep," the exhibition, on view for nine months in 2004, was assembled by John V. Ganly, the assistant director for collections at SIBL, "with help
from the New York Transit Museum, the Museum of American Financial History, the engineering firm Parsons Brinckerhoff and a private subway memorabilia collector George Cuhaj," among others. Focusing on William Barclay
Parsons, the exhibit, in addition to such objects as "a rattan subway seat...and a
rare 1928 subway token," included "a copy of Parson's still influential book Engineers and Engineering in the Renaissance," as well as "reports and published
works...illustrat[ing] the growth and social and economic importance of the
subway...[and] touching on subjects such as the importance of subway advertising, issues relating to women, and the environment."

What philosophical and structural elements would we wish to keep from this
exhibition? First, a display (or exhibit) that might typically be held in a museum
was housed in a subject-specific library such that, for a brief time, SIBL became a
library-museum hybrid. Second, the display was collection based; that is, the
story of the subway had many connections to the collections held at SIBL, from
engineering to advertising, to name but a few. Third, it drew objects from the
collections of other area museums. Fourth, it involved individual and corporate
community members as sources of objects. Fifth, it was overseen by a member of
SIBL's collections department. Sixth, although the subject matter of the exhibition was a popular story that had applicability to the lives of countless individuals,
it was intellectualized and put into two broad cultural contexts: Renaissance engineering and late-nineteenth-century American social history.

What would we wish to alter? First, we would like a better integration of the
display with the text-based collections of the library. As described above, the exhibition is displayed in a lobby that, while adjacent to the reference collections, is
nevertheless a separate area of the library—one that also serves as a reception
area for a conference room.[70] In addition, SIBL has "31.2 miles of closed stack
shelves"[71] on its upper floors—a further physical separation between the permanent collection of text-based materials and objects that is not conducive to the
kind of interplay of text and object that we foresee in our library-museum hybrids. And, although there is a "selected bibliography" accompanying the exhibit,[72] the listed books, reports, and other items are either in SIBL closed stacks
or at far-flung branch libraries of the NYPL system—a circumstance that also

mitigates against the type of close intellectual juxtaposition of text and object we recommend. In sum, we would place the objects in the same room with closely related text-based material.

Second, while we applaud the inclusion of artifacts from other area museums and collectors as a sign of community outreach, it nevertheless remains true that much of the contents of the exhibit returned to special collections that would not be readily accessible to the public once the exhibition had run its course. Our proposal would not do this. Rather, objects would have their natural home within an area that contained related text-based material. If, as we suggested previously, objects were, from time to time, highlighted in an interdisciplinary display or exhibit, this exhibit too would be within one of the areas of our library-museum hybrid (i.e., within one of the cabinets of curiosities). Once the exhibit was replaced by another one, the objects composing that display would be returned to the visible storage center of their appropriate areas. These objects—along with all other objects and text-based materials—would thus be permanently accessible to members of the public as they read, studied, and explored within one or more areas. Although some might view these ideas as outmoded, they could nonetheless become the cornerstone of library-museum hybridization: a series of areas that house both text-based materials on shelving units and objects in visible storage centers. Not only can each of these areas be conceived of as a modern-day cabinet of curiosities, the objects and textual materials contained therein—as well as their interaction—can also be understood as assuming the role of a cabinet of curiosities. In essence, our library-museum hybrid functions both physically and intellectually as a cabinet of curiosities.

A MODEL FOR THE FUTURE

Contemporary museums and libraries that embrace an edutainment approach to attracting patrons are following a similar trajectory to the one that begins with Rubens Peale's cabinets of curiosities and ends with dime museums and theme parks. In the family history of museums and libraries, dime museums are the progenitor of the Disneyland-type theme park, with both venues offering family-oriented popular entertainment packaged as a pseudoeducational experience.[73] By pursuing an edutainment agenda, museums and libraries are metamorphosing into the type of leisure-time venues with which they feel compelled to compete. Yet, just as Rubens Peale's efforts to attract museum visitors with freakish objects and live entertainment could not contend with the amusements offered by dime-museum entrepreneurs such as P. T. Barnum, contemporary museums and libraries cannot hope to lure patrons away from theme parks and shopping malls by offering the same product. Recall Asma's comment about a recent exhibit at the Field Museum in Chicago: "How can such feeble exhibits as 'Dinosaur Families' compete with Spielberg's *Jurassic Park?*"[74]

Museums and libraries should not try to compete with mass media and the type of interactive "authentic experiences" they offer, at least not by following an edutainment approach. Collecting institutions such as museums and libraries have the tools to provide their patrons with meaningful experiences without resorting to the spectacles associated with postobject roles. Museum and library collections themselves can produce wonder, especially when museums and libraries take the time and care to elucidate the relationship between collected material and patron. The history of European *Wunderkammern* illustrates the beneficial role these collections of objects can play in raising public awareness of—and interest in—a museum or library. Wondrous objects reflected the intellectual curiosity of their owners, enabling these individuals to belong to the "new community of the curious."[75] The subsequent opening of cabinets to visitors raised or reinforced the social status of collectors by providing concrete proof of their membership in this elite community. At the same time, cabinets of curiosities—as well as later museum-library hybrid institutions—demonstrate the intrinsic value of collections that combine objects, generally considered the purview of museums, with the text-based resources associated with libraries.

Marc Pachter connects the current predicament of museums to their reactive, rather than proactive, response to new expectations and viewpoints: "Borders Books had the brilliant idea of creating a perfect environment for browsing.... Hard Rock Café had the insight to get real objects and integrate them into café environments. Why didn't museums do those things first?"[76] Similar questions can be asked of libraries. Rather than following trends set by entertainment-based venues, libraries and museums should develop innovative ways to reconnect with their communities—methods that do not lose sight of their educative roles and their responsibility to bring about "deepened curiosity and prolonged, complex attention."[77] We suggest that libraries—working with their user communities—follow this advice by adopting the historical model of combining museum and library collections, that is, by becoming what we have termed library-museum hybrids. Public and academic libraries (reconstituted as library-museum hybrids) can develop a series of cabinets of curiosities geared toward the needs of their respective communities. Knowledge about the objects contained in the visible storage centers of the cabinets of curiosities is imparted through text-based materials that point the way to further exploration of little-known or hidden aspects of the objects or of other objects. Similarly, knowledge about text-based materials in the cabinets of curiosities is imparted through objects contained in the visible storage centers, and these objects point the way to further exploration of the same, or other, text-based materials. "Nested" cabinets of curiosities (displays/exhibits) within the larger cabinet of curiosities also lead to further understanding of selected subjects and topics. In the process, our proposed library-museum hybrids can draw patrons back to the library—and the library collection—and reassert themselves as a physical presence in their communities.

Permanent visible storage centers located in the same area as relevant text-based materials would thus be the defining features of our proposed library-museum hybrids. The whole would thus comprise a series of contemporary cabinets of curiosities. Objects on particular themes would be solicited from local residents, other area museums, or corporate entities by a collection development librarian who would take care to fashion a coherent whole within each area so that objects and text-based materials mutually inform and illuminate one another. Both objects and text-based materials would be available to all patrons for browsing, wonder, and edification; indeed, the shelving units of the visible storage center that contain and hold objects would metaphorically become just like the shelving units holding text-based materials.

Developing cabinets of curiosities that contain visible storage centers and text-based materials would not be a museum-library partnership, but would, instead, be an enterprise run by libraries for library patrons in the interest of reconnecting with their user communities so that they can become legitimate agents of the type of intellectual "nourishment" that engenders public trust.[78] Unlike the "authentic experiences" of edutainment, library text-based collections are unique. By combining these text-based collections with museum objects in a new type of cabinet of curiosities in a library-museum hybrid, they can also become wondrous. The library-museum hybrid creates an imaginative cultural landscape in which objects cannot be divorced from text-based materials and text-based materials cannot be divorced from objects—a landscape in which meaningful knowledge acquisition, contemplation, critical inquiry, and a sense of wonder is predicated on an in-depth study of text-based materials and objects in close juxtaposition in the hopes that such study can lead "to caring, even justice."[79]

NOTES

1. Andrea Stulman Dennett, *Weird and Wonderful: The Dime Museum in America* (New York: New York University Press, 1997), 11–12.

2. Ibid., 12.

3. Ibid., 14.

4. Ibid.

5. Joyce Henri Robinson, "An American Cabinet of Curiosities: Thomas Jefferson's 'Indian Hall' at Monticello," in *Acts of Possession: Collecting in America*, ed. Leah Dilworth (New Brunswick, NJ: Rutgers University Press, 2003), 29.

6. Dennett, *Weird and Wonderful*, 5.

7. Victoria Newhouse, *Towards a New Museum* (New York: Monacelli Press, 1998), 191.

8. Dennett, *Weird and Wonderful*, 5–6.

9. Giuseppe Olmi, "Science-Honour-Metaphor: Italian Cabinets of the Sixteenth and Seventeenth Centuries," in *The Origins of Museums: The Cabinet of Curiosities in Sixteenth- and Seventeenth-Century Europe*, ed. Oliver Impey and Arthur MacGregor (Oxford: Clarendon Press, 1985), 8.

10. Robert S. Martin, "Welcoming Remarks," (presented at the 21st Century Learner Conference, Washington, DC, November 2001), par. 4, http://www.imls.gov/whatsnew/current/sp110701-3.htm (accessed September 6, 2003).

11. Susan Pearce and Ken Arnold, eds., "Zacharias Conrad von Uffenbach Describes Hans Sloane's Collection," in *Early Voices*, vol. 2, *The Collector's Voice: Critical Readings in the Practice of Collecting* (Aldershot, England: Ashgate, 2000), 113.

12. John Cotton Dana, "The Gloom of the Museum," in *The New Museum: Selected Writings by John Cotton Dana,* ed. William A. Penniston (Newark, NJ: The Newark Museum Association, 1999), 57. Originally published in John Cotton Dana, *The New Museum Series, no. 2* (Woodstock, VT: The Elm Tree Press, 1917).

13. John Cotton Dana, "The New Museum," in *The New Museum: Selected Writings by John Cotton Dana,* ed. William A. Penniston (Newark, NJ: The Newark Museum Association, 1999), 31. Originally published in John Cotton Dana, *The New Museum Series, no. 1* (Woodstock, VT: The Elm Tree Press, 1917).

14. Dana, "The Gloom of the Museum," 57.

15. This phrase, which is explained in greater detail later in the chapter, is used by Celestine Bohlen, "Museums as Walk-in Closets: Visible Storage Opens Troves to the Public," *New York Times,* 6 May 2001, B1, B6.

16. Arthur MacGregor, "The Cabinet of Curiosities in Seventeenth-Century Britain," in *The Origins of Museums: The Cabinet of Curiosities in Sixteenth- and Seventeenth-Century Europe,* ed. Oliver Impey and Arthur MacGregor (Oxford: Clarendon Press, 1985), 153.

17. Lorraine Daston and Katharine Park, *Wonders and the Order of Nature, 1150–1750* (New York: Zone Books, 1998), 366.

18. Ibid.

19. Adam Goodheart, "Smithsonian's Veteran Man-in-the-Middle Stands His Ground," *New York Times,* 24 April 2002, E2.

20. James Cuno, ed., "The Object of Art Museums," in *Whose Muse? Art Museums and the Public Trust* (Princeton, NJ: Princeton University Press, 2004), 50.

21. Institute of Museum and Library Services, "2003 National Leadership Grants for Libraries and Museums," part 1.6, http://www.imls.gov (accessed March 19, 2003).

22. Scott Carlson, "The Deserted Library: As Students Work Online, Reading Rooms Empty Out—Leading Some Campuses to Add Starbucks," *The Chronicle of Higher Education,* 16 November 2001, par. 44, http://chronicle.com/free/v48/i12/12a03501.htm (accessed November 29, 2001).

23. Ibid., par. 12.

24. Roberta I. Shaffer, "Bringing Things to the Center: The Center for the Cultural Record of the Graduate School of Library and Information Science at the University of Texas at Austin," *RBM: Journal of Rare Books, Manuscripts, and Cultural Heritage* 1 (fall 2000): 136.

25. Dana, "The New Museum," 28.

26. Donna Wilkinson, "Stuffing Nooks and Crannies with Bones, Insects, and Creepy Fish," *New York Times,* 24 April 2002, E31.

27. Catherine C. Robbins, "No Room for Riches of the Indian Past: Museums Are Inundated by Ceramics, Bones, Arrowheads and Other Cultural Artifacts," *New York Times,* 24 November 2001, A15.

28. Wilkinson, "Stuffing Nooks," E31.

29. Donna Wilkinson, "A Collection Based on Good Connections," *New York Times,* 23 April 2003, F23.

30. Hilary Appelman, "Sharing Buried Treasure Via a Network," *New York Times,* 2 May 2001, D15.

31. Ibid.

32. Wilkinson, "Stuffing Nooks," E31.

33. Julie V. Iovine, "In Basel, Art Is Storage, and Storage Is Art," *New York Times*, 5 June 2003, D3.

34. Ibid.

35. Bohlen, "Museums as Walk-in Closets," B11.

36. Ibid., B6.

37. Ibid.

38. Ibid.

39. Ibid.

40. Ibid., B1.

41. Dana, "The New Museum," 29.

42. Bohlen, "Museums as Walk-in Closets," B1.

43. Paul Martin, *Popular Collecting and the Everyday Self: The Reinvention of Museums?* (London: Leicester University Press, 1999), 37.

44. Ibid., 1.

45. Wilkinson, "A Collection," F23.

46. Jacques Steinberg, "Who Said Plumbing Doesn't Belong on a Pedestal? Not These Museums," *New York Times*, 19 April 2000, D27.

47. Bill Brown, "The Collecting Mania," *University of Chicago Magazine*, October 2001, 38.

48. Martin, *Popular Collecting*, 1.

49. Ibid., 113.

50. Ibid., 6.

51. Ibid., 110.

52. Ibid., 118.

53. Brian Edwards, with Biddy Fisher, *Libraries and Learning Resource Centres* (Oxford: Architectural Press, 2002), 19.

54. Ibid.

55. Richard Bazillion and Connie L. Braun, *Academic Libraries as High-Tech Gateways: A Guide to Design and Space Decisions*, 2nd ed. (Chicago: American Library Association, 2001), 76–88.

56. Edwards, *Libraries and Learning Resource Centres*, 14.

57. Kenneth A. Breisch, *Henry Hobson Richardson and the Small Public Library in America: A Study in Typology* (Cambridge, MA: MIT Press, 1997), 224.

58. Ibid., 54–115.

59. For a list of Dewey Decimal main classes, see http://www.oclc.org/dewey/resources/summaries/default.htm (accessed April 21, 2004); for Library of Congress main classes, see http://www.loc.gov/catdir/cpso/lcco/lcco.html (accessed April 21, 2004).

60. See, for example, Jennifer Ackerman, "No Mere Bird: Cranes," *National Geographic*, April 2004, 38–57; Anna Bahney, "A Place Where Spring Arrives on the Wings of a Sandhill Crane," *New York Times*, 26 March 2004, F1.

61. Sharon L. Baker and Karen L. Wallace, *The Responsive Public Library: How to Develop and Market a Winning Collection*, 2nd ed. (Englewood, CO: Libraries Unlimited, 2002); Peggy Johnson, *Fundamentals of Collection Development and Management* (Chicago: American Library Association, 2004).

62. Johnson, *Fundamentals of Collection Development and Management*, 113–14. See also Hendrick Edelman and Robert P. Holley, eds., *Marketing to Libraries for the New Millennium: Librarians, Vendors, and Publishers Review the Landmark Third Industry-Wide Survey of Library Marketing Practices and Trends* (Lanham, MD: Scarecrow Press, 2002), 135–36, 163. This survey of 305 libraries—more than 60 percent of which have fewer than 75,000 books and may thus be considered to be relatively small—shows that 47.3 percent of institutions rely on approval plans. As libraries become larger, reliance on approval plans grows exponentially. For example, 93 percent of libraries belonging to the Association of Research Libraries (ARL) used approval plans, as reported by Susan Flood, *Evolution and Status of Approval Plans* (Washington, DC: Association of Research Libraries, 1997).

63. Johnson, *Fundamentals of Collection Development and Management*, 115.

64. Baker and Wallace, *The Responsive Public Library*, 247–74.

65. Kirsti Nilsen and Lynne (E. F.) McKechnie, "Behind Closed Doors: An Exploratory Study of the Perceptions of Librarians and the Hidden Intellectual Work of Collection Development in Canadian Public Libraries," *Library Quarterly 72* (July 2002): 313.

66. Ibid., 317.

67. Steven Greenhouse, "Wal-Mart, A Nation unto Itself," *New York Times*, 17 April 2004, B7. Greenhouse refers to an academic conference presentation by Professor James Hoopes, a historian at Babson College in Wellesley, Massachusetts.

68. Our explanation here, adapted to fit the world of libraries, follows Greenhouse's summary of Hoope's conference presentation.

69. All quotations about this exhibition are taken from one of two places: Randy Kennedy, "The Rumble That's Lasted for 100 Years," *New York Times*, 19 March 2004, E31; the Web site of the exhibition at http://www.nypl.org/research/calendar/exhib/sibl/siblexhibdesc.cfm?id=349 (accessed April 17, 2004).

70. See floor plans and an online tour of the Science, Industry and Business Library at http://www.nypl.org/research/sibl/tour/index.html (accessed April 17, 2004).

71. Science, Industry, and Business Library, http://www.nypl.org/research/sibl/tour/onlinecat.html (accessed April 17, 2004).

72. http://www.nypl.org/research/sibl/science/scisubway.htm (accessed April 17, 2004).

73. Dennett, *Weird and Wonderful*, 144.

74. Stephen T. Asma, *Stuffed Animals and Pickled Heads: The Culture and Evolution of Natural History Museums* (Oxford: Oxford University Press, 2001), 45.

75. Daston and Park, *Wonders and the Order of Nature*, 218.

76. Goodheart, "Smithsonian's Veteran," E2.

77. John Walsh, "Pictures, Tears, Lights, and Seats," in *Whose Muse? Art Museums and the Public Trust*, ed. James Cuno (Princeton, NJ: Princeton University Press, 2004), 88. Walsh quotes Philip Fisher.

78. James N. Wood, "The Authorities of the American Art Museum," in *Whose Muse? Art Museums and the Public Trust*, ed. James Cuno (Princeton, NJ: Princeton University Press, 2004), 108–9.

79. Cuno, "The Object of Art Museums," 51.

6 THE SYMBOLIC PLACE OF THE LIBRARY-MUSEUM HYBRID IN THE DIGITAL AGE

As documented by Susan Pearce and Alexandra Bounia, the term *museum*—from the Greek *mouseion*—was originally used to describe an open-air shrine devoted to the muses. *Mouseions* frequently "had literary connections and they formed the focus of circles for the study of literature and especially of the Homeric epics."[1] They were also associated with the study of philosophy, and there is evidence that a *mouseion* existed in Aristotle's Lyceum.[2] In short, groups of individuals called *thiasos* met, studied, and wrote at the *mouseions*, which, according to a description in the will of Theophrastus as preserved by Diogenes Laertius in *Lives of Eminent Philosophers*, typically consisted of gardens with statuaries, walks, and small cloisters adjoining the gardens.[3] The most famous of the *mouseions* was the Alexandria Mouseion, a precinct—"it has a public walk, an Exedra with seats, and a large house"[4]—within the royal palace where "permanent members [were] engaged in various branches of study...especially research into the physical world in its widest sense, including all those aspects of the study of man and of nature represented...by the Aristotelian corpus."[5] In the third century B.C., a library—most scholars say that there were, in fact, two libraries, one a smaller outgrowth of the other[6]—became part of the Alexandria Mouseion, but ancient sources are silent as to the existence of a separate library building. Founded by Philadelphus and with Zenodotus—creator of "alphabetical order as a mode of organization"—as the first librarian,[7] the Alexandria library likely "formed part of...the Mouseion," where there were "abundant courtyards and colonnades which could have served as reading-rooms and study-quarters, while the 'book-stacks' may have been accommodated in rooms attached to the stoa."[8] In broad terms, it probably resembled the second century B.C. library at Pergamum, built by the Attalids dynasty, which consisted of a large room—possibly for receptions, meetings, and conferences—that also housed statues and busts and three smaller rooms that contained stacks of written materials.[9] Gradually, libraries developed in other cities and towns in the Greek and Hellenistic world. Often they were in local gymnasiums, which had slowly evolved from a purely military and athletic function to centers "of learning and education, with facilities for teaching classes, holding lectures and conferences."[10] In the Roman Empire, libraries were part of public baths, which contained not only bathing facilities, but also areas where leisure activities such as informal ball games could be held.[11] From the very beginning, then, libraries and museums were imbricated in what has been described as "a typically Greek composition of loosely flowing parts"—a model that set "the pattern through the Renaissance and beyond of library, museum and art gallery in [a] planned relationship" such that the library and museum were either directly above each other or in separate wings of a single building.[12]

Although this is a truncated version of early library history, it nevertheless indicates that libraries were rarely conceptualized as stand-alone entities: on the one hand, there were sculptures and artworks in the same place as collections of written materials; on the other hand, there was the possibility of engaging in a range of physical activities at the same location where written materials could be perused. And while it is true that, from a theoretical perspective, we can see the forerunners of modern public and academic libraries in the gymnasium/public bath model and the *mouseion*, respectively, it is also true that the contrast between the gymnasium/public bath model and the *mouseion* has some of the characteristics of the divide between library-museum partnerships that—respectively—either are, or are not, based on edutainment. A visit to a public bath and its library has about it a feel of edutainment; in contrast, a visit to a *mouseion* has about it an air of serious inquiry and detailed study.

We have tried to suggest that libraries should reassume the role of a museum through the development of a library-museum hybrid in which museum objects and text-based materials are physically juxtaposed in close proximity so that these objects and text-based materials inform one another. Most important, our proposed library-museum hybrids should conceptualize their new role in terms of serious inquiry and detailed study, not edutainment. Otherwise, there is the risk that museums—increasingly focused on defining themselves as edutainment venues—will colonize the role of libraries and, in the process of doing so, will eviscerate serious inquiry and detailed study in a ceaseless quest for edutainment.

In this regard, the America on the Move exhibit at the Smithsonian's National Museum of American History, like the Chocolate exhibit we discussed in chapter 1, is instructive—and for many of the same reasons. The story of "how trains, streetcars, ships and automobiles...have shaped and reshaped American life," the exhibit—which took up some 26,000 square feet of gallery space and cost approximately $22 billion—is an example of both the "new trend toward gigantism" and the movement away from "the uncontextualized display of old machines and toward an emphasis on how technology affects people and communities."[13] But it is also an example of edutainment. The following description gives insight into the tenor of the show.

> The Jupiter used to be displayed in a room with three other locomotives and a wall lined with models so visitors could compare and contrast railroad technology. Now it sits at a station platform in a re-created slice of Santa Cruz, Calif., the city it helped link with the national rail network in 1876. Theatrical lighting makes its brass work gleam. Lifelike beige figures—they're constructed of acrylic polymer over fiberglass—celebrate its arrival. A background mural adds blue sky and puffy clouds, while a sound-track mixes the Jupiter's whistle with the cries of invisible gulls. Before design began on the show, members of the [exhibit] team visited Disney World, where they learned "how important it is to feel like you're immersed in the setting." To walk through "America on the Move" is to be immersed...in a variety of settings all around the country.

Returning from Disney World "thinking that the Imagineers were really good at what they do, but that an overdose of their techniques could 'shut your brain off,'" exhibit developers attempted to create "its vignettes to hook [the public] into learning more." Undoubtedly many of the vignettes featured real people talking about compelling historical incidents, but, ironically, this was not always the case: "You'll also hear the tales of a traveling salesman named Rollo 'Tubby' Hutchins, though you might be disconcerted if you discovered—as visitors currently have no way of doing—that no such person actually lived. Tubby is a composite created for the show." As the notion of historical verisimilitude gives way to Disneyesque displays in a national museum of history, one is left wondering whether something has been lost.

Just as America on the Move includes a seemingly limitless supply of multimedia extravaganza funded, to a large degree, by a $10 million contribution from General Motors, it hardly includes any information about "the politics of transportation choices [and] how major decisions came to be made, not just how they affected people's lives...how, for example government and private interests combine[d] to promote enormously expensive highway construction, while allowing passenger rail to stagnate." Moreover, there is no mention of the controversy surrounding the role of General Motors in the disappearance of electric streetcars in major American cities, merely "a carefully worded...non-conspiracy version." Such salient transportation issues as safety, air pollution, and the 1973 gas crisis are not addressed: "Want to know more about environmental issues, dependence on foreign oil, or how American automakers...figured out how to avoid fuel economy standards by repackaging cars as SUVs? You're out of luck. Push the button for the audio and you get Click and Clack, the guys from 'Car Talk,' making fun of a woman because she keeps forgetting to release her Honda's emergency brake."

In other words, authentic experience has been replaced by an ersatz pastiche of "daily life" that leaves out the hard reality of the political and national implications of those "daily life" choices. We deliberately used the word *hard* in the previous sentence because the act of acquiring a body of knowledge about any topic is, bluntly put, hard and difficult; it cannot be reduced to the snippets of information gained in edutainment-based exhibits. In the quest for attendance statistics—one type of outcome measure—that will justify future stable or increased budget appropriations and gift shop sales that will provide evidence of managerial prowess and self-generated operating funds, museums that focus on edutainment shows are privileging simulation and simulacra at the expense of a thoughtful and considered educational approach that grapples with difficult questions and provides guideposts for a further examination of those difficult questions. They substitute an adulterated version of reality for the often awkward, hidden, and harsh reality of American—or any other nation's—life. Physically large, the exhibit is intellectually small. It is not the sheer quantity of objects that makes history come alive; indeed, sheer quantity can often overwhelm and devalue. Rather, in-depth understanding and knowledge can often best be gained through extensive study and focus on a limited number of objects.

In effect, America on the Move has the same relationship to thoughtful and well-rounded history as the popularity of commodified blues music among urban whites has to the reality of the blues as "an evocation of the black experience steeped in African musical traditions."[14] As David Hajdu observes, "the gritty authenticity" of the blues, which started as "holler songs" sung in the sun-bleached fields of the Mississippi Delta by African American slaves, has transmogrified "into a theme-park ride—a simulation that feels a little dangerous but doesn't really take you there." Just as museums substitute edutainment for historical fact and nuanced reflection while claiming that they are providing a fun learning atmosphere, so the blues has become "feel-good" and "background music" performed at more than 250 blues festivals "for families and young singles checking out the concessions and each other." On a lighter—though no less structurally analogous—note, baseball stadiums have been transformed from venues in which one watches baseball into places where one goes to do just about anything except watch baseball. Attendance at baseball stadiums has therefore soared, but, as recounted by Steve Rushin, increased attendance does not mean that more people are actually following the game. Instead, fans frequent SBC Park in San Francisco, which "boasts of wireless Internet access from every seat," in order to spend the entire game downloading music because it would take them too long to do so at home. Petco Park in San Diego features Picnic Hill, "a place for ticket holders to enjoy both a picnic and, should they desire it, a 'limited view' of the Padres game." Bank One Ballpark in Phoenix advertises the joys of a 385-square foot pool and an adjoining hot tub; Detroit's Comerica Park has "a Ferris wheel (behind third base), a carousel (behind first) and a tavern with a 70-foot bar"; and the proposed stadium for the Florida Marlins includes plans for an aquarium.[15] A committed baseball aficionado, Rushin seems both bemused and aghast that "many people visiting a ballpark now seem to have little idea of what takes place there" and that "watching a baseball game…has become, in most parks, largely unnecessary." It is little wonder that he waxes eloquent about the sheer beauty of entering "the brutalist Metrodome in Minneapolis to watch the Twins and Tigers play on plastic, beneath a Teflon roof, in a sterile, Sta-Puf stadium incapable of fireworks, Ferris wheels, or fish tanks [and in which] there was only baseball. It was, oddly, a purist's paradise."

Just as blues music has been transformed into a "theme-park ride" that has very little relationship with the essential philosophical underpinnings of the genre, so baseball stadiums at the beginning of the twenty-first century have taken large strides in making the actual *game* of baseball a background diversion to sundry forms of entertainment not connected with the intricacies and complexities of the game itself. Attempting to become an attractive public space, baseball stadiums have lost sight of their primary purpose: the game. Attempting to popularize the Mississippi Delta blues, contemporary blues festivals "conjure an atmosphere of casual fun in the name of boosting tourism and civic pride." Although this atmosphere may temporarily stimulate the local economy, it also eviscerates the very meaning of the blues. For the thousands of individuals participating in these events, nothing remains of the blues—or of baseball—but a gaudy simulation. In many ways, the developments at festivals and baseball stadiums parallel attempts by museums and libraries to become infotainment- and edutainment-based venues where, to extend Hajdu's analogy, it feels as if you know something, but not really.

As we pointed out in chapter 1, fascination with edutainment-based exhibits and activities has cultural and political consequences. Focusing on edutainment means *not* focusing on something else. Recall how Hal Niedzviecki criticized libraries for neglecting to collect alternative resources while directing their efforts at edutainment-type activities. In essence, he finds that, too often, they have become an (unwitting) cog in the corporate media system, emphasizing Feng Shui in the Bedroom courses to the detriment of collecting, for example, radical political and cultural materials that challenge and interrogate the premises of accepted social structures. Just as homogenous library collections bring about a situation in which difficult questions are not broached, the emphasis on edutainment-centered exhibits at museums results in situations in which the most crucial questions are left unasked. As a result, large gaps appear in our knowledge—gaps that we may not even know exist.

From an ideological perspective, the focus on edutainment in libraries and museums is the inevitable result of what Jean Baudrillard identifies as the troubling drift toward a world built on simulation and simulacra instead of reality—a world in which there has been a gradual erosion of the image as a "reflection of a profound reality" such that it either "masks and denatures a profound reality,... masks the *absence* of a profound reality [or finally] has no relation to any reality whatsoever" (original emphasis).[16] Meaning is lost, as information "exhausts itself in the staging of meaning. [This is] a gigantic process of simulation that is very familiar....Immense energies are deployed to hold this simulacrum at bay, to avoid the brutal desimulation that would confront us in the face of the obvious reality of a radical loss of meaning."[17] All this has political implications insofar as the simulacrum is the "preeminent form of a dominant discourse no longer obliged to have any recourse to any legitimating ground or presupposition of resemblance outside its own immanent effects."[18] Fredric Jameson agrees that the political implications of a "society of the image or the simulacrum" are disturbing.[19] Not only is the real transformed into "so many pseudoevents" in such a way that individuals live in "a new and original historical situation in which we are condemned to seek History by way of our own pop images and simulacra of that history, which itself remains forever out of reach,"[20] but the transformation of reality into images is related "to the emergence of…consumer or multinational capitalism"[21] and therefore "issues in a loss of any referent that might provide resources for resisting the spread of consumer capitalism."[22] Postmodern culture has thus succeeded in pulling "a mystificatory veil over the realities of contemporary exploitation."[23]

Although some scholars have taken Jameson to task for being "practically misguided" and an intellectual relic—arguing, for instance, that the "'symbolic order' is not necessarily separate from or transcendent to the 'real' [because] in the virtual dimension, the symbolic becomes real in a world where reality is undeniably symbolic"[24]—others, such as Nick Dyer-Witherford, have recognized the pertinence of his ideas and have proposed a series of alternative measures that would ameliorate the negative effects of postmodernism.[25] One of the key planks of Dyer-Witherford's platform is the "socialization of media," which, to be sure, would "reappropriat[e] resources from corporate conglomerates." But such socialization has an even more significant function.

> Every communicational node and link established outside the control of capital diminishes its ability to naturalize commodification, to impose its "class-ifying" grids of surveillance, to suppress news of struggles, to censor, to mystify, and deceive. Conversely, each instance of such countercommunication increases the possibility to explore variegated images of decommodified human identity, circulate struggles, and discuss the reorganization of society outside the parameters of the market.[26]

In a roundabout fashion, this takes us back to Niedzviecki's disappointment with the current state of libraries and the criticisms of Asma, Perl, and Hein with regard to museums. As libraries and museums focus on edutainment-based programs and activities, they do not participate in what Dyer-Witherford calls "decommodification." Ultimately, the users whom libraries and museums try to attract through edutainment suffer because libraries and museums do not provide them with sufficient opportunities—through diverse collections in which detailed explorations can be made about subjects both large and small—to "circulate struggles" or to "discuss the reorganization of society outside the parameters of the market." In this context, it is little wonder that bowdlerized Feng Shui in the Bedroom courses are assuming pride of place in libraries, with little awareness on the part of librarians that such courses are, in reality, the most recent examples of "popular orientalism" in which global capitalism works to bring about a situation wherein "difference is commodified, sanitized, and thus *neutralized* for easy consumption" such that countries like China are transformed from "contemporary world economies" with complex histories and traditions into "nations of spiritual peasants whose non-materialist goals are essentially to live in peace and to seek enlightenment" (original emphasis).[27]

As Dyer-Witherford hopes, the digital world may, of course, facilitate the conditions for decommodification. But to pin all our aspirations on the digital world—or digital libraries and museums—is to underestimate the power of new and evolving forms of edutainment and consumer capitalism, as explicated by Baudrillard and Jameson, among others. A return to the historical real—in the form of collections of objects and text-based materials juxtaposed with those objects—in an on-site library-museum hybrid of the type proposed in chapter 5 would ensure meaningful experiences without having to resort to spectacles associated with postobject roles. Otherwise, libraries and museums may find that they have become Disneyland-type theme parks offering popular entertainments masquerading as educational experiences.

Certainly, it is true that North Americans have become a *joystick nation*, a phrase appearing on the cover of the *New York Times Magazine* in late December 2003 to draw attention to an article entitled "Playing Mogul," an insightful overview of the changes wrought by the video-game industry in contemporary notions of entertainment.[28] There has indeed been "a cultural sea change" because of "the rise of interactive entertainment," of which video games are a crucial part. Video-game industry representatives even go so far as to refer to their products as interactive "art" because "you can have different kinds of experience." It is completely understandable that "to anyone who came of age after, say, the introduction of the first Sony Playstation in 1995, video gaming is every bit as central to the pop-entertainment universe as movies or music, while to anyone older than that, it seems like one of those strange customs indigenous to the country of the young." Because the concept of entertainment has changed, edutainment has become an inescapable part of the cultural landscape of the late twentieth and early twenty-first centuries, and it will likely become even more inescapable and leave an even more indelible mark. Little wonder that libraries and museums feel compelled to offer edutainment-type programs and activities in an attempt to remain relevant: they do not want to be perceived as out-of-touch laggards who are not cognizant of cultural sea change.

Yet libraries and museums have a stark choice. And this choice is encapsulated in the discussion that Bruno Bonnell, the chief executive officer of Atari—a well-known video-game company—had with his son:

> I was trying to convince my boy to learn Chinese. You know what his answer was? "Why do I care about learning Chinese? By the time I master Chinese, we'll have computer phones where you'll be able to talk in French or English and it will be translated into Chinese in real time." And he is right! I am wrong! I mean, who cares about speaking in Chinese, because we'll be able to communicate like in 'Star Trek.' We'll have automatic translation, and we'll be able to talk. And you know the wonder of this? This is all video games. This is why it's so interesting. And we haven't even touched the depth of all the education that you can derive from there.

There are a number of observations to be made here. Not surprisingly, there is a sanguine trust in the inevitability of technological developments that will make life easier. Why should anyone bother to learn a language—or, for that matter, any difficult subject matter—if there is a strong chance that technological advances will render that effort—and the time spent expending the effort—moot? Second, there is the conviction that the ability to talk in Chinese through some form of—at first rudimentary, then increasingly sophisticated—automatic translation is tantamount to an in-depth comprehension of the nuances of the Chinese language and the Chinese people, with their centuries of rich and complex linguistic, social, cultural, religious, and political history. While long years of painstaking study of Chinese would—in addition to increasing language facility—open a window on some of these historical aspects and lead to an increased understanding of the Chinese world and worldview, reliance on automatic translations of the kind mentioned by Bonnell would not. By analogy, when libraries and museums put their trust in edutainment-type events and partnerships, they forsake their traditional mission to provide the tools their patrons need to acquire detailed knowledge of diverse subjects and topics. In a very real way, they are Bonnell. Initially anxious to encourage new knowledge acquisition, they settle for—and become enthusiastic about—what is often a technologically driven superficiality that they hope will be, on some level, seductive enough to entice their patrons to be lifelong learners and which they convince themselves somehow represents, in Bonnell's formulation, "depth of all the education that you can derive from there." And the more emphasis that there is on quantifiable outcome measures that provide value to taxpayers, the more libraries will be tempted—and ineluctably led—to become popular edutainment attractions that are challenged to justify their existence through high attendance (e.g., popular programs such as dance classes and yoga) and circulation statistics (e.g., reliance on marketing-based and product-analysis selection policies and practices).

Some learning will doubtless occur, but, as we have seen in such examples as America on the Move, the Steven F. Udvar-Hazy Center, and Chocolate, many salient topics and questions are not even included in edutainment-type offerings. And when topics and subjects are included, they are treated without the type of contextually rich depth, detail, and background necessary for the creation of knowledge and critical inquiry. For example, curators at the refurbished Brooklyn Museum of Art, which was the beneficiary of a $63 million "face-lift and modernization" that featured "a futuristic glass entrance with fountains designed by the same company that created the ones at the Bellagio Hotel and Casino in Las Vegas," have "recently been instructed to write explanatory labels in short, simple paragraphs that some [of them] describe as being designed for no more than a third-grade reading level."[29] One argument for undertaking extensive renovations at BMA—many of the new galleries and rooms have been outfitted with "plump armchairs, computer touch screens, background music and flat-panel televisions showing short documentaries" as well as "theatrical installations"—was that, taken together, these innovations would attract "more people from surrounding neighborhoods," especially "the ethnically diverse population of Brooklyn to whom the museum's strengths in African, Egyptian and South American art should appeal." But if "splashy colors and designs" and "simple paragraphs...designed for no more than a third-grade reading level" are what museum officials think they need to overcome issues of race and class in museum attendance, then these same officials are not so much breaking down socioeconomic barriers but perpetuating an insidious racism based on "an insufficient respect for the audience."

It is these identified lacunae in edutainment-based learning that should be of primary concern as libraries and museums—together or separately—seek to establish for themselves a distinct, meaningful, and sustainable role in an already edutainment-saturated cultural landscape. As Richard Morrison writes about the controversy surrounding the reinvention of the Victoria and Albert Museum in London, the reigning mantra of "'access for the many, not just for the few' sounds uncontroversial, but sooner or later it means every institution is deemed to have failed if it doesn't lure millions of punters through its doors."[30] And to lure these "punters"—individual citizens—through the doors and thus ensure that their institution has public relevancy in the eyes of—and continued support from—funding entities and agencies, directors have decided that "museums should be branded and packaged like pop videos and then targeted at a nine-year-old with the attention span of a gnat"[31] and that they should advertise themselves as "a café with 'art on the side.'"[32] Or, as Arnold Lehman, the director of the BMA bluntly puts it, the museum should be a place where people decide to go "on a date, instead of the movies, say, or the park...'a place to celebrate an event, a place to come to—with no art involved, per se—a place to come to celebrate something about their community.'"[33] In other words, cultural institutions—in this case, museums—instead of intellectually challenging patrons, have dumbed themselves down, in the process becoming indistinguishable from other edutainment-based venues. In a sense, they pass inadvertent judgment on the intellectual capacities of their patrons by not affording them opportunities to ask difficult questions.

The attempt to lure thousands of individuals to frequent libraries and museums by emphasizing edutainment to ensure the survival of the same libraries and museums is, in so many words, the result of the need to pay attention to easily understood and easily quantifiable outcome measures: the more patrons a library or museum can attract, the more relevant and worthy it is to governments and private donors. The library and museum no longer can exist qua library or museum, that is, as an institution with "wondrous educational resources"[34] based on expertise and scholarship—an institution that leads to contemplation of and critical inquiry about important issues. Rather, the argument goes, it must, by means of edutainment, be turned into a "public space," as if libraries and museums that exist as rigorous learning institutions are somehow not public space. Accordingly, the attempt to turn libraries and museums into an edutainment-based public space is a veiled attempt to redefine museums and libraries away from being venues for contemplation, wonder, knowledge acquisition, and critical inquiry.

Consider the work of Gloria Leckie and Jeffrey Hopkins, who argue that a central library has untold value for a community primarily because it is one of the few remaining public spaces—a concept that they link to the circumstance that "patrons themselves create a dynamic and animated ambience through their own activities, diversity, and vitality."[35] To support their contention, they refer to Ray Oldenburg's book *The Great Good Place*, which suggests that there is a vital role to be played by "third places." And it is here that the crux of the matter lies. At the same time that they use Oldenburg's concept of "third place" and transform it into "public space," they somehow overlook that Oldenburg understood third places to be, as the subtitle of his book asserts, "cafés, coffee shops, community centers, beauty parlors, general stores, bars, [and] hang-outs"—places where the "cardinal and sustaining activity is...pleasurable and entertaining conversation" whose main goal is "pure sociability."[36]

Metaphorically, Leckie and Hopkins want to turn central libraries into the equivalent of coffee shops and bars because, among other reasons, they want to ensure the survival of libraries in an age when some commentators view libraries as being "redundant [because] of electronic information."[37] To be sure, there is nothing wrong with coffee shops and bars, but they do not offer the educational opportunities and resources that are present in a library or museum. On the other hand, coffee shops and bars could be said to offer a form of edutainment through their various themes and motifs, and casual conversation that is "pleasurable and entertaining" in a themed bar or coffee shop can often be informative, though not necessarily conducive to rigorous learning. Leckie and Hopkins, among others, thus have little confidence that libraries can be justified as places of contemplation, wonder, knowledge acquisition, and critical inquiry. Instead, they must be justified as "public spaces" that, through such edutainment-based offerings as dance classes and band concerts, foster "pure sociability" and "create a dynamic and animated ambience"—the type of dynamism and animation that pleases funding entities because it allows them to justify the expenditure of public monies. As a result, the library—or the museum—is no longer a library or museum, defined as an institution of learning, contemplation, wonder, knowledge acquisition, and critical inquiry. Rather, it has evolved into something else, something that is, ironically, more akin to the "shopping malls, theme parks, and other large, commercialized ventures"—all purveyors of edutainment experiences—that Leckie and Hopkins criticize.[38]

Hovering in the background, of course, is Jürgen Habermas's definition of the "public sphere" as "the sphere of private people come together as a public"[39]—a definition that some scholars have seen as an appropriate one for libraries, especially public libraries in their roles as social and cultural places.[40] But, as we shall see, invoking the concept of a public sphere as a goal to which libraries should aspire may not be especially helpful, since Habermas makes a distinction between a critical public sphere—something that has a positive value—and a public sphere that only claims to be a public sphere but is not. In tracing the historical and structural evolution of the public sphere, Habermas identified seventeenth- and eighteenth-century coffeehouses in Great Britain as one of the early preeminent symbols of the public sphere—a place where "private people com[ing] together as a public…claimed the public sphere regulated from above against the public authorities themselves, to engage them in a debate over the general rules governing relations in the basically privatized but publicly relevant sphere of commodity exchange and social labor. The medium of this political confrontation was peculiar and without historical precedent: people's public use of their reason," defined as "simultaneously the invocation of reason and its disdainful disparagement as merely malcontent griping."[41] In so many words, it was meant to be a place of resistance and confrontation with existing authority structures—a place where the public could discuss "the problematization of areas that until then had not been questioned."[42] In this sense, it was a positive critical public sphere.

But, ironically enough, as Habermas makes clear, the public sphere was only inclusive in principle, not in practice, since it included only those who were "propertied and educated": "in relation to the mass of the rural population and the common 'people' in the towns, of course, the public 'at large' that was being formed diffusely outside the early institutions of the public was still extremely small."[43] In other words, the public sphere was "the new form of bourgeois representation" and became its "mouthpiece."[44] The public sphere was, as Karl Marx understood all too well, nothing but "property-owning private people"[45]: "the social preconditions for the equality of opportunity were obviously lacking, namely: that any person with skill and 'luck' could attain the status of property owner and thus the qualifications of a private person granted access to the public sphere, property and education."[46] As a result, "the view on which the private people, assembled to form a public, reached agreement through discourse and counter-discourse must not therefore be confused with what was right and just…as long as power relationships were not effectively neutralized in the reproduction of social life."[47]

Thus, when libraries try to appropriate for themselves what they consider to be the positive elements of the mantle of the Habermasian public sphere, they advocate for—and indeed perpetuate—the very same type of social exclusion that excluded non-property-owning lower social classes from the public sphere. And they do so while cloaking themselves in the rhetoric of inclusiveness. In other words, they position themselves as agents of a middle-class ethos—a part of the existing authority structure. Sadly, statistics bear this out. In the United States, "library users reported a significantly higher annual income than library nonusers."[48] In England and Wales, "the upper middle class and middle class make up 15% of the population, but 41% of this class are frequent library users and 29% are non users…[while] the semi skilled and unskilled working class make up 31% of the population, but only 26% of this class are frequent users and 57% are non users."[49]

Of course, the notion of public sphere, as Habermas recognizes, is not a static one. In the nineteenth and twentieth centuries, it became increasingly subject to "the laws of the market," and the "rational-critical debate" that had characterized the early public sphere "had a tendency to be replaced by consumption,"[50] including books, advertiser-supported magazines, movie attendance, and television watching.[51] One of the results was the creation of "mass culture," which "earned its rather dubious name precisely by achieving increased sales by adapting to the need for relaxation and entertainment on the part of consumer strata with relatively little education, rather than through the guidance of an enlarged public toward the appreciation of culture undamaged in its substance."[52] In other words, while the idea of the public sphere may have become more inclusive because more and more people were participating in the public sphere, this participation was not a real participation insofar as it was characterized by a consumerism that, in its very nature, was the antithesis of a critical public sphere.

To be sure, discussion continued, but it took on the characteristics of a consumer item: "discussion, now a 'business,' becomes formalized [as] the presentation of positions and counterpositions [was] bound to certain prearranged rules of the game."[53] Accordingly, "critical debate arranged in this manner certainly fulfills important social-psychological functions, especially that of a tranquillizing substitute for action; however, it increasingly loses its publicist [public sphere] function."[54] As "the institutions of the public engaged in rational-critical debate . . . were commercialized and underwent economic, technological, and organizational concentration," they became "complexes of societal power, so that precisely their remaining in private hands . . . threatened the critical functions of publicist institutions."[55] In short, the public sphere was transformed into "a medium of advertising"[56] in which individuals reproduced opinions that were "ready-made, flexibly reproduced, barely internalized, and [did] not evok[e] much commitment."[57]

If we place Habermas's analysis side-by-side with Leckie and Hopkins's work, we begin to see what the public library is and is not. First, while it may want to see itself as an integral part of the public sphere, it really only serves a small fraction of the public. And, to keep that fraction of individuals coming back, it has increasingly become café- and coffeehouse-like—a public space stressing "pure sociability" and the creation of "a dynamic and animated ambience." And it has also, to a large extent, adopted market-driven, collection development policies and edutainment-based events and programming. In concert with the evolution of the public sphere as identified by Habermas, the public library has evolved into a pseudo–public sphere—one that has become "commercialized and [that has] under[gone] economic, technological, and organizational concentration" to such an extent that it "threaten[s] the critical functions" of the public sphere. In sum, the public library, as presently constituted, cannot be said to be an unambiguous example of a critical public sphere. The concept of the public sphere—which, as Marx recognized, was not inclusive of a large portion of the public—was associated first with coffeehouses and later with consumer-based consumption; public libraries that want to become key components of the public sphere by assuming the attributes of coffeehouses and consumer-driven models of collecting and programming have little claim to being components of a critical public sphere. Indeed, it could be argued that they fail to understand the difference between the notions of public sphere and critical public sphere, thus contributing to the collapse of a "communicative network of a [critical] public made up of rationally debating private citizens."[58] Accordingly, as public libraries become "caught in the vortex of *publicity that is staged for show or manipulation*" (original emphasis), they contribute to a situation in which "the public of nonorganized public people is laid claim to not by public communication but by the communication of publicly manifested opinions"[59] of the consumerist culture industry, defined as "the ephemeral results of the relentless publicist barrage and propagandist manipulation by the media to which consumers are exposed, especially during their leisure time."[60] While championing their centrality to the public sphere, public libraries do not see that their deeply cherished public sphere is no longer a critical public sphere. As public libraries become, in the words of Niedzviecki, "mere cogs in the machine of capitalism," they run a real risk of not only continuing to exclude low-income individuals, but also depriving all their patrons of a space free of consumerist imperatives in all their multiple manifestations.

And, to say the least, the ways in which these consumerist imperatives are manifested in libraries and museums are not only legion, but also intertwined. As we have seen throughout this book, the focus on edutainment, in its myriad forms, is essentially a consumer-centric philosophy driven by the need to increase attendance and satisfaction levels of attendees, which leads to positive outcome and performance measures, which in turn provide the kind of quantitative evidence that governments and private funding agencies increasingly demand as they allocate, on a competitive basis, future funding upon which cultural institutions depend. Libraries and museums can no longer simply be places that quietly encourage the acquisition of knowledge through reading, contemplation, reflection, and critical inquiry; rather, they must demonstrate relevance and usefulness as embodiments of "social capital" that contribute, in economic terms, to the development of an information-based society. And, as John Buschman has explained, these consumerist imperatives are all the more insidious because they also pervade less-obvious aspects of library philosophy and service, from the profit-oriented knowledge management theories that many library administrators have embraced to the "transformative" postmodern architectural design of library buildings such as the Cerritos (California) Public Library and the Seattle Public Library designed by Rem Koolhaas, which have become "multi-sensory learning environments" and "'hyper-energized' entertainment centers with librarians as concierges to 'customers.'"[61]

On the other hand, if libraries and museums were to reassert themselves as places devoted to contemplation, wonder, knowledge acquisition, and critical inquiry—and not just places that (unwittingly) perpetuate the structures of global capitalism—then, we believe, the conditions for the formation of a truly critical, inclusive, and less-commercialized public sphere that could think seriously about thorny social and political issues would have a better chance of taking root. When libraries and museums understand their role to be edutainment-based public spaces on the model of cafés and coffeehouses, they abrogate their role as educational entities committed to rigorous learning and the kind of knowledge acquisition that asks hard questions about various social, political, historical, economic, and cultural phenomena. Accordingly, to borrow the words of Jean Baudrillard,[62] they contribute to "a radical loss of meaning" as they transform the historical real into "so many pseudoevents"[63] and pseudoknowledge by trying to emulate the coffeehouse ambience of a (pseudo) public sphere, overlooking the fact that the transformation of reality into images is related "to the emergence of…consumer or multinational capitalism"[64] and therefore "issues in a loss of any referent that might provide resources for resisting the spread of consumer capitalism."[65]

Can libraries become venues of "critical publicity"?[66] That is, can they become instantiations of the critical public sphere where "public communications are so organized that there is a chance immediately and effectively to answer back any opinion expressed in public [and] where opinion formed by such discussion…readily finds an outlet in effective action, even against—if necessary—the prevailing system of authority"?[67] Such opinions, it is to be noted, are distinct from mass communicative interchanges in which "the community of publics becomes an abstract collection of individuals who receive impressions from the mass media," in which the prevailing communication channels are organized in a way that makes it "difficult or impossible for the individual to answer back immediately or with any effect," and in which "the realization of opinion in action is controlled by authorities who organize and control the channels of such action."[68] In other words, the more that a venue—such as a library or museum—allows the development and creation of opinions that are not mediated by the cultural industry "through the channels of a publicity staged for the purpose of manipulation or show,"[69] the more it can lay claim to being a site for critical publicity—to being a critical public sphere. All this is of real importance because the ability of the public sphere to assume its proper critical function "determines whether the exercise of domination and power persists as a negative constant."[70]

Although there are tantalizing possibilities for the creation of just such a critical sphere in the electronic realm, our argument, quite simply, is that there are also real possibilities for the creation of such a critical public sphere in a library-museum hybrid of the type described in chapter 5. Libraries and museums that focus on infotainment- and edutainment-based events do not give their patrons the possibility of becoming deeply informed and critically knowledgeable to the extent that they can become real members of a critical public sphere; our library-museum hybrid, on the other hand, does so by fostering meaningful knowledge acquisition and critical inquiry through the juxtaposition of objects and text-based materials. As library officials and museum directors try to salvage their respective institutions from what appears to them to be musty irrelevance by focusing on edutainment-based events or what Richard Morrison calls "pretentious 'rebranding' exercise[s] by some slick-suited Soho marketing guru,"[71] they run the risk of hollowing out their missions of education, knowledge acquisition, and critical inquiry. And once these missions have been downplayed, the potential for individuals to ask difficult questions and hold views not necessarily compatible with mainstream consumerist society markedly wanes.

But, as a headline about the demanding exhibits at the Jewish Museum of New York indicates, "Why Should It Be Easy?"[72] Libraries and museums would do well to consider that question. Education, knowledge acquisition, and critical inquiry *are* difficult and demanding; they rarely take place through edutainment-type displays and events that touch on trendy topics, feature prose written at a third-grade reading level, and rely overmuch on the splashy "wow" factor to the detriment of substantial and detailed content. Our proposal for single-building library-museum hybrids, with its focus on the interaction of objects (contained in visible storage centers) and text-based materials in a series of contemporary cabinets of curiosities (rooms or designated areas/wings/floors), has the potential to recenter knowledge acquisition, wonder, and critical inquiry at the heart of the public mission of libraries, now transformed into library-museum hybrids. We are not saying that our model is perfect; indeed, it might seem outmoded or unduly traditional. We would like to think, however, that the acquisition of meaningful knowledge and the development of critical inquiry skills through a sense of wonder and serious study never go out of fashion. Just as two or more libraries join forces to become joint-use libraries to enhance the learning experiences of their respective user communities, so our library-museum hybrids can be considered as joint-use library-museums whose overarching goal is to enhance the learning experiences and critical faculties of *all* community members in meaningful ways, not merely in ways that are dependent upon consumerism-based edutainment events, displays, and programs.

NOTES

1. Susan Pearce and Alexandra Bounia, eds., *Ancient Voices*, vol. 1, *The Collector's Voice: Critical Readings in the Practice of Collecting* (Aldershot, England: Ashgate, 2000), 84.

2. See the extensive description in P. M. Fraser, *Ptolemaic Alexandria* (Oxford: Clarendon Press, 1972), 313–15.

3. Pearce and Bounia, *Ancient Voices*, 84.

4. Ibid., 87–89.

5. Fraser, *Ptolemaic Alexandria*, 315, 317.

6. Ibid., 323–24.

7. Lionel Casson, *Libraries in the Ancient World* (New Haven, CT: Yale University Press, 2001), 37.

8. Fraser, *Ptolemaic Alexandria*, 324–25.

9. Casson, *Libraries in the Ancient World*, 51.

10. Ibid., 58.

11. Ibid., 91–92.

12. Brian Edwards, with Biddy Fisher, *Libraries and Learning Resource Centres* (Oxford: Architectural Press, 2002), 19.

13. All quotations about the America on the Move exhibit are from Bob Thompson, "The Wheel Thing: Smithsonian's Massive Transportation Show Keeps to the Highway,"

Washington Post, 22 November 2003, http://www.washingtonpost.com (accessed November 22, 2003).

14. All quotes about the blues are from David Hajdu, "Who's Got the Blues?" *Mother Jones,* September–October 2003, 79.

15. All quotes and information in this paragraph are taken from Steve Rushin, "Take Me Out to the...Whatever," *Sports Illustrated,* 14 June 2004, 15.

16. Jean Baudrillard, *Simulacra and Simulation,* trans. Sheila Faria Glaser (Ann Arbor, MI: University of Michigan Press, 1994), 6.

17. Ibid., 80.

18. Scott Durham, *Phantom Communities: The Simulacrum and the Limits of Postmodernism* (Stanford, CA: Stanford University Press, 1998), 53–54.

19. Fredric Jameson, *Postmodernism, or The Cultural Logic of Late Capitalism* (Durham, NC: Duke University Press), 48.

20. Ibid., 25.

21. Fredric Jameson, "Postmodernism and Consumer Society," in *The Anti-Aesthetic: Essays on Post-Modern Culture,* ed. Hal Foster (Seattle, WA: Bay Press, 1983), 124–25.

22. Mark C. Taylor, *About Religion: Economies of Faith in Virtual Culture* (Chicago: University of Chicago Press, 1999), 144–45.

23. Nick Dyer-Witherford, *Cyber-Marx: Cycles and Circuits of Struggle in High-Technology Capitalism* (Urbana, IL: University of Illinois Press, 1999), 170. Dyer-Witherford refers to Arif Dirlik, "Post-Socialism/Flexible Production: Marxism in Contemporary Radicalism," *Polygraph* 6/7 (1993): 156–57.

24. Taylor, *About Religion,* 148.

25. Dyer-Witherford, *Cyber-Marx,* 192–218.

26. Ibid., 206.

27. Kimberly J. Lau, *New Age Capitalism: Making Money East of Eden* (Philadelphia: University of Pennsylvania Press, 2000), 7–12. Lau makes use of the insights of Edward Said and Stuart Hall to ground her argument.

28. All quotations about the video-game industry are taken from Jonathan Dee, "Playing Mogul," *New York Times Magazine,* 21 December 2003, 36–41, 52–53, 66–68.

29. All quotations in this paragraph about the Brooklyn Museum of Art are taken from Randy Kennedy and Carol Vogel, "Brooklyn Museum, Newly Refurbished, Seeks an Audience," *New York Times,* 12 April 2004, A19.

30. Richard Morrison, "Minister, It Ain't Broke," *The Times* (London), 9 April 2001, http://www.lexis.com (accessed April 12, 2004).

31. Ibid. For more information about the Victoria and Albert Museum renovation project, see Hugo Pearman, "From Here to Modernity," *The Times* (London), 21 April 2002, http://www.lexis.com (accessed April 12, 2004); and Joanna Pitman, "Smile! You're Being Done Up," *The Times* (London), 22 July 1998, http://www.lexis.com (accessed April 12, 2004).

32. This fact is mentioned by Phillipe de Montebello, "Art Museums, Inspiring Public Trust," in *Whose Muse? Art Museums and the Public Trust,* ed. James Cuno (Princeton, NJ: Princeton University Press, 2004), 167.

33. Kennedy and Vogel, "Brooklyn Museum," A19.

34. Morrison, "Minister, It Ain't Broke."

35. Gloria J. Leckie and Jeffrey Hopkins, "The Public Place of Central Libraries: Findings from Toronto and Vancouver," *Library Quarterly* 72 (July 2002): 332.

36. Ray Oldenburg, *The Great Good Place: Cafés, Coffee Shops, Community Centers, Beauty Parlors, General Stores, Bars, Hangouts and How They Get You Through the Day* (New York: Paragon House, 1989), 26, 28.

37. Leckie and Hopkins, "The Public Place of Central Libraries," 359.

38. Ibid., 360.

39. Jürgen Habermas, *The Structural Transformation of the Public Sphere: An Inquiry into a Category of Bourgeois Society,* trans. Thomas Burger with Frederick Lawrence (Cambridge, MA: MIT Press, 1989), 27.

40. See, for example, Wayne A. Wiegand, "To Reposition a Research Agenda: What American Studies Can Teach the LIS Community About the Library in the Life of the User," *Library Quarterly* 73 (October 2003): 369–82; and Sarah A. Anderson, "'The Place to Go': The 135th Street Branch Library and the Harlem Renaissance," *Library Quarterly* 73 (October 2003): 383–421.

41. Habermas, *The Structural Transformation of the Public Sphere,* 27.

42. Ibid., 36.

43. Ibid., 37.

44. Ibid.

45. Ibid., 123.

46. Ibid., 124.

47. Ibid., 125.

48. Eleanor Jo Rodger and others, *The Impacts of the Internet on Public Library Use: An Analysis of the Current Consumer Market for Library and Internet Services,* (pp. 8, 29), http://www.urbanlibraries.org/pdfs/finalulc.pdf (accessed April 21, 2004).

49. John Pateman, "Public Libraries, Social Exclusion and Social Class," *Information for Social Change* 10, http://www.libr.org/ISC/articles/10-public.html (accessed February 28, 2004). Pateman's statistics are based on Steve Bohme and David Spiller, *Perspectives of Public Library Use 2: A Compendium of Survey Information* (Loughborough, Leicestershire, England: Department of Information Science, Loughborough University, 1999), 34.

50. Habermas, *The Structural Transformation of the Public Sphere,* 161.

51. Ibid., 163–64.

52. Ibid., 165.

53. Ibid., 164.

54. Ibid.

55. Ibid., 188.

56. Ibid., 189.

57. Ibid., 246.

58. Ibid., 247.

59. Ibid., 247–48.

60. Ibid., 245.

61. John Buschman, *Dismantling the Public Sphere: Situating and Sustaining Librarianship in the Age of the New Public Philosophy* (Westport, CT: Libraries Unlimited, 2003), 92–99.

62. Baudrillard, *Simulacra and Simulation,* 80.

63. Jameson, *Postmodernism*, 25.

64. Ibid., 124–25.

65. Taylor, *About Religion*, 144–45.

66. Habermas, *The Structural Transformation of the Public Sphere*, 248.

67. Ibid., 249. Habermas quotes from C. W. Mills, *The Power Elite* (New York: Oxford University Press, 1956), 303–4.

68. Ibid., 249. Habermas quotes from C. W. Mills, *The Power Elite*, 303–4.

69. Ibid., 249.

70. Ibid., 250.

71. Morrison, "Minister, It Ain't Broke."

72. Julie Salamon, "At 100, Still Asking 'Why Should It Be Easy?'; The Jewish Museum, A Place for Art and Debate," *New York Times*, 21 January 2004, E1.

BIBLIOGRAPHY

Achilles, Rolf, ed. *Humanities' Mirror: Reading at the Newberry, 1887–1987*. Chicago: The Newberry Library, 1987.

Ackerman, Jennifer. "No Mere Bird: Cranes." *National Geographic,* April 2004, 38–57.

AHA Books. "Put Your Books in the Brautigan Virtual Library." http://www.ahapoetry.com/braushlf.htm (accessed December 6, 2003).

American Library Association. *Combined Libraries: A Bibliography* (ALA Library Fact Sheet Number 20). http://www.ala.org/library/fact20.html (accessed April 4, 2004).

Anderson, Sarah A. "'The Place to Go': The 135th Street Branch Library and the Harlem Renaissance." *Library Quarterly* 73 (October 2003): 383–421.

Appelman, Hilary. "Sharing Buried Treasure Via a Network." *New York Times,* 2 May 2001, D15.

Arizona Science Center. "Satellite Science." http://www.satellitescience.org (accessed May 11, 2003).

Asma, Stephen T. *Stuffed Animals and Pickled Heads: The Culture and Evolution of Natural History Museums*. Oxford: Oxford University Press, 2001.

Bahney, Anna. "A Place Where Spring Arrives on the Wings of a Sandhill Crane." *New York Times,* 26 March 2004, F1.

Baker, Sharon L. *The Responsive Public Library Collection: How to Develop and Market It*. Englewood, CO: Libraries Unlimited, 1993.

Baker, Sharon L., and Karen L. Wallace. *The Responsive Public Library: How to Develop and Market a Winning Collection.* 2nd ed. Englewood, CO: Libraries Unlimited, 2002.

Bakker, Isabella. "Introduction: The Gendered Foundations of Restructuring in Canada." In *Rethinking Restructuring: Gender and Change in Canada,* edited by Isabella Bakker, 3–25. Toronto, ON: University of Toronto Press, 1996.

Barry, Andrew. "On Interactivity: Consumers, Citizens and Culture." In *The Politics of Display: Museums, Science, Culture,* edited by Sharon Macdonald, 98–117. London: Routledge, 1998.

Baudrillard, Jean. *Simulacra and Simulation.* Translated by Sheila Faria Glaser. Ann Arbor, MI: University of Michigan Press, 1994.

Bazillion, Richard, and Connie L. Braun. *Academic Libraries as High-Tech Gateways: A Guide to Design and Space Decisions.* 2nd ed. Chicago: American Library Association, 2001.

Bell, Whitfield J., Jr. "The Cabinet of the American Philosophical Society." In *A Cabinet of Curiosities: Five Episodes in the Evolution of American Museums,* edited by Whitfield J. Bell Jr., 1–34. Charlottesville, VA: University Press of Virginia, 1967.

Bennett, Nuala A. "Building a Web-Based Collaborative Database—Does it Work?" In *Papers: Museums and the Web 2001.* http://www.archimuse.com/mw2001/papers/bennett/bennett.html (accessed June 10, 2003).

Bennett, Nuala A., Beth Sandore, Amanda M. Grunden, and Patricia L. Miller. "Integration of Primary Resource Materials into Elementary School Curricula." In *Papers: Museums and the Web 2000.* http://www.archimuse.com/mw2000/papers/bennett/bennett.html (accessed June 10, 2003).

Bennett, Nuala A., and Brenda Trofanenko. "Digital Primary Source Materials in the Classroom." In *Papers: Museums and the Web 2002.* http://www.archimuse.com/mw2002/papers/bennett/bennett.html (accessed June 10, 2003).

Bennett, Tony. "The Multiplication of Culture's Utility." *Critical Inquiry* 21 (summer 1995): 861–89.

Birmingham Civil Rights Institute. "The Richard Arrington Jr. Resource Gallery." http://bcri.bham.al.us/multimedia.htm (accessed May 11, 2003).

Bjorncrantz, Leslie, Jeffrey Garrett, and Harrie Hughes. "Northwestern's Art of the Story: Public Relations on a Grand Scale." *American Libraries* 31 (December 2000): 50–53.

Blumenthal, Ralph. "A Press Pass to the Workings Behind the Headlines." *New York Times,* 12 April 2001, B2.

Bohlen, Celestine. "Museums as Walk-in Closets: Visible Storage Opens Troves to the Public." *New York Times,* 6 May 2001, B1, B6.

Bohme, Steve, and David Spiller. *Perspectives of Public Library Use 2: A Compendium of Survey Information*. Loughborough, Leicestershire, England: Department of Information Science, Loughborough University, 1999.

Bornstein, Jeanne, Meg Maher, and Holland Goss. "The Public's Treasures: A Cabinet of Curiosities." http://www.nypl.org/research/chss/events/images/curiositiesbrochure.pdf (accessed July 8, 2003).

Boström, Hans-Olof. "Philipp Hainhofer and Gustavus Adolphus's *Kunstschrank* in Uppsala." In *The Origins of Museums: The Cabinet of Curiosities in Sixteenth- and Seventeenth-Century Europe*, edited by Oliver Impey and Arthur MacGregor, 90–101. Oxford: Clarendon Press, 1985.

Boxer, Sarah. "Snubbing Chronology as a Guiding Force in Art." *New York Times*, 2 September 2000, A19.

Brautigan, Richard. *The Abortion: A Historical Romance 1966*. New York: Simon and Schuster, 1970.

Breckenridge, Tom. "Check It Out—Libraries Shelve Stuffy Image for Broader Appeal." *The Plain Dealer*, 14 January 2002, B5.

Breisch, Kenneth A. *Henry Hobson Richardson and the Small Public Library in America: A Study in Typology*. Cambridge, MA: MIT Press, 1997.

Brooke, Elizabeth Heilman. "Car Showrooms Give Way to Cultural Showcases." *New York Times*, 3 June 1999, B2.

Brooklyn Children's Museum. "Brooklyn Expedition Lesson Plans." http://www.brooklynexpedition.org/lessonplans.html (accessed June 6, 2003).

Brooklyn Historical Society. "Brooklyn Works: 400 Years of Making a Living in Brooklyn." http://www.brooklynhistory.org/main/brooklyn_works4.html (accessed December 5, 2003).

Brooklyn Museum of Art. "First Saturdays at the Brooklyn Museum of Art: August 2 Schedule of Evening Programs." http://www.brooklynmuseum.org (accessed July 29, 2003).

Brown, Bill. "The Collecting Mania." *University of Chicago Magazine*, October 2001, 38–43.

Brown, Karen, and Miriam Pollack. "Illinois Libraries and Museums: Connecting and Collaborating for the Future." *Illinois Libraries* 82 (summer 2000): 209–15.

Browne, Julia. "Coffee, Tea and/or Literacy: The Public Library's Role in Accommodating Today's 'Average Joe.'" *Current Studies in Librarianship* 24 (spring/fall 2000): 80–87.

Brunsdale, Maureen. "From Mild to Wild: Strategies for Promoting Academic Libraries to Undergraduates." *Reference and User Services Quarterly* 39 (summer 2000): 331–35.

Bryman, Alan. "The Disneyization of Society." *The Sociological Review* 47 (February 1999): 25–47.

Buckland, Michael K. "Five Grand Challenges for Library Research." *Library Trends* 51 (spring 2003): 675–86.

Bundy, Alan. "Joint-Use Libraries: The Ultimate Form of Cooperation." In *Planning the Modern Public Library Building,* edited by Gerard B. McCabe and James R. Kennedy, 129–48. Westport, CT: Libraries Unlimited, 2003.

———. *Widened Horizons: The Rural School Community Libraries of South Australia.* Adelaide, Australia: Auslib Press, 1997.

Buschman, John E. *Dismantling the Public Sphere: Situating and Sustaining Librarianship in the Age of the New Public Philosophy.* Westport, CT: Libraries Unlimited, 2003.

California Digital Library. "Free Speech Movement Digital Archive." http://bancroft.berkeley.edu/FSM (accessed November 19, 2003).

———. "Japanese American Relocation Digital Archives." http://jarda.cdlib. org (accessed November 19, 2003).

———. "Museums and the Online Archive of California." http://www. bampfa.berkeley.edu/moac (accessed November 19, 2003).

Carlson, Scott. "The Deserted Library: As Students Work Online, Reading Rooms Empty Out—Leading Some Campuses to Add Starbucks." *The Chronicle of Higher Education,* 16 November 2001. http://chronicle.com/ free/v48/i12/12a03501.htm (accessed November 29, 2001).

Carr, David. "Rex's Lending Center and the Information Life of the Child at the Children's Museum of Indianapolis." http://www.scils.rutgers.edu/~kvander/ books/CARR.pdf (accessed May 15, 2003). Also available in *Ways of Knowing,* edited by Kay E. Vandergrift, 89–118. Lanham, MD: Scarecrow Press, 1996.

Casson, Lionel. *Libraries in the Ancient World.* New Haven, CT: Yale University Press, 2001.

Center for Columbia River History. "Oral History Archives." http://www. ccrh.org/oral/index.htm (accessed December 4, 2003).

Central Library of Rochester and Monroe County, New York. "Rochester Images." http://www.libraryweb.org/rochimag (accessed June 6, 2003).

Cherokee Heritage Center. "Cherokee Traveling Exhibits." http://www.cherokee heritage.org/coe/ov_imls.html (accessed May 10, 2003).

Children's Museum of Houston. "Museum Map." http://www.cmhouston.org/ map/map.htm (accessed June 10, 2003).

Coffman, Steve. "What If You Ran Your Library Like a Bookstore?" *American Libraries* 29 (March 1998): 40–43.

Colorado Digitization Program. "Heritage Colorado." http://www.cdpheritage. org (accessed December 6, 2003).

Connecticut History Online. "Photographs, Drawings and Prints about Connecticut History." http://www.cthistoryonline.org (accessed May 9, 2003).

Conner Prairie Living History Museum. "The Conner Estate." http://www. connerprairie.org (accessed May 9, 2003).

Cuno, James. "The Object of Art Museums." In *Whose Muse? Art Museums and the Public Trust*, edited by James Cuno, 49–75. Princeton, NJ: Princeton University Press, 2004.

Dana, John Cotton. "The Gloom of the Museum." In *The New Museum: Selected Writings by John Cotton Dana*, edited by William A. Penniston, 44–61. Newark, NJ: Newark Museum Association, 1999. Originally published in Dana, John Cotton. *The New Museum Series, no. 1*. Woodstock, VT: Elm Tree Press, 1917.

———. "Libraries and Museums: How Museums Came to Be So Deadly Dull." In *The New Museum: Selected Writings by John Cotton Dana*, edited by William A. Penniston, 118–127. Newark, NJ: Newark Museum Association, 1999. Originally published in *The Library Journal* 46 (15 May 1921).

———. "The New Museum." In *The New Museum: Selected Writings by John Cotton Dana*, edited by William A. Penniston, 21–43. Newark, NJ: Newark Museum Association, 1999. Originally published in Dana, John Cotton. *The New Museum Series, no. 2*. Woodstock, VT: Elm Tree Press, 1917.

———. "A Museum of, for, and by Newark." In *The New Museum: Selected Writings by John Cotton Dana*, edited by William A. Penniston, 173–78. Newark, NJ: Newark Museum Association, 1999. Originally published in *The Survey: Graphic Number 55*, no. 11 (1 March 1926).

Daston, Lorraine, and Katharine Park. *Wonders and the Order of Nature, 1150–1750*. New York: Zone Books, 1998.

Davis, Douglas. *The Museum Transformed: Design and Culture in the Post-Pompidou Age*. New York: Abbeville Press, 1990.

DeCarlo, Tessa. "A Place to Hang Out and Learn a Thing or Two." *New York Times*, 23 April 2003, F16.

Dee, Jonathan. "Playing Mogul." *New York Times Magazine*, 21 December 2003, sec. 6, 36–41, 52–53, 66–68.

de Montebello, Phillipe. "Art Museums, Inspiring Public Trust." In *Whose Muse? Art Museums and the Public Trust*, edited by James Cuno, 151–69. Princeton, NJ: Princeton University Press, 2004.

Dennett, Andrea Stulman. *Weird and Wonderful: The Dime Museum in America*. New York: New York University Press, 1997.

Diamant-Cohen, Betsy. "Role of Pratt's Exploration Center Clarified." *Baltimore Chronicle*, 27 June 2001. http://baltimorechronicle.com/pratt_jul01.html (accessed June 21, 2003).

Diamant-Cohen, Betsy, and Dina Sherman. "Hand in Hand: Museums and Libraries Working Together." *Public Libraries* 42 (March/April 2003): 102–5.

Dilevko, Juris. "Why Sallie [Sally] Tisdale Is *Really* Upset About the State of Libraries: Socio-political Implications of Internet Information Sources." *Journal of Information Ethics* 8 (spring 1999): 37–62.

Dilevko, Juris, and Lisa Gottlieb. "The Politics of Standard Selection Guides: The Case of the *Public Library Catalog.*" *Library Quarterly* 73 (July 2003): 289–337.

Dirlik, Arif. "Post-Socialism/Flexible Production: Marxism in Contemporary Radicalism." *Polygraph* 6/7 (1993): 133–69.

Discovery Center of Springfield. "Science Source." http://www.discoverycenter.org/sciencesource.asp (accessed May 10, 2003).

Dixon, Joyce K. "Experiencing Architecture: The Young People's Library Department in Las Vegas." *School Library Journal* 37 (February 1991): 30–32.

DMCD Incorporated. "DMCD Overview May 2001." http://www.dmcd.com (accessed September 9, 2003).

Dornseif, Karen A. "Joint-Use Libraries: Balancing Autonomy and Cooperation." In *Joint-Use Libraries*, edited by William Miller and Rita M. Pellen, 103–16. Binghampton, NY: Haworth Press, 2001.

Durham, Scott. *Phantom Communities: The Simulacrum and the Limits of Postmodernism*. Stanford, CA: Stanford University Press, 1998.

Dyer-Witherford, Nick. *Cyber-Marx: Cycles and Circuits of Struggle in High-Technology Capitalism*. Urbana, IL: University of Illinois Press, 1999.

Edelman, Hendrick, and Robert P. Holley, eds. *Marketing to Libraries for the New Millennium: Librarians, Vendors, and Publishers Review the Landmark Third Industry-Wide Survey of Library Marketing Practices and Trends*. Lanham, MD: Scarecrow Press, 2002.

Edwards, Brian, with Biddy Fisher. *Libraries and Learning Resource Centres*. Oxford: Architectural Press, 2002.

Emory University Digital Library. "American South." http://www.americansouth.org (accessed November 19, 2003).

Fitzgibbons, Shirley A. "School and Public Library Relationships: Essential Ingredients in Implementing Educational Reforms and Improving Student Learning." *School Library Media Research* 3 (2000). http://www.ala.org/ala/

aasl/aaslpubsandjournals/slmrb/slmrcontents/volume32000/relationships.htm (accessed March 28, 2003).

Flood, Susan. *Evolution and Status of Approval Plans*. Washington, DC: Association of Research Libraries, 1997.

Frank, Michael. "Will Wonders Never Cease?" *New York Times*, 21 June 2002, B36.

Fraser, P. M. *Ptolemaic Alexandria*. Oxford: Clarendon Press, 1972.

Frieze, Henry Simmons. "Art Museums and Their Connection with Public Libraries." In *Public Libraries in the United States of America: Special Report: Part I*, by U.S. Bureau of Education, 434–44. Washington, DC: Government Printing Office, 1876.

Fučiková, Eliška. "The Collection of Rudolf II at Prague: Cabinet of Curiosities or Scientific Museum?" In *The Origins of Museums: The Cabinet of Curiosities in Sixteenth- and Seventeenth-Century Europe*, edited by Oliver Impey and Arthur MacGregor, 47–53. Oxford: Clarendon Press, 1985.

Fugate, Cynthia. "Common Ground: Making Library Services Work at a Collocated Campus." In *Joint-Use Libraries*, edited by William Miller and Rita M. Pellen, 55–64. Binghampton, NY: Haworth Press, 2001.

Getty Museum. "Getty to Partner with U.S. Department of Education, NEA, NASA, and the White House on Mars Millennium Project." http://www. getty.edu/news/press/la/marsmill.html (accessed December 21, 2003).

Gilmore, Don. "Anatomy of a Bestseller." *Toronto Life*, September 2003, 86–92.

Goldberg, Beverly. "Faculty Object to Shared San Jose Library: Joint University–Main Public Library Facility." *American Libraries* 29 (December 1998): 21–22.

Goldberger, Paul. "High-tech Bibliophilia: Rem Koolhaas's New Library in Seattle Is an Ennobling Public Space." *The New Yorker*, 24 May 2004, 90–91.

Gomez, Elsa, Eila Hultén, and Ulla Drehmer. "A Joint Library Project in Härnösand, Sweden." *Scandinavian Public Library Quarterly* 31 (1998): 22–24.

Goodheart, Adam. "Smithsonian's Veteran Man-in-the-Middle Stands His Ground." *New York Times*, 24 April 2002, E2.

Gorman, James. "In Virtual Museums, an Archive of the World." *New York Times*, 12 January 2003. http://www.nytimes.com (accessed January 12, 2003).

Greenhouse, Steven. "Wal-Mart, A Nation unto Itself." *New York Times*, 17 April 2004, B7.

Gumbel, Andrew. "The Perfect City Library: Rem Koolhaas's Design for the Seattle Library Was Initially Derided." *The Independent* (London), 25 May 2004, http://www.lexis.com (accessed July 13, 2004).

Gundersen, Edna. "Downloading Squeezes the Art out of the Album." *USA Today*, 5–7 December 2003, A1–2.

Gundestrup, Bente. "From the Royal *Kunstkammer* to the Modern Museums of Copenhagen." In *The Origins of Museums: The Cabinet of Curiosities in Sixteenth- and Seventeenth-Century Europe*, edited by Oliver Impey and Arthur MacGregor, 128–33. Oxford: Clarendon Press, 1985.

Gurian, Elaine Heumann. "What Is the Object of This Exercise? A Meandering Exploration of the Many Meanings of Objects in Museums." *Daedalus* 128 (summer 1999): 163–83.

Habermas, Jürgen. *The Structural Transformation of the Public Sphere: An Inquiry into a Category of Bourgeois Society.* Translated by Thomas Burger with the assistance of Frederick Lawrence. Cambridge, MA: MIT Press, 1989 (12th printing, 2001).

Hajdu, David. "Who's Got the Blues?" *Mother Jones*, September–October 2003, 76–84.

Hall, Peter. "Now Showing: Something Dazzling." *New York Times*, 2 May 2001, D17.

Hein, Hilde S. *The Museum in Transition: A Philosophical Perspective.* Washington, DC: Smithsonian Institution Press, 2000.

Henry E. Huntington Library and Art Gallery. "The World From Here: Introduction to the Website." http://www.calbook.org (accessed November 15, 2003).

Heritage Museum. "Museum History." http://www.lincolncountylibraries.com/museum/museum_history.htm (accessed May 11, 2003).

Honig-Bear, Sharon. "School-Public Library Partnerships in Washoe County, Nevada." In *Joint-Use Libraries*, edited by William Miller and Rita M. Pellen, 5–16. Binghampton, NY: Haworth Press, 2001.

Hunt, John Dixon. "*Curiosities* to Adorn *Cabinets* and *Gardens*." In *The Origins of Museums: The Cabinet of Curiosities in Sixteenth- and Seventeenth-Century Europe*, edited by Oliver Impey and Arthur MacGregor, 193–203. Oxford: Clarendon Press, 1985.

Hunter, Michael. "The Cabinet Institutionalized: The Royal Society's 'Repository' and Its Background." In *The Origins of Museums: The Cabinet of Curiosities in Sixteenth- and Seventeenth-Century Europe*, edited by Oliver Impey and Arthur MacGregor, 159–68. Oxford: Clarendon Press, 1985.

Imhoff, Kathleen R. T. "Public Library Joint-Use Partnerships: Challenges and Opportunities." In *Joint-Use Libraries*, edited by William Miller and Rita M. Pellen, 17–40. Binghampton, NY: Haworth Press, 2001.

Impey, Oliver, and Arthur MacGregor. "Introduction." In *The Origins of Museums: The Cabinet of Curiosities in Sixteenth- and Seventeenth-Century Europe*, edited by Oliver Impey and Arthur MacGregor, 1–4. Oxford: Clarendon Press, 1985.

Indiana University–Purdue University at Indianapolis Library and Indianapolis Museum of Art. "Community Project." http://www.ulib.iupui.edu/imls (accessed June 7, 2003).

Institute of Museum and Library Services. "2003 National Leadership Grants for Libraries and Museums." http://www.imls.gov (accessed March 19, 2003).

———. *Libraries and Museums Give Kids a Head Start*. Washington, DC: Institute of Museum and Library Services, 2003. http://www.imls.gov/closer/archive/hlt_c0503.htm (accessed June 14, 2003).

———. *True Needs True Partners: Museums Serving Schools: 2002 Survey Highlights*. Washington, DC: Institute of Museum and Library Services, 2003. http://www.imls.gov (accessed June 15, 2003).

———. "What's the Buzz?" http://www.imls.gov/closer/archive/hlt_m0902.htm (accessed May 10, 2003).

Iovine, Julie V. "In Basel, Art Is Storage, and Storage Is Art." *New York Times*, 5 June 2003, D3.

Jameson, Fredric. "Postmodernism and Consumer Society." In *The Anti-Aesthetic: Essays on Postmodern Culture*, edited by Hal Foster, 111–25. Seattle, WA: Bay Press, 1983.

———. *Postmodernism or, The Cultural Logic of Late Capitalism*. Durham, NC: Duke University Press, 1991.

Johnson, Peggy. *Fundamentals of Collection Development and Management*. Chicago: American Library Association, 2004.

Jones, Barbara M. "Providing Virtual Archives for the Classroom: The Librarian's Perspective." Abstract in *SHARP 2001: 9th Annual Conference*. http://www.wm.edu/CAS/ASP/SHARP/abstract.php?author=bjones-session11 (accessed June 10, 2003).

Jones, Karen. "New 'Smart' Galleries, Wireless and Web-Friendly." *New York Times*, 24 April 2002, E27.

Karlen, Neal. "A Curator Puts 'Star Wars' in Turnaround." *New York Times*, 19 April 2000, D17.

———. "Displaying Art with a Smiley Face." *New York Times,* 19 April 2000, D17.

Kennedy, Randy. "The Rumble That's Lasted for 100 Years." *New York Times,* 19 March 2004, E31.

Kennedy, Randy, and Carol Vogel. "Brooklyn Museum, Newly Refurbished, Seeks an Audience." *New York Times,* 12 April 2004, A1, A19.

Kimmelman, Michael. "All Too Often, the Art Itself Gets Lost in the Blueprints." *New York Times,* 21 April 1999, D7.

———. "J. Carter Brown, Who Transformed the Museum World, Dies at 67." *New York Times,* 19 June 2002. http://www.nytimes.com (accessed June 19, 2002).

———. "Museums in a Quandary: Where Are the Ideals?" *New York Times,* 26 August 2001, sec. 2, 26.

Kinzer, Stephen. "The Dead Sea Scrolls: Middle West Miracle." *New York Times,* 23 April 2003, F9.

———. "It's Museum Time in the South." *New York Times,* 18 December 2001, E1.

———. "Mount Vernon, Alarmed by Fading Knowledge, Seeks to Pep Up Washington's Image." *New York Times,* 29 July 2002, http://www.nytimes.com (accessed July 29, 2002).

Kratz, Charles. "Transforming the Delivery of Service." *College and Research Library News* 64 (February 2003): 100–101.

Krippendorff, Klaus. "The Power of Communication and the Communication of Power: Toward an Emancipatory Theory of Communication," *Communication* 12 (1989): 175–96.

Larson, Reed W. "Toward a Psychology of Positive Youth Development." *American Psychologist* 55 (January 2000): 170–83.

Lau, Kimberly J. *New Age Capitalism: Making Money East of Eden.* Philadelphia: University of Pennsylvania Press, 2000.

Laurencich-Minelli, Laura. "Museology and Ethnographical Collections in Bologna During the Sixteenth and Seventeenth Centuries." In *The Origins of Museums: The Cabinet of Curiosities in Sixteenth- and Seventeenth-Century Europe,* edited by Oliver Impey and Arthur MacGregor, 17–23. Oxford: Clarendon Press, 1985.

Leckie, Gloria J., and Jeffrey Hopkins. "The Public Place of Central Libraries: Findings from Toronto and Vancouver." *Library Quarterly* 72 (July 2002): 326–72.

Leigh Yawkey Woodson Art Museum. *Calendar of Events. Down Under and Over Here: Children's Book Illustration from Australia and America.* Wausau, WI, (no date).

————. *Family Activity Guide. Down Under and Over Here: Children's Book Illustration from Australia and America.* Wausau, WI, (no date).

Lester, Ray. "The Convergence of Museums and Libraries?" *Alexandria* 13 (March 2001): 183–91.

Library Company, The. "At the Instance of Benjamin Franklin: A Brief History of the Library Company of Philadelphia." http://www.librarycompany.org/instance.htm (accessed July 8, 2003).

Lobner, Jerome, and Lillian Kaslon. "School/Public Library Combinations." *Nebraska Library Association Quarterly* 31 (summer 2000): 17–21.

Macdonald, Sharon, ed. "Exhibitions of Power and Powers of Exhibition: An Introduction to the Politics of Display." In *The Politics of Display: Museums, Science, Culture*, 1–24. London: Routledge, 1998.

————. "Supermarket Science? Consumerism and 'The Public Understanding of Science.'" In *The Politics of Display: Museums, Science, Culture*, 118–38. London: Routledge, 1998.

MacGregor, Arthur. "The Cabinet of Curiosities in Seventeenth-Century Britain." In *The Origins of Museums: The Cabinet of Curiosities in Sixteenth- and Seventeenth-Century Europe*, edited by Oliver Impey and Arthur MacGregor, 147–58. Oxford: Clarendon Press, 1985.

MacGregor, Arthur, ed. "Collectors and Collections of Rarities in the Sixteenth and Seventeenth Centuries." In *Tradescant's Rarities: Essays on the Foundation of the Ashmolean Museum 1683 with a Catalogue of the Surviving Early Collections*, 70–97. Oxford: Clarendon Press, 1983.

————. "The Tradescants as Collectors of Rarities." In *Tradescant's Rarities: Essays on the Foundation of the Ashmolean Museum 1683 with a Catalogue of the Surviving Early Collections*, 17–23. Oxford: Clarendon Press, 1983.

Martin, Paul. *Popular Collecting and the Everyday Self: The Reinvention of Museums?* London: Leicester University Press, 1999.

Martin, Robert S. "Blurring the Boundaries of Cultural Institutions." Presented at the Natural Science Collections Alliance conference, Washington, DC, 7 June 2002. http://www.imls.gov/whatsnew/current/sp041902 (accessed September 9, 2003).

————. "Welcoming Remarks." Presented at the 21st Century Learner Conference, Washington, DC, November 2001. http://www.imls.gov/whatsnew/current/sp110701–3.htm (accessed September 6, 2003).

Maryland ArtSource. "Baltimore Art Resource Online Consortium." http://www.marylandartsource.org (accessed May 11, 2003).

Mattson, Kevin. "The Librarian as Secular Minister to Democracy: The Life and Ideas of John Cotton Dana." *Libraries and Culture* 35 (fall 2000): 514–34.

Memorial Hall Museum. "American Centuries: Views from New England." http://www.memorialhall.mass.edu/site_intro.html (accessed May 11, 2003).

Menzhausen, Joachim. "Elector Augustus's *Kunstkammer:* An Analysis of the Inventory of 1587." In *The Origins of Museums: The Cabinet of Curiosities in Sixteenth- and Seventeenth-Century Europe,* edited by Oliver Impey and Arthur MacGregor, 69–75. Oxford: Clarendon Press, 1985.

Mihm, Stephen. "Museums: Firsts, Facts and Figures." *New York Times,* 19 April 2000, D20.

Mills, C. W. *The Power Elite.* New York: Oxford University Press, 1956.

Morris, Bonnie Rothman. "Lots of Rubbernecking in These Traffic Jams." *New York Times,* 23 April 2003, F4.

Morrison, Richard. "Minister, It Ain't Broke." *The Times* (London), 9 April 2001. http://www.lexis.com (accessed April 12, 2004).

Morton, Norman. "Anatomy of a Community Relations Success." *American Libraries* 32 (February 2001): 40–42.

Murphy, Dean E. "Moving Beyond 'Shh' (and Books) at Libraries." *New York Times,* 7 March 2001, A1, A20.

Muschamp, Herbert. "The Library that Puts on Fishnets and Hits the Disco." *New York Times,* 16 May 2004, sec. 2, 1, 31.

Museum of History and Industry (Seattle, Washington). "King County Snapshots." http://content.lib.washington.edu/imls/kcsnapshots/explore.html (accessed November 7, 2003).

National Archives and Records Administration. "Exit Nara Notice." http://clinton4.nara.gov/cgi_bin/good_bye_cgi?url (accessed December 21, 2003).

NatureMaker. "Company Profile: Worldwide Makers of Museum-Quality Sculpted Trees." http://www.naturemaker.com (accessed September 6, 2003).

———. "Installations." http://www.naturemaker.com (accessed September 6, 2003).

Neverov, Oleg. "'His Majesty's Cabinet' and Peter I's *Kunstkammer.*" Translated by Gertrud Seidmann. In *The Origins of Museums: The Cabinet of Curiosities in Sixteenth- and Seventeenth-Century Europe,* edited by Oliver Impey and Arthur MacGregor, 54–61. Oxford: Clarendon Press, 1985.

Newhouse, Victoria. *Towards a New Museum.* New York: Monacelli Press, 1998.

Newseum. "Newseum Design Unveiled: Museum Will Be Expanded and 'Reinvented' Next to the National Mall." http://www.newseum.org (accessed July 29, 2003).

Nickerson, Matthew. "Voices: Bringing Multimedia Museum Exhibits to the World Wide Web." *First Monday* 7 (May 2002). http://www.firstmonday.dk (accessed May 11, 2003).

Niedzviecki, Hal. "Libraries Need to Mind Their Own Business." *The Globe and Mail*, 27 October 2003, R3.

Nielsen, Arno Victor. *Museum Europa: An Exhibition About the European Museum from the Renaissance to Our Time*. Copenhagen: Danish National Museum, 1993.

Nilsen, Kirsti, and Lynne (E. F.) McKechnie. "Behind Closed Doors: An Exploratory Study of the Perceptions of Librarians and the Hidden Intellectual Work of Collection Development in Canadian Public Libraries." *Library Quarterly* 72 (July 2002): 294–325.

Oldenburg, Ray. *The Great Good Place: Cafés, Coffee Shops, Community Centers, Beauty Parlors, General Stores, Bars, Hangouts and How They Get You Through the Day*. New York: Paragon House, 1989.

Olliver, James, and Susan Anderson. "Seminole Community Library: Joint-Use Library Services for the Community and the College." In *Joint-Use Libraries*, edited by William Miller and Rita M. Pellen, 89–102. Binghampton, NY: Haworth Press, 2001.

Olmi, Giuseppe. "Science-Honour-Metaphor: Italian Cabinets of the Sixteenth and Seventeenth Centuries." In *The Origins of Museums: The Cabinet of Curiosities in Sixteenth- and Seventeenth-Century Europe*, edited by Oliver Impey and Arthur MacGregor, 5–16. Oxford: Clarendon Press, 1985.

Pateman, John. "Public Libraries, Social Exclusion and Social Class." *Information for Social Change* 10. http://www.libr.org/ISC/articles/10-public.html (accessed February 28, 2004).

Pearce, Susan M. *On Collecting: An Investigation into Collecting in the European Tradition*. London: Routledge, 1995.

Pearce, Susan, and Ken Arnold, eds. *Early Voices*. Vol. 2, *The Collector's Voice: Critical Readings in the Practice of Collecting*. Aldershot, England: Ashgate, 2001.

Pearce, Susan, and Alexandra Bounia, eds. *Ancient Voices*. Vol. 1, *The Collector's Voice: Critical Readings in the Practice of Collecting*. Aldershot, England: Ashgate, 2000.

Pearman, Hugo. "From Here to Modernity." *The Times* (London), 21 April 2002. http://www.lexis.com (accessed April 12, 2004).

Penrose Library, University of Denver. "Images of Pioneer Jewish Families." http://www.library.du.edu/specoll/beck/images.cfm (accessed December 6, 2003).

Perl, Jed. "Welcome to the Funhouse: Tate Modern and the Crisis of the Museum." *The New Republic*, 19 June 2000, 30–36.

Peterson, Christina, and Patricia Senn Breivik. "Reaching for a Vision: The Creation of a New Library Collaborative." In *Joint-Use Libraries*, edited by William Miller and Rita M. Pellen, 117–30. Binghampton, NY: Haworth Press, 2001.

Philbin, Ann, and David Stuart Rodes. "Foreword." In *The World from Here: Treasures of the Great Libraries of Los Angeles*, edited by Cynthia Burlingham and Bruce Whiteman, 5–11. Los Angeles: UCLA Grunwald Center for the Graphic Arts and the Armand Hammer Museum of Art and Cultural Center, 2001.

Pitman, Joanna. "Smile! You're Being Done Up." *The Times* (London), 22 July 1998. http://www.lexis.com (accessed April 12, 2004).

Public Library Association. *Public Library Data Service Statistical Report 2003*. Chicago: American Library Association, 2003.

Public Library of Charlotte and Mecklenburg County. "Weaving a Tale of Craft: About this Project." http://www.handsoncrafts.org (accessed June 10, 2003).

Rabe, Annina. "A Library in Balance." *Scandinavian Public Library Quarterly* 35 (2002): 31–33.

Rhode Island School of Design. "Artist Residencies: David McGee, 15 Minutes: The Ballad of Then and Now." http://www.risd.edu/artcontext/artists/david/david_mcgee.htm (accessed June 10, 2003).

———. "Artist Residencies: Jerry Beck, Wheel of Wonder." http://www.risd.edu/artcontext/artists/jerry/jerry_artwork.htm (accessed June 10, 2003).

———. "Artist Residencies: Lynne Yamamoto, This, and my Heart." http://www.risd.edu/artcontext/artists/lynne/lynne_artwork.htm (accessed June 10, 2003).

———. "Interview with the Artist: David McGee, 15 Minutes: The Ballad of Then and Now." http://www.risd.edu/artcontext/splash_frame.htm (accessed December 12, 2003).

———. "Interview with the Artist: Ernesto Pujol, Memory of Surfaces." http://www.risd.edu/artcontext/artists/ernesto/ernesto_interview.htm (accessed June 10, 2003).

———. "Interview with the Artist: Indira Freitas Johnson, Freenotfree." http://www.risd.edu/artcontext/artists/indira/indira_interview.htm (accessed June 10, 2003).

Riding, Alan. "The Royal Academy Puts On a New, Fresher Face." *New York Times*, 21 April 1999, D7.

Ritzer, George. *Enchanting a Disenchanted World: Revolutionizing the Means of Consumption.* Thousand Oaks, CA: Pine Forge, 1999.

Robbins, Catherine C. "No Room for Riches of the Indian Past: Museums Are Inundated by Ceramics, Bones, Arrowheads and Other Cultural Artifacts." *New York Times,* 24 November 2001, A15.

Robinson, Joyce Henri. "An American Cabinet of Curiosities: Thomas Jefferson's 'Indian Hall' at Monticello." In *Acts of Possession: Collecting in America,* edited by Leah Dilworth, 16–41. New Brunswick, NJ: Rutgers University Press, 2003.

Rodger, Eleanor Jo, George D'Elia, Corinne Jörgensen, and Joseph Woelfel. *The Impacts of the Internet on Public Library Use: An Analysis of the Current Consumer Market for Library and Internet Services.* http://www.urbanlibraries.org/pdfs/finalulc.pdf (accessed April 21, 2004).

Rosenbaum, David E. "Smithsonian Loses Millions After Dispute with Donor." *New York Times,* 6 February 2002, A14.

Roshaven, Patricia, and Rudy Widman. "A Joint University, College and Public Library." In *Joint-Use Libraries,* edited by William Miller and Rita M. Pellen, 65–88. Binghampton, NY: Haworth Press, 2001.

Rudd, Peggy D. "Documenting the Difference: Demonstrating the Value of Libraries Through Outcome Measurement." In *Perspectives on Outcome Based Evaluation for Libraries and Museums.* Washington, DC: Institute of Museum and Library Services, 2000. http://www.imls.gov (accessed June 15, 2003).

Rushin, Steve. "Take Me Out to the…Whatever." *Sports Illustrated,* 14 June 2004, 15.

Salamon, Julie. "At 100, Still Asking 'Why Should It Be Easy?'; The Jewish Museum, A Place for Art and Debate." *New York Times,* 21 January 2004, E1.

———. "Museums Defend Fudge Factor." *New York Times,* 30 July 2003, B7.

Scheicher, Elisabeth. "The Collection of Archduke Ferdinand II at Schloss Ambras: Its Purpose, Composition and Evolution." In *The Origins of Museums: The Cabinet of Curiosities in Sixteenth- and Seventeenth-Century Europe,* edited by Oliver Impey and Arthur MacGregor, 29–38. Oxford: Clarendon Press, 1985.

Schiller, Herbert I. *Culture, Inc.: The Corporate Takeover of Public Expression.* New York: Oxford University Press, 1989.

Science, Industry and Business Library (New York Public Library). "Exhibitions. The Subway at 100: General William Barclay Parsons and the Birth of the NYC Subway." http://www.nypl.org/research/calendar/exhib/sibl/siblexhibdesc.cfm?id = 349 (accessed April 17, 2004).

Sciolino, Elaine. "Smithsonian Chief Draws Ire in Making Relics of Old Ways." *New York Times*, 30 April 2001, A1.

———. "Smithsonian Is Promised $38 Million, with Strings." *New York Times*, 10 May 2001, A12.

Seelig, Lorenz. "The Munich Kunstkammer, 1565–1807." In *The Origins of Museums: The Cabinet of Curiosities in Sixteenth- and Seventeenth-Century Europe*, edited by Oliver Impey and Arthur MacGregor, 76–89. Oxford: Clarendon Press, 1985.

Shaffer, Roberta I. "Bringing Things to the Center: The Center for the Cultural Record of the Graduate School of Library and Information Science at the University of Texas at Austin." *RBM: Journal of Rare Books, Manuscripts, and Cultural Heritage* 1 (fall 2000): 136–44.

Shelton, Anthony Alan. "Cabinets of Transgression: Renaissance Collections and the Incorporation of the New World." In *The Cultures of Collecting*, edited by John Elsner and Roger Cardinal, 177–203. London: Reaktion Books, 1994.

Shipley, Jane. "Role of Pratt's Exploration Center Clarified: Jane Shipley Responds." *Baltimore Chronicle*, 27 June 2001, http://baltimorechronicle. com/pratt_jul01.html (accessed June 21, 2003).

———. "A Tale of Two Libraries: Clifton and Port Discovery." *Baltimore Chronicle*, 30 May 2001. http://baltimorechronicle.com/library_jun01.html (accessed June 21, 2003).

Simpson, Matthew. " 'You Have Not Such a One in England': St Andrew's University Library as an Eighteenth-Century Mission Statement." *Library History* 17 (March 2001): 41–55.

Solomon, Deborah. "He Turns the Past into Stories, and the Galleries Fill Up." *New York Times*, 21 April 1999, D12.

———. "Tastemaker, New in Town, Dives into a Cauldron." *New York Times*, 2 May 2001, D1.

Southern Utah University. "Voices of the Colorado Plateau." http://archive.li. suu.edu/voices (accessed November 8, 2003).

Stamler, Bernard. "Temples of Culture Are Needy, Too. Tai Chi, Anyone?" *New York Times*, 23 April 2003, F2.

Stein, Karen. "Meyer, Scherer and Rockcastle's Sahara West Library and Fine Arts Museum Is a World Apart from the Las Vegas Strip." *Architectural Record* 185 (March 1997): 54–61.

Steinberg, Jacques. "Who Said Plumbing Doesn't Belong on a Pedestal? Not These Museums." *New York Times*, 19 April 2000, D27.

Stevens, Kimberly. "The Name May Be Artsy, But It's Still Date Night." *New York Times*, 24 April 2002, E25.

Stewart, Susan. "Death and Life, in that Order, in the Works of Charles Willson Peale." In *The Cultures of Collecting,* edited by John Elsner and Roger Cardinal, 204–23. London: Reaktion Books, 1994.

Taylor, Mark C. *About Religion: Economies of Faith in Virtual Culture.* Chicago: University of Chicago Press, 1999.

Theuerkauff, Christian. "The Brandenburg *Kunstkammer* in Berlin." In *The Origins of Museums: The Cabinet of Curiosities in Sixteenth- and Seventeenth-Century Europe,* edited by Oliver Impey and Arthur MacGregor, 110–14. Oxford: Clarendon Press, 1985.

Thompson, Bob. "History for Sale." *Washington Post,* 20 January 2002. http://www.washingtonpost.com (accessed January 20, 2002).

———. "The Wheel Thing: Smithsonian's Massive Transportation Show Keeps to the Highway." *Washington Post,* 22 November 2003. http://www.washingtonpost.com (accessed November 22, 2003).

Tisdale, Sallie. "Silence, Please: The Public Library as Entertainment Center." *Harper's,* March 1997, 65–74.

Towner, Lawrence W. "A History of the Newberry Library." In *Humanities' Mirror: Reading at the Newberry, 1887–1987,* edited by Rolf Achilles, 17–26. Chicago: Newberry Library, 1987.

———. *Past Imperfect: Essays on History, Libraries, and the Humanities.* Chicago: University of Chicago Press, 1993.

Trescott, Jacqueline. "Egyptian Exhibit to Rival Tut Show." *Washington Post,* 4 June 2002. http://www.washingtonpost.com (accessed September 13, 2003).

Tuscon Botanical Gardens. "Desert Connections." http://www.tucsonbotanical.org/desert_connections (accessed May 9, 2003).

University of Pittsburgh. "Historic Pittsburgh." http://digital.library.pitt.edu (accessed November 7, 2003).

U.S. Congress. House. *Bill Summary and Status for the 94th Congress.* HR 7216. 94th Cong., 2nd sess. http://thomas.loc.gov (accessed September 6, 2003).

Vandergrift, Kay E., ed. *Ways of Knowing.* Lanham, MD: Scarecrow Press, 1996.

Vavrek, Bernard. "Wanted! Entertainment Director." *American Libraries* 32 (June/July 2001): 68–71.

Vergo, John, Claire-Marie Karat, John Karat, Claudio Pinhanez, Renee Arora, Thomas Cofino, Doug Riecken, and Mark Podlaseck. "Less Clicking, More Watching: Results from the User-Centered Design of a Multi-Institutional Web Site for Art and Culture." *Papers from Museums and the Web 2002.* http://www.archimuse.com (accessed November 8, 2003).

Vogel, Carol. "House Approves Increase in Insurance for Museums." *New York Times*, 18 September 2003, B5.

Wald, Matthew L. "A Big Museum Opens, to Jeers as Well as Cheers." *New York Times*, 16 December 2003, A28.

Walsh, John. "Pictures, Tears, Lights, and Seats." In *Whose Muse? Art Museums and the Public Trust*, edited by James Cuno, 77–101. Princeton, NJ: Princeton University Press, 2004.

"Weddings at the Library?" *The Unabashed Librarian* 112 (1999): 19.

Weil, Stephen E. *A Cabinet of Curiosities: Inquiries into Museums and Their Prospects*. Washington, DC: Smithsonian Institution Press, 1995.

———. *Making Museums Matter*. Washington, DC: Smithsonian Institution Press, 2002.

———. "Transformed from a Cemetery of Bric-a-Brac...." In *Perspectives on Outcome Based Evaluation for Libraries and Museums*. Washington, DC: Institute of Museum and Library Services, 2000. http://www.imls.gov (accessed June 15, 2003).

Welch, Martin. "The Ashmolean as Described by Its Earliest Visitors." In *Tradescant's Rarities: Essays on the Foundation of the Ashmolean Museum 1683 with a Catalogue of the Surviving Early Collections*, edited by Arthur MacGregor, 59–69. Oxford: Clarendon Press, 1983.

———. "The Foundation of the Ashmolean Museum." In *Tradescant's Rarities: Essays on the Foundation of the Ashmolean Museum 1683 with a Catalogue of the Surviving Early Collections*, edited by Arthur MacGregor, 40–58. Oxford: Clarendon Press, 1983.

Well, James M. "Building the Collection." In *Humanities' Mirror: Reading at the Newberry, 1887–1987*, edited by Rolf Achilles, 27–35. Chicago: Newberry Library, 1987.

Weschler, Lawrence. *Mr. Wilson's Cabinet of Wonder*. New York: Vintage, 1996.

White House Millennium Council 2000. "The Mars Millennium Project." http://www.clinton4.nara.gov/initiatives/millennium/mars.html (accessed December 21, 2003).

Wiegand, Wayne A. "The Development of Librarianship in the United States." *Libraries and Culture* 24 (winter 1989): 99–109.

———. "To Reposition a Research Agenda: What American Studies Can Teach the LIS Community About the Library in the Life of the User." *Library Quarterly* 73 (October 2003): 369–82.

Wilkinson, Donna. "A Collection Based on Good Connections." *New York Times*, 23 April 2003, F23.

———. "Stuffing Nooks and Crannies with Bones, Insects, and Creepy Fish." *New York Times,* 24 April 2002, E31.

Wilson, Craig. "A Library Made More Lovely by a Tree." *USA Today,* 18 April 2003, D1.

Wood, James N. "The Authorities of the American Art Museum." In *Whose Muse? Art Museums and the Public Trust,* edited by James Cuno, 103–28. Princeton, NJ: Princeton University Press, 2004.

Woods, Julia A. "Joint-Use Libraries: The Broward Community College Central Campus Experience." In *Joint-Use Libraries,* edited by William Miller and Rita M. Pellen, 41–54. Binghampton, NY: Haworth Press, 2001.

Worters, Garance, ed. *American Biographical Archive* (microfiche, sheet 577, frame 336). London: K. G. Saur, 1986.

Yahoo! "Yahoo! Picks: May 26, 2002." http://picks.yahoo.com/picks/i/20020526.html (accessed May 11, 2003).

Ziarnik, Natalie Reif. *School and Public Libraries: Developing the Natural Alliance.* Chicago: American Library Association, 2003.

Zolberg, Vera L. "An Elite Experience for Everyone: Art Museums, the Public, and Cultural Literacy." In *Museum Culture: Histories, Discourses, Spectacles,* edited by Daniel J. Sherman and Irit Rogoff, 49–65. Minneapolis, MN: University of Minnesota Press, 1994.

INDEX

New York Public Library (NYPL),
Science, Industry and Business Library
(SIBL), 196–97
Niedzviecki, Hal, 5–7, 144, 207, 215
North Carolina Museum of Life and
Science (Durham), 69, 115

Oldenburg, Ray, 212
Olearius, Adam, 157, 195
Oregon State Historical Society, 101
outcome measures: definition, 5, 41;
history, 41–44; philosophical
implications, 5, 8–10, 41–43,
214–18

Palau Community College (Republic of
Palau), 77, 82–83
Peale, Charles Willson, 162–64, 181–82
Peale, Rubens, 163, 181–82, 197
Pei, I. M., 18–19
performance measures: *See* outcome
measures
Perl, Jed, 3, 4, 23–24, 25, 31, 208
Phoenix Public Library (Arizona), 115–16,
119–20
Poets House (New York), 83–84
Pompidou Center, 17–18
Ponce Museum of History (Puerto Rico),
100
Poole, William Frederick Poole, 192
postobject role: definition, 16; examples in
libraries and museums, 16–29, 144
Providence Public Library (Rhode Island),
108–9, 112–14
public libraries: architecture, 26–27;
blockbuster exhibits, 29–30;
challenges, 2; changing community
roles, 2, 5–7, 8–10, 143–46; economic
instrumentality, 8–10; edutainment,
5–8, 25–26, 28; outcome measures in,
5, 8–10, 211–16; partnerships with
museums, 29–30, 45–120 passim,
121–22, 143–45; postobject role, 8–10,
26–28; social exclusion in, 213–15. *See
also names of specific libraries*
Public Museum of Grand Rapids
(Michigan), 14–15
public sphere, 8–10, 211–16; critical
public sphere, 211–16, pseudo public
sphere, 211–16

Putnam Museum (Davenport, Iowa),
70–71

Queens Borough Public Library, 28

Rex's Lending Center/InfoZone, 61–63,
67, 114, 120, 124, 171
Rhode Island School of Design
(Providence): Museum of Art, 108–9,
112–14
Richardson, Henry Hobson, 165–66
Richmond Museum of History
(California), 100–101
Richmond Public Library (California),
100–101
Ritzer, George, 24, 28–29, 125
Rochester Museum and Science Center,
53–54, 60, 67
Rochester Public Library (New York),
53–54, 60, 67
Rockford Public Library (Illinois), 93–94
Rutgers University Libraries (New
Jersey), 101–2
Ruth and Sherman Lee Institute for
Japanese Art at the Clark Center
(Hanford, California), 87

Sahara West Library and Fine Arts
Museum (Las Vegas, Nevada), 171
San Francisco Museum of Modern Art,
23, 24, 171
San Francisco Performing Arts Library
and Museum, 111
Sargent Murals Restoration Project,
86–87, 89–90, 124
Schiller, Herbert I., 8
Schumacher, Johann, 157–58, 195
Seattle Public Library (Washington),
26–27, 215
simulacra, 207–8
Smithsonian Institution (Washington,
D.C.), 13, 30–31, 122–24, 162,
204–6
social capital, 8–10, 211–16
Southern Utah University (Cedar City):
Sherratt Library, 79–80, 81–82
Southern Ute Museum and Cultural
Center, 76
Springfield-Greene County Library
System (Missouri), 70–71, 72

St. Andrew's University Library
(Scotland), 160–163, 186

Tampa-Hillsborough County Public
Library System, 115, 118–19
Texas Christian University Library, 28
Tisdale, Sallie (Sally), 8
Tradescant John, 151, 153–54, 158–62
Triton College Library (River Grove,
Illinois), 116, 119
Tucson Botanical Gardens (Arizona),
116–17, 120
Tucson-Pima Public Library (Arizona),
116–17, 120

University of Connecticut Libraries
(Storrs), 103
University of Denver, Penrose Library,
102–3
University of Florida Libraries
(Gainesville), 117–18, 120
University of Idaho Library, 2
University of Illinois Libraries, 54–58
University of Kansas, Spencer Research
Library, 52–53
University of Maine Libraries (Orono),
54, 60–61
University of Michigan Natural History
Museums, 96–97
University of Michigan University Library
(Ann Arbor), 96–97
University of Nebraska-Lincoln Libraries,
75–76
University of Nebraska State Museum,
75–76

University of Oregon Libraries, 115
University of Oregon Museum of Natural
History (Eugene), 117, 120
University of Pittsburgh Libraries, 78–79,
81–82
University of Washington Libraries
(Seattle), 76–77, 79, 81

Victoria and Albert Museum (London,
England), 211
visible storage centers, 189–91. *See also*
museums, overcrowded storage areas

Washington State University Libraries
(Pullman), 101
Washington University (St. Louis,
Missouri), 103–5
Wayne State University Library System
(Detroit, Michigan), 88–89, 91
Weil, Stephen E., 16, 22, 127 nn.10, 11
WGBH Educational Foundation (Boston),
Media Library, 103–5
Wildlife Conservation Society/Central
Park Zoo (New York), 83–84
Winn, Charles Bowers, 165
Woburn Public Library (Massachusetts),
165–66
Wunderkammern: See Cabinets of
curiosities
Wyoming State Library, 102–3

Young at Art of Broward (Florida),
125

Zolberg, Vera L., 18

ABOUT THE AUTHORS

JURIS DILEVKO is Assistant Professor in the Faculty of Information Studies of the University of Toronto.

LISA GOTTLIEB is a writer living in Toronto, Canada. Together, Dilevko and Gottlieb have published articles about a wide variety of library and information science topics in scholarly journals such as *American Studies*, *Government Information Quarterly*, *Journal of the American Society for Information Science and Technology*, *Library & Information Science Research*, and *Library Quarterly*.

They are co-authors of the book *Reading and the Reference Librarian: The Importance to Library Service of Staff Reading Habits* (2004).